Topics in Parallel and Distributed Computing: Introducing Concurrency in Undergraduate Courses

Topics in Parallel and Distributed Computing: Introducing Concurrency in Undergraduate Courses

Edited by

Sushil K Prasad

Anshul Gupta

Arnold L Rosenberg

Alan Sussman

Charles C Weems

AMSTERDAM • BOSTON • HEIDELBERG • LONDON
NEW YORK • OXFORD • PARIS • SAN DIEGO
SAN FRANCISCO • SINGAPORE • SYDNEY • TOKYO

Morgan Kaufmann is an imprint of Elsevier

Acquiring Editor: Todd Green
Editorial Project Manager: Amy Invernizzi
Project Manager: Mohanambal Natarajan
Designer: Alan Studholme

Morgan Kaufmann is an imprint of Elsevier
225 Wyman Street, Waltham, MA 02451 USA

Library of Congress Cataloging-in-Publication Data
A catalog record for this book is available from the Library of Congress.

British Library Cataloguing in Publication Data
A catalogue record for this book is available from the British Library.

ISBN: 978-0-12-803899-4

For information on all MK publications
visit our website at www.mkp.com

Contents

Contributors

Steven Bogaerts
DePauw University

David P. Bunde
Knox College

Thomas H. Cormen
Dartmouth College

Victor Eijkhout
The University of Texas at Austin

Ryan E. Grant
Sandia National Laboratories

Dan Grossman
University of Washington

Anshul Gupta
IBM Research

Stephen L. Olivier
Sandia National Laboratories

Sushil K. Prasad
Georgia State University

Suresh Rai
Louisiana State University

Arnold L. Rosenberg
Northeastern University

Joshua Stough
Washington & Lee University

Alan Sussman
University of Maryland

Jerry L. Trahan
Louisiana State University

Ramachandran Vaidyanathan
Louisiana State University

Charles C. Weems
University of Massachusetts

Editor and author biographical sketches

EDITORS

Anshul Gupta is a principal research staff member in the Mathematical Sciences Department at the IBM Thomas J. Watson Research Center. His research interests include sparse matrix computations and their applications in optimization and computational sciences, parallel algorithms, and graph/combinatorial algorithms for scientific computing. He has coauthored several journal articles and conference papers on these topics and a textbook titled "Introduction to Parallel Computing." He is the primary author of Watson Sparse Matrix Package, one of the most robust and scalable parallel direct solvers for large sparse systems of linear equations.

Sushil K. Prasad (BTech 1985, Indian Institute of Technology Kharagpur; MS 1986, Washington State University, Pullman; PhD 1990, University of Central Florida, Orlando; all in computer science/engineering) is a professor of computer science at Georgia State University and Director of the Distributed and Mobile Systems Laboratory. He has carried out theoretical as well as experimental research in parallel and distributed computing, resulting in more than 140 refereed publications, several patent applications, and about $3 million in external research funds as principal investigator and over $6 million overall (National Science Foundation (NSF)/National Institutes of Health/graduate research assistantship/industry).

Sushil was honored as an Association for Computing Machinery (ACM) Distinguished Scientist in fall 2013 for his research on parallel data structures and applications. He was the elected chair of the IEEE Technical Committee on Parallel Processing (TCPP) for two terms (2007-2011), and received its highest honor in 2012—IEEE TCPP Outstanding Service Award. Currently, he is leading the NSF-supported IEEE-TCPP curriculum initiative on parallel and distributed computing with a vision to ensure that all computer science and engineering graduates are well-prepared in parallelism through their core courses in this era of multicore and many-core desktops and handheld devices. His current research interests are in parallel data structures and algorithms, and computation over geospatiotemporal datasets over cloud, graphics processing unit (GPU) and multicore platforms. His homepage is www.cs.gsu.edu/prasad.

Arnold L. Rosenberg is a research professor in the Computer Science Department at Northeastern University; he also holds the rank of Distinguished University Professor Emeritus in the Computer Science Department at the University of Massachusetts Amherst. Before joining the University of Massachusetts Amherst, Arnold was a professor of computer science at Duke University from 1981 to 1986, and a research staff member at the IBM Thomas J. Watson Research Center from 1965 to 1981. He has held visiting positions at Yale University and the University of Toronto. He was a Lady Davis Visiting Professor at the Technion (Israel Institute of Technology) in 1994, and a Fulbright Senior Research Scholar at the University of Paris-South in 2000. His research focuses on developing algorithmic models and techniques to exploit the new modalities of "collaborative computing" (wherein multiple computers cooperate to solve a computational problem) that result from emerging computing technologies. He is the author or coauthor of more than 170 technical papers on these and other topics in theoretical computer science and discrete mathematics. He is the coauthor of the research book *Graph Separators, with Applications* and the author of the textbook *The Pillars of Computation Theory: State, Encoding, Nondeterminism*; additionally, he has served as coeditor of several books. He is a Fellow of the ACM, a Fellow of the IEEE, and a Golden Core member of the IEEE Computer Society. He received an AB degree in mathematics from Harvard College and AM and PhD degrees in applied mathematics from Harvard University. More details are available at http://www.cs.umass.edu/~rsnbrg/.

Alan Sussman is a professor in the Department of Computer Science and Institute for Advanced Computer Studies at the University of Maryland. Working with students and other researchers at The University of Maryland and other institutions, he has published over 100 conference and journal papers and received several best paper awards in various topics related to software tools for high-performance parallel and distributed computing, and has contributed chapters to six books. His research interests include peer-to-peer distributed systems, software engineering for high-performance computing, and large-scale data-intensive computing. He is an associate editor of the *Journal of Parallel and Distributed Computing*, a subject area editor of the journal *Parallel Computing*, and an associate editor of *IEEE Transactions on Services Computing*. Software tools he has built have been widely distributed and used in many computational science applications, in areas such as earth science, space science, and medical informatics. He received his PhD degree in computer science from Carnegie Mellon University.

Charles C. Weems is co-director of the Architecture and Language Implementation laboratory at the University of Massachusetts. His current research interests include architectures for media and embedded applications, GPU computing, and high-precision arithmetic. Previously he led the development of two generations of a heterogeneous parallel processor for machine vision, called the Image Understanding Architecture, and co-directed initial work on the Scale compiler that was eventually used for the TRIPS architecture. He is the author of numerous articles, has served on many program committees, chaired the 1997 IEEE CAMP Workshop and the 1999 IEEE Frontiers Symposium, co-chaired the IEEE International Parallel and Distributed Processing Symposium (IPDPS) in 1999, 2000, and 2013, was general vice-chair for IPDPS from 2001 to 2005, and co-chairs the Large-Scale Parallel Processing workshop. He has coauthored 26 introductory computer science texts, and coedited the book *Associative Processing and Processors*. He is a member of the ACM, a Senior Member of IEEE, a member of the Executive Committee of the IEEE Technical Committee on Parallel Processing, has been an editor of *IEEE Transactions on Parallel and Distributed Systems* and *Journal of Parallel and Distributed Computing*, and is an editor of *Parallel Computing*.

AUTHORS

Steven Bogaerts holds a BS degree from Rose-Hulman Institute of Technology and MS and PhD degrees from Indiana University. He is an assistant professor of computer science at DePauw University in Greencastle, Indiana, and previously held a faculty position at Wittenberg University. His research interests include artificial intelligence and machine learning, most recently with applications of Monte-Carlo Tree Search to game playing. He is a strong supporter of including undergraduate students in research, and is also active in parallelism in computer science education, especially in integration in lower-level courses.

David Bunde is an associate professor of computer science at Knox College, a liberal arts college in Galesburg, Illinois. His PhD degree is in computer science from the University of Illinois at Urbana-Champaign. He earned a BS degree in mathematics and computer science from Harvey Mudd College. He is active in parallel computing education and was selected as an Early Adopter of the NSF/IEEE-TCPP Curriculum on Parallel and Distributed Computing in spring 2011. His other research focuses on resource management for high-performance computers, particularly the allocation of compute nodes to jobs and the assignment of job tasks to allocated nodes. He is particularly passionate about undergraduate research, and includes undergraduate students in most of his work.

Thomas H. Cormen is a professor in the Dartmouth College Department of Computer Science, where he has been since 1992. He served as the department chair from 2009 to 2015, and he directed the Dartmouth Institute for Writing and Rhetoric from 2004 to 2008. He received BSE degree in electrical engineering and computer science from Princeton University in 1978 and SM and PhD degrees in electrical engineering and computer science from the Massachusetts Institute of Technology in 1986 and 1992, respectively. An ACM Distinguished Educator, he is coauthor of the leading textbook on computer algorithms, *Introduction to Algorithms*, which he wrote with Charles E. Leiserson, Ronald L. Rivest, and Clifford Stein. He is also the author of *Algorithms Unlocked*. His primary research interests are in algorithm engineering and parallel computing. He focuses on algorithms and software infrastructure to mitigate the high latency inherent in accessing the outer levels of the memory hierarchy and in interprocessor communication.

Victor Eijkhout's scientific computing career started with a degree in numerical analysis, gradually moving into computational science. He has published numerous papers, as well as the book *Templates for the Solution of Linear Systems: Building Blocks for Iterative Methods* and the textbook *Introduction to High-Performance Scientific Computing*. He currently holds a position as a research scientist at the Texas Advanced Computing Center.

Ryan E. Grant is a postdoctoral appointee and the scalable interconnects team lead in the Center for Computing Research at Sandia National Laboratories in Albuquerque, New Mexico, USA. His research focuses on high-performance networking for extreme-scale systems. He is an active member of the Portals Networking Interface specification team, working on next-generation high-performance interconnects. In addition, he serves on the MPI specifications body (MPI Forum), as well as being a developer for the Open MPI project. He graduated with a PhD degree in computer engineering in 2012 from Queen's University, Kingston, Canada, where he was an Alexander Graham Bell Canada Research Scholar.

Dan Grossman is a professor in the Department of Computer Science and Engineering at the University of Washington, where he has been a faculty member since 2003. He holds the J. Ray Bowen Professorship for Innovation in Engineering Education.

Dan completed his PhD degree at Cornell University and his undergraduate studies at Rice University. His research interests lie in the area of programming languages, ranging from theory to design to implementation, with a focus on improving software quality. In recent years, he has focused on better techniques for expressing, analyzing, and executing multithreaded programs. He has collaborated actively with researchers in several other disciplines of computer science, particularly computer architecture.

Dan has served on roughly 30 conference and workshop program committees. He has served on the ACM SIGPLAN Executive Committee and the Steering Committee for the ACM/IEEE-CS 2013 Computer Science Curriculum. He currently serves on the Computing Research Association Board and the ACM Education Board.

Dan teaches a popular massive open online course on undergraduate topics in programming languages and functional programming.

Stephen L. Olivier is a senior member of the technical staff in the Center for Computing Research at Sandia National Laboratories in Albuquerque, New Mexico. His research focuses on run-time systems and programming models for high-performance computing, including issues in productivity, scalability, and power. He is co-lead for the Qthreads multithreading library and a contributor to the Power API for energy-efficient measurement and control in high-performance computing systems. He represents Sandia National Laboratories on the OpenMP Architecture Review Board and Language Committee, chairing its subcommittee on task parallelism.

He received his PhD degree in computer science from the University of North Carolina at Chapel Hill, where he was a US Department of Defense National Defense Science and Engineering (NDSEG) Fellow and received the Best Student Paper Award at the ACM/IEEE Supercomputing Conference.

Joshua Stough (PhD, University of North Carolina at Chapel Hill, 2008) is a liberal arts college educator with years of experience teaching CS1 and CS2/data structures courses in the Python programming language. He teaches computer science around three core concepts: a hybrid lecture/laboratory class format; the extensive use of props, toys, games, and physical exercises; and guided peer tutoring through a policy of unfettered student collaboration on most programming assignments. These methods allow students to interact with concepts from multiple perspectives, improving fluency and retention, and permit the instructor's guiding presence during the difficult analysis and synthesis stages of learning.

Suresh Rai is the Michel B. Voorhies Distinguished Professor in the Division of Electrical and Computer Engineering and the Emmet and Toni Stephenson College of Engineering Distinguished Professor at Louisiana State University, Baton Rouge, Louisiana. His teaching and research interests include wavelet applications in steganography and network traffic, logic testing, and parallel and distributed processing. He is a coauthor of the book *Wave Shaping and Digital Circuits*, and the tutorial texts *Distributed Computing Network Reliability* and *Advances in Distributed System Reliability*. He has guest edited a special issue of *IEEE Transactions on Reliability* on the topic reliability of parallel and distributed computing networks and an *International Journal of Performability Engineering* special issue on dependability of wireless systems. He was an associate editor of *IEEE Transactions on Reliability* from 1990 to 2004. Currently, he is on the editorial board of *International Journal of Performability Engineering*.

Suresh Rai has published about 150 technical papers in refereed journals and conference proceedings. His paper entitled "Analyzing packetized voice and video traffic in an ATM multiplexer" received the Best Paper Award at the 1998 IEEE IPCC Conference (February 16-18, Tempe, Arizona). His research has been funded by the Air Force Office of Scientific Research, NSF, and Army Research Office.

He is a senior member of the IEEE.

Jerry L. Trahan received his BS degree from Louisiana State University in 1983 and his MS and PhD degrees from the University of Illinois at Urbana-Champaign in 1986 and 1988, respectively. Since 1988, he has been a faculty member in the Division of Electrical and Computer Engineering, Louisiana State University, where he is currently chair and Chevron Associate Professor of Electrical Engineering. His research interests include algorithms, models of parallel computation, theory of computation, and reconfigurable computing.

Ramachandran Vaidyanathan received his B-Tech and M-Tech degrees from the Indian Institute of Technology, Kharagpur, in 1983 and 1985, respectively, and a PhD degree from Syracuse University in 1990. Since then he has been a faculty member in the Division of Electrical and Computer Engineering at Louisiana State University, Baton Rouge, where he is currently the Elaine T. and Donald C. Delaune Distinguished Associate Professor. His research interests include parallel and distributed computing, algorithms, reconfigurable systems, and interconnection networks.

Symbol or phrase

Symbol or phrase	Latex format (italicize symbols)	Definition	Author	Comment	Editing comments
p	p	Number of processors or cores	Sushil Prasad	Processors, cores, and nodes are alternative ways of describing the number of processing units employed. The same symbol can be used if the description of a parallel algorithm or program uses "processes" or another abstraction for processing units	
T1*	T_1^*	Fastest sequential time		This (usually) corresponds to the best sequential algorithm	
Tp	T_p	Execution time of a parallel program/algorithm using p processors		T1 is thus the time taken by a parallel program using one processor and may involve parallel overheads. As compared with this, T1* is the pure sequential time	
Sp	S_p	(Absolute) speedup of a parallel program using p processors compared with the fastest sequential time		Thus, the "absolute speedup" is defined as $S_p = T_1^*/T_p$. T_1/T_p is the "relative speedup," comparing a parallel program's performance relative to its own performance using one processor	

Continued

Symbol or phrase	Latex format (italicize symbols)	Definition	Author	Comment	Editing comments
Cost		Cost of a parallel program		Cost = pT_p	
Work		Total work collectively done by all processors		Work <= cost	
Ep	E_p	Efficiency of a parallel program		$E_p = S_p/p = T_1^*/pT_p = T_1^*/cost$	
Cost-optimal		A parallel algorithm whose cost is of the same order as T_1^*			
G	G	Graph G		$G = (V, E)$	
V	V	Set of nodes in graph G			
E	E	Set of edges in graph G			
n, m	n, m	Variables related to the size of the input	Anshul Gupta	Lower case letters such as n, m, etc., should be used to denote variables that determine the size of the input; for example, a set of n records, or an $n \times m$ matrix, or a graph with n vertices and m edges, etc.	
Design pattern		A description of an effective solution to a recurring problem in a particular context	Dick Brown		
N	N	Input size	Ramachandran Vaidyanathan	Uppercase is useful when $N = 2^k$ is a power of 2	

l	ℓ	Level of node in a tree	Ramachandran Vaidyanathan	
t	t_i	Time-related quantity	Ramachandran Vaidyanathan	
x', X'	x' or X'	Complement of a Boolean variable x or X	Ramachandran Vaidyanathan	
$< a, b >$	$< a, b >$	Doublet or ordered pair $< a, b >$	Ramachandran Vaidyanathan	
oplus	$\oplus$	Generic associative operator	Thomas Cormen	When describing reduce and scan operations, we need a generic operator
@	@	Operator to perform segmented scans via unsegmented scans	Thomas Cormen	When performing segmented scan operations, we use a special operator to use the mechanism for unsegmented scans

Editors' introduction and road map

Sushil K. Prasad*, Anshul Gupta[†], Arnold L. Rosenberg[‡], Alan Sussman[§] and Charles C. Weems[¶]

Georgia State University* IBM Research[†] Northeastern University[‡] University of Maryland[§] University of Massachusetts[¶]

1.1 WHY THIS BOOK?

Parallel and distributed computing (PDC) now permeates most computing activities. It is no longer sufficient for even novice programmers to acquire only traditional sequential programming skills. In recognition of this technological evolution, a working group was organized under the aegis of the US National Science Foundation (NSF) and the IEEE Computer Society Technical Committee on Parallel Processing (TCPP) to draft guidelines for the development of curricula in PDC for low-level (core) undergraduates courses in computational subjects such as computer science (CS), computer engineering (CE), and computational science. The NSF/TCPP working group proposed a set of core PDC topics, with recommendations for the level of coverage each in undergraduate curriculum. The resulting curricular guidelines have been organized into four tables, one for each of computer architecture, computer programming, algorithms, and cross-cutting topics.[1]

The initial enthusiastic reception of these guidelines led to a commitment within the working group to continue to develop the guidelines and to foster their adoption at a broad range of academic institutions. Toward these ends, the Center for Curriculum Development and Educational Resources (CDER) was founded, with the five editors of this volume comprising the initial Board of Directors. CDER has initiated several activities toward the end of fostering PDC education:

---

[1] NSF-supported TCPP/CDER curriculum (preliminary version released in 2010, version 1 released in 2012): http://www.cs.gsu.edu/~tcpp/curriculum. This material is based on work partially supported by the NSF under grants IIS 1143533, CCF 1135124, CCF 1048711, and CNS 0950432. Any opinions, findings, and conclusions or recommendations expressed in this material are those of the author(s) and do not necessarily reflect the views of the NSF.

1. A *courseware repository* has been established for pedagogical materials—sample lectures, recommended problem sets, experiential anecdotes, evaluations, etc. This is a living repository: CDER invites the community to contribute existing and new material to it.[2]

2. An *Early Adopter Program* has been established to foster the adoption and evaluation of the guidelines. This activity has fostered educational work on PDC at more than 100 educational institutions in North America, South America, Europe, and Asia. The program has thereby played a major role in establishing a worldwide community of people interested in developing and implementing PDC curricula.

3. The *EduPar workshop series* has been established. The original instantiation of EduPar was as a satellite of the International Parallel and Distributed Processing Symposium (IPDPS). EduPar was—and continues to be—the first education-oriented workshop at a major research conference. The success of EduPar led to the development of a sibling workshop, EduHPC, at the Supercomputing Conference. In August 2015, EduPar and EduHPC will be joined by a third sibling workshop, Euro-EduPar, which will be a satellite of the International Conference on Parallel Computing (EuroPar). CDER has also sponsored panels and birds-of-a-feather sessions at Association for Computing Machinery (ACM) Special Interest Group on Computer Science Education (SIGCSE) conferences.

The preceding activities have succeeded not only as individual activities, but even more exciting, by spawning a vibrant international community of educators who are committed to PDC education. It is from this community that the desirability of the *CDER Book Project*, a series of volumes to support both instructors and students of PDC, became evident. This is the first volume in the series.

Motivation and goals of the CDER Book Project: Curricular guidelines such as those promulgated by both the CDER Center and the CS2013 ACM/IEEE Computer Science Curriculum Joint Task Force[3] are an essential first step in propelling the teaching of PDC-related material into the twenty-first century. But such guidelines are only a first step: both instructors and students will benefit from suitable textual

---

[2]CDER courseware repository: http://www.cs.gsu.edu/~tcpp/curriculum/?q=courseware_management.

[3]The ACM/IEEE Computer Science Curricula 2013 document (http://www.acm.org/education/CS2013-final-report.pdf) explicitly refers to our proposed curriculum on page 146 as follows:

> *"As multi-processor computing continues to grow in the coming years, so too will the role of parallel and distributed computing in undergraduate computing curricula. In addition to the guidelines presented here, we also direct the interested reader to the document entitled "NSF/TCPP Curriculum Initiative on Parallel and Distributed Computing—Core Topics for Undergraduates", available from the website: http://www.cs.gsu.edu/~tcpp/curriculum."*

material to effectively translate guidelines into a curriculum. Moreover, experience to this point has made it clear that the members of the PDC community have much to share with each other and with aspiring new members, in terms of creativity in forging new directions and experience in evaluating existing ones. The CDER Book Project's goal is to engage the community to address the need for suitable textbooks and related textual material to integrate PDC topics into the lower-level core courses (which we affectionately, and hopefully transparently, refer to as CS1, CS2, Systems, Data Structures and Algorithms, Logic Design, etc.). The current edited book series intends, over time, to cover all of these proposed topics. This first volume in the projected series has two parts:

(1) Part One—for instructors: These chapters are aimed at instructors to provide background, scholarly materials, insights into pedagogical strategies, and descriptions of experience with both strategies and materials. The emphasis is on the basic concepts and references on what and how to teach PDC topics in the context of the existing topics in various core courses.
(2) Part Two—for students: These chapters aim to provide supplemental textual material for core courses which students can rely on for learning and exercises.

Print and free Web publication: While a print version through a renowned commercial publisher will foster our dissemination efforts in a professional format, the preprint versions of all the chapters will be freely available on the CDER Book Project website.[4]

Organization: This introductory chapter is organized as follows. Section 1.2 gives brief outlines of each of the nine subsequent chapters. Section 1.3 provides a road map for readers to find suitable chapters and sections within these which are relevant for specific courses or PDC topics. Section 1.4 contains examples of future chapters and an invitation for chapter proposals.

1.2 CHAPTER INTRODUCTIONS
1.2.1 PART ONE—FOR INSTRUCTORS

In Chapter 2, titled "Hands-on parallelism with no prerequisites and little time using Scratch," Steven Bogaerts discusses hands-on exploration of parallelism, targeting instructors of students with no or minimal prior programming experience. The hands-on activities are developed in the Scratch programming language. Scratch is used at various higher-education institutions as a first language for both majors and nonmajors. One advantage of Scratch is that programming is done by dragging and connecting blocks; therefore, students can create interesting programs extremely quickly. This is a crucial feature for the prerequisite-free approach of this proposed

---

[4]CDER Book Project (free preprint version): http://cs.gsu.edu/~tcpp/curriculum/?q= CDER_Book_Project.

chapter, which, as the chapter shows, is sufficient for introducing key parallelism ideas such as synchronization, race conditions, and the difference between blocking and nonblocking commands. The chapter can be used by instructors of CS0 or CS1, or computer literacy courses for nonmajors, or even high-school students.

In Chapter 3, titled "Parallelism in Python for novices," Steven Bogaerts and Joshua Stough target instructors of courses for novice programmers, with material on parallelism and concurrency in the Python programming language. The topics covered include tasks and threads, recursion, and various features of the Python multiprocessing module. The chapter includes multiple small examples, demonstration materials, and sample exercises that can be used by instructors to teach parallel programming concepts to students just being introduced to basic programming concepts. More specifically, the chapter addresses Python multiprocessing features such as fork/join threading, message passing, sharing resources between threads, and using locks. Examples of the utility of parallelism are drawn from application areas such as searching, sorting, simulations, and image processing.

Chapter 4, titled "Modules for introducing threads," by David Bunde, is meant to be used by instructors to add coverage of threads to either a data structures class, or to a systems programming class that has data structures as a prerequisite. The chapter presents two parallel examples: prime counting and computing the Mandelbrot set. The prime counting example is coded in three different frameworks: POSIX pthreads, the C++11 std::thread class, and Java's java.lang.thread class. Thus, the material can be easily adopted for use in a wide range of curricula, and can also be the basis for a comparative study of different threading environments in a more advanced class. The Mandlebrot example uses OpenMP, and includes a discussion of accomplishing the same effect using a threaded model. Both examples address the ideas of speedup, race conditions, load balancing, and making variables private to enhance speedup. In addition, the prime counting example considers critical sections and mutual exclusion, while the Mandelbrot section looks at parallel overhead and dynamic scheduling.

In Chapter 5, titled "Introducing parallel and distributed computing concepts in digital logic," Ramachandran Vaidyanathan, Jerry Trahan, and Suresh Rai provide insights into how instructors of introductory digital logic classes can present topics from PDC through common logic structures. Some examples include the following: How circuit fan-in and fan-out can be seen as analogous to broadcast, multicast, and convergecast. Circuit timing analysis offers an opportunity to explore dependencies between tasks, data hazards, and synchronization. The topology of Karnaugh maps provides an opening for introducing multidimensional torus networks. Carry-look-ahead circuits represent parallel prefix operations. Many other connections and analogies are noted throughout the chapter, providing instructors with opportunities to encourage parallel thinking in students, in a context different from that of traditional programming courses.

In Chapter 6, titled "Networks and MPI for cluster computing," Ryan Grant and Stephen Olivier address parallel computing on clusters, using high-performance message passing and networking techniques. This material is mainly targeted at instructors of introductory classes in systems or data structures and algorithms, and can complement discussions of shared memory parallelism in those courses. The topics in the chapter introduce the ideas necessary to scale parallel programs to the large configurations needed for high-performance supercomputing, in a form that is approachable to students in introductory classes. Through examples using the Message Passing Interface (MPI), the ubiquitous message passing application programming interface for high-performance computing, the material enables students to write parallel programs that run on multiple nodes of a cluster, using both point-to-point message passing and collective operations. Several more advanced topics are also addressed that can be included as enrichment material in introductory classes, or as the starting point for deeper treatment in an upper-level class. Those topics include effective use of modern high-performance networks and hybrid shared memory and message passing programming.

1.2.2 PART TWO—FOR STUDENTS

Chapter 7, titled "Fork-join parallelism with a data-structures focus," by Dan Grossman, is intended for use by students in a data structures class. It introduces the basic concepts of parallelism. While it introduces the idea of concurrency control and dependencies between parallel tasks, examples of these are deferred to Chapter 8 so that students may focus exclusively on methods for achieving parallel execution. Using the java.lang.Thread library to introduce basic issues of parallelism, it then moves to the java.util.concurrent library to focus on fork-join parallelism. Other models of parallelism are described to contrast them with the shared-memory, fork-join model. Divide-and-conquer and map-reduce strategies are covered within the fork-join model before moving onto a section on analysis of parallel algorithms in terms of make and span, with an overview of Amdahl's law and its relationship to Moore's law. The chapter concludes with additional examples of parallel prefix, pack, quicksort, and mergesort.

Chapter 8, titled "Shared-memory concurrency control with a data-structures focus," is a continuation of Chapter 7 for use when a data structures class will be delving more deeply into structures and algorithms where concurrency control is necessary to ensure correctness. It begins by presenting the need for synchronization, and how it can be achieved using locks, both at a conceptual level and in Java. It then demonstrates some of the subtle kinds of bad interleaving and data race scenarios that can occur in careless use of concurrency control. Guidelines are then introduced for managing shared memory to isolate and minimize the opportunities for concurrency control to go awry, while still retaining efficient parallelism. Deadlock is then introduced with a series of examples, followed by guidelines for establishing deadlock-free lock acquisition orders. The chapter concludes with a survey of some additional synchronization primitives, including reader-writer locks, condition variables, semaphores, barriers, and monitors.

Chapter 9, titled "Parallel computing in a Python-based computer science course," by Thomas Cormen, is written for use by students in a Python-based data structures or algorithms class. It introduces parallel algorithms in a conceptual manner using sequential Python, with indications of which loops would be executable in parallel. The algorithms are designed using scan (prefix) and reduction operations, with consideration of whether the number of values (n) is less than or equal to the number of processors (p), versus the case where n is greater than p. Exclusive and inclusive scans are differentiated, as are copy-scans. After the basic scan operations have been covered, melding, permuting, and partitioning are described, and partitioning is analyzed for its parallel execution time. Segmented scans and reductions are then introduced and analyzed in preparation for developing a parallel quicksort algorithm.

Chapter 10, titled "Parallel programming illustrated through Conway's Game of Life," by Victor Eijkhout, is a student-oriented chapter that presents different means of executing Conway's Game of Life in parallel. After introducing the game, it provides an overview of array processing, short-vector processing, vector pipelining, and graphics processing unit computing. After showing how OpenMP can be used, it describes aggregation into a coarser granularity of parallelism. Shared memory programming is then contrasted with distributed memory, and MPI is introduced. Blocking and nonblocking sends are then distinguished, leading to the issue of deadlock. Dataflow as well as master-worker paradigms are described, which brings up the topic of task scheduling. The chapter concludes with discussions of data partitioning, combining work to reduce communication, and load balancing.

1.3 HOW TO FIND A TOPIC OR MATERIAL FOR A COURSE

The following table lists the other chapters in the book, the core undergraduate courses for which they can be used (see the list below), and their prerequisites, if any. More detailed tables in the Appendix list the topics covered in each chapter.

Core courses:

CS0: Computer literacy for nonmajors;
CS1: Introduction to computer programming (first course);
CS2: Second programming course in the introductory sequence;
Systems: Introductory systems/architecture course;
DS/A: Data structures and algorithms;
CE1: Digital logic (first course).

Chapter	Short Title	Primary Core Course	Other Courses	Prerequisites
Part One				
2	Hands-on parallelism using Scratch	CS0	CS1	–
3	Parallelism in Python	CS0	CS1, CS2, DS/A	–
4	Introducing threads	Systems	CS2	Java, C++, C
5	PDC concepts in digital logic	CE1	CS2, DS/A	Math maturity
6	Networks and MPI	Systems	CS2, DS/A	CS0, CS1
Part Two				
7	Fork-join data structures	DS/A	CS2	CS1, CS2
8	Shared-memory concurrency	DS/A	CS2	CS1, CS2
9	Parallel computing in Python	DS/A		CS1, CS2
10	Parallel programming in Conway's Game of Life	CS2, DS/A		CS1, Python syntax, algorithms analysis

1.4 INVITATION TO WRITE FOR VOLUME 2

This volume has evolved organically on the basis of contributions received in response to two calls for book chapters, in 2013 and 2014; all contributions have been rigorously reviewed. We invite proposals for chapters on PDC topics, for either instructors or students, for a subsequent volume of this book. More specifically, we are interested in chapters on topics from the current TCPP/CDER curriculum guidelines at http://www.cs.gsu.edu/~tcpp/curriculum for introductory courses that have not been addressed by the chapters in this volume. Examples of such topics include memory hierarchy issues, single instruction, multiple data (SIMD) architectures (such as accelerators) and programming models for them, and parallel versions of common algorithms and their analysis. Future volumes are also planned that will address more advanced, specialized topics in PDC that are targeted at students in upper-level classes.

For instructors

Hands-on parallelism with no prerequisites and little time using Scratch

2

Steven Bogaerts*
*DePauw University**

Relevant core courses: Computer literacy, CS0, early CS1.

Relevant parallel and distributed computing topics: Cross-cutting: Why and what is PDC (A), Cross-cutting: Concurrency (C), Cross-cutting: Nondeterminism (C), Programming: Shared memory (C), Programming: Distributed memory (C), Programming: Data races (A), Algorithm: Time (C), Algorithm: Communication (A), Algorithm: Broadcast (A), Algorithm: Synchronization (A), Architecture: Multicore (K).

Context for use: For nonmajors and novice majors, with no prerequisites and little course time.

Learning outcomes: Know that parallel computation is a natural means to model the real world, and have a basic understanding of programming and coordinating multiple processes to execute simultaneously to accomplish some task. Identify and resolve simple race conditions. Choose between blocking and nonblocking versions of commands, and between shared and private variables.

The computer science education community increasingly recognizes that parallel and distributed computing (PDC) is a crucial core component of computer science. Nevertheless, the transition to coverage in more courses has been challenging. Given the historical coverage of PDC primarily in upper-level electives, there is a perception among some faculty and many students that PDC is unnatural or difficult, and therefore inappropriate for introductory-level students.

On the contrary, as this chapter will argue, PDC is neither unnatural nor excessively difficult. The world is naturally parallel, and so PDC can lead to much cleaner solutions to real-world modeling problems. If presented in the right context and with the right scaffolding, core PDC concepts are understandable to students at any level. This can be accomplished even for students with no prior programming knowledge and no intention of advanced study in computer science. This chapter describes one avenue for accomplishing this: the Scratch programming language. While

Scratch should not necessarily be the only context of exploration of these topics even at the introductory level, it does provide a highly effective, no-prerequisite introduction not just to programming in general, but also to a variety of parallelism concepts.

Support for the work on which this chapter is based has come from a 4-year National Science Foundation grant[1] to create reusable PDC modules for integration into existing courses across the computer science curriculum. The overall strategy of the effort is to use PDC as a *medium* to explore traditional course topics [1, 2]—that is, instructors are invited to do what they ordinarily do in a course, only to do some of it in parallel.

Presenting and expanding on the work in [3], this chapter describes how this can be accomplished using Scratch in a computer literacy, CS0, or CS1 course. The chapter will provide some background in Scratch, and then describe in detail several exercises that illustrate parallelism topics: parallelism and communication for clean solutions, race conditions, blocking and nonblocking commands, and shared and private variables.

2.1 CONTEXTS FOR APPLICATION

The value of the approach described in this chapter depends on the context of its application. So I will begin with a discussion of the context in which I have applied this work, along with other contexts in which this approach may be useful.

I have successfully applied the work described in this chapter in a computer literacy course. This course is entirely for nonmajors, though sometimes a student will decide to move on to CS1 after having taken it. Furthermore, the course is often taken by math-phobic students, under the questionable assumption that it will be easier than a math course that meets the same graduation requirement. Nevertheless, students often approach this course with some trepidation as well.

The course involves 45 "lecture" contact hours, roughly evenly split between programming, spreadsheets, and databases. Each topic is taught with the expectation of no prior student experience. So in this course there is about 15 h of contact time to give the students very basic literacy in programming. Given the ubiquity of PDC capabilities even in relatively low-end computers today, it can be argued that to be truly literate in computing requires some basic understanding of parallelism. This leads to the following question:

> *With no prerequisites and little time, can nervous nonmajors gain hands-on experience in parallelism?*

[1]National Science Foundation grant CCF-0915805, SHF:Small:RUI:Collaborative Research: Accelerators to Applications Supercharging the Undergraduate Computer Science Curriculum.

In such a context it would not be too difficult to give a general overview of some PDC concepts, without providing technical details or hands-on activities. For example, one could define processes, interprocess communication, race conditions, etc., all in a very high level, abstract way. But could it really be possible to enable students to work with these concepts directly, with no prerequisites and so little time? Yes. The Scratch programming language is an effective way to accomplish this, as this chapter will discuss in detail.

The above context is not the only one in which this approach can be applied, however. Scratch has also been used effectively as a component of CS0 [4, 5] and CS1 [6, 7] before moving on to other languages and topics, both for majors and for nonmajors [8, 9]. This chapter adds to these previous applications of Scratch by making more explicit the opportunities for exploration of PDC concepts for absolute beginners in a very limited time frame.

For students who will never take another computer science course, this early exposure to PDC concepts can provide some basic literacy in this crucial area. For students planning on further study in computer science, this work is intended to pave the way for deeper exploration in later courses.

2.2 INTRODUCTION TO SCRATCH

Scratch [10, 11] is a visually oriented programming language designed to provide a gentle introduction to programming concepts. As such, Scratch shares some similarities of purpose and design with the Alice programming language [12]. In contrast to most programming languages, Scratch involves very little typing, and thus little traditional syntax for the beginning programmer to learn. Instead, instructions are created by dragging *blocks* representing different statements and expressions from a *palette* into a coding area. Where most languages would formally specify syntactic rules, Scratch enforces very basic syntax simply by shaping the blocks in ways such that invalid combinations will not "fit" together. Thus, Scratch can help mitigate the common challenges in teaching introductory programming [13], in which an emphasis on certain programming mechanics can cause novice students to miss the larger issues of programming and computing.

Scratch is also designed to be fun, with a large variety of cartoonish characters and photographs of people doing amusing things that can be easily integrated into programs. The standard installation also comes with many example programs, including some animations and games. *Scratch 1.4* [14] is a student-friendly textbook on learning Scratch.

One criticism that some might offer toward Scratch is that it is a "toy" language and cannot be used in the real world. One response is that very introductory programming, especially at the CS0/computer literacy level, should be about basic understanding of core programming and computing ideas, not yet professional-level programming competence. Students should come away from the experience understanding on some level what it means to program, and should have gained some of the practice in general problem-solving that comes from programming. Sometimes this introduction will motivate students to engage in deeper study in additional courses.

Another potential criticism is that Scratch obscures how programming is really done, or more specifically, obscures some details of PDC concepts. While there is some truth to this, a response to this criticism again lies in the context of application. This chapter discusses how to give students *hands-on* experience in parallelism in *very little time*, with *no prerequisites*—a task which would seem to be quite challenging using more traditional tools for parallelism (e.g., C++ with OpenMP or MPI). In a context in which students have prior experience, or in which more time is available, Scratch is not necessarily the ideal approach; though, again, Scratch can still be an appropriate *first* tool before moving on to more sophisticated tools [6, 7].

2.3 PARALLEL COMPUTING AND SCRATCH

This section provides specific examples of using Scratch as a tool for studying some core PDC concepts. It is important to note first that Scratch code does not literally execute in parallel. Rather, code executes concurrently, sharing a single execution thread through context switches. While this should be explained to students, the behavior of most programs is not affected by this difference. The main example in which this concurrency is distinguishable from parallelism is in the "race condition" example below, but as described below, this too provides an opportunity to illustrate important PDC ideas.

2.3.1 PARALLELISM AND COMMUNICATION FOR CLEAN SOLUTIONS

The world naturally works in parallel, and so parallelism is a helpful tool for modeling the real world. An effective way to demonstrate this is to introduce parallelism early and without any particular fanfare. In fact, the instructor may wish to consider not mentioning the word "parallelism" until after this exercise has been completed. In this exercise, a parallel solution arises as a natural consequence of the desire to model the real world, and thus students are more comfortable with it as just another part of programming.

In this first exercise, students are presented with a cartoon boy with four frames of animation (Figure 2.1), and the image of a basketball. The task is for the students to create an animation of the boy walking and dribbling the basketball across the screen. For simplicity, the instructor may wish to disregard whether or not the ball is actually "hitting" the boy's hands. Rather, the instructor might consider requiring simply that the ball must move in a fairly natural-looking way as the boy continues to walk forward smoothly.

In Scratch, an object loaded into a script is called a *sprite*. So in this example there is a boy sprite, containing four related images, and a basketball sprite. Each sprite has a script-editing area. This is the only area in which commands may be given to

FIGURE 2.1

The four frames of animation for the boy.

that sprite, except indirectly through intersprite communication, as discussed below. Often, blocks of commands are triggered through some user action, such as pressing the space bar or the "flag" button in the Scratch interface.

In the code in Figure 2.2, both the boy script and the basketball script are activated by hitting the flag button. Even here, a simple form of parallelism is in use. The boy and the ball start at the same location. The boy moves forward a small distance at a time, changing to the next frame of animation at each step. In parallel, the ball moves down and then up, also spinning slightly and moving right slightly.

The problem with this code is the precise relationship required between several numbers. As shown, the boy moves seven "steps" at a time (not corresponding to an animated step), with a 0.2 s wait time between each move, and an unknown short time to execute the `next costume` command to go to the next frame of animation. The ball has far more moves to be executed in the same amount of time, as the ball's vertical movement should be faster than the boy's horizontal movement. But at the same time, the ball must move horizontally, *at the same pace as the boy*. Thus, there are complex relationships between the numbers controlling the movement of the sprites. Determining the perfect balance between these numbers is a frustrating exercise in trial and error with limited educational value. In fact, the numbers shown in Figure 2.2 are not precisely correct in order to obtain natural movement. Rather, the ball and the boy will become out of sync, with one increasingly distant from the other as they move across the screen. Even a small imperfection in the relationship between these numbers will be revealed when the sprites are allowed to move sufficiently far.

With more effective use of parallelism, a simple and flexible solution is easily obtainable with very little trial and error required. The solution involves parallelism not just in the boy and ball acting simultaneously, but also in two separate blocks of code for the ball running simultaneously.

Consider the solution in Figure 2.3. In this solution, the boy sprite uses the `broadcast` block to send a message to the ball sprite. The ball sprite listens for this message with the `when I receive` block. This will occur in parallel with the ball's

Boy

Ball

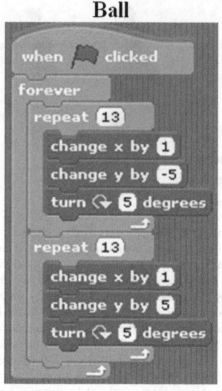

FIGURE 2.2

A basketball-dribbling solution that is difficult to tweak precisely.

larger code block, which now handles only vertical movement. With the boy "telling" the ball exactly when to move, no more guessing or precise balancing of commands is required between the two sprites.

In contrast to the previous code, this code is quite easy to tweak for good visual performance, with a good balance obtainable in just a couple of trials. This is because there are fewer dependent numbers. In particular, note that the ball's horizontal movement (change x by 7) can now perfectly and trivially match the boy's horizontal movement (move 7 steps). The only numbers to tweak, then, are those controlling the vertical movement for the ball, through the relationship between repeat 13 and change y by ± 5.

Through some hints in the problem description, students can be guided to this more effective solution. This can be done without mentioning the word "parallelism" yet, so as to avoid the suggestion that this is something particularly difficult or different from what ordinary programming is. Only when the exercise has been completed and the solution is being discussed as a class is it necessary to explicitly

FIGURE 2.3

A basketball-dribbling solution that is much cleaner through the use of intersprite communication.

introduce concepts of parallelism and intersprite communication, drawing an analogy to the coordination of processes through communication. Thus, the students' first exposure to these concepts is in a fun context, in which the more sequential solutions are unnatural and unwieldy, while the parallel solution is very natural and helpful. And so students' appreciation of parallelism begins.

2.3.2 A CHALLENGE OF PARALLELISM: RACE CONDITIONS

Of course, for all its benefits, parallelism does sometimes bring unique challenges to a problem, and to be literate in programming requires students to be aware of these challenges. One challenge of parallelism is that of race conditions. Since Scratch actually executes code concurrently, not truly in parallel (as discussed above), "race conditions" in Scratch actually give behavior that is consistent, though often unexpected. So in this context one might define these "race conditions" as unexpected program behavior occurring because of the arbitrary interleaving of concurrent code.

This issue arises very naturally in an exercise based on the simple video game Pong. An implementation of this game comes with the Scratch installation, and the code discussed here is a modified version of that provided code. In this game, a ball bounces off the top and sides of the screen, and the player controls a horizontally moving paddle at the bottom of the screen on which the ball can also bounce. The player's goal is to prevent the ball from bypassing the paddle and thus hitting the bottom of the screen.

Figure 2.4 shows Scratch code for the ball sprite, while Figure 2.5 shows code for the paddle sprite. Note that the three loops (two `repeat until` loops and one `forever if` loop) each depend on the "Boolean" variable `stop` to determine when they should stop looping. When a new game is started by the player clicking on the flag, the clear intent of the programmer is for the initialization code to run first. Note, however, that all four blocks of code are triggered by the flag, and thus they are all running concurrently.

In Scratch, the interleaving of these concurrent commands is consistent, but arbitrary from the programmer's perspective. In the code in Figures 2.4 and 2.5, once one game has been completed (when the ball touches the red color at the bottom of the screen), the `stop` variable remains set to 1. When a new game is begun, if the loop conditions are checked before the `set stop to 0` initialization code is executed, then the `repeat until` loops will immediately terminate and the game will not run properly.

For example, it is possible that the `ordinary ball movement` code block ceases while the paddle does respond to mouse movement. Thus, it is an interesting exercise for the students to devise arbitrary interleavings consistent with the evidence. One such interleaving for the example stated here is as follows:

1. Ordinary ball movement (first command)
2. If ball touches paddle, bounce (first command)
3. Initialization (first command)
4. Paddle script (first command)

The most important exercise, of course, is to devise program modifications to address this race condition and allow the code to execute correctly every time. There are many possibilities. For example, the `initialization` block of code could be extended, with `wait 0.5 secs` and `set stop to 0` blocks added to the end. Alternatively, all blocks of code except the `initialization` block could have a `wait 0.2 secs` block added to the *beginning*. These modifications use a common trick of inserting a small wait in order to ensure an appropriate interleaving.

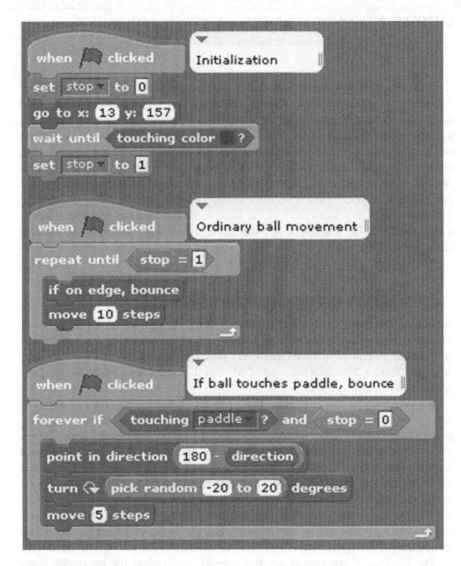

FIGURE 2.4

Code for the Pong ball.

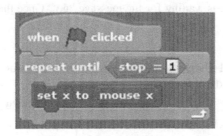

FIGURE 2.5

Code for the Pong paddle.

It is important to emphasize that this exercise depends on Scratch's arbitrary interleaving of concurrent code. As such, seemingly inconsequential modifications to the code can alter this interleaving in a way that may change, or even eliminate, the negative effects of the race condition. While this might take the instructor by surprise and result in a perceived loss of an educational opportunity, it need not be so. Rather, the instructor could take "correct" code, in which the arbitrary interleaving does not lead to any negative effects, and introduce a seemingly inconsequential change. For example, in the `initialization` code, swapping the first two statements, and/or adding a very short `wait` at the start, could produce the negative effect of a race condition. These kinds of changes can lead to striking surprises and learning opportunities for students.

2.3.3 BLOCKING AND NONBLOCKING COMMANDS

Scratch also provides an excellent context in which to explore the use and behavior of blocking versus nonblocking commands. Table 2.1 provides these commands. It is important to remind students that every time they use one of these commands, they must make a conscious decision of whether they want blocking or nonblocking behavior.

For the most part, the commands behave as one would expect. The blocking `say` and `think` commands will block for the specified number of seconds, while the nonblocking versions cause the text to be said or thought indefinitely while the rest of the code executes. (The text disappears only when another `say` or `think` command is executed to replace it.) The blocking `play sound` command waits until the sound has finished before proceeding to the next command, while the nonblocking version moves on to the next command immediately. Finally, in the blocking `broadcast`, the sending sprite waits for the receiving sprite's `when I receive` block of code to complete execution before continuing, while the nonblocking version continues immediately.

The `broadcast` commands are the primary mechanism for intersprite communication, and are an effective introduction to the PDC concept of interprocess communication. One interesting classroom exercise is to consider the code in Figure 2.6. Sprite 2 is waiting for the message "go." Once the message has been

Table 2.1 Blocking and Nonblocking Versions of Commands in Scratch

Blocking	Nonblocking
say \<text\> for \<float\> secs	say \<text\>
think \<text\> for \<float\> secs	think \<text\>
play sound \<snd\> until done	play sound \<snd\>
broadcast \<msg\> and wait	broadcast \<msg\>

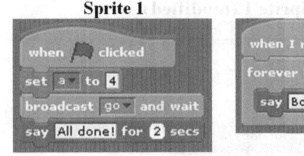

FIGURE 2.6

Code demonstrating the behavior of the blocking broadcast command.

received, sprite 2 enters a `forever if` loop. By way of explanation, consider how this code would look in pseudocode:

while True **do**
   if $a > 5$ **then**
      print "Boogety"
   end if
end while

So the $a > 5$ question is asked repeatedly, forever, once the "go" message is received the first time. Even though the answer will always be `False`, the question is continually asked.

When we examine the code for sprite 1, it is apparent that it will never say "All done!" The first `broadcast go and wait` will never unblock, because sprite 2 will never stop asking if $a > 5$. The reminder, "forever never ends," is helpful, and yet it is easy to forget in certain contexts.

Of course, a simple modification to sprite 1's code can have a large effect. If the original code and the modified code are not shown side by side, some students may not notice the difference between the original code in Figure 2.6, and the modified code in Figure 2.7. In this modified code, the *nonblocking* `broadcast` command is used. Thus, even though "forever never ends," sprite 1 does not wait for sprite 2 to finish, and so sprite 1 does indeed say "All done!" here.

Another interesting modification is to change sprite 1's code such that a is set to 6. While some students may be fooled initially, this is of no consequence for whether or not "All done!" is said. The only difference is that with a set to 6, sprite 2 would say "Boogety!" repeatedly, forever.

2.3.4 SHARED AND PRIVATE VARIABLES

Scratch allows students to wrestle with the use of shared versus private variables as well. Shared variables are specified as available "for all sprites" at variable creation time, while private variables are "for this sprite only."

Sprite 1 (modified)

FIGURE 2.7

Code demonstrating the behavior of the nonblocking broadcast command.

One fun exercise in which both types of variables must be used effectively is in the creation of a "whack-a-mole" game. In the traditional carnival version of this game, a player uses a foam hammer to hit "moles" as they pop up from various holes and pop down those holes randomly and quickly. In this Scratch version, students add eight identical mole sprites arranged in two rows of four, with each assigned a key on the keyboard as shown in Figure 2.8.

The moles execute their code concurrently, each appearing and disappearing randomly and independently. Pressing a key while the corresponding mole is visible makes it immediately disappear and earns the player one point. Pressing a key while the corresponding mole is *not* visible results in a one-point penalty.

Scratch does not have a built-in mechanism for querying whether or not a sprite is visible. This means that each sprite must keep track of a Boolean variable indicating

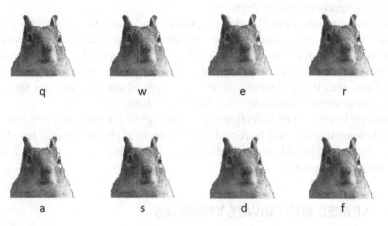

FIGURE 2.8

Arrangement of moles and assigned keys for a whack-a-mole game.

its visibility status. Since each mole's visibility status is independent of the visibility status of the other moles, this status must be maintained in a private variable. In contrast, variables such as the score counter and parameters controlling game difficulty should be shared by all moles. So these variables must be created as "for all sprites."

While the game difficulty value does not change within a single game, it is worthwhile pointing out to students that the shared score counter variable demonstrates a form of interprocess communication. Each sprite has access to this variable and can inform the other sprites that another "hit" has been registered by incrementing the variable. To push this interprocess communication even further, one could imagine an adaptive game in which sprites inform each other of player success via a score variable increase, which leads to increases in the shared difficulty parameter.

As in the blocking/nonblocking issue, it is important to instill in the students the fact that every time they create a new variable, they need to make an explicit decision about whether the variable should be shared or private. In short, if every sprite needs its own copy of some information, and that information need not be accessed by other sprites, then the variable should be private. Similarly, a shared variable can be used to enable all sprites to read, and perhaps write, some aspect of the current state.

2.4 CONCLUSION

To be a student of computing today requires learning core concepts of PDC. This applies not just to upper-level undergraduate majors, but also to introductory-level students and even nonmajors taking only a single computing course. This chapter has described in detail how to provide students with hands-on learning experiences in parallelism with the Scratch programming language. The experiences are designed to be accessible and interesting to any computing student, even at the lowest levels. For a computer science major, these experiences provide a foundation on which a more detailed study of parallelism can be based. For nonmajors, these experiences give a level-appropriate overview of several relevant issues in parallelism.

REFERENCES

[1] S. Bogaerts, K. Burke, B. Shelburne, E. Stahlberg, Concurrency and parallelism as a medium for computer science concepts, in: Curricula for Concurrency and Parallelism Workshop at Systems, Programming, Languages, and Applications: Software for Humanity (SPLASH), Reno, NV, USA, October 2010.

[2] S. Bogaerts, K. Burke, E. Stahlberg, Integrating parallel and distributed computing into undergraduate courses at all levels, in: First NSF/TCPP Workshop on Parallel and Distributed Computing Education (EduPar-11), Anchorage, AK, 2011.

[3] S. Bogaerts, Hands-on exploration of parallelism for absolute beginners with Scratch, in: IPDPSW '13: Proceedings of the 2013 IEEE 27th International Symposium on Parallel and Distributed Processing Workshops and PhD Forum, IEEE Computer Society,

Washington, DC, USA, ISBN 978-0-7695-4979-8, 2013, pp. 1263-1268, doi:10.1109/IPDPSW.2013.63.

[4] M. Rizvi, T. Humphries, D. Major, M. Jones, H. Lauzun, A CS0 course using Scratch, J. Comput. Sci. Coll. 26 (3) (2011) 19-27.

[5] S. Uludag, M. Karakus, S.W. Turner, Implementing IT0/CS0 with Scratch, app inventor for Android, and Lego Mindstorms, in: Proceedings of the 2011 Conference on Information Technology Education, ACM, 2011, pp. 183-190.

[6] U. Wolz, H.H. Leitner, D.J. Malan, J. Maloney, Starting with Scratch in CS 1, in: ACM SIGCSE Bulletin, vol. 41, ACM, 2009, pp. 2-3.

[7] D. Ozorana, N.E. Cagiltayb, D. Topallia, Using Scratch in introduction to programming course for engineering students, in: MEUK2012, Antalya, Turkey, 2012.

[8] D.J. Malan, H.H. Leitner, Scratch for budding computer scientists, ACM SIGCSE Bull. 39 (1) (2007) 223-227.

[9] B. Harvey, J. Mönig, Bringing no ceiling to Scratch: can one language serve kids and computer scientists, Proc. Constructionism (2010).

[10] M. Resnick, J. Maloney, A. Monroy-Hernández, N. Rusk, E. Eastmond, K. Brennan, A. Millner, E. Rosenbaum, J. Silver, B. Silverman, et al., Scratch: programming for all, Commun. ACM 52 (11) (2009) 60-67.

[11] J. Maloney, M. Resnick, N. Rusk, B. Silverman, E. Eastmond, The Scratch programming language and environment, ACM Trans. Comput. Educ. 10 (4) (2010) 16.

[12] S. Cooper, W. Dann, R. Pausch, Alice: a 3-D tool for introductory programming concepts, J. Comput. Sci. Coll., 15 (4) (2000) 107-116. Consortium for Computing Sciences in Colleges.

[13] V. Allan, M. Kolesar, Teaching computer science: a problem solving approach that works, in: Proceedings of the National Educational Computing Conference, 1996, pp. 9-15.

[14] M. Badger, Scratch 1.4, Packt Publishing, 2009.

Parallelism in Python for novices

Steven Bogaerts* and Joshua Stough†

DePauw University* Washington & Lee University†

Relevant core courses: CS0, CS1, CS2/DS.

Relevant parallel and distributed computing topics: Concurrency (C), Tasks and threads (A), Decomposition into atomic tasks (A), Performance metrics (C), Divide and conquer (parallel aspects) (A), Recursion (parallel aspects) (A), Sorting (A).

Learning outcomes: The student should be able to apply the demonstrated techniques to new computational problems, and generally be able to maintain intelligent conversation on parallel computing.

Context for use: The very early introduction of parallel computing techniques in computer science curricula and the reinforcement of concepts already covered in introductory curricula.

3.1 INTRODUCTION

This chapter[1] provides practical advice and materials for instructors of novice programmers. The Python programming language and its `multiprocessing` module are used in a hands-on exploration of concepts of parallelism. The chapter starts with some background information, followed by specific materials and advice on how best to deliver them to students. Many of the code examples are available online [1], with more comments than are possible here.

---

[1]Funding support in part from National Science Foundation grant CCF-0915805, SHF:Small:RUI:Col-laborative Research: Accelerators to Applications—Supercharging the Undergraduate Computer Science Curriculum. Additional funding from NSF/TCPP CDER Center Early Adopter Awards and institutional sources.

3.2 BACKGROUND

This section provides information about the target audience, our goals for the reader, and our reasons for selecting particular tools.

3.2.1 TARGET AUDIENCE OF THIS CHAPTER

This chapter is intended for instructors of *novice* programmers. We expect this will most typically be instructors of CS1, CS2, and introductory computational science courses with a programming component. Instructors of other courses may also find some components of this material helpful, at least to organize an overview for their students.

3.2.2 GOALS FOR THE READER

Our goals for the reader are as follows:

- The reader will share in our experience of prerequisites, best practices, and pitfalls of working with the `multiprocessing` module and integrating it into existing courses.
- Through numerous demonstration materials and example in-class exercises, the reader will be able to write programs and customize course materials that use `multiprocessing`, including fork/join, message passing, resource sharing, and locks.
- The reader will have experience with many practical applications of parallelism, including searching, sorting, pipelining, Monte Carlo simulations, and image processing.

3.2.3 TOOLS

Python

Python is an increasingly popular choice as a first programming language in computer science curricula. Its simple syntax allows students to quickly write interesting applications, minimizing the time spent on syntactic rules. For example, Python requires no variable type declarations, variables are dynamic and can hold any time, garbage collection is automatic, and there is no explicit memory management. Clearly, students should learn such traditional programming mechanics at some point, but we argue that to require very early examination of such topics (i.e., in CS1) delays the exploration of interesting applications, possibly to the point that some students lose interest and do not take further computer science courses. We believe that interesting introductory experiences can be created in any programming language, but Python's simplicity greatly facilitates this effort.

We use Python 2.x in this chapter since, at time of writing, many third-party libraries still support only Python 2.x, and most current Linux distributions and Mac OS releases use Python 2.x as a default. This is not a significant problem, however, as the code examples in this chapter are essentially the same in Python 2.x and Python 3.x.

The multiprocessing *module*

Within the Python community, there are many tools available for the exploration of parallelism, including pprocess, Celery, MPI4Py, and Parallel Python [2]. Our primary need in this work is pedagogical clarity and ease of integration into existing courses, not all-out speed. For this reason we choose the multiprocessing module. This module is simpler than many other tools, features excellent documentation, and comes as standard with Python 2.6+.

One small downside of the multiprocessing module is that it is not compatible with IDLE, the integrated development environment (IDE) that comes with Python installations. The simplest work-around is to use a third-party IDE, such as spyder [3], for which this is not an issue. A listing of IDE's is available through the Python.org website [4].

3.3 STUDENT PREREQUISITES

Here we discuss prerequisites for exploration of the multiprocessing module, in terms of both Python programming and a high-level overview of parallelism concepts. Some examples later in this chapter may have some additional prerequisites related to the area of application, as discussed in the context of those examples.

3.3.1 MOTIVATING EXAMPLES INVOLVING PARALLELISM CONCEPTS

It is the experience of many instructors that students are not ready to absorb a new technique until it clearly solves a problem familiar to them. Fortunately for the introduction of concurrency and parallel computational techniques, *every* student will be very familiar with real-world situations that parallel and distributed computing thinking clearly addresses. Thus, even in spite of the inevitable difficulties with implementation details (ameliorated though they are through Python), the parallel and distributed computing teacher is gifted with students who have been primed for this topic by their experience. Here we address some broad themes that invoke parallelism, along with particular scenarios that might serve as motivation. Just as with all of computer science, parallel algorithms and organization mimic human solutions to real-world problems.

- **Accelerating a large task by harnessing parallel hardware**: Real-world experiences exemplifying this theme include a group assembling a puzzle or toy, band or choir practice, or even any team sports. Among numerous computational examples involving this form of parallelism are animation (both film and video game), Internet search, and data mining.
- **Communicating with remote entities that are inherently autonomous**: Everyone has experience with the concept of process coordination through

message passing, usually in the context of the real-world examples above. Additionally, many games (Go Fish, Taboo, Trivial Pursuit) involve language or physical communication (Charades, Tag). While the students may not have previously thought about these scenarios as involving parallelism, the instructor may make the link by replacing keywords, "process" for "player," or "pass a message" for "tell/say." In the world of computers, students can understand their use of e-mail, Web browsing, and social media clients as parallelism in this vein, with their device's client software communicating with the server software on the Internet.

- **Isolating independent processes for security or resource management**: Most school cafeterias illustrate this concept through multiple independent counters or store fronts serving different fare, such as a pizza bar separate from the salad bar separate from the sandwich bar. This makes it possible for people who want pizza to avoid waiting behind people who want a sandwich. Dealing with a particular line, Subway, Chipotle, Qdoba, and other establishments further use assembly-line production to improve efficiency, where isolated processes (employees) contribute to a job (order) and pass it along. Through this pipelining and the avoidance of context switching (no sandwich orders in the pizza line), a long line of customers can be served very quickly. This real-world organization is reflected in computers through chip design (memory unit separate from the register table separate from the arithmetic-logic unit) and the modularized organization of the computer itself.

The above information provides the reader with some jumping-off points to motivate the use of parallelism, integral in computer science just as in our corporal reality. To further elicit this motivation in students, the authors are particularly fond of the physical exercises in [5]. Depending on time constraints and preferences, this can be covered in 1-3 h of in-class time.

3.3.2 PYTHON PROGRAMMING

The bare minimum Python prerequisites for exploring the multiprocessing module are actually very few: just printing, variables, tuples, and writing and using functions with keyword arguments. Theoretically, then, students could begin exploring the multiprocessing module extremely early in their study of programming (i.e., within the first few weeks). However, there are two problems with starting so early.

First, such limited programming ability would severely restrict what applications are feasible. Since an important part of this work is to apply parallelism to interesting problems, it would be wise to provide some introduction in traditional early topics such loops and conditionals.

Second, the multiprocessing module works through the use of classes (e.g., a Process class, a Lock class, etc.). Students are not required to understand object-oriented programming to use the multiprocessing module—they could simply be told "this is the syntax to make a new process," rather than "this is how you call the Process *constructor*, a special *method* defined in the Process *class*." Our experience has shown, however, that this would make student learning much more challenging. Thus, it is preferable for students to have a small amount of experience in working with classes as well, before beginning a study of the multiprocessing module. The experience should cover the notion that a class defines methods and object state, constructors, method invocation, and that methods can modify state.

It is important to emphasize that only *introductory* experience in the above topics is necessary. That is, students should know the basics of what a loop is; they do not need to have mastered multiple kinds, less common forms, etc. Students should know some basics about classes as described above, but they do not need to understand object-oriented design and the language constructs that facilitate good designs. Thus, we expect that most introductory programming courses would be ready to consider the multiprocessing module after 50-75% of the course has been completed.

3.4 GENERAL APPROACH: PARALLELISM AS A MEDIUM

This section describes our general approach for integrating parallelism into introductory courses, based on work first reported in [6]. Detailed materials and explanation for this approach will be provided following this section.

In considering how to integrate parallelism into introductory courses, one finds it useful to make an analogy. Consider object-oriented programming. At its core, object-oriented programming is a different paradigm from imperative programming, the primary paradigm in use decades ago. As object-oriented programming was developed, we can imagine posing questions similar to those we face today regarding parallelism: How can object-oriented programming be integrated into introductory programming courses? Is this wise, or even possible?

Of course there are still many variations in curricula, but in general we can see how these questions have been answered. While there is a place for a high-level object-oriented programming course, object-oriented concepts are by no means relegated only to such a course. CS1 typically includes the use of objects and basic class construction. A data structures course often includes the creation of abstract data types with classes. Graphics courses can make use of abstraction through classes as well as through functions. The inclusion of these object-oriented topics has necessitated some additional time to learn mechanics, but it is fair to say that many of the topics of these courses are simply being taught through the medium of object-oriented programming now, rather than solely through the medium of imperative programming. Furthermore, while perhaps some sacrifices have been made, most key concepts of imperative programming have not been sacrificed to achieve this object-oriented programming coverage.

We argue that the same can and will be said for questions of parallelism education. Our approach for integrating parallelism into introductory courses while not sacrificing large amounts of traditional content is to recognize parallelism as a complementary *medium* for learning various computer science topics. This does require some additional background in basic mechanics, but once these basics have been covered, parallelism can be used in combination with traditional approaches for learning computer science. The key is that this can be done without significant elimination of other material; rather, other material is simply learned through the medium of parallelism. We will consider this theme explicitly in many of the course materials provided below.

3.5 COURSE MATERIALS

The remaining sections of this chapter contain many examples, along with an explanation of what is happening and some tips on presenting the material in a course.

Also included with most examples is a list of "key ideas." We find that after an in-class example, it is useful to give students some time in class to enter into their copy of the file what they believe are the key ideas for that example. Students can then share key ideas with the class as a whole. While this explicit consideration of key ideas does take extra class time and may seem repetitious to the instructor, we find that it is worth it in the long run; students retain the material much better and are thus better prepared for later material, and therefore require less time reviewing prerequisite concepts. Some sample key ideas are provided for most concepts below, demonstrating what students should take away from the example. These are key ideas taken directly from students, meaning that occasionally some ideas listed were actually first introduced in earlier examples. The presence of such "review" key ideas reinforces the notion that students may need regular reminders of certain concepts. The sequence of examples is designed to provide these reminders.

Some course materials below are presented as in-class lecture-oriented examples, while others are presented as in-class exercises. We try to balance the two, keeping students as active as possible through the exercises while still providing adequate scaffolding through lectures. For the exercises, we will assume that students have access to computers in class, though the exercises could be adapted to individual pencil-and-paper exercises or class-wide collaborative activities.

3.6 PROCESSES

A very brief discussion of processes is useful before going into programming. While the reality of the execution of processes on various architectures can be quite complex, a simplified overview is all that is required here. The instructor can explain that a process is a running program, in which the current instruction and the data is maintained. On a single-core processor, only one process actually runs at a time. This may be surprising to students, as they are accustomed to having many applications active at once. But the reality is that the operating system actually switches from one process to the next and back very quickly via *context switches*, giving the *illusion* of multiple processes executing at once. Such context switching, sharing the single-processor resource, is an example of *concurrency*. It can be fun to view a list of running processes on a machine (Crtl-Alt-Delete to the Task Manager in Windows, for example) as an illustration of how this works.

This is in contrast to a multicore processor, in which multiple processes can be executed literally at the same time (limited by the number of cores, of course). Thus, true *parallelism* is achieved in this case, rather than simply the illusion that concurrency provides. Of course, the reality of all this is more complex, but this is a useful abstraction at this level.

A potentially helpful side-note can be made here, comparing concurrency with the common human effort in multitasking. People often believe that in multitasking (e.g., texting and listening to a lecture, etc.) that they are working in parallel, truly doing both tasks at the same time. Psychological studies suggest, however, that the reality is closer to concurrency—multitasking through context switches—as most of a "multitasker's" performance on both tasks suffers. This can be a revelation in study skills for students who are willing to take the message to heart.

3.6.1 SPAWNING A PROCESS

We are now ready to work with the multiprocessing module itself. The first step is to import the module with from multiprocessing import *. Students can then view the first example, in Figure 3.1. Note that current_process returns a Process object corresponding to the currently running process. The Process class defines a pid instance variable for the process identifier. The print at line 5 prints the pid of the default *parent* process for the program.

Line 10 then constructs, but does not start, a *child* process. Note the use of keyword arguments. The target is sayHi, meaning that the child process, once started, will execute the sayHi method. The args argument is a tuple of the

```
1  def sayHi():
2    print "Hi from process", current_process().pid
3
4  def procEx():
5    print "Hi from process", current_process().pid, "(main process)"
6
7    # Construct the process (but it doesn't start automatically).
8    # target must be a function, without the parentheses.
9    # args must be a tuple, containing the arguments to pass to the target,
10   #   or () if no arguments.
11   otherProc = Process(target=sayHi, args=())
12
13   # Start the process we just constructed.
14   otherProc.start()
```

FIGURE 3.1

Spawning a single process.

arguments to pass to the `target`; since `sayHi` takes no arguments, `args` is an empty tuple in this example. Note the inclusion of comments for the assistance of the student in this constructor call.

Finally, the child process is started with the `start` method. At this point, both the parent process and the child process want to run. On a multicore system, they can run in parallel; on a single-core system, they will run concurrently.

Immediately in this example we can see the idea of parallelism as a *medium* for traditional course topics. Ideally, at this point students will have had some experience with using classes, constructors, other methods, and instance variables. And yet they might not yet be fully comfortable with these ideas, and/or may not see their value. This early example gives students additional practice with these concepts. Through the `Process` class, a very significant amount of functionality is gained for very little programming effort. The `Process` class interacts with the operating system to create a new process registered with the scheduler, ready to access shared processor resources. This is an excellent illustration of the power of encapsulation and object-oriented programming.

Sample key ideas

- To create a child process, call the `Process` constructor, specifying a target (the function to be run—without parentheses), and also specifying the arguments that will go to that target function.
- The `Process` class has many instance variables, including `pid` and `name`, which are public and can be used to identify the process. `current_process().pid` gives the pid of the currently running process (same idea for name).
- `current_process()` is a function defined in the `multiprocessing` module. It is an expression, giving a `Process` object representing the currently running process.
- The `Process` class has a start method that must be called for the process to start doing its task.

3.6.2 SPAWNING MULTIPLE PROCESSES

Immediately after the example above, a short active exercise is helpful:

Copy the "Spawning a single process" example in Figure 3.1, and modify it to create three processes, each of which says "Hi" as above.

A solution is provided in Figure 3.2. It is important to point out to the students that each process uses the same `sayHi` function defined above, but each process executes that function independently of the others.

While this exercise is just a trivial extension of the previous example, we find it helpful to give the students hands-on experience with the `multiprocessing` module as soon as possible. This short exercise can give the students an early successful experience.

```
1  def procEx2():
2    print "Hi from process", current_process().pid, "(main process)"
3
4    p1 = Process(target=sayHi, args=())
5    p2 = Process(target=sayHi, args=())
6    p3 = Process(target=sayHi, args=())
7
8    p1.start()
9    p2.start()
10   p3.start()
```

FIGURE 3.2

Exercise solution for spawning multiple processes.

Sample key ideas

• You can make multiple child processes simply by calling the Process constructor multiple times. These processes are independent of each other.

Immediately after this exercise, a trivial extension can introduce the passing of arguments to a child process's function, as shown in Figure 3.3.

Note that sayHi2 takes a single argument, and that each call to the Process constructor passes a tuple with a single value inside the args parameter. It may also be helpful here to remind students of the purpose of the comma in (name,). Python requires this in order to interpret the parentheses as markers of a tuple rather than simple grouping.

Sample key ideas

• When you create multiple processes, they run independently of each other.
• The args tuple can be set to contain whatever data you want to pass to the target function.

```
1  def sayHi2(n):
2    print "Hi", n, "from process", current_process().pid
3
4  def manyGreetings():
5    print "Hi from process", current_process().pid, "(main process)"
6
7    name = "Jimmy"
8    p1 = Process(target=sayHi2, args=(name,))
9    p2 = Process(target=sayHi2, args=(name,))
10   p3 = Process(target=sayHi2, args=(name,))
11
12   p1.start()
13   p2.start()
14   p3.start()
```

FIGURE 3.3

Passing arguments to child processes.

- The args tuple must contain exactly as many items as the target takes as arguments. The arguments must be provided in the correct order (you cannot use the keywords "arguments style" here).

3.6.3 SPAWNING MULTIPLE PROCESSES USING POOL

While the Process constructor is useful for explicitly spawning independent processes, the multiprocessing module also offers multiple process spawning through the use of the Pool and Pool.map mechanism, as seen in Figure 3.4. Two syntactic constraints to this usage are first that all processes execute the same function (sayHi2 above), and second that this function accepts only one argument. (The second argument of map at line 12 is a list of the single arguments to distribute to the processes.) These are weak constraints, however, in that both can be easily circumvented. Also in this simple example, the return argument of Pool.map is unassigned at line 12, though it would be the list of return arguments of the three independent expressions sayHi2(name), or [None, None, None]. See Section 3.9 for more complicated and useful examples of the Pool/map paradigm, including Monte Carlo simulation, integration, and sorting.

3.6.4 ANONYMOUS PROCESSES

At this point, we recommend another exercise:

Write a function that first asks for your name, and then asks how many processes should be spawned. That many processes are created, and each greets you by name and gives its pid.

See Figure 3.5 for a solution. Many students may devise a solution involving the commented-out approach (storing a new Process object in p and then calling p.start()), though for the purposes of this problem, the code in line 8 is more compact. While to an experienced programmer this may seem hardly worth a separate

```
1  from multiprocessing import Pool, current_process
2
3  def sayHi2(n):
4      print('Hi ' + n + ' from process ' + str(current_process().pid))
5
6  def manyGreetings():
7      print('Hi from process ' + str(current_process().pid) + ' (main process)')
8
9      name = 'Jimmy'
10     p = Pool(processes = 3)
11
12     p.map(sayHi2, [name, name, name])
13
14 if __name__ == '__main__':
15     manyGreetings()
```

FIGURE 3.4

Using a Pool to perform the example in Figure 3.3.

```
1  def manyGreetings2():
2      name = raw_input("Enter your name: ")
3      numProc = input("How many processes? ")
4
5      for i in range(numProc):
6          #p = Process(target=sayHi2, args=(name,))
7          #p.start()
8          (Process(target=sayHi2, args=(name,))).start()
```

FIGURE 3.5

"Anonymous" processes.

exercise, the *medium* of parallelism in this example actually offers a wealth of traditional topics for novice programmers to consider.

First, we find that novice programmers do not readily transfer knowledge from one context to another without explicit practice. It is not uncommon to find student attempts such as the following:

```
1      for i in range(numProc):
2          pi = Process( target =sayHi2, args=(name,))
3          pi. start ()
```

This would work, as it merely substitutes variable p in Figure 3.5 for pi. However, students may believe that this is actually creating several variables, p0, p1, p2, etc. This is not due to a complete lack of understanding of how loop variables work. Rather, it is a failure to transfer knowledge to a new context. Students can be quickly corrected with the following example:

```
1      for a in range(10):
2          grade = 97
```

It will likely be obvious to students that this code does not generate the variables gr0de, gr1de, gr2de, etc. Similarly, then, this code analogy should make it clear that pi does not become p0, p1, p2, etc.

This exercise provides opportunities to consider other important concepts as well. For example, which approach is better, the explicit use of p, or the anonymous version? Which is more readable? Should the program be designed such that the programmer can refer to the object later, thus necessitating p or perhaps a list of all constructed processes? Students may not yet be accustomed to considering such questions in a wide variety of contexts, so this practice is very important.

This example also reinforces the notion that the Process constructor is an *expression* when called, and can be used as any other expression. Introductory programmers sometimes learn to do things more by rote than through deep understanding. A student might think "to make an instance of a class, I have to call the constructor and store it in a variable." Of course, in reality the programmer has more flexibility, and it is important for students to see this in various contexts.

The instructor can remind students that the start method is a *statement* when called. This means that (Process(target=sayHi2, args=(name,))).

start() or p.start() is acceptable by itself on a line. Furthermore, p.start().pid, for example, will *not* work. It would only work if the start method were an expression when called, returning a Process object. But this is not the case. Students will likely have wrestled with these ideas of expressions and statements earlier in the course, and this is another excellent opportunity to consider them in detail in a new context. The issue of expressions versus statements is not just some unimportant distinction designed to give instructors something to test students on. Rather, the understanding of this concept enables programmers to more effectively use unfamiliar tools such as the multiprocessing module!

Thus, we see that, while the example is at its surface about creating processes, the most important lessons are about more general, traditional programming topics. These topics would need to be discussed in any event in introductory programming courses. Parallelism provides a very practical *medium* in which to do so.

Sample key ideas

- A process (or any object) does not have to be stored in a variable to be used. But if you do not store it in a variable, you will not be able to use it after the first time. An object not stored in a variable is called an "anonymous object."
- If you need to access the process objects later, you could store them in a list when you make them. To do this, make a list accumulator (starting with []) that you append Process objects to, so that you can loop through the list later.
- Once a process has been started, changing the variable that stored it will not stop the process.
- For loops do not substitute values into the middle of variable names.

3.6.5 SPECIFYING PROCESS NAMES

The next example (Figure 3.6) on its surface is about a small piece of multiprocessing functionality: specifying a name for a process. The more important lesson, using parallelism as a *medium* for traditional course topics, is that name is an instance variable of the Process class, thus providing a reminder of what instance variables are in general.

Another important issue brought up in this example is the idea of *resource contention*. It is likely that the output of this example will be very jumbled up; the reason why, and a solution, is discussed in the next example.

3.6.6 USING A LOCK TO CONTROL PRINTING

It is now time to consider an important part of parallelism: controlling access of shared resources. One excellent way to begin this process is by analogy to a concept from the novel *Lord of the Flies* by William Golding (or the 1963 and 1990 film adaptations). The novel tells the story of a group of boys shipwrecked on a deserted

```
1  def sayHi3(personName):
2    print "Hi", personName, "from process", current_process().name, "−
3  pid", current_process().pid
4
5  def manyGreetings3():
6    print "Hi from process", current_process().pid, "(main process)"
7
8    personName = "Jimmy"
9    for i in range(10):
10     Process(target=sayHi3, args=(personName,), name=str(i)).start()
```

FIGURE 3.6

Specifying process names.

island, with no adult survivors. Before an eventual breakdown into savagery, the boys conduct regular meetings to decide on issues facing the group. The boys quickly realize that, left unchecked, such meetings will be unproductive as multiple boys wish to speak at the same time. Thus a rule is developed: Only the boy that is holding a specially designated conch is allowed to speak. When that boy has finished speaking, he relinquishes the conch so that another boy may speak. Thus, order is maintained at the meetings as long as the boys abide by these rules. We can also imagine what would happen if this conch were not used: chaos in meetings as the boys try to shout above each other. (And in fact this does happen in the story.)

It requires only a slight stretch of the events in this novel to make an analogy to the coordination of multiple processes accessing a shared resource. In programming terms, each boy is a separate process, having his own things he wishes to say at the meeting. But the air around the meeting is a shared resource—all boys speak into the same space. So there is contention for the shared resource that is this space. Control of this shared resource is handled via the single, special conch. The conch is a *lock*—only one boy may hold it at a time. When he releases it, indicating that he has finished speaking, some other boy may pick it up. Boys that are waiting to pick up the conch cannot say anything—they just have to wait until whoever has the conch releases it. Of course, several boys may be waiting for the conch at the same time, and only one of them will actually get it next. So some boys might have to continue waiting through multiple speakers.

The code in Figure 3.7 shows the analogous idea in Python. Several processes are created and started. Each wants to print something, in sayHi4. But print writes to stdout (standard output), a single resource that is shared among all the processes. So when multiple processes all want to print at the same time, their output would be jumbled together were it not for the lock, which ensures that only one process is able to execute its print at a time. Suppose process *A* acquires the lock and begins printing. If processes *B*, *C*, and *D* then execute their acquire calls while process *A* has the lock, then processes *B*, *C*, and *D* must each wait. That is, each will *block* on its acquire call. Once process *A* releases the lock, one of the processes blocked

```
 1 def sayHi4(lock, name):
 2    lock.acquire()
 3    print "Hi", name, "from process", current_process().pid
 4    lock.release()
 5
 6 def manyGreetings3():
 7    lock1 = Lock()
 8
 9    print "Hi from process", current_process().pid, "(main process)"
10
11    for i in range(10):
12        Process(target=sayHi4, args=(lock1, "p"+str(i))).start()
```

FIGURE 3.7

A demonstration of a lock to handle resource contention.

on that lock acquisition will arbitrarily be chosen to acquire the lock and print. That process will then release the lock so that another blocked process can proceed, and so on.

Note that the lock must be created in the parent process and then passed to each child—this way each child process is referring to the same lock. The alternative, in which each child constructs its own lock, would be analogous to each boy bringing his own conch to a meeting. Clearly this would not work.

It is important to point out to students that the order of execution of the processes is arbitrary. That is, the acquisition of the lock is arbitrary, and so subsequent runs of the code in Figure 3.7 are likely to produce different orderings. It is not necessarily the process that was created first, or that has been waiting the longest, that gets to acquire the lock next.

Sample key ideas
- Locks prevent multiple processes from trying to do something at the same time that they should not do. For example, multiple processes should not try to print (access stdout) at the same time.
- Define the lock in the parent process, so it can be passed to all the children.
- Do not forget to use lock.release() sometime after every lock.acquire(), otherwise any other processes waiting for the lock will wait forever.

3.6.7 DIGGING HOLES

The final example in this section is a simple exercise extending the concept of locks above:

Imagine that you have 10 hole diggers, named A, B, C, D, E, F, G, H, I, and J. Think of each of these as a process, and write a function assignDiggers() *that creates 10 processes with these worker names working on holes 0, 1, 2, ..., 9, respectively. Each one should print a message about what it is doing. When you have finished, you should get output like the following (except that the order will be arbitrary):*

```
>>> assignDiggers()
>>>
Hiddy-ho! I'm worker G and today I have to dig hole 6
Hiddy-ho! I'm worker A and today I have to dig hole 0
Hiddy-ho! I'm worker C and today I have to dig hole 2
Hiddy-ho! I'm worker D and today I have to dig hole 3
Hiddy-ho! I'm worker F and today I have to dig hole 5
Hiddy-ho! I'm worker I and today I have to dig hole 8
Hiddy-ho! I'm worker H and today I have to dig hole 7
Hiddy-ho! I'm worker J and today I have to dig hole 9
Hiddy-ho! I'm worker B and today I have to dig hole 1
Hiddy-ho! I'm worker E and today I have to dig hole 4
```

A solution is provided in Figure 3.8. This exercise provides a good medium to discuss the strengths and limitations of different looping constructs. Note that the solution provided uses a "loop by index" approach, in which the holeID index is the loop variable. An alternative that some students might attempt would be "loop by element" (a for-each loop), as in Figure 3.9. The issue here is that workerNames.index(workerName) is a linear time operation, so this is a far less efficient approach. Note that the actual execution time will be nearly instantaneous in both approaches, but it is nevertheless a good idea to reiterate the general principle of using the right programming constructs for maximum efficiency. Novice

```
1  def dig(workerName, holeID, lock):
2    lock.acquire()
3    print "Hiddy-ho! I'm worker", workerName, "and today I have to dig hole",
       holeID
4    lock.release()
5
6  def assignDiggers():
7    lock = Lock()
8    workerNames = ["A", "B", "C", "D", "E", "F", "G", "H", "I", "J"]
9
10   for holeID in range(len(workerNames)):
11     Process(target=dig, args=(workerNames[holeID], holeID, lock)).start()
```

FIGURE 3.8

Digging holes: practice with locks.

```
1    ... # Other code as before
2    for workerName in workerNames:
3      Process(target=dig, args=(workerName, workerNames.index(workerName),
         lock)).start()
```

FIGURE 3.9

Digging holes: a less effective loop-by-element approach.

programmers may not be accustomed to considering such things, and so this is a good opportunity to explore this important introductory programming concept arising in the medium of parallelism.

Sample key ideas

- If it does not matter what order the processes run in, then code like in this example can run very efficiently.
- This is a good example of a situation where you need to choose carefully between looping by index and looping by element. Looping by index is ideal here.

3.7 COMMUNICATION

This section provides several examples of interprocess communication. As in the other sections of this chapter, the purpose is not to exhaustively cover every possibility, but rather to allow students to gain some basic exposure. While the multiprocessing module does support some shared memory mechanisms, message passing is the primary means of communication for the module, and so that is the paradigm we recommend exploring in the limited time of an introductory course.

3.7.1 COMMUNICATING VIA A QUEUE

The authors find it helpful to start immediately with a simple example. Figure 3.10 demonstrates the use of a *queue* for communication between processes. Note that the parent process creates the queue and passes it as an argument to the child process. So the child process is in fact using the same queue as the parent. In this case, the child will only receive (get) while the parent will only send (put). The child's get is a *blocking* command. This means that the child process will go to sleep until it has

```
1  def greet(q):
2    print "(child process) Waiting for name..."
3    name = q.get()
4    print "(child process) Well, hi", name
5
6  def sendName():
7    q = Queue()
8
9    p1 = Process(target=greet, args=(q,))
10   p1.start()
11
12   time.sleep(5) # wait for 5 seconds
13   print "(main process) Ok, I'll send the name"
14   q.put("Jimmy")
```

FIGURE 3.10

The use of a queue for communication between processes.

a reason to wake up—in this case, when there is something to `get` from the queue. Since the parent sleeps for 5 s, the child ends up blocking for approximately 5 s as well. Finally the parent process sends the string "`Jimmy`", the child process unblocks and stores "`Jimmy`" in the variable `name`, and prints.

Note also the addition of some print statements to give the programmer a visual indication of what is happening while the code is running. This is an important programming and debugging skill for introductory programmers to practice.

Sample key ideas

- A queue is like standing in line. The first thing in is the first thing out.
- `put` and `get` can be used for any processes to communicate by sending and receiving data.
- If a process tries to get data from an empty queue, it will sleep until some other process puts data in the queue.

3.7.2 EXTENDED COMMUNICATION VIA A QUEUE

After the simple example above, it is helpful to provide an immediate opportunity for student practice, even for a very small expansion of the problem. This enables students to do something active, thereby facilitating the transfer of these concepts into long-term memory. The following exercise is provided:

> *Copy the code in Figure 3.10 as a basis for greet2 and sendName2. Modify the code so that greet2 expects to receive five names, which are sent by sendName2. Each function should accomplish this by sending/receiving one name at a time, in a loop.*

While this exercise seems rather simple to experienced programmers, the newness of queues is sufficient to make many students pause. Thus, this exercise provides an excellent opportunity to remind students of the utility of pseudocode. This crucial problem-solving technique frees students from most concerns of syntax, and so the overall program structure is then not too difficult to determine. And so, part way through this exercise, it is useful to work with the students in developing the pseudocode in Figure 3.11. Once this pseudocode has been developed, the actual code comes much more easily. Figure 3.12 shows a solution.

Sample key ideas

- Sometimes you can get by without using locks if processes are waiting for other reasons.
- `import moduleName` means I have to say `moduleName`. `functionName`. `from moduleName import functionName` means I can just say `functionName`.

```
1  '''
2  def greet2():
3    for 5 times
4      get name from queue
5      say hello
6
7  def sendName2():
8    queue
9    make a child process, give it the queue
10   start it
11
12   for 5 times
13     sleep for a bit
14     put another name in the queue
15  '''
```

FIGURE 3.11

Pseudocode for an extended exercise for communicating via a queue.

```
1  from random import randint
2
3  def greet2(q):
4    for i in range(5):
5      print
6      print "(child process) Waiting for name", i
7      name = q.get()
8      print "(child process) Well, hi", name
9
10 def sendName2():
11   q = Queue()
12
13   p1 = Process(target=greet2, args=(q,))
14   p1.start()
15
16   for i in range(5):
17     sleep(randint(1,4))
18     print "(main process) Ok, I'll send the name"
19     q.put("George"+str(i))
```

FIGURE 3.12

Python solution for an extended exercise for communicating via a queue.

3.7.3 THE JOIN METHOD

In parallel programming, a *join* operation instructs the executing process to block until the process on which the join is called finishes. For example, if a parent process creates a child process in variable p1 and then calls p1.join(), then the parent process will block on that join call until p1 finishes. One important point to emphasize again in this example is that the *parent* process blocks, not the process on which join is called (p1)—hence, the careful language at the start of this paragraph: the executing process blocks until the process on which the join is called finishes.

The word "join" can sometimes be confusing for students. The example in Figure 3.13 provides a very physical analogy, of the parent process waiting (using

```
 1  def slowpoke(lock):
 2      sleep(10)
 3      lock.acquire()
 4      print "Slowpoke: Ok, I'm coming"
 5      lock.release()
 6
 7  def haveToWait():
 8      lock = Lock()
 9      p1 = Process(target=slowpoke, args=(lock,))
10      p1.start()
11      print "Waiter: Any day now..."
12
13      p1.join()
14      print "Waiter: Finally! Geez."
```

FIGURE 3.13

Using `join` for coordination between processes.

`join`) for a "slowpoke" child process to catch up. The child process is slow because of the `sleep(10)` call. Note also the use of a lock to manage the shared `stdout`.

It should be pointed out, however, that `join` is not always necessary for process coordination. Often a similar result can be obtained by blocking on a queue `get`, as described in Sections 3.7.4 and 3.7.5.

Sample key ideas

- `p.join()` makes the currently running process wait for p to finish. Be careful! It is not the other way around.
- `join` will slow things down (since it makes a process wait), but it can be used to enforce a particular order of activity.
- Anonymous processes cannot be used with `join`, because you have to both start it and join with it, which means you will need a variable to be able to refer to the process.

3.7.4 OBTAINING A RESULT FROM A SINGLE CHILD

While earlier sections demonstrated a parent process sending data to a child via a queue, this exercise allows students to practice the other way around: a child that performs a computation which is then obtained by the parent. Consider two functions: `addTwoNumbers`, and `addTwoPar`. `addTwoNumbers` takes two numbers as arguments, adds them, and places the result in a queue (which was also passed as an argument). `addTwoPar` asks the user to enter two numbers, passes them and a queue to `addTwoNumbers` in a new process, waits for the result, and then prints it.

The starting code provided to the students is shown in Figure 3.14. The completed exercise is shown in Figure 3.15. We choose to use starter code here because, as an in-class exercise with limited time available, it is important to get to the key points addressed by the example. Thus, the starter code enables students to bypass side issues. Of course, given more time, these "side issues" could provide a good review,

```
1 def addTwoNumbers(a, b, q):
2   # sleep(5) # In case you want to slow things down to see what is happening.
3   q.put(a+b)
4
5 def addTwoPar():
6   x = input("Enter first number: ")
7   y = input("Enter second number: ")
8
9   q = Queue()
10  p1 = Process(target=addTwoNumbers, args=(x, y, q))
11  p1.start()
```

FIGURE 3.14

Starter code for the exercise on obtaining a result from a child process.

```
1 def addTwoNumbers(a, b, q):
2   # sleep(5) # In case you want to slow things down to see what is happening.
3   q.put(a+b)
4
5 def addTwoPar():
6   x = input("Enter first number: ")
7   y = input("Enter second number: ")
8
9   q = Queue()
10  p1 = Process(target=addTwoNumbers, args=(x, y, q))
11  p1.start()
12
13  # p1.join()
14  result = q.get()
15  print "The sum is:", result
```

FIGURE 3.15

Complete code for the exercise on obtaining a result from a child process.

or a relatively short homework problem, and so each instructor should consider personal goals and the time allotted for the exercise.

The parent's use of q.get() is important, but should be familiar from previous exercises. The new idea here is that although join was just introduced, it should not be used thoughtlessly. join is not necessary in this example, because get will already cause the parent to block. The parent will not unblock until the child executes put, which is the child's last action. Thus, in this example, get is already accomplishing essentially what join would accomplish, while also obtaining the child's result.

Also note the commented-out sleep in the child process, which can be useful for seeing more clearly the sequencing created through the queue operations.

Sample key ideas
- This illustrates the bigger concept of making a child process to do some (possibly complex) task while the parent goes on to do other things. You could even have multiple child processes working on parts of the problem.
- You do not need join here, because q.get() will wait until the child puts something in the queue anyway.

3.7.5 USING A QUEUE TO MERGE MULTIPLE CHILD PROCESS RESULTS

The example in Figure 3.16 is a fairly straightforward extension of the one in Section 3.7.4. Here, two child processes are created, each given half of the work. The results are then merged by the parent through two get calls.

It can be interesting to ask students which child's result will be in answerA and which will be in answerB. The answer is that this is indeterminate. Which child process finishes first will have its result in answerA, and the other will have its result in answerB. This is not a problem for commutative merging operations, like the addition in this example, but of course could be a complication for noncommutative merging.

As in the previous exercise, the joins are not necessary and should not be used, so they are commented out.

The use of some rudimentary timing mechanisms in this example is a precursor to further considerations of speedup in some examples below.

Sample key ideas
- This demonstrates the idea of splitting a task up evenly among multiple processes. Each one reports back to the parent processes via a queue.

```
1  from random import randint
2  import time
3  def addManyNumbers(numNumbers, q):
4      s = 0
5      for i in range(numNumbers):
6          s = s + randint(1, 100)
7      q.put(s)
8
9  def addManyPar():
10     totalNumNumbers = 1000000
11
12     q = Queue()
13     p1 = Process(target=addManyNumbers, args=(totalNumNumbers/2, q))
14     p2 = Process(target=addManyNumbers, args=(totalNumNumbers/2, q))
15     startTime = time.time()
16     p1.start()
17     p2.start()
18
19 #      p1.join()
20 #      p2.join()
21
22     answerA = q.get()
23     answerB = q.get()
24     endTime = time.time()
25     timeElapsed = endTime - startTime
26     print "Time:", timeElapsed
27     print "Sum:", answerA + answerB
```

FIGURE 3.16

A parent process obtaining results from children.

3.7.6 MERGESORT USING PROCESS SPAWNING AND QUEUE OBJECTS

This subsection demonstrates parallel mergesort, extending the simpler example in Figure 3.16. There, each child process produces a single integer response, and the parent process combines the responses of the children. Here, each child process produces a list and the parent process merges the lists produced into a larger list. Figure 3.17 shows sequential mergesort code, while Figure 3.28 shows a parallel implementation using Process spawning and communication via Queue objects.

Mergesort is a deceptively simple procedure to intuitively understand, while at the same time the code is so simple it can make students feel they must be missing something. Mergesort is simply "sort the left half; sort the right half; merge the results." One physical exercise the authors find useful involves sorting a deck of cards. To begin, sorting the entire deck as a whole is slow, given that at this stage in the curriculum only $O(N^2)$ sorts have been covered. However, if the instructor splits the deck in two parts and distributes one part to each of two students in the front row, the students quickly see the efficiency implied. If they do the same with their half decks, distributing the work to students behind them, then soon many independent workers are sorting very small decks. As these students finish, the merging operation takes place as the cards make their way back to the front. In-class discussion of this process determines that relative to the $O(N^2)$ sorts, speedup is obtained both by doing less work and by parallelizing that work among multiple processes/students.

```
1  #Sequential mergesort code
2  def merge(left, right):
3      ret = []
4      li = ri = 0
5      while li < len(left) and ri < len(right):
6          if left[li] <= right[ri]:
7              ret.append(left[li])
8              li += 1
9          else:
10             ret.append(right[ri])
11             ri += 1
12     if li == len(left):
13         ret.extend(right[ri:])
14     else:
15         ret.extend(left[li:])
16     return ret
17
18 def mergesort(lyst):
19     if len(lyst) <= 1:
20         return lyst
21     ind = len(lyst)//2
22     return merge(mergesort(lyst[:ind]), mergesort(lyst[ind:]))
```

FIGURE 3.17

Sequential mergesort code (referred to as seqMergesort in Figures 3.28 and 3.27).

The code in Figure 3.28 demonstrates how interactions of the physical exercise can be mapped almost directly to Python. The `mergeSortParallel` process, which represents any particular student in the physical exercise, receives as parameters both the list it is responsible for sorting and the `Queue` object on which it will put the sorted result. A third, integer parameter merely serves to limit the number of recursive process instantiations: that is, can this student recruit two other students or should the student perform the sorting himself/herself?

As an aside, the sequential mergesort in Figure 3.17 uses $O(N \log N)$ memory rather than the ideal $O(N)$, as a result of list slicing in argument passing. While not ideally efficient, this implementation allows the student to move easily from the intuitively understood mergesort idea to the code. Finally, see Section 3.9.3 for a "flattened" mergesort implementation using a `Pool` of processes.

3.7.7 SHARING A DATA STRUCTURE

The examples in Figures 3.18, 3.19, and 3.20 illustrate that memory is not shared between processes, so mutation of arguments does not occur in the same way as

```
1 import random
2 def addItem(ls):
3   ls.append(random.randint(1,100))
4
5 def sequentialDS():
6   ls = []
7   addItem(ls)
8   addItem(ls)
9   print ls
```

FIGURE 3.18

Sequential program showing mutation of a parameter, to serve as a reminder to students.

```
1 # Doesn't work as you might hope!
2 def parallelShareDS1():
3   ls = []
4
5   p1 = Process(target = addItem, args = (ls,))
6   p2 = Process(target = addItem, args = (ls,))
7   p1.start()
8   p2.start()
9
10  p1.join()
11  p2.join()
12
13  print ls
```

FIGURE 3.19

Attempting to pass a parameter to child processes in a way analogous to the sequential case, but not obtaining the same results. Uses `addItem` in Figure 3.18.

```
1  def addItem2(ls , q):
2    q.put(random.randint(1,100))
3
4  def parallelShareDS2():
5    ls = []
6
7    q = Queue()
8    p1 = Process(target = addItem2, args = (ls,q))
9    p2 = Process(target = addItem2, args = (ls,q))
10
11   p1.start()
12   p2.start()
13
14   # Now do whatever we need to with the results from the spawned processes
15   ls.append(q.get())
16   ls.append(q.get())
17   print ls
```

FIGURE 3.20

Communication between processes must occur via special structures, such as a queue.

in a single-process program. First, Figure 3.18 reviews and reinforces the concept that in Python object references are passed, and so mutations will be seen by the caller—that is, the changes to ls that addItem makes will be reflected in the print in sequentialDS.

The code in Figure 3.19 then attempts to accomplish the same idea by passing a list to two child processes. If this worked similarly to the sequential version, then both child processes would append their results to the same list, and the parent would then print a list with two items. However, this is not what occurs. The actual result is that the parent prints an empty list. Thus, the child processes do not share ls, they receive copies. These copies are mutated, but are then thrown away when the child processes terminate. The parent process's ls is not affected.

Finally, Figure 3.20 demonstrates one correct way to accomplish this task. The use of a queue as demonstrated here should be familiar. The necessity of the queue, however, may be new to the students, hence the utility of this example.

3.8 SPEEDUP

These examples demonstrate how to conduct basic timing in Python. This is then applied to examine the speedup of the use of multiple processors on a problem.

3.8.1 TIMING THE SUMMATION OF RANDOM NUMBERS

The example in Figure 3.21 introduces students to the notion of timing the execution of a part of a program, and the generation of random numbers in Python. time.time() returns a float representing the number of seconds since the *epoch*, which in Python is defined as midnight UTC on January 1, 1970. Thus, the elapsed

```
1  import random
2  import time
3
4  def timeSum():
5      numNumbers = 10000
6
7      startTime = time.time()
8      s = 0
9      for i in range(numNumbers):
10         s = s + random.randint(1, 100)
11         # randint(x, y) gives a random integer between x and y, inclusive
12     stopTime = time.time()
13
14     elapsedTime = stopTime - startTime
15     print "The summation took", elapsedTime, "seconds."
16
17 # This version just shows a small shortcut in the timing code.
18 def timeSum2():
19     numNumbers = 10000
20
21     startTime = time.time()
22     s = 0
23     for i in range(numNumbers):
24         s = s + random.randint(1, 100)
25     elapsedTime = time.time() - startTime
26
27     print "The summation took", elapsedTime, "seconds."
```

FIGURE 3.21

Use of the time module for simple timing of algorithms.

time can easily be computed as shown in timeSum, or with a small "trick" in timeSum2 that saves the use of a stopTime variable.

3.8.2 USING JOIN TO TIME A CHILD PROCESS

At this point, students may already be familiar with join from previous examples, but Figure 3.22 is a helpful illustration of its utility in timing a child process's activity. The start time is measured when the child process is started. Once the parent's join call unblocks, the elapsed time is calculated immediately.

3.8.3 COMPARING PARALLEL AND SEQUENTIAL PERFORMANCE

The example in Figure 3.23 demonstrates and allows students to experiment with the speedup that having multiple processors allows. This example is set up to make use of two processors. Note the clear comments marking the section for timing the parallel code and the section for timing the sequential code. Interprocess communication is avoided in this example; that is, the example is embarrassingly parallel. The spawned processes also do not merge their results into a final computed sum, and therefore one less addition is done.

```
1  def addEmUp(maxNum):
2      s = 0
3      for i in range(maxNum):
4          s = s + i
5
6  def joinEx():
7      # Compare execution times of the two processes below
8      p1 = Process(target=addEmUp, args=(50,))
9      # p1 = Process(target=addEmUp, args=(5000000,))
10
11     startTime = time.time()
12     p1.start()
13     print "Still working..."
14     p1.join()
15     elapsedTime = time.time() - startTime
16
17     print "Done!"
18
19     print "The process took", elapsedTime, "seconds."
```

FIGURE 3.22

Use of `join` in timing processes.

```
1  from multiprocessing import *
2
3  def addNumbers(numNumbers):
4      s = 0
5      for i in range(numNumbers):
6          s = s + random.randint(1, 100)
7      print s
8
9  def compareParSeq():
10     totalNumNumbers = 1000000
11
12     # START TIMING PARALLEL
13     startTime = time.time()
14     p1 = Process(target=addNumbers, args=(totalNumNumbers/2,))
15     p2 = Process(target=addNumbers, args=(totalNumNumbers/2,))
16     p1.start()
17     p2.start()
18
19     # Wait until processes are done
20     p1.join()
21     p2.join()
22
23     parTime = time.time() - startTime
24     # DONE TIMING PARALLEL
25     print "It took", parTime, "seconds to compute in parallel."
26
27     # START TIMING SEQUENTIAL
28     startTime = time.time()
29
30     s = 0
31     for i in range(totalNumNumbers):
32         s = s + random.randint(1, 100)
33
34     seqTime = time.time() - startTime
35     # DONE TIMING SEQUENTIAL
36     print "It took", seqTime, "seconds to compute sequentially."
37
38     print "Speedup: ", seqTime / parTime
```

FIGURE 3.23

Comparing parallel and sequential performance on two processors.

This problem can make a good base for an exercise in or out of the classroom. Students can be instructed to experiment with the code and perhaps write a report with graphs showing performance across multiple variables:

- Adjusting totalNumNumbers
- Modifying the difficulty of the operation to be performed (e.g., summing square roots of numbers)

In such an exercise, students should observe the following key points:

- When operations are longer and/or more complex, working in parallel has the potential to bring more significant speedups. (This is definitely true in embarrassingly parallel problems like this summation.)
- Speedup of n processors over one processor on the same algorithm will typically not exceed n (barring potential effects of caching, for example).

The version in Figure 3.24 uses n processors, instead of hardcoding for exactly 2 processors. It requires the use of accumulation in lists to manage the child processes.

```
1  def compareParSeqN():
2      totalNumNumbers = 1000000
3      numProcesses = 5
4
5      # START TIMING PARALLEL
6      startTime = time.time()
7      pList = []
8      for i in range(numProcesses):
9          pList.append(Process(target = addNumbers, args =
                  (totalNumNumbers/numProcesses,)))
10         pList[-1].start()
11
12     # Wait until processes are done
13     for i in range(numProcesses):
14         pList[i].join()
15
16     parTime = time.time() - startTime
17     # DONE TIMING PARALLEL
18     print "It took", parTime, "seconds to compute in parallel."
19
20     # START TIMING SEQUENTIAL
21     startTime = time.time()
22
23     s = 0
24     for i in range(totalNumNumbers):
25         s = s + random.randint(1, 100)
26
27     seqTime = time.time() - startTime
28     # DONE TIMING SEQUENTIAL
29     print "It took", seqTime, "seconds to compute sequentially."
30
31     print "Speedup: ", seqTime / parTime
```

FIGURE 3.24

Comparing parallel and sequential performance on n processors. This uses addNumbers defined in Figure 3.23.

In experimenting with this code, students should see that simply adding more processes, when there are no dedicated processors for them, does not speed up the computation. In fact, the extra overhead may slow things down further.

3.9 FURTHER EXAMPLES USING THE POOL/map PARADIGM

The following examples all take advantage of the Pool/map mechanism described in Section 3.6.3. The examples are each embarrassingly parallel, allowing the student to consider the following abstract procedure for parallel problem solving:

1. Split up the work into chunks.
2. Process the chunks independently in parallel using the parallel map mechanism.
3. Synthesize the overall solution using the results of the independently processed chunks.

This procedure is applicable to many interesting problems, from computer graphics and image processing to brute-force security attacks, to distributed computing projects such as Folding@home and computational science more generally.

3.9.1 MONTE CARLO ESTIMATION OF π

A simple—if slowly converging—method for computing π is to generate N random pairs in the interval $[0, 1]$. When each pair is considered a point in the unit square, the fraction of generated points whose distance from the origin is less than or equal to 1 will approach $\pi/4$ as N grows large. Further, generating N points can be seen as the same random estimation as independently generating P sets of N/P points and combining the results. The program in Figure 3.25 shows such a sequential versus parallel timing. On an example quad-core machine, the typical output might be as follows:

```
$ python parallelMontePi.py 10000000
Sequential: With 10000000 iterations and in 4.528216 seconds,
            pi is approximated to be 3.141044.
Parallel: With 10000000 iterations and in 1.106317 seconds,
          pi is approximated to be 3.141217.
```

To explain why the parallel process could run more than four times faster on a quad-core machine, recall that the time computed is "real" or "wall" time rather than time consumed only by the process. This example demonstrates the simple steps of the abstract procedure defined above, while also showing the Pool/map mechanism simply, where the spawned process accepts and returns a single integer argument.

```
1  #Monte Carlo estimation of pi.
2  from multiprocessing import Pool, cpu_count
3  import random, time, sys
4
5  def main():
6      N = 1000000 #default unless provided on command line.
7      if len(sys.argv) > 1:
8          N = int(sys.argv[1])
9
10     #sequential timing
11     start = time.time()
12     result = montePi(N)
13     pi_seq = 4.0*result/N
14     elapsed = time.time() - start
15
16     print("Sequential: With %d iterations and in %f seconds," % (N, elapsed))
17     print("                pi is approximated to be %f." % (pi_seq))
18
19
20     time.sleep(3) #To see the parallel effect on OS' process manager.
21
22     #parallel timing
23     start = time.time()
24
25     #Step 1: split up the work: how many iterations to run each montePi.
26     cpus = cpu_count()
27     args = [N // cpus] * cpus
28     #Distribute extra work if work cannot be evenly distributed.
29     for i in range(N % cpus):
30         args[i] += 1
31
32     #Instantiate the pool of processes
33     pool = Pool(processes = cpus)
34
35     #Step 2: process chunks independently. Here, compute subtotals.
36     subtotals = pool.map(montePi, args)
37
38     #Step 3: Synthesize the overall solution.
39     result = sum(subtotals)
40     pi_par = 4.0*result/N
41     elapsed = time.time() - start
42
43     print("Parallel: With %d iterations and in %f seconds," % (N, elapsed))
44     print("                pi is approximated to be %f." % (pi_par))
45
46 def montePi(num): #returns the number of pairs in [0,1] lie within unit disk.
47     numInCircle = 0
48     for i in range(num):
49         x, y = random.random(), random.random()
50         if x**2 + y**2 <= 1:
51             numInCircle += 1
52     return numInCircle
```

FIGURE 3.25

Monte Carlo estimation of π.

3.9.2 INTEGRATION BY RIEMANN SUM

A more complicated demonstration of the `Pool/map` mechanism is shown in the program in Figure 3.26, which computes an integral via Riemann sum. Here the sequential `integrate` function accepts four arguments, from the function to integrate to the limits and the step size of that integration. However, if we wish to call on this function to integrate subdomains in parallel, recall that the `map` method requires a function that accepts only a single argument. This is accomplished with the `wrapIntegrate` function, where a single tuple containing the `integrate` arguments is unpacked and sent on (argument unpacking in the method header is deprecated). A typical output might be as follows:

```
$ python integratePool.py
sequential integral ans, time: 0.459698, 3.232372 sec.
parallel integral ans, time: 0.459698, 0.665953 sec.
```

3.9.3 MERGESORT

The code in Figure 3.27 demonstrates a variant on mergesort using a `Pool` of processes. Motivation follows from the intuitive mergesort algorithm of sorting two half-lists and merging the result. Why split the list into only two parts, since each sublist sort is independent, and each pair of sorted sublists can be merged independently as well? The algorithmic variant demonstrated here is first to sort *P* independent sublists in parallel (line 33 in Figure 3.27), then to merge pairs of sorted sublists *also in parallel* (line 35) until there is only one list left. This "flattened" mergesort is in contrast to the recursive instantiation used in Section 3.7.6. The following is example output, again obtained with a quad-core machine (Figure 3.28):

```
$ python mergesortPool.py
Sequential mergesort: 6.134139 sec
Parallel mergesort: 2.011089 sec
```

3.10 CONCLUSION

We hope with this chapter to have provided some guidance and a plethora of examples to consider for introducing parallel computing concepts with Python in early computer science curricula. Using the demonstration programs provided, instructors can expose students to such critical considerations in parallel computing as shared resources, divide and conquer, communication, and speedup. The programs also demonstrate the basic syntax for process spawning using `Process` or `Pool`, allowing students and instructors to re-purpose the code for their own ends.

```
1  #Parallel integration by Riemann Sum.
2  from multiprocessing import Pool, cpu_count
3  from math import sin
4  import time, sys
5
6  def main():
7      n = 10000000
8
9      #First, sequential timing:
10     start = time.time()
11     ans = integrate(sin, 0,1,1.0/n)
12     elapsed = time.time() - start
13     print("sequential integral ans, time: %f, %f sec." % (ans, elapsed))
14
15     #Now, the parallel solver
16     start = time.time()
17     stpsize = 1.0/n
18     cpus = cpu_count()
19
20     #Step 1: split up the work. Domain split into equal parts.
21     args = []
22     endpoints = linspace(0,1,cpus+1)
23     for i in range(cpus):
24         args.append((sin, endpoints[i], endpoints[i+1], stpsize))
25
26     #Step 2: process chunks independently. Here, sub-integrals.
27     pool = Pool(processes = cpus)
28     results = pool.map(wrapIntegrate, args)
29
30     #Step 3: Synthesize the overall solution. The integral of the domain
31     #is the sum of the integrals over the non-overlapping partial domains.
32     ans = sum(results)
33     elapsed = time.time() - start
34     print("parallel integral ans, time: %f, %f sec." % (ans, elapsed))
35
36  def integrate(f, a,b,h):
37      """computes the integral of f from a to b in n steps"""
38      s = 0
39      x = a + h/2.0
40      while x < b:
41          s += h*f(x)
42          x += h
43      return s
44
45  def wrapIntegrate(fabh):
46      (f, a,b,h) = fabh
47      return integrate(f, a,b,h)
48
49  def linspace(a,b,nsteps):
50      #returns linear steps from a to b in nsteps.
51      ssize = float(b-a)/(nsteps-1)
52      return [a + i*ssize for i in range(nsteps)]
53      #list comprehension, equivalent to map(lambda i:a+i*ssize, range(nsteps))
```

FIGURE 3.26

Sequential versus parallel integration of sin over [0,1].

```
1  from multiprocessing import Pool
2  import time, random, sys
3  from seqMergesort import merge, mergesort
4
5  def main():
6      N = 500000
7      lystbck = [random.random() for x in range(N)]
8
9      #Sequential mergesort a copy of the list.
10     lyst = list(lystbck)
11     start = time.time()                    #start time
12     lyst = mergesort(lyst)
13     elapsed = time.time() - start    #stop time
14     print('Sequential mergesort: %f sec' % (elapsed))
15
16     #Now, parallel mergesort.
17     lyst = list(lystbck)
18     start = time.time()
19     lyst = mergeSortParallel(lyst)
20     elapsed = time.time() - start
21     print('Parallel mergesort: %f sec' % (elapsed))
22
23 def mergeWrap(AandB):
24     a,b = AandB
25     return merge(a,b)
26
27 def mergeSortParallel(lyst, n = 3):
28     numproc = 2**n #default 8 sublists to sort.
29     endpoints = [int(x) for x in linspace(0, len(lyst), numproc+1)]
30     args = [lyst[endpoints[i]:endpoints[i+1]] for i in range(numproc)]
31
32     pool = Pool(processes = numproc)
33     sortedsublists = pool.map(mergesort, args)
34
35     while len(sortedsublists) > 1:
36         #get sorted sublist pairs to send to merge
37         args = [(sortedsublists[i], sortedsublists[i+1]) \
38             for i in range(0, len(sortedsublists), 2)]
39         sortedsublists = pool.map(mergeWrap, args)
40     return sortedsublists[0]
41
42 def linspace(a,b,nsteps):
43     """
44     returns list of simple linear steps from a to b in nsteps.
45     """
46     ssize = float(b-a)/(nsteps-1)
47     return [a + i*ssize forig:pool-merges i in range(nsteps)]
```

FIGURE 3.27

Parallel mergesort using `Pool`/`map`. The code relies on sequential mergesort from Figure 3.17.

```
1  from multiprocessing import Process, Queue
2  import random
3  from seqMergesort import merge, mergesort
4
5  def main():
6      N = 500000
7      lyst = [random.random() for x in range(N)]
8      n = 3 #2**(n+1) - 1 processes will be instantiated.
9
10     #Instantiate a Process and send it the entire list,
11     #along with a Queue so that we can receive its response.
12     q = Queue()
13     p = Process(target=mergeSortParallel, \
14                 args=(lyst, q, n))
15     p.start()
16     #get blocks until there is something (the sorted list) to receive.
17     lyst = q.get()
18     p.join()
19
20 def mergeSortParallel(lyst, q, procNum):
21     #Base case, this process is a leaf or the problem is very small.
22     if procNum <= 0 or len(lyst) <= 1:
23         q.put(mergesort(lyst))
24         q.close()
25         return
26
27     ind = len(lyst)//2
28
29     #Create processes to sort the left and right halves of lyst,
30     #with queues to communicate the sorted sublists back to us.
31     qLeft = Queue()
32     leftProc = Process(target=mergeSortParallel, \
33                        args=(lyst[:ind], qLeft, procNum - 1))
34     qRight = Queue()
35     rightProc = Process(target=mergeSortParallel, \
36                         args=(lyst[ind:], qRight, procNum - 1))
37     leftProc.start()
38     rightProc.start()
39
40     #Receive the left and right sorted sublists (each get blocks, waiting to
41     #finish), then merge the two sorted sublists, then return through our q.
42     q.put(merge(qLeft.get(), qRight.get()))
43     q.close() #ensure no more data.
44
45     #Join the left and right processes to finsh.
46     leftProc.join()
47     rightProc.join()
```

FIGURE 3.28

Parallel mergesort using `Process` and `Pipe`. Uses the sequential mergesort code from Figure 3.17.

REFERENCES

[1] S. Bogaerts, J. Stough, Strategies for Introducing Parallelism with Python, 2013, URL sc13.cs.wlu.edu.

[2] Parallel Processing and Multiprocessing in Python, 2013, URL https://wiki.python.org/moin/ParallelProcessing.

[3] Spyder: The Scientific PYthon Development EnviRonment, 2014, URL https://bitbucket. org/spyder-ide/spyderlib.

[4] Python.org:IntegratedDevelopmentEnvironments, 2014, URL https://wiki.python.org/ moin/IntegratedDevelopmentEnvironments.

[5] B.R. Maxim, G. Bachelis, D. James, Q. Stout, Introducing parallel algorithms in undergraduate computer science courses (tutorial session), ACM SIGCSE Bull. 22 (1) (1990) 255.

[6] S. Bogaerts, K. Burke, B. Shelburne, E. Stahlberg, Concurrency and parallelism as a medium for computer science concepts, in: Curricula for Concurrency and Parallelism workshop at Systems, Programming, Languages, and Applications: Software for Humanity (SPLASH), Reno, NV, USA, 2010.

Modules for introducing threads

4

David P. Bunde*

*Knox College**

Relevant core courses: Systems, CS2.

Relevant parallel and distributed computing topics: Shared memory: compiler directives/pragmas (A), libraries (A); Task/thread spawning (A); Data parallel: parallel loops for shared memory (A); Synchronization: critical regions (A); Concurrency defects: data races (C); Load balancing (C); Scheduling and mapping (K); Speedup (C).

Learning outcomes: The student will be able to use common thread libraries for new problems and also have a working knowledge of some basic concepts of parallel programming.

Context for use: First course introducing shared memory programming. Assumes prior background in either Java or C/C++.

4.1 INTRODUCTION

This chapter[1] presents a pair of modules for teaching basic thread programming. Each module is built around an example application, stepping through the process of parallelizing that application. The first module uses the example of counting the number of primes up to some value. The second uses the example of generating an image of the Mandelbrot set. Each module includes a summary of the author's experiences teaching it and advice for using it at other institutions.

[1]Partial support for the work described in this chapter was provided by National Science Foundation grant DUE-1044299.

Target audience

The materials in this chapter are intended for instructors who are introducing their students to parallel programming and concurrency. The author has primarily used these examples in a systems programming course that covers basic operating systems and networking concepts. That course has a CS2 prerequisite, though some students have done additional prior computer science coursework. The modules can also potentially be used late in CS2 or as the first examples in a more advanced course on parallel programming.

Threads and OpenMP

Both modules teach shared memory programming with threads. Such programs use multiple threads to simultaneously execute different parts of the program. Each thread has its own program counter and stack (i.e., distinct local variables), but all the threads run in the same memory space, with interactions through shared variables, either global variables in C/C++ or static variables in Java.

The modules use two different approaches for creating and managing threads. The first is explicit threading, in which the programmer uses system calls to directly create threads and manage interactions between them. The example code does this using the POSIX-standard pthreads library in C, the `std::thread` class in C++11, and the `Thread` class in Java. The second thread creation and management approach, used only in the second module, is OpenMP. OpenMP is a standardized extension of C (and C++) in which the compiler generates the thread-related code on the basis of hints (called *pragmas*) added to a sequential program.

Topics covered

Both modules cover the idea of threads and at least one notation for using them. In addition, they both cover the following concepts:

- Speedup
- Race conditions
- Load balance
- Privatization of variables, the act of giving threads private copies of a variable to reduce the amount of sharing

In addition to these shared concepts, each module covers some additional concepts not included in the other. The prime counting module adds the following:

- Critical sections and mutual exclusion

The Mandelbrot module adds the following:

- Parallel overhead, the extra work added to a program in the process of parallelizing it
- Dynamic scheduling, in which the tasks performed by each thread are determined at run time

Using these modules

The author has typically used only one of these modules in any given course since the modules cover many of the same concepts and class time is always limited. Of the two, the prime counting example seems to be simpler since its given code is shorter and less complicated. Thus, it should be used first if both modules are taught. Language choice may also factor into the decision of which module to use; the prime counting example can be done in Java, C, or C++, while the Mandelbrot exercise must be done in C or C++ since OpenMP is available only in those languages.

Computing environment

The running times discussed in this chapter were measured on two different systems. The majority are from a 16-core AMD Opteron 6272 processor running Fedora Linux release 19. In Section 4.3, we also contrast results on that system with times from a MacBook Pro with a dual-core Intel Core i5 processor (dual-core with hyperthreading support for two tasks per core) running Mac OS X version 10.6.8 (Snow Leopard). The C and C++ examples were compiled using gcc version 4.8.3 on the Linux system and 4.2.1 on the Mac system. On both systems, we used the command line options -Wall (enable all warnings), -lpthread (include the POSIX-standard pthread library to implement threading), -lm (include the math library), and -fopenmp (activate OpenMP; included only when using OpenMP). In addition, the C standard was specified. For C we specified the C 99 standard with -std=c99 (later standards should work as well), and for C++ we specified C++11 with -std=c++11 (required for the C++11 threading). The Java examples were compiled as Java version 1.7. The running times were measured using the Unix command time.

The specific running times will differ depending on your hardware and software configuration, so instructors adopting these materials are encouraged to time the code on their own systems and to rescale the problem sizes.

4.2 PRIME COUNTING

This section describes the first module, which is based on a program counting prime numbers. A *prime* is an integer whose only positive integral divisors are 1 and itself. Primes are one of the main topics of study of number theory, and also have great practical importance in computer cryptography. Their distribution among the integers is related to the Riemann hypothesis, one of the most important open problems in mathematics.

This module was previously presented in [1]; this version expands on that presentation, adding more about the author's experiences, the C and C++ versions of the module, and a discussion of issues arising with more than two cores. Given code and the author's handouts for this module are available from [2].

4.2.1 USING THIS MODULE

The main part of this module involves walking through the parallelization of a program that counts the number of primes in a range. The author has always done this in a laboratory. The students are given the sequential program and follow the instructions in a handout that lead them through the process of parallelizing it (i.e., the entire process outlined in Section 4.2.3). The instructor is available for questions, but the intent is that the students work through most of the process themselves. Prior to this laboratory, the instructor has briefly introduced the idea of threads in a lecture. Following the laboratory, the instructor also talks about each part of the laboratory to reinforce the lessons learned and to answer questions. Afterward, the students are given a follow-up assignment as homework. (One possible assignment is discussed in Section 4.2.4.)

For courses without class time allocated to working in a laboratory, there are a couple of alternatives. The first is for the parallelization to be done in a lecture, with the instructor illustrating the process. This loses the hands-on aspect since the students are watching rather than changing the code themselves. The second alternative is to give the laboratory handout to students as an assignment. In this case, it would be harder for students to get assistance, but the author does not believe this would be a serious issue since most students in his course completed the laboratory assignment on their own. A potentially bigger concern is that some students may not work on the laboratory assignment, though this would be mitigated by requiring the follow-up assignment.

4.2.2 SEQUENTIAL CODE

Now we describe the initial sequential program that students are given. It has a function isPrime that returns whether its argument is prime. To test the number n for primality, this function tries all integers from 2 to $\sqrt{n}$ as possible divisors. (We have to check up only to $\sqrt{n}$ since any divisor above $\sqrt{n}$ will be paired with one below $\sqrt{n}$.) The program uses isPrime to count the number of primes up to some value finish, using the code shown in Figure 4.1. This code "prerecords" that 2 is prime and then tests odd integers up to finish.

```
long pCount = 1;  //number of primes found (starts with 2)
long nextCand = 3;  //next number to consider

while(nextCand < finish) {
  if(isPrime(nextCand))
    pCount++;
  nextCand += 2;
}
```

FIGURE 4.1

Loop to count the number of primes up to finish.

For the value of `finish`, the author used 2,000,000. Adopters of this module should choose a value that is appropriate for the machines with which they are working. The fastest version should take a measurable amount of time, and the sequential version should take at least a couple of seconds. Students are used to instant feedback from their programs and so are strongly motivated to speed this program up so they do not have to wait. (When this example has been used with larger values of `finish`, some students require reassurance that the initial program is correct because they thought it was in an infinite loop and killed it before completion.)

4.2.3 STEP-BY-STEP PARALLELIZATION

Now we step through the process of parallelizing this program. As described above, this is intended as a discovery process, either during a lecture or in a laboratory. Thus, the first versions are incorrect; subsequent versions correct the bugs and then tune the performance.

Creating multiple threads

The first step is creating multiple threads. The main part of this is to move the `nextCand` loop shown in Figure 4.1 into a function for a thread to run. Each thread will run this function for a different range of candidate numbers. To do this, the thread function needs to know the endpoints of the range of candidate numbers to check. This is simplest in C++,[2] where the endpoints can be passed as a pair of integer arguments. These arguments, along with the thread function, are passed to the constructor for `std::thread`. In C, thread functions take only a single argument, so the endpoints must be placed in a `struct`. A pointer to this `struct` is then passed to the `pthread_create` function, which creates a thread. In Java, threads are represented with `Thread` objects. The thread body is specified via a `Runnable` object passed to the constructor, and the range endpoints must be stored as attributes of the `Runnable` object.

In all three implementations, the threads must be able to increase the count of primes found, which we store in a variable `pCount`. As a first cut toward updating `pCount`, we make it a shared variable which each thread increments as primes are found.[3] Sketches of the code are shown in Figures 4.2 (C), 4.3 (C++), and 4.4 (Java).

---

[2]For brevity, we specify the language rather than the specific thread implementation. Thus, we use "C++" to denote the C++11-standard `std::thread` class and "C" to denote the POSIX-standard pthreads library.

[3]This turns out to be a bad decision, and we revisit it below.

Joining the threads

Running the code in Figure 4.2, 4.3, or 4.4 gives a very underwhelming result. The program is very fast, finishing without noticeable delay, but is incorrect. The C and Java versions find very few primes (possibly none other than 2, which we identified ahead of time). The C++ version exits with an error message: "terminate called

```
struct prime_arg {
  long start, finish;
};

long pCount = 1;  //global variable; we already recognize 2 as prime

void* prime_thread (void *arg) {
  struct prime_arg *parg = (struct prime_arg *) arg;
  for(long i=parg->start; i<parg->finish; i+=2)
    if (isPrime(start))
      pCount++;
  return &pCount;  //not used, but function must return a pointer
}

int main () {
  pthread_t t1, t2;
  struct prime_arg t1arg = { 3, 1000000 };
  struct prime_arg t2arg = { 1000001, 2000000 };

  pthread_create(&t1, NULL, prime_thread, &t1arg);
  pthread_create(&t2, NULL, prime_thread, &t2arg);

  printf ("%ld_primes_found\n", pCount);
}
```

FIGURE 4.2

The first multithreaded prime counter in C (broken).

```
long pCount = 1;

void prime_thread(int start, int finish) {
  for(long i = start; i < finish; i+=2)
    if (isPrime(i)) {
      pCount++;
    }
}

int main () {
  std::thread first(prime_thread, 3, 1000000);
  std::thread second(prime_thread, 1000001, 2000000);

  std::cout << pCount << "_primes_found" << std::endl;
}
```

FIGURE 4.3

The first multithreaded prime counter in C++ (broken).

```java
public class ThreadedPrimes {

    public static int pCount;

    static class PrimeFinder implements Runnable {
        private long from;
        private long to;

        //constructor that takes values for from and to

        public void run() {
            for (long i = from; i<to; i+=2)
                if (isPrime(i))
                    pCount++;
        }
    }

    public static void main(String args[]) throws InterruptedException {
        pCount = 1;   //(starting with 2)

        Thread t1 = new Thread(new PrimeFinder(3, 1000000));
        Thread t2 = new Thread(new PrimeFinder(1000001, 2000000));

        t1.start();
        t2.start();

        System.out.println(pCount + " primes found");
    }
}
```

FIGURE 4.4

The first multithreaded prime counter in Java (broken). This code also appears in [1].

without an active exception." In all cases, the problem is that the program creates and starts the threads, but fails to wait for them to finish before printing the result and exiting. Waiting for thread completion is called *joining*, a term that captures the idea of the computation that has been distributed over several threads joining together. A single join call waits for a single thread. Thus, we need to add

```
pthread_join(t1, NULL);
pthread_join(t2, NULL);
```

to the C version of our program,

```
first.join();
second.join();
```

to the C++ version, or

```
t1.join();
t2.join();
```

to the Java version. These calls should be added after both threads have started—that is, after the calls to pthread_create, the declaration of the std::thread objects, or the calls to Thread.start.

Fixing the race condition

After the calls that join the threads have been added, the running time will be more reasonable, but the number of primes found still does not match the (correct) number found by the sequential version. In fact, the number of primes reported by the program likely varies every time the program runs, with the reported number always below the correct value. The variation is caused by a *race condition*, a concurrency bug in which a bad interleaving of operations executed by different threads can give an incorrect result.

In this case, the problem has to do with the variable pCount, which both threads are updating. Whenever either thread identifies a prime number, it uses the ++ operator to increment this variable. Although the use of a single operator makes this increment appear to be a single operation, executing the operator actually requires three distinct operations: reading the current value of pCount, adding 1 to it, and then storing the new value. If both threads try to increment pCount simultaneously, one of the updates can be lost.

Figure 4.5 depicts one possible way that operations from two threads can interleave and lose an update. It shows the operations of each thread, each thread's local (register-stored) value of pCount after each operation, and the globally visible value of pCount stored in memory. Initially, pCount has value 5. After both ++ operators have been executed, pCount should have value 7 since it was incremented twice, but instead it has the incorrect value 6; one of the increments has been lost. To make our program properly count the number of primes, we need to avoid this race condition. Specifically, we need one thread to complete the entire ++ operation before the other thread begins it. We can call the line with the ++ operation a *critical section*, meaning that it is a piece of code that must run all together to guarantee correct execution.

To protect the critical section from interruptions, we will use a *lock*, also called a *mutex* because it provides *mutual exclusion*, the phenomenon of only one thread being in the critical section at a time. Mutexes provide two main operations, *lock* and *unlock*. At all times, their state is either *locked* or *unlocked*. Mutexes are unlocked when they are created, move to locked if their lock operation is invoked, and move to unlocked if their unlock operation is invoked. Complicating this is that operations that would "change" the state to its current value do not proceed until the state changes. For example, if the lock operation is performed on a mutex that is already locked, that operation will block (i.e., wait) until the mutex becomes unlocked.

Time	Thread 1		Thread 2		Value of pCount in memory
	Operation	Local value	Operation	Local value	
1	read value	5	...	n/a	5
2	add 1	6	read value	5	5
3	store value	6	add 1	6	6
4	...	n/a	store value	6	6

FIGURE 4.5

Possible operation interleave that loses an increment. NA, not applicable.

A mutex can be used to achieve mutual exclusion for a critical section by adding a call to lock the mutex at the beginning of the critical section and one to unlock it at the end. With this arrangement, any thread wishing to enter the critical section must first lock the mutex, and the mutex remains locked until that thread exits the critical section. Thus, if one thread is in the critical section and another thread attempts to enter it, the second thread will block until the first thread exits the critical section.

To achieve mutual exclusion for our application in C, we replace the single line incrementing pCount with

```
pthread_mutex_lock(&m);
pCount++;
pthread_mutex_unlock(&m);
```

where m is a global variable for use as a mutex. It is declared and initialized with the following lines:

```
pthread_mutex_t m;              //declared as a global variable
...
pthread_mutex_init(&m, NULL); //initialized in main
```

This ensures that only one thread tries to increment pCount at a time, ensuring that no updates are lost.

The C++ version is similar, albeit with minor syntactic differences since the mutex is now an object. It is declared and initialized with

```
std::mutex m;   //declared as a global variable
```

and then used to protect the increment line with

```
m.lock();
pCount++;
m.unlock();
```

Note that this code requires including the mutex header file.

There are a couple of differences in how we achieve mutual exclusion in Java. First of all, Java does not have separate lock/mutex objects. Instead, every Java object has an associated mutex. Since the program does not create any objects thus far, we can add one as a class variable:

```
static Object m = new Object(); //declared outside the methods
```

We could use a different class, but we chose Object to emphasize that the object m is only used as a mutex. Then, to protect the increment operation, we enclose it in a synchronized block:

```
synchronized(m) {
 pCount++;
}
```

Despite the difference in syntax, this performs essentially the same operations as the other versions; the mutex associated with m is locked at the beginning of the synchronized block (blocking if necessary), then the increment is performed, and finally the mutex is unlocked. This syntax is less flexible in general, but it makes the relationship between locking and unlocking explicit. It also prevents the programmer from forgetting to unlock a mutex at the end of a critical section.

Now that the code is correct, we can check its performance. On my system, the C version of the sequential code runs in 2.08 s, and the corrected parallel version runs in 1.48 s. (I get slightly different running times for the other versions, but our main focus will be on the ratios between running times, none of which are materially different between the languages.) Thus, it achieves a *speedup* of $2.08/1.48 = 1.41$, meaning that the parallel program runs 1.41 times as fast as the sequential one. This is an improvement, but not very impressive; we would like something closer to *linear speedup*, a speedup equal to the number of cores we are using. In our case, since we are using two threads and the work they perform is completely independent (since no primality test depends on any other), the goal would be a speedup close to 2.

Privatizing the counter

One possible issue with our parallel program that could be preventing it from achieving a high speedup is the way that it increments pCount. For each increment, the program has to lock and then unlock a mutex. This could undermine our efforts to achieve a high speedup in two ways. First of all, it incurs a relatively high amount of *overhead*, instructions that are added as part of parallelizing the program. If we execute enough extra instructions, we lose all the benefit of being able to execute instructions faster. Secondly, the mutex causes threads to wait since only one thread can execute the critical section at a time. This is good in that it allows us to achieve mutual exclusion, but having threads wait also undermines the benefit of parallelism. In an extreme case, a program can be completely *serialized*, meaning that only one thread runs at a time because of mutexes that cause all other threads to block. If this happens, the program gains no benefit from parallelism, while keeping all the additional overhead.

To avoid these issues, we will use a common technique called *privatizing variables*, in which shared variables are replaced with private copies to eliminate the overhead involved in safely sharing them. In our case, the variable pCount is shared. Looking at this variable, we see the individual threads do not really use its current value. Thus, instead of incrementing pCount each time a prime is found, each thread can have a private counter to record the number of primes it discovers. Then, after the thread has identified all the primes in its range, it can use this private counter to update the shared variable pCount. Since only this last step involves a shared variable, it is the only one that requires protection with a mutex. Figures 4.6 (C), 4.7 (C++), and 4.8 (Java) show the key functions with this modification.

When we run the program after privatizing pCount, we get a minimal improvement in speedup (1.44 from 1.41). For this program, the shared variable was not a big problem. One way to understand this is to observe that the critical section is

```
void* prime_thread (void *arg) {
  struct prime_arg *parg = (struct prime_arg *) arg;
  long localCount = 0;
  for (long i=parg->start; i<parg->finish; i+=2)
    if (isPrime(start))
      localCount++;

  pthread_mutex_lock(&m);
  pCount += localCount;
  pthread_mutex_unlock(&m);

  return &pCount;  //not used, but function must return a pointer
}
```

FIGURE 4.6

Function `prime_thread` for C program with `pCount` privatized.

```
void prime_thread(int start, int finish) {
  long localpCount = 0;
  for (long i = start; i < finish; i+=2)
    if (isPrime(i)) {
      localpCount++;
    }

  count_mutex.lock();
  pCount += localpCount;
  count_mutex.unlock();
}
```

FIGURE 4.7

Function `prime_thread` for C++ program with `pCount` privatized.

```
public void run() {
  long localCount = 0;

  for (long i = from; i<to; i+=2)
    if (isPrime(i))
      localCount++;

  synchronized (m) {
    pCount += localCount;
  }
}
```

FIGURE 4.8

Method `run` for Java program with `pCount` privatized.

small relative to the other work each thread is doing, most of which is in the call to isPrime. Since the sequential program spends very little of its time in what becomes the critical section, the threads spend very little time blocked trying to get into it.

Because privatization did not lead to a big performance win in this case, some instructors may want to skip this part of the module. I choose to include it because the technique is important in some cases. In particular, the benefit of privatization increases as the number of threads grows since this makes it more likely that a thread will be in the critical section at any given time. Thus, the technique is likely to become more important over time as processors have more cores.

Improving load balance

Another common factor limiting parallel programming performance, and one that is more important for the prime counting program, is *load balance*, how evenly the work is divided between the threads. If the work is split unevenly (*poor load balance*), some threads will take much longer than others. Since the program does not complete execution until the last thread finishes, this makes the overall program slower.

How does this apply to our program? At first glance, the program's load balance seems good because each thread receives a nearly equal-sized range of numbers to test for primality; the first thread receives 3 through finish/2, while the second receives finish/2 through finish. This impression of equal parts turns out to be an illusion, however, because it takes longer to test the primality of some numbers than others. Consider Figure 4.9, which contains the body of isPrime in Java (the C/C++ version merely replaces Math.sqrt with sqrt and substitutes 0/1 for false/true). This code returns as soon as a divisor of num is found. Thus, its running time is proportional to the value of the smallest divisor for composite (i.e., not prime) numbers and to limit for primes. This leads to the following two opposing arguments about the load balance:

(1) The first thread does more work: There are more prime numbers in the first thread's range (the lower half), and primes take longer to test than composite numbers.

(2) The second thread does more work: It is testing larger numbers, so its value of limit will be higher. This means its primes require more work than the first thread's. Composite numbers whose smallest divisor is near the limit will also require more work than composite numbers in the first half.

```
long limit = (long) Math.sqrt(num);
for (long i=2; i<=limit; i++)
    if (num % i == 0)
        return false;
return true;
```

FIGURE 4.9

Body of isPrime method.

Empirically, the second argument turns out to be the dominant factor. This can be verified by splitting the numbers unevenly; the program's running time improves if the ranges are split at a value slightly above finish/2. For example, when finish is 2,000,000, splitting at 1,100,000 improves the speedup to 1.69.

The problem with improving the load balance by adjusting the split point is the difficulty of identifying a good value. For the particular problem of counting prime numbers, there is a clever trick that easily gives good load balance. The idea is to give both threads numbers throughout the entire range; give the first thread numbers of the form $3 + 4k$ and the second thread numbers of the form $5 + 4k$ (i.e., start the first thread at 3, start the second thread at 5, and increment by 4 instead of 2 to get the next number). This simple change eliminates the need for tuning the load balance and brings the speedup to 1.86. (One note about this trick: It does not work for odd numbers of threads. For example, applying it with three threads would split the numbers into the forms $3 + 6k$, $5 + 6k$, and $7 + 6k$, but all numbers of the first form are multiples of 3, which are tested very quickly.)

The main part of the module concludes with the corrected load balance, which gives a speedup of 1.86.

4.2.4 FOLLOWUP ASSIGNMENT

As an exercise related to this module, students were given a homework assignment based on another variation of prime counting. Instead of determining the primality of n by testing all integers from 2 to $\sqrt{n}$, it is sufficient to just test the primes in this range. Figure 4.10 shows the body of a Java function isPrime based on this idea. The variable primes is an ArrayList containing the primes discovered thus far; this list is built as the primes are discovered (by code outside isPrime). Comparison with Figure 4.9 shows that the two methods are quite similar. Avoiding the extra divisor tests yields a large saving, however; the students are given a sequential program utilizing this approach that is actually faster than the best parallelized version based on the previous method.

The students' task was to parallelize this new program, with the suggestion that they sequentially compute the primes up to $\sqrt{\text{final}}$. They were also asked in a

```
long limit = (long) Math.sqrt(num);
long val;
long i = 1;  //prime to test; start at 1 since 2 is first and num is odd
while ((i<primes.size()) && ((val = primes.get(i)) <= limit)) {
  if (num % val == 0)
    return false;
  i++;
}
return true;
```

FIGURE 4.10

Body of isPrime method that uses previously identified primes as possible divisors. This code also appears in [1].

written question what would go wrong if they just parallelized everything, using the new isPrime with the program developed in the previous section. (The issue is a race condition.) This assignment forces the students to write some threading code outside the laboratory environment. The resulting code is closely related to what they did in the laboratory, but the written question helps check for conceptual understanding.

One issue with adapting this assignment for use in C is the lack of a built-in structure equivalent to ArrayList. (Note that it could be replaced with vector in C++.) This issue can be massaged by allocating a sufficiently large array to store the discovered primes, though this approach limits the potential value of final. An alternative is to provide an implementation of an array-based list, but then the students must either trust or understand the given code. (A linked list could also be used, but array-based lists are faster for the operations needed here; the performance is important since the list will be built during the program's sequential part, before the threads are launched.)

4.3 MANDELBROT

This section describes the second module, which is based on a program creating an image of the Mandelbrot set. The Mandelbrot set is the well-known fractal image depicted in Figure 4.11, where the black points are those inside the set. To determine if a point (x, y) is inside the set, it is interpreted as a complex number $c = x + yi$, and the series $z_1 = c$, $z_{n+1} = z_n^2 + c$ is computed. Formally, the Mandelbrot set is all points for which this series is bounded. For example, the point $(-1, 0)$ is represented as $c = z_1 = -1$, which gives the following series:

$$z_1 = -1, \quad z_2 = 0, \quad z_3 = -1, \quad z_4 = 0, \quad \ldots.$$

This is clearly bounded, never exceeding magnitude 1. Different behavior is seen for $(1, 0)$, which yields a series whose elements' magnitudes grow without bound:

$$z_1 = c = 1, \quad z_2 = 2, \quad z_3 = 5, \quad z_4 = 26, \quad \ldots.$$

In practice, depictions of the Mandelbrot set are typically computed by iteratively generating z_i until either the magnitude of some z_i exceeds a threshold (points outside the set) or a specified number of iterations have been performed (points in the set). The image in Figure 4.11 was generated with a threshold of 2 and by stopping after 1000 elements. For the points above, this would generate all 1000 elements of the series for $(-1, 0)$, but would stop the series for $(1, 0)$ at z_3, the first point whose magnitude exceeds 2.

Users of this module are not required to understand the mathematics behind the Mandelbrot set. The main point is that computing an image such as that shown in Figure 4.11 is a computational task requiring sufficient work to justify parallelization. The only requirement is that the students are able to examine the code determining

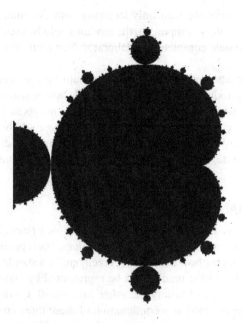

FIGURE 4.11

The Mandelbrot set.

if a point is in the Mandelbrot set (see Figure 4.13) and observe that its running time varies depending on the iteration at which z_i surpasses the threshold.

More information on the Mandelbrot set, including multicolored images that distinguish points on the basis of how soon their series exceeds the threshold, is available from [3]. Given code and the author's handouts related to this module are available from [4].

4.3.1 USING THIS MODULE

As with the prime counting module, the main part of this module is parallelizing a sequential application. Section 4.3.3 steps through the process of doing this using OpenMP, and Section 4.3.4 discusses doing it with explicit threading calls. Since each approach has advantages (discussed in Section 4.3.4), there are many possible ways that this module can be used. Most recently, the author has had students parallelize the program using the approaches one after the other in consecutive laboratory periods (scheduled specifically to facilitate this). Other terms, he has stepped through the OpenMP approach in a lecture either before or after a laboratory in which the students followed the explicit threading approach. His sense is that using a hands-on laboratory was more effective than only lecturing with this material. That said, in courses without a laboratory component, the module could be used as an example for a lecture or students could complete the "laboratory" on their own as an out-of-class activity.

For any of these alternatives, the module should be prefaced by a lecture or reading that briefly introduces the idea of threads. The author also recommends an in-class discussion following the module to reinforce the concepts and answer questions.

The program as given creates an 800 × 800 image of the Mandelbrot set. Depending on the hardware being used, the instructor may wish to adjust this (at the top of the given code) so that the running time is significant but reasonable.

4.3.2 SEQUENTIAL PROGRAM

The initial sequential implementation creates a bitmap file (.bmp). In this type of file, an image is represented as a large array of pixel values. Each pixel is represented by a triple of bytes specifying how much blue, green, and red should appear in a given location. For example, a blue pixel could be represented by setting the blue value as high as possible (255) and setting the other values to 0. Colors other than blue, green, and red are represented as a combination of these three colors. For example, an orange color can be created by setting the red value to 255, the green value to 128, and the blue value to 0. The bulk of the Mandelbrot program's output is the contents of the array `pixels`, which stores these color values in `struct`s of type `RGBTRIPLE`. Each `struct` has the color of a single pixel, represented by three fields `rgbtBlue`, `rgbtGreen`, and `rgbtRed` that store the values of its blue, green, and red components, respectively. In this program, the only colors we use are black (all values 0) and white (all values 255).

In addition to the array of pixel values, the .bmp file format requires a header. Generating this header requires a significant amount of code, but it does not need to be modified, so it can be treated as a "black box" during parallelization. When the author has used this example in a laboratory, students have been content to ignore this code.

There are only two parts of the program that need to be examined or manipulated. The first part is the pair of loops that we will be parallelizing, shown in Figure 4.12. These loops go through every pixel in the image, whose size is determined by `numCols=800` and `numRows=800`. For each pixel, it calls the function `mandelbrot` and uses the return value for all three color values for that pixel. Since the calculation for each pixel is independent, these loops are completely parallelizable.

The other part of the program relevant for parallelization is the `mandelbrot` function, which decides whether a given point (x, y) is in the Mandelbrot set or not. It runs the algorithm described above for 1000 iterations and uses a threshold of 2. (The value appears as 4 in the code because the other side of the inequality is the square of the magnitude.) The function then returns either 0 or 255 depending on whether the given point appears to be in the Mandelbrot set with these parameters—that is, whether $z_{1000}^2 \leq 4$. Code for this method is shown in Figure 4.13.

```
for (int i = 0; i < numCols; i++) {
  for (int j = 0; j < numRows; j++) {
    x = ((double)i / numCols -0.5) * 2;
    y = ((double)j / numRows -0.5) * 2;

    color = mandelbrot(x,y);   //returns 0 or 255

    pixels[i][j].rgbtBlue = color;
    pixels[i][j].rgbtGreen = color;
    pixels[i][j].rgbtRed = color;
  }
}
```

FIGURE 4.12

Nested loops to set pixel values.

```
int mandelbrot(double x, double y) {
  int maxIteration = 1000;          //# of iterations tested
  int iteration = 0;                //current iteration number

  double re = 0;   //current real part
  double im = 0;   //current imaginary part
  while ((re*re + im*im <= 4)                //haven't exceeded threshold
        && (iteration < maxIteration)) {     //and haven't used all iterations
    double temp = re*re - im*im + x;
    im = 2*re*im + y;
    re = temp;

    iteration++;
  }

  if (iteration != maxIteration)
    return 255;    //didn't exceed threshold (yet) so (x,y) is in the set
  else return 0;   //exceeded threshold so (x,y) is outside set
}
```

FIGURE 4.13

Function `mandelbrot`, which tests for membership of the Mandelbrot set.

4.3.3 STEP-BY-STEP PARALLELIZATION WITH OpenMP

Now we are ready to begin the process of parallelizing this program. As described above, this is intended as a discovery process, either during a lecture or in a laboratory. Thus, our first attempt is incorrect, and subsequent versions fix it and improve the performance.

To make the performance effects as visible as possible, we first set the environment variable OMP_NUM_THREADS to 2, which causes OpenMP to use only two threads. The command to do this varies with the shell being used, but the commands are

```
setenv OMP_NUM_THREADS 2
```

for csh or tcsh and

```
export OMP_NUM_THREADS=2
```

for bash.

Pragma on the outer loop

Since the main work is done in the nested pair of loops shown in Figure 4.12, we focus our parallelization efforts on them. We begin by adding a pragma to run the outer loop in parallel as follows:

```
#pragma omp parallel for
for (int i = 0; i < numCols; i++) {
  for (int j = 0; j < numRows; j++) {
   //set pixel[i][j]
  }
}
```

After this change, the program does indeed run faster. Unfortunately, it also fails to generate the correct image. Figure 4.14 shows close-ups of the versions generated by the original program and this version. The image generated by the parallel version appears somewhat grainy, with both white pixels inside the set and additional isolated dark ones outside it. (The Mandelbrot set is actually connected, but even the sequential version of our program draws some isolated black pixels since it generates a discrete version of the real set.) In addition, close examination reveals that the parallel version created some pixels with colors other than black and white.

The reason for these artifacts is that both threads created by the pragma are using the same copies of the variables x, y, and color. This causes them to sometimes use a value written by the other thread. Threads interfering with each other in this way is an example of a *race condition*, a concurrency bug in which a bad interleaving of operations executed by different threads can give an incorrect result.

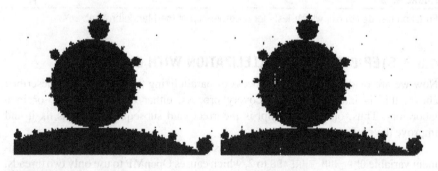

FIGURE 4.14

Zoomed-in view of the Mandelbrot set as generated by the sequential program (left) and the first parallel version (right).

For example, if the first thread writes 255 in `color` but the second thread overwrites it with 0 before the first thread sets the pixel values, both threads will store 0 as the pixel values. This causes a pixel that should be white to become black. (The reverse can also happen.) A similar problem can result if the value of x or y is overwritten between when the values are set and when they are used to call the `mandelbrot` function. Note that these problems occur only when one of the shared variables is changed in the brief time between when it is set and when it is used, which is why most of the pixels have the correct color.

Fixing the race condition

To fix the race condition, we simply want each thread to use its own copies of the variables x, y, and `color`. To indicate this, we add `private(x,y,color)` to the end of the pragma, giving the following:

```
#pragma omp parallel for private(x,y,color)
for (int i = 0; i < numCols; i++) {
  for (int j = 0; j < numRows; j++) {
    //set pixel[i][j]
  }
}
```

(In this case, the problem could also be solved by declaring these variables within the loop rather than outside it; this is why there are no races on the variable j.) Adding the extra qualifier causes the indicated variables to be *privatized*—that is, made private to each thread instead of shared by all of them.

After this change, the parallel program produces the same image as the original sequential program. Dividing the sequential running time by the parallel running time gives 1.40. This value, called the *speedup*, means that the parallel program runs 1.40 times as fast as the sequential version. This is an improvement, but not very impressive. Because every pixel is independent, we would like to achieve something closer to *linear speedup*, speedup equal to the number of cores in use—that is, two since we limited OpenMP to use two threads.

Swapping the loops

To try improving this, we consider an alternative. What happens if we swap the order of the loops? The resulting code is as follows:

```
#pragma omp parallel for private(x,y,color)
for (int j = 0; j < numRows; j++) {
  for (int i = 0; i < numCols; i++) {
    //set pixel[i][j]
  }
}
```

With this change, the speedup becomes 1.94, quite an improvement for such a minor change.

To understand the cause of this change, we have to examine the code of the `mandelbrot` function in Figure 4.13. Nearly all of this function's running time is in the `while` loop. For points in the set (displayed as black in the output and for which the function returns 0), the loop executes 1000 (= `maxIteration`) times. For points outside the set, the loop exits earlier. Thus, points that are black in the output take longer to process than points that become white.

Now consider how this relates to the change we made by swapping the loops. When the pragma was associated with the `i` loop, each thread was responsible for a share of the columns. When the loops were reordered, the pragma became associated with the `j` loop, making each thread responsible for a share of the rows. The two ways of decomposing the image are illustrated in Figure 4.15. As you can see, dividing the rows between threads results in each thread having the same number of black pixels.

Thus, the issue is *load balance*, how evenly the work is divided between the threads. If the work is split unevenly (*poor load balance*), some threads take longer than others. Since the program does not complete execution until the last thread finishes, this makes the overall program slower. In our case, splitting the image by rows gives a better load balance than splitting the image by the columns, which explains why parallelizing the `j` loop gives a better speedup.

The reason for setting the environment variable `OMP_NUM_THREADS` was to better illustrate this effect. If the variable is not set, OpenMP uses as many threads as can run simultaneously on the hardware. In our case, 16 threads are used, and the resulting speedups are 5.32 when parallelizing the outer loop and 5.98 when parallelizing the inner loop. Swapping the loop order still improves load balance, but less dramatically since the parts are all smaller.

 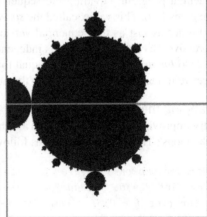

FIGURE 4.15

Two possible decompositions of the Mandelbrot set: division of the columns (left) or the rows (right) into two parts.

Pragma on the inner loop

A different way to parallelize the j loop is to move the pragma into the outer loop body instead of swapping the loops. This gives the following:

```
for (int i = 0; i < numCols; i++) {
  #pragma omp parallel for private(x,y,color)
  for (int j = 0; j < numRows; j++) {
    //set pixel[i][j]
  }
}
```

This change gives qualitatively different results depending on the system. The results stated thus far in this chapter are from a 16-core Linux system. On that system, this version of the code gives a speedup of 1.94, the same as the version with swapped loops. On our other system, a dual-core Mac, this version gave a speedup of 1.67, intermediate between the values achieved by the original parallel program (speedup 1.32) and the version with swapped loops (speedup 1.72). (Both systems are described in more detail in Section 4.1.)

Why do the systems give qualitatively different results, and what could cause the intermediate speedup? We begin with the second question and explain the factors that can lead to an intermediate speedup. The version with a parallelized inner loop still has better load balance than the original parallel program; for each column, the work is split between two threads, with each processing the same number of black pixels. There are two reasons why the version with swapped loops may still be better. The first is that it requires fewer instructions. When the inner loop is parallelized, the threads need to start, do their work, and then join each of the numRows times that the outer loop runs. Starting and joining the threads requires extra instructions that do not occur in the sequential version. This extra work is called *overhead*, instructions that are added as part of parallelizing a program. There is less overhead when the loop order is switched since the threads start and join only once.

A second reason why the swapped version may run faster than the version with a parallelized inner loop has to do with idle time introduced with each join of the threads. When the inner loop is parallelized, there is a join for each column. This means that whichever thread finishes its part of the column first will wait for the other thread before proceeding to the next column. If the threads take different amounts of time for their parts, this difference can accumulate even if the total load is balanced between the threads, as illustrated in Figure 4.16. These differences between thread completion times can occur even if the threads have an identical amount of work because the operating system might not give each of them the same share of the processor. Remember that the operating system is doing other things even if only a single program is running. Random differences in the running time of otherwise identical pieces of work are called *jitter*.

Given these two factors that tend to favor the version with loops swapped, why does parallelizing the inner loop give the same performance on the Linux system? It

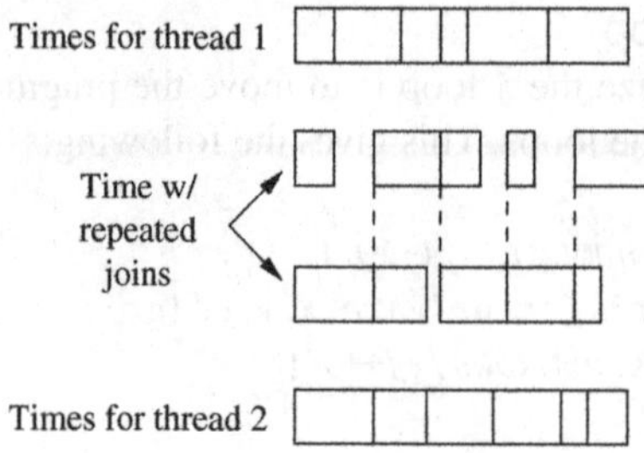

FIGURE 4.16

Idle time created by repeatedly joining threads.

turns out that both of these factors are mitigated on that system. To test the overhead, we ran a program that repeatedly created and joined threads with minimal workloads. Overhead caused the parallel version of this program to run more slowly than the serial version on both systems, but the slowdown was less on the Linux system, indicating lower overhead. (The exact cause is unclear, but the Linux system has newer hardware running a more recent operating system and a newer version of the compiler.) The expected effect of jitter is also reduced on the Linux system since it has many cores beyond the two needed for our threads, allowing it to run other things without interrupting our threads.

As a side note, the differences we observed between systems should impress upon readers the need to test the module code on their system before using it in class. With OpenMP, this is particularly important because of the compiler's increased role. For example, a more aggressive compiler might reorder the nested loops to improve cache performance and thus eliminate the programmer's ability to try both orders.

Dynamic scheduling

The final step in our illustration of parallelizing the Mandelbrot program is actually an alternative to our manual adjustments to improve load balancing. The idea is to change how the loop iterations are distributed between the threads. Up to this point, all the variations implicitly use what is called *static scheduling*, meaning that the iterations assigned to each thread are determined before the loop begins. The alternative is *dynamic scheduling*, in which the iterations are broken into small groups that are then assigned to threads as the loop runs. This requires more coordination between the threads, and the resulting overhead is why static scheduling is the default behavior. For our problem, however, dynamic scheduling improves the load balance by allowing a thread that runs faster iterations to do more of them than a thread that runs slower iterations.

To enable dynamic scheduling, we add `schedule(dynamic)` to the pragma as follows:

```
#pragma omp parallel for private(x,y,color) schedule(dynamic)
for (int i = 0; i < numCols; i++) {
  for (int j = 0; j < numRows; j++) {
    //set pixel[i][j]
  }
}
```

With this change, the program achieves a speedup of 1.94, equal to the best speedup previously achieved. The overhead of dynamic scheduling can hurt performance if the iterations are well balanced, but this example shows that it can be very effective when iterations require significantly different amounts of work; dynamic scheduling achieved the same performance without the previous efforts to hand-tune the load balance.

4.3.4 PARALLELIZATION USING EXPLICIT THREADS

An alternative way to use the Mandelbrot module is to parallelize this program using pthreads, `std::thread`, or Java threads instead of OpenMP. Hand-written thread code can be used to demonstrate any of the concepts discussed in this section except for dynamic scheduling, which is more complicated to implement by hand. Both the OpenMP approach and the explicit threading approach have advantages. The advantage of OpenMP is that the ease of adding pragmas allows the four main versions of the parallel program (parallelizing i loop or j loop, swapping the loops or not swapping them) to be tested in a relatively short time. Implementing these four versions using explicit threading code would take significantly longer and have a much greater risk that bugs are introduced. Thus, the OpenMP approach is preferable for demonstrating the high-level concepts of load balance and parallel overhead. The disadvantage of using OpenMP instead of explicit threading code is the danger that students see it as "magic" that parallelizes their program without requiring an understanding of the underlying mechanism.

Because of the different advantages of each approach, the author advocates using both when teaching the Mandelbrot module. By the end of the module, the students have both written explicit threading code for a couple of the versions and used OpenMP to explore the entire space of possibilities. The author's inclination is to take a top-down approach by presenting the idea of threads, having students do the OpenMP version of the module for the high-level concepts, and then having them write explicit threading code. Other instructors could also use this material for a bottom-up approach in which students first write explicit threading code and then move on to OpenMP.

REFERENCES

[1] D. Bunde, A short unit to introduce multi-threaded programming, in: Proceedings of the Consortium for Computing Science in Colleges—Midwest Region Conference, 2009, pp. 9-20.

[2] Resources for multi-threaded intro assignment, URL http://faculty.knox.edu/dbunde/teaching/threadIntro/.

[3] Mandelbrot set, URL http://en.wikipedia.org/wiki/Mandelbrot_set.

[4] Resources for parallel mandelbrot assignment, URL http://faculty.knox.edu/dbunde/teaching/mandelbrot/.

Introducing parallel and distributed computing concepts in digital logic

5

Ramachandran Vaidyanathan, Jerry L. Trahan and Suresh Rai

Louisiana State University

Relevant core courses impacted: This chapter is primarily directed at a first digital logic course but will indirectly impact learning in several courses such as courses in computer architecture and algorithms (including parallel and distributed), networking and interconnects, and computational complexity.

Relevant parallel and distributed computing topics: For a course whose primary focus is outside parallel and distributed computing (PDC), many of the PDC topics covered would be at the lower end of the Bloom taxonomy. However, we expect the real benefit of the proposed early exposure to PDC concepts would be in subsequent courses that address PDC topics more directly. The early (indirect) exposure to PDC would build a framework onto which subsequently covered PDC topics can latch, leading to improved learning and retention. Table 5.1 shows the expected pedagogical level for a set of PDC concepts corresponding to the digital logic topics discussed in this chapter.

Learning outcomes: The main purpose of this chapter is to provide a framework for introducing PDC topics while teaching digital logic. The following set of possible learning outcomes must be viewed in this context:

(1) Recognize basic interconnection structures—for example, tree, bus, mesh, and torus.

(2) Identify and apply parallel and sequential structures in hardware—for example, identify the critical path in a circuit; explain concurrency in a carry-look-ahead adder; identify time-size trade-offs in circuits such as adders; adjust parallelism in circuits to adjust delay.

(3) Understand the concepts of recursive decomposition and divide and conquer—for example, apply recursive decomposition to circuit design (such as in a multiplexer); recognize the parallelism in independent branches of a recursion.

Table 5.1 Pedagogical Levels for PDC Concepts, Using K (know the term), C (comprehend so as to paraphrase or illustrate it), and A (apply it in some way)

PDC Concept	Section					
	5.1	5.2	5.3	5.4	5.5	5.6
Concurrency, sequential/parallel		C	C	C	C	A
Interconnects, topologies	K	C	C			A
Performance measures (latency, scalability, efficiency, trade-offs)				K	C	C	C
Recursive decomposition, divide and conquer	K	C		A		
Prefix computation				C	A	
(A)synchrony			K		C	A
Pipelining					C	
Data hazards			K			
Buses, shared resources		K				K
Complexity, asymptotics	K					
Dependencies, task graphs			K			
Broadcast, multicast		K				
Reduction, convergecast		K			C	

(4) Understand the concept of a prefix computation—for example, explain the prefix computations present in a carry-look-ahead adder and in a synchronous counter.

(5) Explain the difference between synchronous and asynchronous operations—for example, asynchronous nature of latches and ripple counters.

(6) Understand the concept of an ideal pipeline—for example, as a generalization of a shift register; as a form of parallelism.

Context for use: Hardware is inherently parallel, and digital logic provides a fertile ground for exploring fundamental ideas in PDC at an early stage of the curriculum. It affords instructors an early opportunity to introduce key PDC concepts to which many students in electrical and computer engineering would otherwise not be exposed until much later in the academic program. Even for those students who receive exposure to PDC concepts early in their programs, the digital logic context provides a different setting that serves to broaden their perspectives and understanding of key concepts in both PDC and digital logic.

This chapter is intended to help the instructor incorporate PDC in the coverage of standard digital logic topics, rather than allocate separate instruction time specifically for PDC. It does not seek to add new topics to the digital logic course. Rather, it suggests a framework in which PDC topics can be introduced seamlessly through the instruction of digital logic topics. The discussion of PDC topics could be in class as a side note in a lecture, or a separate exploration off-line, perhaps as part of homework or a reading assignment.

The level of the chapter assumes the digital logic instructor has some PDC background. The goal, in most instances, is to augment standard approaches to the material and view digital logic topics from a different perspective, revealing PDC concepts already present in these topics. In some instances, the goal is to generalize a digital logic topic to a PDC application, both revealing the digital logic concept as a building block and explaining it by tangible applications. To facilitate simple integration, the material in this chapter is organized by digital logic topics (rather than by PDC concepts). Along the way, several PDC concepts will be visited, possibly multiple times and in increasing levels of complexity. This allows the instructor to select the set of PDC concepts to be discussed and the level of detail of the discussion. We also observe that in programs requiring digital logic, the material in this chapter could be used by instructors of mainstream PDC courses to draw analogies to (digital logic) concepts that students may have grasped earlier. The material in this chapter is meant to augment and illustrate digital logic concepts using PDC examples.

Chapter organization: The chapter has five sections (Sections 5.1–5.5) that discuss PDC ideas in the context of specific digital logic topics. Formalism has been employed in places to convey some ideas accurately, tersely, and with some generality. This is directed at the instructor. We recommend that the instruction itself use simple examples without the formalism.

As we noted earlier, the focus is on relating digital logic concepts to PDC ideas. Consequently, we do not discuss the PDC ideas themselves in much detail, often just offering an alternative view of the digital logic topic. A basic understanding of many of these PDC ideas can be obtained from resources on the Internet; nevertheless, we suggest some references that the reader may find useful. Each section also lists applications where the PDC concepts discussed could be used.

At the end of each section, we offer suggestions for incorporating the ideas discussed in the instruction of digital logic. Typically, this picks each of the broad topics of a section and lists (in order of increasing complexity) various aspects of the topics to which students can be exposed. The instructor can tailor this to suit the class.

Finally, Section 5.6 outlines idea threads for several other digital logic settings that the instructor could elaborate upon as desired.

5.1 NUMBER REPRESENTATION

One of the first topics introduced in digital logic is the binary representation of integers. Consider an exercise where each student picks a number u from the set $\{0, 1, 2, \ldots, 15\}$ (abbreviated here as $[0, 15]$). The purpose of the exercise is to derive the four-bit binary representation of u. For this discussion, we will refer to the set $[0, 15]$ as the *level 4 set of u*. As a first step, determine whether the selected number u is in the bottom half, $[0, 7]$, or the top half, $[8, 15]$, of the set $[0, 15]$ of possible numbers. If $u \in [0, 7]$, record a "0" to indicate the bottom half; similarly, if $u \in [8, 15]$, record a "1" to indicate the top half. Denote the symbol (0 or 1) as the level 3 symbol of u and the set ($[0, 7]$ or $[8, 15]$) that u belongs to as the level 3 set of u. For the running example with $u = 13$, the level 3 symbol is 1 and the level 3 set is $[8, 15]$.

Next, record the level 2 symbol of u as 0 or 1 depending on whether u is in the bottom half or top half of its level 3 set. For the running example, the level 2 symbol is 1 as 13 is in the top half of its level 3 set $[8, 15]$; the level 2 set of 13 is $[12, 15]$. Proceeding similarly, we find the level 1 and level 0 symbols of u and obtain a string $b_3 b_2 b_1 b_0$, where $b_i \in \{0, 1\}$ is the level i symbol of u. For the running example, the level 1 and level 0 symbols of 13 are 0 and 1, respectively; the string for 13 is 1101.

We have presented the binary representation of u as a sequence of decisions about which half of a range u belongs to. The binary decision tree in Figure 5.1 represents all possible outcomes of these decisions for set $[0, 15]$.

The tree representation described here can be used as a basis for several concepts in digital logic, parallel and distributed computing (PDC), and some fundamental to computing itself.

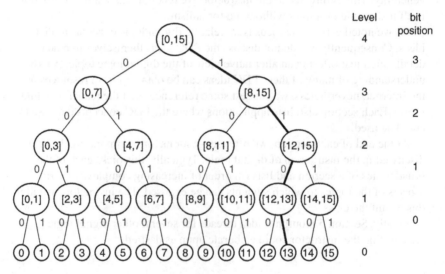

FIGURE 5.1

A decision tree representing the four-bit numbers in the range $[0,15]$. The representation for 13 is emphasized. The figure also shows the node levels and bit positions corresponding to edge labels.

Binary numbers: The tree representation in Figure 5.1 can be used to augment standard discussion of binary numbers. Consider any leaf u; we assume u denotes both the node and its value. Observe that the sequence of edge labels (decision outcomes) in a path from the root to leaf u is the binary representation of the edges in the path. Figure 5.1 shows the path to leaf 13 in bold; the corresponding sequence of edge labels 1101 is the binary representation of 13.

In general, observe that nodes at level ℓ represent the level ℓ sets and an edge between nodes at levels ℓ and $\ell + 1$ is labeled with the level ℓ symbol. Let u be a leaf and let the labels on edges in the path from the root to the leaf u be $b_{n-1}, b_{n-2}, \ldots, b_0$. Observe that the value of a leaf is the number of leaves to its left in the tree. For example, there are 13 leaves (labeled 0 to 12) to the left of leaf 13 in Figure 5.1. Thus, obtaining the binary representation of a number u is an exercise in determining the number of leaves to the left of u in the corresponding binary tree.

Consider an edge labeled b_ℓ in the path from the root to leaf u; this is an edge between a node α (say) at level $\ell + 1$ and its child β (say) at level ℓ; let the other child of α be γ (also at level ℓ). If $b_\ell = 1$, then all 2^ℓ leaves of the subtree rooted at γ are to the left of u. If $b_\ell = 0$, on the other hand, then all leaves of γ are to the right of u; one cannot tell at this point how many leaves of α are to the left of u. Extending this to all levels, we find the value of the leaf (number of other leaves to its left) is $u = \sum_{i=0}^{n-1} b_i 2^i$. This is the basis for converting a binary number to its decimal value.

To see the correspondence in the other direction, we first label each internal node slightly differently. Let u be a node at level ℓ. Then label u with a string of length n of the form

$$b_{n-1}b_{n-2}\cdots b_{n-\ell} \underbrace{**\cdots *}_{n-\ell \text{ times}},$$

where $b_{n-1}, b_{n-2}, \ldots, b_{n-\ell}$ is the sequence of bits in the path from the root to node u and $*$ is a wild-card symbol. For example, the nodes corresponding to ranges $[12, 15]$ and $[12, 13]$ are represented by the strings $11 * *$ and $110*$, respectively. Notice that the binary representations of all elements of $[12, 15]$ have 11 in the most significant two bits; the corresponding string $11 * *$ reflects this. Similarly, the string $110*$ for $[12, 13]$ reflects the fact that the binary representations of 12 and 13 have 110 in their most significant bits and differ only in the least significant bit.

We now return to relating the tree in Figure 5.1 to the standard method of converting a (decimal) number to its binary representation. This standard conversion method calls for repeated division of the given number by 2 and recording the remainders. These produce the binary number from the least significant bit to the most significant bit or from the leaves to the root in the binary tree. Consider the example of $u = 13$ (see Table 5.2). The last column of the table has a four-bit string, the non-wild-card bits of which constitute the binary representation of the quotient. As described above, these strings also identify the nodes $[12, 13], [12, 15], [8, 15], [0, 15]$ on the path from 13 to the root.

Table 5.2 Converting 13 to Binary

Bit	Quotient				Remainder	String			
0 (lsb)	13	÷ 2	=	6	1	1	1	0	*
1	6	÷ 2	=	3	0	1	1	*	*
2	3	÷ 2	=	1	1	1	*	*	*
3 (msb)	1	÷ 2	=	0	1	*	*	*	*

Abbreviations: lsb, least significant bit; msb most significant bit.

These ideas could also be further explored in the context of an r-ary tree for a general radix r; $r = 8, 16$ (octal and hexadecimal) may be of particular interest in digital logic. At a later stage (particularly in input, state, or output assignment in finite state machine design), one could use an n-bit number to represent fewer than 2^n distinct "values." Here one could also introduce heaps and unbalanced trees by considering subsets of $\{0, 1, \ldots, 2^n - 1\}$.

Recursive thinking: We constructed the tree in Figure 5.1 by dividing the initial range $[0, 2^n - 1]$ into the bottom and top halves, which formed the left and right subtrees. The subtrees themselves were constructed the same way (recursively). This manner of expressing a large instance of a problem (for the range $[0, 2^n - 1]$) in terms of smaller instances of the same problem (ranges $[0, 2^{n-1} - 1]$ and $[2^{n-1}, 2^n - 1]$) is an easy way to introduce recursive thinking and the divide-and-conquer paradigm. The fact that the left subtree can be constructed completely independently of the right subtree can also be used to introduce the idea of parallelism.

Trees and interconnection networks: The systematic partitioning of the range $[0, r^n - 1]$ into a hierarchy of ranges represented in the r-ary tree can be used to introduce the notion of a tree itself and its use in representing hierarchical structures. Familiar examples include family trees and organizational hierarchical structures. Less familiar, perhaps, a phylogenetic tree [1, 2] captures evolutionary relationships between organisms, and vascular trees [3] model the proliferation of blood vessel in organs. In the computing arena itself (including in PDC), trees are central to numerous topics. One example is that of an interconnection network [4–6]. In the current context, an interconnection network uses a tree structure to connect several elements that could communicate with each other. For instance, a set of computer terminals or telephone lines in an office building may be connected to each other and to the outside through a (minimum spanning) tree. A (minimum Steiner) tree [7] is often used to connect elements inside an integrated circuit. These forms of connecting elements use the fact that a tree is a minimally connected graph (that connects its nodes with the smallest number of edges). Another interconnection network that is based on a tree is the fat-tree network [8], which has been used to connect large multiprocessor systems.

The difference between unary and binary: Students may have observed that the depth (or maximum level of nodes) of a balanced binary tree for the set $\{0, 1, \ldots, N - 1\}$ is $\lceil \log_2 N \rceil$. The depth of a balanced ternary tree (for radix 3 representation) is $\lceil \log_3 N \rceil$, which is smaller by a factor of about only $\log_2 3 = 1.58$. In general for radix $r \geq 2$, the balanced r-ary tree has depth $\lceil \log_r N \rceil$, which is about $\log_2 r$ times smaller than that of a balanced binary tree with the same number of nodes. Observe that the ratio of the depths is independent of N. On the other hand, a unary tree (consisting of a chain of nodes) has a depth of N (assuming internal nodes can represent elements of $\{0, 1, \ldots, N-1\}$). This depth is considerably larger than for r-ary trees for $r \geq 2$.

This observation carries much import for PDC. Often a large problem is divided recursively into r independent subproblems, and each subproblem is solved in parallel. Moving from $r = 1$ to $r = 2$ has a substantial impact on the time for the computation, but not so much for $r = k \geq 2$ to $k + 1$. Cormen et al. [9, Section 34.1] discuss the effect of input encoding (unary/binary) on computational complexity.

Instruction notes for Section 5.1: The discussion on binary numbers could start with the (in-class) exercise described earlier (in which each student picks a number u and makes decisions about the bottom and top halves of sets to derive the binary representation). It could also be explored as an off-line activity in a flipped-classroom setting.[1]

The exercise described at the start of this section uses symbols 0 and 1 to denote the bottom and top halves of a range. The instructor could point out that other symbols would work equally well—for example, f and t (for "false" and "true") to denote the answer to the question of whether the number belongs to the top half. This could help students see that a bit has logical significance (over and above the arithmetic significance of a radix 2 representation).

The discussion on recursive thinking should first construct the tree, emphasizing that the recipe for each node to expand into its children is exactly the same (divide into top half and bottom half). Then it can be cast as solving a large problem by solving smaller problems of the same type. The idea of parallelism and divide and conquer could be emphasized by first splitting the root into its children ([0, 15] into [0, 7] and [8, 15] in our example). Then have a think-pair-share[2] activity to (recursively) draw the trees for the two halves and put them together.

At this stage it would be useful to introduce the term "binary tree" and to introduce the need to connect modules in a digital system (this can be expanded to the ideas of graphs (state diagrams) and interconnection networks later).

The portion on the difference between unary and binary should start with emphasizing that numbers expressed with respect to larger bases have shorter representations; this will also help in justifying octal and hexadecimal number systems that will be covered at a later stage. The large difference between unary (linear) and binary (logarithmic) representations can then be illustrated with an example.

---

[1] In a *flipped-classroom* setting, students understand the basics of a topic outside the class, and class time is devoted to problem solving and the discussion of advanced concepts.

[2] In a *think-pair-share* activity, students in a small group individually solve a problem, then collectively discuss their solutions to come to a final answer.

5.2 LOGIC GATES

In this section we will use fan-out, fan-in, and tristate gates to illustrate PDC concepts.

5.2.1 FAN-OUT AND FAN-IN OF GATES

A fan-out of f restricts the number of places to which a gate's output can be connected to be at most f. If a signal output by a gate needs to be delivered to N other gate inputs, then it is customary to use a set of buffers to boost the signal appropriately as shown in Figure 5.2. Here a source signal x, output, for example, by an OR gate, is ultimately fanned out to 15 destinations. For this illustration a fan-out of 3 is used to construct a ternary tree. In general, fanning the signal out to N places with buffers of fan-out f constructs an f-ary tree of buffers of depth $\lceil \log_f N \rceil$.

Similarly, a restriction in fan-in of a gate (number of input bits that a gate may receive) can be circumvented by a tree of gates. A gate with fan-in g can accept g inputs. For associative operations such as AND, OR, EX-OR, max, or min, a g-ary tree is used to apply the operation on $N > g$ inputs. Figure 5.3 illustrates the fanning in of 15 logic values to one value using seven three-input AND gates.

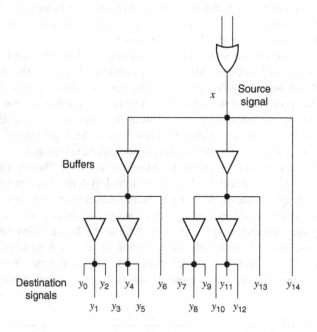

FIGURE 5.2

Fanning out a signal to 15 places using gates with a fan-out of 3.

Trees again: While the use of trees for fan-out and fan-in is folklore in digital logic, it provides a convenient basis for reinforcing ideas from the previous section and to introduce new ideas. First it must be noted that the idea of a tree introduced in the context of number representations has a direct application in digital logic (for fan-out and fan-in). Observe that while the logic values in the circuits in Figures 5.2 and 5.3 move from one to many and many to one, respectively, the underlying tree structure (with its edge directions interpreted differently) is abstract enough to capture both situations. Indeed, one could easily draw a fan-out tree corresponding to the structure in Figure 5.3 and a fan-in tree corresponding to the structure in Figure 5.2. This also illustrates that many such trees are possible for the same problem, and, drawn correctly, all of them for the example in question will have seven gates arranged in three levels.

Broadcast, multicast, and convergecast: In many applications, a value needs to be *broadcast* from a source to all other nodes—for example, an emergency bulletin that needs to be sent to all. This is a fan-out of a value to many places. Broadcasting is a special case of a more common mechanism called a *multicast* in which a value is sent to a subset of nodes. For example, a webinar may require the source to send the same content to several users (a very small subset of the Internet). Other similar examples include the multicasting of news items and stock quotes that may be viewed by several consumers simultaneously. In all of these cases, it would be unnecessarily expensive to send a separate feed to each user. For example, a live World Cup soccer video may be fed to several regional hubs and local stations before it is streamed into

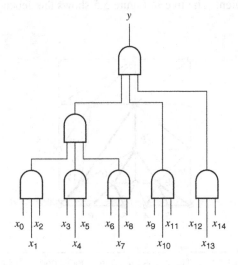

FIGURE 5.3

ANDing 15 bits using gates with a fan-in of 3.

individual devices. This requires the construction of a *multicast tree* through which the source can send content to a subset of nodes. A node in the interior of this tree may or may not be a destination for the multicast (see Figure 5.4 for an example).

At this point it may be useful to generalize trees into graphs—that is, explain to students that a graph is a set of nodes connected by a set of edges. The Internet, for example, may be represented as a graph [10]. In this context, a multicast tree is a subgraph of the Internet graph that includes all the nodes of interest (source and destinations), and which is typically optimized with respect to some cost (such as latency, quality of service, or traffic). Figure 5.4 shows a (multicast) subtree of a larger graph.

In a multicast, the flow of information is from a source to several destinations (as in fan-out). *Convergecast* is the collection of information from several sources into one sink (as in the fan-in tree). Convergecasting is a fundamental operation of distributed systems, and is commonly used in sensor networks in which the information from several sensors must be aggregated into a node. Again the idea is similar to a multicast, in that a tree is employed, this time to move information from the leaves to the root. The tree in Figure 5.4 can be used to collect information from the destination nodes into the source node.

Parallelism: Consider a game (such as Monopoly) that can be played with three players, in which one player wins a three-player match. A tournament pits 15 players in groups of three in a knockout tournament. For our discussion, let us assume that each match lasts 1 day. One way to conduct the tournament is with seven matches as shown in Figure 5.5; the last six players have the highest rankings and get to play one less game than the rest of the field. Clearly, the trees in Figures 5.3 and 5.5 are topologically equivalent. The tree in Figure 5.5 shows the dependencies among the

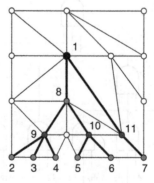

FIGURE 5.4

An example of a multicast tree. Node 1 is the source node, nodes 2-8 are destination nodes, and nodes 9-11 are intermediate nodes (which are part of the multicast tree, but are not destination nodes). Observe that a nonleaf node, such as node 8, can be a destination node.

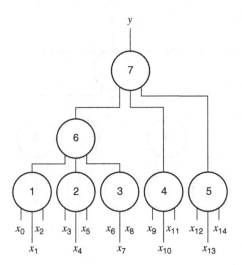

FIGURE 5.5

A seven-game tournament among 15 players. Each circle represents a match. Players are denoted by x_0-x_{14}, and y represents the champion.

matches in the tournament (in the same way that Figure 5.3 shows the connections among gates). The gate delay and the match duration are also analogous quantities. We now indicate how the dependencies in the tree can be used to illustrate *speedup* and *efficiency*, two important concepts in parallel processing.

A *feasible schedule* for the tournament is an arrangement of matches in time (possibly in parallel) such that the dependencies shown in the tree in Figure 5.5 are respected. For example, matches 1 and 2 can be held simultaneously, whereas matches 1 and 6 cannot, as the result of match 1 is needed before match 6 can be held. We now examine different schedules for the tournament.

An obvious schedule for the seven matches is to hold them one at a time. While this schedule would need only one venue (there are no simultaneous matches), the tournament would last 1 week. One could recognize that all matches at the same level of the tree in Figure 5.5 can be held in parallel, and this leads to a second schedule with a 3-day tournament (1 day per level of the tree). Specifically, matches 1-5 are held on day 1, match 6 is held on day 2, and match 7 is held on day 3. This schedule requires five venues, however, as the first day has five concurrent matches. Observe in Figure 5.5 that matches 4, 5, and 6 are independent of each other, and can therefore be held in parallel. This results in a third schedule, shown in Figure 5.6, that corresponds to a 3-day tournament requiring only three venues; matches 1-3 are held on day 1, matches 4-6 are held on day 2, and match 7 is held on day 3. Note also that a first round match (one of matches 1-3) for players x_0-x_8, their second round match (match 6), and the finals (match 7) all have to be held one after the other

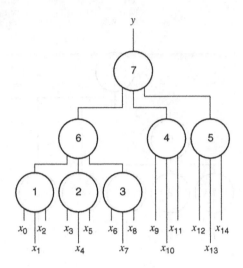

FIGURE 5.6

The schedule tree in Figure 5.5 redrawn to balance the number of nodes per level.

(sequentially); therefore, the tournament cannot be conducted in less than 3 days. Moreover, since there are seven matches over 3 days, we will need a minimum of $\left\lceil \frac{7}{3} \right\rceil = 3$ venues. So the third schedule is optimal.

As this example illustrates, a tree may be used to model the hierarchical relationship between a set of elements (including computational tasks). The relative positions of these elements within the tree could be used to determine which tasks can run in parallel and which are (sequentially) dependent on each other. In a computational setting, the number of venues may correspond to the number of processors, and the number of days needed for the tournament corresponds to the time needed for the computation. Compared with the sequential 7-day solution, the parallel 3-day solution finishes $\frac{7}{3}$ faster. In the setting of parallel computing, this quantity is called the *speedup* of the computation.

Continuing with the Monopoly example, we suppose that each venue rents for one unit per day and that the venues must be reserved for the entire tournament. Then the sequential 7-day solution costs 7 units. The 3-day, five-venue schedule has a cost of $3 \times 5 = 15$ units and the 3-day, three-venue schedule has a cost of 9 units. The 7-day tournament has $\frac{7}{9}$ the cost of our 3-day, three-venue tournament. This quantity is sometimes called the *efficiency* of the parallel solution.

We note that one of the first areas in which parallelism was explored was circuit complexity [11]. The simplicity of circuits as a model was a key reason, as was the relation of the circuit model to physical circuits. Limiting parameters such as fan-in, types of gates, and uniformity of construction allowed investigation of different computational complexity questions. The primary measures were circuit size and depth. Further, circuit complexity strongly relates to the complexity of parallel computation (e.g., circuit depth and size roughly correspond to the time and work needed for a parallel computation).

Recursive decomposition: The fan-in and fan-out problems may also be viewed recursively. For example, consider the fan-in problem in Figure 5.6. Suppose $F(N)$ represents the fan-in solution for N inputs using gates with a fan-in of 3. The tree in Figure 5.6 corresponds to recursively decomposing $F(15)$ (i.e., fanning in 15 inputs) into three subproblems, two $F(3)$'s and one $F(9)$ and combining the outputs of the three subproblems into the solution to $F(15)$. This can also be first explained in terms of a balanced ternary tree for $N = 3^k$, where k is an integer; then it makes sense to use $15 = 3^1 + 3^1 + 3^2$. The fan-out tree in Figure 5.2 similarly reduces the problem of sending a signal to 15 places to that of two instances of sending the signal to seven places, and sending the signal to one place. The broadcasting to seven places can similarly be recursively viewed in terms of that of two instances of sending the signal to three places and one instance of sending the signal to one place.

These examples further reinforce the idea of trees and recursive decomposition, illustrating the use of the same model (trees in this case) in two different scenarios.

5.2.2 TRISTATE GATES AND BUSES

Tristate gates provide the opportunity of introducing a bus (to which several modules could connect through exclusively enabled tristate gates). For a start, something along the lines of Figure 5.7a is a good way to illustrate the operation of a tristate gate; this figure may also be useful in explaining the functionality of a multiplexer. The figure shows two data inputs A and B connected to a bus C. In general, the control input S could be independently generated for each of the two tristate gates (e.g., to disconnect both of them from the bus). One could also easily generalize this to connect several data inputs to the bus (see Figure 5.7b).

In Section 5.1, we introduced the idea of an interconnection network to connect communicating elements. The bus is an important interconnection network in modern computing systems; the PCI bus [12], Ethernet [13], FireWire (IEEE 1394) [14], and USB [15] are commonly used standards. The term "bus" is used today to mean a network with the functionality illustrated in Figure 5.7. The term "*multidrop bus*" is often used to mean a bus constructed by connecting elements to a wire as in Figure 5.7. Buses also model other communication systems with shared resources (such as wireless systems in which a single frequency may be shared by multiple users).

Instruction notes for Section 5.2: The discussion of fan-in and fan-out circuits directly pertains to digital logic, so much of this could be an in-class activity. The instructor could further reinforce the idea of trees and PDC, possibly introduced earlier. One could also illustrate an unbalanced higher-depth tree (as a bad choice for fan-in or fan-out) and explain why it entails a higher gate delay; the prefix circuit

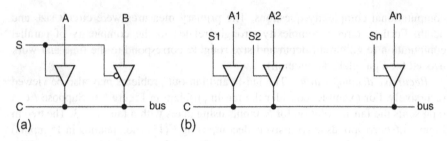

FIGURE 5.7

(a) A multiplexer with data inputs *A* and *B* output through a bus *C*. Control input *S* selects a data input to connect to the bus. (b) The structure of an *n*-input bus in which each control bit S_i independently decides if data input A_i is connected to the bus.

in Figure 5.15 illustrates a high-delay fan-in. This ties in to circuit delay (in logic), algorithmic time, and network latency in very similar ways.

At this point, the generalization of trees to graphs should, in our view, be only with the purpose of emphasizing the acyclic and sparse nature of trees. Later these ideas can generalize to directed acyclic graphs (DAGs; for reconvergent circuits) and directed graphs (state diagrams).

The ideas of broadcast and multicast are, in principle, analogous to signal fan-out; convergecasting is analogous to fan-in. A modest investment of time here could motivate students to see the wider-than-expected scope of the principles studied in a digital logic course (and, in general, other courses).

If recursive decomposition was explored earlier (e.g., in binary number systems), then fan-in and fan-out trees present a simple way to further reinforce the idea.

The discussion of parallelism is perhaps best done as an off-line exercise. The purpose of this discussion could be to lay the groundwork for subsequent discussion (in sequential circuits and Verilog). Some points that could be emphasized at this stage include that, in general, both delay and efficiency decrease with increased parallelism. While delay is easily appreciated in combinational circuits, efficiency requires reuse of combinational blocks; sequential circuits will provide a way for this reuse (see "Bit serial adder" in Section 5.6.2).

In many digital logic texts, tristate gates are introduced in the context of a bus. The discussion typically explains how the gates can effectively connect or disconnect a signal source from the bus. It is easy to use this to further build on the idea of interconnection networks. Another important PDC point to note here is that of exclusive access to a shared resource. While the mechanism for providing this exclusive access may differ across environments, the underlying ideas and issues have many similarities whether the environment is a shared bus, a shared frequency or wavelength in a multiaccess system, or a memory module in a shared memory system.

5.3 COMBINATIONAL LOGIC SYNTHESIS AND ANALYSIS

In this section we will consider two broad topics: timing analysis and Karnaugh maps.

5.3.1 TIMING ANALYSIS

This part of the discussion should be introduced only after students have been exposed to the idea of propagation delay of gates and circuit delay. The Monopoly tournament example in Section 5.2.1 touched on these ideas. Here we build on this initial exposure to introduce Directed Acyclic Graphs (DAGs) [16, 17], which capture task dependencies and play an important role in several scheduling and resource allocation problems. We also use the setting to discuss data hazards and synchronization.

Consider the multiplexer circuit implementing the function $C = AS + BS'$ shown in Figure 5.8.

Directed acyclic graphs: If the propagation delay of gate i (for $1 \leq i \leq 4$) is t_i, then after any change in the input, the values of Z and Y are settled (in the steady state) in at most time t_2 and $t_1 + t_3$, respectively. Thus, the multiplexer output is settled in at most time $t_4 + \max\{t_2, t_1 + t_3\}$. Clearly this has some of the ideas introduced in the Monopoly example. The new idea here is that of reconvergent paths that are not present in trees (here input S flows through two paths to get to output C).

If each gate (or module) of a combinational circuit corresponds to a node and a connection between them corresponds to a directed edge, then the circuit generates a graph. Because combinational logic is inherently without feedback, its graph is acyclic and forms a DAG. In fact, the tree topology that we discussed in Section 5.2.1 is a special case of a DAG. The DAG of the multiplexer example in Figure 5.8 is shown in Figure 5.9. The node named "A" in the DAG represents the module generating the signal named "A" in the circuit in Figure 5.8; the other nodes in Figures 5.8 and 5.9 have a similar correspondence.. Each node in the DAG may represent a task, and the DAG edges could represent dependencies. Therefore, a node named α in a DAG cannot be "executed" unless nodes with incoming edges to α have been executed. If node α requires time t_α, the time needed to execute the DAG in Figure 5.9 (once input nodes A, S, and B have been obtained) is at least $t_C + \max\{t_Z, t_X + t_Y\}$, which, not surprisingly, closely corresponds to the time for the circuit in Figure 5.8.

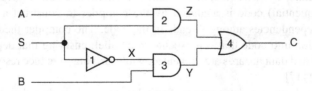

FIGURE 5.8

A 2-to-1 multiplexer circuit.

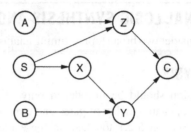

FIGURE 5.9

The DAG corresponding to the circuit in Figure 5.8.

In general, a DAG could be used to represent dependencies in a variety of computations. Consider, for example, a finite impulse response filter of the first order that transforms an input signal $s(t)$ at time t to an output $c(t)$ given by

$$c(t) = a \cdot s(t) + b \cdot s(t - 1).$$

If $x(t) = s(t - 1)$, $z(t) = a \cdot s(t)$ and $y(t) = b \cdot x(t)$, then $c(t) = y(t) + z(t)$. Clearly, the computation that this finite impulse response filter represents corresponds to the DAG in Figure 5.9.

Typically, a faster circuit or algorithm uses more resources (e.g., area, power, memory, or processors); therefore, there is a benefit from slowing down a part of the circuit or algorithm, if possible. As noted earlier, the DAG's execution time is $t_C + \max\{t_Z, t_X + t_Y\}$. Suppose $t_Z < t_X + t_Y$, then the path S, X, Y, C is the *critical path* of the DAG; the time to execute the nodes on a critical path is the minimum time to execute the entire DAG. All nodes outside the critical path can be suitably slowed down for potential improvements in resource usage. For the example, the execution of nodes X, Y, and Z should be adjusted so that (ideally) $t_Z = t_X + t_Y$. This could entail using a slower (and cheaper) execution at node Z than at nodes X and Y. This idea is central in digital design, and is discussed further in Section 5.4.1 in the context of fast adders.

It should also be pointed out that DAGs have several applications in computer science and engineering [16, 17]. One important application is in modern compilers for parallel systems (including multicore environments). A given piece of (typically sequential) code is analyzed by the compiler to construct a DAG that establishes dependencies among threads in the code. The compiler then translates this information into code that can execute in parallel, ensuring that dependencies are respected and data hazards are prevented, while striving to reduce resources used (time, power) [17].

Data hazards and synchronization: Static logic hazards in digital circuits can be used to illustrate synchronization and data hazards. Consider the circuit in Figure 5.8 with inputs $A = B = S = 1$. Clearly, the output is $C = 1$. Changing S from 1 to 0 should not change C, unless the inputs to gate 4 settle at different times. Suppose

$t_2 \ll t_1 + t_3$, then the output of gate 2 (signal Z) could settle much earlier than that of gate 3 (signal Y). Consequently, gate 4 could first react to the change of Z, and then to the change of Y. In the example at hand, when S changes from 1 to 0, Z may change to 0 before Y changes to 1. Consequently, both inputs to gate 4 are 0, and the output $C = 0$. When X then Y ultimately change to 1, C goes back to 1. This glitch in the output, if wide enough, could cause elements using C as an input to produce incorrect results. It is also possible that $t_2 \gg t_1 + t_3$, in which case a change of S from 0 to 1 causes a glitch. In short, the problem arises owing to gate 4 using information that is not yet current.

This situation has a counterpart in parallel and distributed systems. Suppose that processes Y and Z in Figure 5.9 are generating data for a third process C and passing this data through shared memory locations M_y and M_z. Process C should ensure that the values in M_y and M_z are updated before it proceeds to use them; otherwise the computation could produce an incorrect result. This situation could be particularly problematic if, say, processor 1 is sequentially executing processes Y and C and processor 2 is executing process Z. If one is not careful, processor 1 could, after executing process Y, move on to process C, without ensuring that processor 2 has completed process Z. This problematic situation is an example of a *data hazard* [17], one with which most parallel and distributed systems must grapple.

For the multiplexer circuit, one solution to the problem described above is to ensure that gate 4 receives the new values of Z and Y only after both have reached the steady state. This can be done by inserting a two-bit register before gate 4. (As a practical matter since gate 4 itself does not cause an erroneous behavior of consequence, a one-bit register can instead be placed after gate 4.)

The corresponding solution for processes Y, Z, and C is to place a *barrier* or a synchronizing stage before process C can start. A barrier [18], which causes a set of processes (or threads) to stop until all processes in the set have finished, is a common method of synchronization in parallel and distributed systems. This form of synchronization is also used in other everyday situations, such as not starting a game until all players are present or not counting (or announcing) election results until voting has closed in all precincts.

5.3.2 KARNAUGH MAPS

Karnaugh maps, a staple in digital logic, can serve as much more than a tool to minimize the number of prime implicants in a Boolean expression. In this section we detail how a Karnaugh map can be used to introduce the torus, mesh, and possibly the hypercube topologies. The cells of a Karnaugh map are arranged so that adjacent cells (to within wraparound and across dimensions) can be combined into a prime implicant. Specifically, define two cells to be *adjacent* if and only if their corresponding expressions (minterms) differ in only one literal. For example, in a three-variable map, the cell (minterm) corresponding to xyz is adjacent to $x'yz, xy'z, xyz'$, but not to $x'y'z$. Define the *adjacency graph* of a Karnaugh map to be a graph with cells as vertices and an edge connecting each vertex pair corresponding to a pair of adjacent cells. This adjacency graph is a hypercube [6]. This is because two Karnaugh map cells are adjacent if and only if their expressions differ in exactly one variable. The corresponding condition for two nodes of a hypercube to be connected is for the binary addresses of the two nodes to differ in exactly one bit. Karnaugh maps flatten and slice the hypercube to fit a two-dimensional depiction.

Figure 5.10 shows the adjacency graph for three- and four-variable Karnaugh maps. Figure 5.11 shows a five-variable Karnaugh map and the corresponding five-dimensional hypercube. It is not difficult to observe that the adjacency graphs of the three- and four-variable Karnaugh maps are, in fact, 2×4 and 4×4 tori. (Observe that these are the same graphs as three- and four-dimensional hypercubes.) One could now easily extend the small tori to a general $R \times C$ two-dimensional torus and an $R \times C$ two-dimensional mesh (torus without the wraparound connections). An extension to higher-dimensional meshes and tori is also possible. The mesh and torus are arguably among the most widely used topologies [6]. The IBM Blue Gene/L has a three-dimensional torus [19] connecting its processors. The Cray Seastar interconnect is also a three-dimensional torus [20], and the Fujitsu K computer uses a six-dimensional torus [21]. The planar structure of the two-dimensional mesh also makes mesh-like interconnects common in integrated circuit chips (e.g., in field-programmable gate arrays [22, 23]). Ring-based topologies (one-dimensional torus) are also common in local area networks and distributed computing frameworks [24, 25].

Instruction notes for Section 5.3: The relation of fan-in and fan-out circuits to directed trees easily generalizes to the relation of logic circuits to directed graphs. One could observe here that a main difference between combinational and sequential logic is the lack of feedback cycles in the former. This allows for the introduction

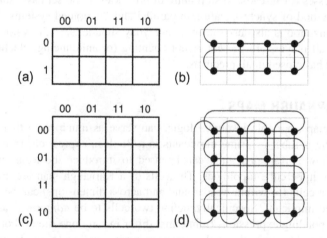

FIGURE 5.10

Cell layouts (a, c) and adjacency graphs (b, d) of three- and four-variable Karnaugh maps.

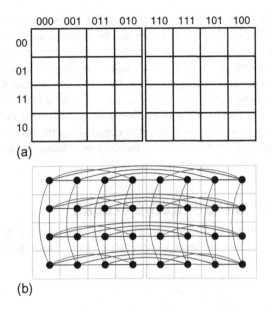

FIGURE 5.11

Cell layout (a) and adjacency graph (b) of a five-variable Karnaugh map.

of DAGs. However, introducing this term would be much more meaningful if one could tie it to the critical path, data hazards, and synchronization ideas. While this would probably require too much time for an in-class exposition, it holds the potential to explain and clarify slightly advanced digital logic ideas such as design optimization principles and fault tolerance; some of these may be explored in a design course/laboratory setting for digital logic.

Synchronization could be presented here as a method to keep signals with vastly different or unpredictable delays on the same page. This is in line with the barrier examples (game and voting) cited earlier, to which students would probably relate easily. Later in the context of sequential circuits, it would be beneficial to draw upon this intuitive understanding of synchronization to fully appreciate the advantage of clocked circuits.

Karnaugh maps should be presented as simply a different way of drawing a truth table, a way that allows us to see spatial relationships easily. An initial (obvious) reflection of this spatial relationship (for up to four-variable Karnaugh maps) is through a two-dimensional mesh (without the wraparound connections). The notion of adjacency (with the purpose of minimizing a function) for cells in these Karnaugh maps requires wraparound connections, and this naturally leads to a torus. All along the way the ideas of graphs and interconnection networks can also be easily reinforced.

The Karnaugh maps in Figures 5.10 and 5.11 number rows and columns according to the reflected Gray code sequence. This could be used to further reinforce recursive thinking.

Extension to a hypercube is difficult in a first digital logic course, but is not much more difficult than explaining adjacencies in five- and six-variable Karnaugh maps. In this context, we note that some texts view, for example, a five-variable Karnaugh map in terms of two four-variable maps, but without reflecting the indices of the second four-variable map. This will alter the edges along the fifth dimension in the corresponding hypercube in Figure 5.11b, but does not change the underlying idea.

5.4 COMBINATIONAL BUILDING BLOCKS

In this section we will use two commonly discussed combinational structures, adders and multiplexers, to illustrate several important concepts, including parallel prefix, and a variant of Amdahl's law.

5.4.1 ADDERS

Adders are one of the most commonly discussed combinational circuits in a course on digital logic and offer unique opportunities for exploring PDC topics. Consider the standard ripple-carry adder illustrated in Figure 5.12. The bottleneck of the ripple-carry adder's speed is the sequential generation of carry bits—that is, the longest path in the circuit traverses the carry lines. Students should note the important design principle of improving overall performance of a module by reducing its bottleneck (or critical path). This principle can also be seen as being somewhat similar to Amdahl's law [26, 27], which states that the part of an algorithm that is inherently sequential is the speed bottleneck in parallelizing this algorithm. For the ripple-carry adder (all of whose component full adders run in parallel) the carry generation used reflects an inherently sequential task. Here the speed of the circuit is bottlenecked by this sequential part (namely, ripple-carry generation).

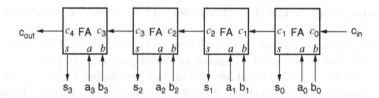

FIGURE 5.12

A four-bit ripple-carry adder. Each box labeled "FA" is a full adder accepting data bits a_i and b_i and carry-in bit c_i, and generating the sum bit s_i and the carry-out bit c_{i+1}.

In the normal course of explaining a ripple-carry adder, one would note that for $i \geq 0$, the $(i+1)$th carry c_{i+1} is given by the following recurrence in which "+" and "·" represent the logical OR and AND operations.

$$c_{i+1} = a_i \cdot b_i + (a_i + b_i) \cdot c_i = g_i + p_i \cdot c_i. \tag{5.1}$$

Here a_i and b_i are the ith bits of the numbers to be added, and g_i and p_i are the ith *carry-generate* and *carry-propagate* bits. Given this first-order recurrence in which c_{i+1} is expressed using c_i, a student in a first digital logic class (typically a freshman or sophomore) may incorrectly assume that carry computation (or for that matter any recurrence) is inherently sequential and that the adder circuit cannot overcome the delay of a ripple-carry adder. This presents the opportunity to use a carry-look-ahead adder (Figure 5.13) to show how seemingly sequential operations can be parallelized. In particular, one could introduce the idea of parallel prefix, a versatile PDC operation used in numerous applications ranging from polynomial evaluation and random number generation to the N-body problem and genome sequence alignment [28, 29]. *Prefix computation*: Let $\otimes$ be any associative operation. A *prefix computation* with respect to $\otimes$ on inputs $\alpha_0, \alpha_1, \ldots, \alpha_{n-1}$ produces outputs $\beta_0, \beta_1, \ldots, \beta_{n-1}$, where

$$\beta_i = \bigotimes_{j=0}^{i} \alpha_j = \alpha_0 \otimes \alpha_1 \otimes \cdots \otimes \alpha_i, \quad \text{for any } 0 \leq i < n.$$

A prefix computation is a special case of a first-order recurrence in that $\beta_i = \beta_{i-1} \otimes \alpha_i$. We now develop the relationship in the other direction and indicate how the first-order recurrence for the carry in Equation (5.1) can be expressed as a prefix computation.

Let $x_1, y_1, x_2,$ and y_2 be four binary signals. Define a binary operation $\odot$ on two doublets (pairs) $\langle x_1, y_1 \rangle$ and $\langle x_2, y_2 \rangle$ to produce the doublet $\langle x, y \rangle = \langle x_1, y_1 \rangle \odot \langle x_2, y_2 \rangle$ defined as follows:

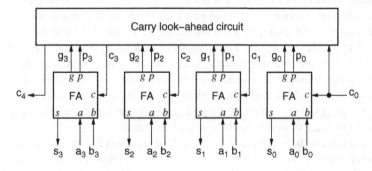

FIGURE 5.13

A four-bit carry-look-ahead adder. Each box labeled "FA" is a modified full adder accepting data bits a_i and b_i and carry-in bit c_i, and generating the sum bit s_i and the carry-generate and carry-propagate bits g_i and p_i.

$$x = x_2 + x_1 \cdot y_2 \quad \text{and} \quad y = y_1 \cdot y_2,$$

where $+$ and $\cdot$ denote the OR and AND operations. The operation $\odot$ can be proved to be associative. It can be shown that for $j \geq 0$ and doublets $\langle x_j, y_j \rangle$,

$$\bigodot_{j=0}^{i} \langle x_j, y_j \rangle = \langle G_i, P_i \rangle, \quad \text{where} \quad G_i = \sum_{j=0}^{i} x_j \left(\prod_{k=j+1}^{i} y_k \right) \quad \text{and} \quad P_i = \prod_{j=0}^{i} y_j. \quad (5.2)$$

Notice that this represents a prefix computation on the doublets $\langle x_i, y_i \rangle$ with respect to the operation $\odot$.

Coming back to the carry recurrence, let $x_0 = g_0$, $y_0 = c_0 p_0$, and for all $i > 0$ let $x_i = g_i$, $y_i = p_i$. Let bits G_i and P_i be obtained by a prefix computation as described in Equation (5.2). It can be shown that the ith carry is $c_i = G_i + P_i$. In other words, the carry bits can be computed by a prefix computation.

The ripple-carry circuit corresponds to a very slow prefix computation. A carry-look-ahead adder employs a fast prefix computation circuit to generate the carry bits. In general, by adopting different prefix circuits for carry generation, one could create adders with different cost-performance trade-offs. In Section 5.5.1 we will revisit prefix computations in the context of counters. It should also be noted that, in general, any linear recurrence can be converted to a prefix computation [30, 31].

5.4.2 MULTIPLEXERS

Earlier, we introduced recursive thinking in the context of number representations (Section 5.1), expressed fan-in and fan-out recursively (Section 5.2.1), and discussed carry look-ahead in terms of a recurrence relation (Equation (5.1)). We will show in Section 5.5.1 that prefix computation circuits (which compute a recurrence relation) also lend themselves to recursive decomposition. In this section, we will use multiplexers to reinforce recursive decomposition. It is well known that large multiplexers can be constructed using smaller multiplexers (see Figure 5.14). However, the construction is often not cast recursively or in terms of a divide-and-conquer strategy. For example, the multiplexer in Figure 5.14 can be viewed as follows. The problem is to select one input out of a set of 64 inputs. Partition the 64-input problem into four subproblems, each with 16 inputs. Then, recursively solve these four subproblems to obtain one (intermediate) selection from each subproblem. Finally, select one of the four intermediate selections using a 4-to-1 multiplexer. Similar decompositions can be illustrated through one-hot decoders and priority encoders (which are typically taught with multiplexers).

These ideas can be generalized to the task of recursively constructing a 2^n-to-1 multiplexer using 2^r-to-1 multiplexers for $r < n$. Observe that this recursive decomposition corresponds to a 2^r-ary tree and should be related to the ideas in Section 5.1. It should also be observed that this recursive decomposition is an algorithmic notion. It is applied here to a piece of hardware, but can equally apply to software. For example, merge sort [9] provides a classic illustration of such a

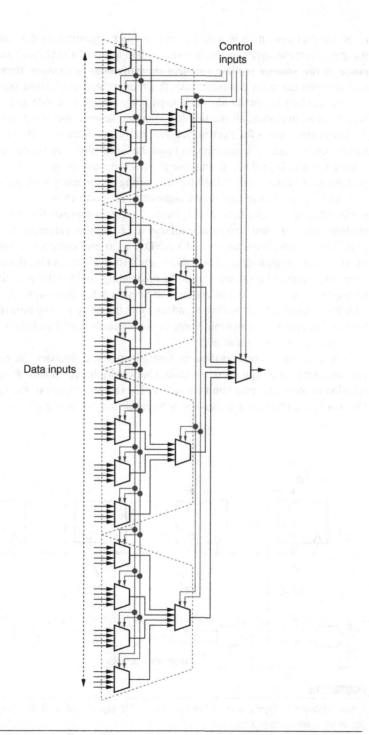

FIGURE 5.14

A 64-to-1 multiplexer constructed out of 21 4-to-1 multiplexers. Portions outlined in dashed lines indicate recursively constructed 16-to-1 multiplexers.

recursive decomposition in a divide-and-conquer algorithm. In the context of PDC, the merge sort example can also be expressed in terms of a DAG with an initial divide phase to run smaller sorting instances on individual processors, then merging the sorted sequences in the conquer phase; this merge can also illustrate synchronization.

The fact that important algorithmic paradigms such as divide and conquer apply broadly is an important abstraction for computer science and engineering students.

Instruction notes for Section 5.4: Normally, instruction on adders will cover the recurrence relation of Equation (5.1) and the linear delay of ripple-carry adders. It is easy to include in this a discussion of how the carry propagation bottlenecks the performance of the entire adder. Before getting to the carry-look-ahead adder, one may find a brief detour into prefix computations worthwhile. A simple example of prefix AND has several benefits: (1) by the instructor representing it as a recurrence, students can appreciate structural similarity to carry-propagation, (2) by the instructor providing the simple circuit for prefix AND (e.g., from Figure 5.15), students can see the similarity to ripple-carry, (3) from Figure 5.16, students can see that the seemingly sequential nature of a recurrence can be misleading, and (4) these prefix circuits can be used later in the context of counters in Section 5.5.1. Although one could go into additional details, it may suffice to indicate that the carry-propagation recurrence can be cast as a prefix computation. Some of these details would surface in the course of discussing carry-look-ahead adders.

The recursive decomposition in multiplexers and decoders is covered in the normal course of a digital logic course. One could direct students to notice that the solution to the larger problem is in terms of smaller instances of the same problem. One could use other circuits, such as a barrel shifter, to similar effect.

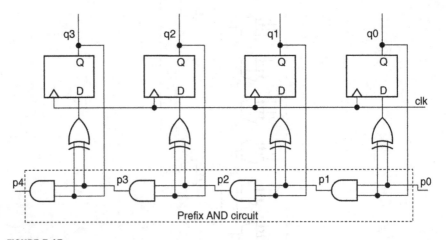

FIGURE 5.15

A four-bit counter. Typically p_0 is the counter-enable signal and p_4 is the "ripple carry-out" signal used for counter expansion.

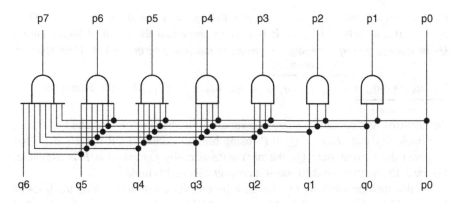

FIGURE 5.16

A prefix AND circuit for an eight-bit counter. For clarity, the ripple carry-out signal p_8 has not been generated.

5.5 COUNTERS AND REGISTERS

In this section we use counters to reinforce prefix computation and shift registers to illustrate pipelining.

5.5.1 COUNTERS

Counters are an important sequential building block, not just because of their utility in logic circuits, but also as a vehicle to explain concepts in digital logic (e.g., a counter's operation lends itself to a simple and intuitive introduction to state diagrams and transition expressions). Here we cast counters in a direction that we expect will help the student grasp both counters and prefix computations better. We will also use asynchronous (ripple) counters to illustrate the benefits and pitfalls of synchronous and asynchronous computation environments.

Prefix computations in counters: An n-bit binary counter gets to the next state by incrementing (modulo 2^n) the binary representation of the current state. This boils down to complementing bits up to the least significant 0 in the current state (and leaving the remaining higher bits unchanged). For instance, let the current state of an eight-bit counter be $1011\underline{0}111$. Here the least significant 0 (underlined) is in position 3. The next state is $10110111 + 1 = \underbrace{1011}_{\text{unchanged}}\ \overbrace{1000}^{\text{complemented}}$. Determining the position of the least significant 0 reduces to computing the prefix AND of the bits. Specifically, let the current state (or count) be $Q_t = q_{n-1}q_{n-2}\cdots q_1 q_0$ (in binary). We now construct an n-bit "prefix" sequence $P = \langle p_{n-1}, p_{n-2}, \ldots, p_1, p_0 \rangle$ in which $p_0 = 1$ and for $0 < i < n$ we have $p_i = q_0 \cdot q_1 \cdot \cdots \cdot q_{i-1} = p_{i-1} \cdot q_{i-1}$, where "$\cdot$" denotes the logical AND operation. Let $0 \leq i_0 \leq n$ be the position of the least significant 0 ($i_0 = n$ indicates that $q_i = 1$ for all $0 \le i < n$). Then $p_i = 1$ if and only if $i \le i_0$. It is easy to show that the result of incrementing $Q_t = q_{n-1}q_{n-2} \cdots q_{i_0+1}q_{i_0}q_{i_0-1} \cdots q_1 q_0 = q_{n-1}q_{n-2} \cdots q_{i_0+1}01 \cdots 11$ is $Q_{t+1} =$

$$q_{n-1}q_{n-2} \cdots q_{i_0+1} \underbrace{\overbrace{q'_{i_0}q'_{i_0-1} \cdots q'_1 q'_0}^{\text{complemented}}}_{\text{unchanged}} = q_{n-1}q_{n-2} \cdots q_{i_0+1}10 \cdots 00. \text{ Noting that for}$$

the exclusive-OR operation $\oplus$ and any variable v we have $v \oplus 1 = v'$ and $v \oplus 0 = v$, one could say that $Q_{t+1} = Q_t \oplus P$ (using bitwise exclusive-OR operations). That is, given the current state Q_t, the next state is easily computed if P is available. Figure 5.15 shows a standard four-bit counter cast in this mold.

Notice that the clocking rate for an n-bit counter constructed along the lines of Figure 5.15 must accommodate at least $n - 1$ AND gate delays. Clearly, this does not scale for large n (in much the same way that a ripple-carry adder does not scale for large addends). Standard textbook solutions include using larger-input AND gates such as the design shown in Figure 5.16 for an eight-bit counter. Here the delay is that of an n-input AND gate and the delay for fanning a signal out to n places; this delay typically grows sublinearly with n. One could replace the circuit in Figure 5.16 by any other prefix circuit (see, e.g., Figure 5.17).

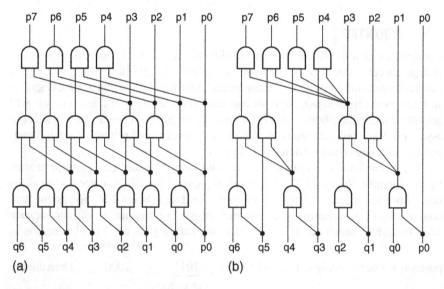

FIGURE 5.17

Examples of prefix AND circuits for an eight-bit counter: (a) the Kogge-Stone circuit [32]; (b) the Ladner-Fischer circuit [33]. These circuits exhibit trade-offs between the number of gates used and their fan-out. These circuits can be used with any associative operation, including one for carry propagation.

A combination of one of these circuits with the method in Figure 5.16 to accommodate the availability of high fan-in gates may provide an optimal middle ground for large values of n.

Ripple counters: It is well known that ripple counters (Figure 5.18) can be very cheap to implement and quite fast for small counters. However, as the size of the counter grows, flip-flop delays accumulate, necessitating a reduction in the clock speed. As shown in Figure 5.18, the clock of an n-bit ripple counter should be wide enough to accommodate n flip-flop delays.

The clock in synchronous counters of the form illustrated in Figure 5.15 also needs to accommodate n gate delays. However, there is a significant difference in the two situations.

In general, a synchronous circuit must use a clock that is wide enough to accommodate delays to flip-flop inputs. Although this worst-case clock considerably simplifies circuit design and ensures correct flip-flop state changes, it fails to exploit the speed of a typical case behavior, while an asynchronous circuit can (albeit at the cost of more complex design procedures and potentially unreliable operation).

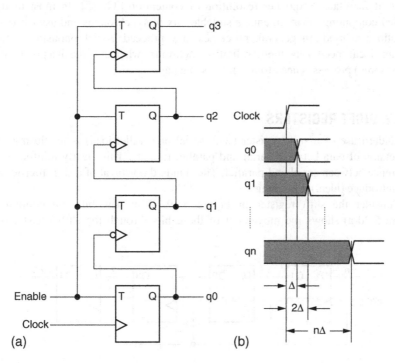

FIGURE 5.18

Structure of a ripple counter and its timing diagram; flip-flop propagation delay is denoted by Δ.

These trade-offs present significant design choices for parallel and distributed systems. The Internet (or a computer network, in general) is typically distributed over a large geographic area. Consequently there are large (variations in) delays associated with communication between nodes in the network. Clearly, a synchronous system is not suitable here, as that would entail very long waits to accommodate all delays. In other cases, the nature of the problem or computing environment induces large variations or uncertainties among communicating elements; again an asynchronous environment is better here. Consider a school of sardines that collectively swim as a school, but where each fish individually takes its cues from its immediate neighborhood. If all the sardines need to proceed in lockstep, the school's response would not be fast enough to evade a predator. Such event- and neighborhood-driven responses are typical in distributed computing systems that operate asynchronously. Other situations, however, call for synchronous operation. An example, many medium access control (MAC) protocols or leader election algorithms use a slotted (synchronous) mode to resolve contention. As opposed to the previous situations where all entities need to react quickly, contention resolution tries to systematically reduce attempts to secure a shared resource (such as a wireless channel), ideally to one contender. While the slotted mode reduces the speed of operation of individual nodes, it facilitates a quicker resolution of contention [34, 35]. In most modern parallel computing environments, a suitable mix of synchronous and asynchronous operations is used. In general, processes may proceed asynchronously (to fully leverage local speeds) and then explicitly synchronize when they reach a point where all (or some) processes need to be on the same page.

5.5.2 SHIFT REGISTERS

A standard use of a shift register (with serial or parallel load) is to illustrate the conversion of data between serial and parallel formats. This clearly reinforces the difference between serial and parallel. The standard portrayal of a shift register can also introduce (ideal) pipelining.

Consider the shift register in Figure 5.19. With new bits *a-e* coming in, Figure 5.20(a) shows the movement of these bits through the shift register over

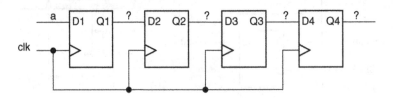

FIGURE 5.19

A four-bit shift register. The input D_1 has a binary value *a*. The question marks at flip-flop outputs indicate do not care values.

clock	D_1	Q_1	Q_2	Q_3	Q_4
0	a	–	–	–	–
1	b	a	–	–	–
2	c	b	a	–	–
3	d	c	b	a	–
4	e	d	c	b	a
5	–	e	d	c	b
6	–	–	e	d	c
7	–	–	–	e	d
8	–	–	–	–	e

(a)

time	Input x	$F_1(x)$	$F_2(x)$	$F_3(x)$	$F_4(x)$
0	a	–	–	–	–
Δ	b	a_1	–	–	–
2Δ	c	b_1	a_2	–	–
3Δ	d	c_1	b_2	a_3	–
4Δ	e	d_1	c_2	b_3	a_4
5Δ	–	e_1	d_2	c_3	b_4
6Δ	–	–	e_2	d_3	c_4
7Δ	–	–	–	e_3	d_4
8Δ	–	–	–	–	e_4

(b)

FIGURE 5.20

An illustration of pipelining. (a) The shifting of bits through a four-bit shift register. (b) The movement of inputs through a four-stage pipeline. A dash indicates a do not care value.

clock cycles. The first point to note (even in the understanding of the shift register) is that with each clock tick, all bits shift simultaneously by one position; for example, at clock tick 5, e moves from D_1 to Q_1 at the same time as d moves from Q_1 to Q_2, and so on. Therefore, despite the seemingly serial structure of the shift register, the movement of bits is inherently parallel, a fact that many students initially miss. Now consider the four-stage ideal pipeline in Figure 5.21 (in which each stage requires the same time, Δ, to process any input). For any input x and $1 \leq i \leq 4$, let $x_i = f_i(f_{i-1}(\cdots(f_1(x))\cdots)) = F_i(x)$ (say), then Figure 5.20b represents the flow of data through the pipeline. The similarity between the two tables is unmistakable. While the quantities moving through the pipeline may be different, the pattern of their movement is the same.

It could also be noted that many practical pipelines are not ideal, suffering stalls and timing imbalances, and requiring flushing of partly processed inputs. However, the fundamental (and preferred) operation of the pipeline is embodied in the flow of bits in a shift register. Pipelines are common in processors [36]. A classic RISC pipeline includes stages for instruction fetch, decode, execute, memory access, and register writeback. Image and video pipelines [37] are standard in cameras. The idea of pipelining also applies to software—for example, in out-of-order execution of instructions in loops [17].

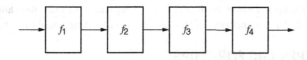

FIGURE 5.21

A four-stage pipeline. Stage i computes a function f_i.

Instruction notes for Section 5.5: The standard discussion of synchronous counters uses a circuit similar to that in Figure 5.15. Expressing the counter in terms of prefix AND would serve to explain why the circuit works as a counter; for a first digital logic course, these ideas could be expressed through examples rather than general expressions. If the prefix AND circuits were discussed earlier in the context of adders (see Section 5.4.1), then relatively little time would be needed to explain the "slow" and "fast" counters associated with Figures 5.15 and 5.16. One could go further and note that prefix computations have many applications besides counters and there are several methods for performing prefix computations (such as those shown in Figure 5.17). On a more advanced note, it could be observed that the Ladner-Fischer circuit (Figure 5.17b) translates to a simple recursive algorithm on the CREW PRAM, a model of parallel computation on which numerous parallel algorithms, algorithmic techniques, and complexity results have been developed [31].

The discussion with ripple counters should aim to first distinguish synchronous and asynchronous circuits in basic terms. For example, one could emphasize that for flip-flops (or latches), synchronous operation amounts to triggering at the same time, and for correct operation no flip-flop triggers until all flip-flops are ready to trigger. This has similarities to the data hazards and synchronization example in Section 5.3.1. The larger discussion of the advantages and limitations of synchronous/asynchronous design should be placed in the context of most sequential logic in a first digital logic course being synchronous.

A key common point of shift registers and pipelines is that the flow of "data" is parallel. This observation (without reference to pipelines) may help students understand shift registers better. Next, one could consider a (simplified) four-stage ideal video pipeline (consisting of, e.g., analog-to-digital conversion, noise filtering, color correction, compression) and illustrate how successive frames move through these stages. If one wishes to take this further, the idea of a processor pipeline could also be introduced without too many details. The key point to note here is that a program is a sequence of instructions stored in memory outside the processor. The processor must first get (fetch) the instruction from the memory, then it must determine what the instruction means (decode). Only after that can the processor do what the instruction calls for (execute). While instruction 3 is being fetched, instruction 2 could be decoded and instruction 1 executed.

5.6 OTHER DIGITAL LOGIC TOPICS

We have discussed a selection of digital logic topics that can serve to introduce several PDC concepts. However, digital logic is replete with examples and instances that can illustrate PDC concepts. In this section we touch on some of them.

5.6.1 LATCHES AND FLIP-FLOPS

Latches and flip-flops clearly show the difference between asynchronous and synchronous systems. A simple analysis of a latch can also be used to show how different delays on different paths can result in different flip-flop states. (One standard example is that of metastability when an SR latch input changes simultaneously from $SR = 11$ to $SR = 00$. The output state depends on the gate delays in the paths to the outputs.) This illustration can generalize to situations in which the order of an execution (used in a distributed algorithm sense) can affect the outcome of an algorithm. Read/write hazards and cache consistency are examples [36].

5.6.2 FINITE STATE MACHINES

State diagrams of finite state machines can be used to reinforce the idea of a graph introduced in Section 5.2.1. In addition, finite state machine design examples can also convey PDC ideas. In this section we identify three such commonly used examples.

Bit serial adder: A bit-serial adder is a ripple-carry adder with only one full adder. An additional flip-flop conveys the carry-out of one bit position to the carry-in of the next bit position. This design, which uses few components, but which is slower and has synchronization requirements on the inputs and outputs, illustrates the cost performance trade-offs inherent in parallelism.

Bus arbiter: An arbiter selects one of a set of contenders according to some rule (which can be simple or as complex as the instructor wishes). When placed in the context of the earlier discussion of the bus, this illustrates the overheads inherent in sharing resources.

Pattern recognizer: A pattern recognizer accepts a stream of input symbols and outputs a 1 whenever the last k inputs coincide with a fixed reference string of length k. The reference string passes through the state diagram unimpeded from the initial state to the ACCEPT state. Any deviation from the reference string sets the progress back a little further away from the ACCEPT state. This is similar to a complex pipeline in which inputs move in tandem until something like a missed prediction causes the pipeline to start over.

5.6.3 VERILOG

Most modern offerings of digital logic courses also include an introduction to a hardware description language such as Verilog. Despite its similarity to C (in syntax and some semantics), Verilog code works very differently from (sequential) C code. This difference could be useful to illustrate the difference between sequential and parallel systems. Verilog code is inherently parallel. For example, two or more instantiations of a module in Verilog result in two or more pieces of hardware that have the potential to operate simultaneously. On the other hand, multiple calls to a C procedure run the procedure sequentially multiple times. Blocking and nonblocking assignments in Verilog also illustrate parallelism and (a)synchrony.

5.6.4 PROGRAMMABLE LOGIC DEVICES TO FIELD-PROGRAMMABLE GATE ARRAYS

Almost all digital logic texts cover programmable logic devices and some devote pages to more advanced devices such as complex programmable logic devices and field-programmable gate arrays. Field-programmable gate arrays, in particular, have assumed a mainstream presence in parallel computing as accelerators and in embedded systems. Some modern field-programmable gate arrays also have embedded processor cores. Depending on the depth of coverage in the digital logic course, field-programmable gate arrays could be used to inform students of the wide scope of digital logic in PDC, and perhaps to introduce concepts ranging from interconnect structures to the role of special-purpose accelerators and reconfigurable computing in general [22, 23].

5.6.5 PRACTICAL CONSIDERATIONS

Clock distribution and skew can reinforce ideas of scaling (seen in the context of fan-in, fan-out, adders, and counters). A clock distribution tree can also be used to revisit trees, interconnects, and broadcasting. The tree to depict binary numbers (Figure 5.1) can be extended to explain prefix codes.

REFERENCES

[1] I. Letunic, P. Bork, Interactive Tree Of Life (iTOL): an online tool for phylogenetic tree display and annotation, Bioinformatics 23 (2007) 127-128, doi:10.1093/bioinformatics/btl529.

[2] iTOL: Interactive Tree of Life, URL http://itol.embl.de/.

[3] A. Espinoza-Valdez, R. Femat, F.C. Ordaz-Salazar, A model for renal arterial branching based on graph theory, Math. Biosci. 225 (2010) 36-43, doi:10.1016/j.mbs.2010.01.007.

[4] W.J. Dally, B. Towles, Principles and Practices of Interconnection Networks, Morgan Kaufman Publishers, San Francisco, CA, USA, 2004, ISBN 0122007514, 978-0122007514.

[5] J. Duato, S. Yalamanchili, L. Ni, Interconnection Networks, Morgan Kaufman Publishers, San Francisco, CA, USA, 2003, ISBN 1558608524, 978-1558608528.

[6] F.T. Leighton, Introduction to Parallel Algorithms and Architectures: Arrays, Trees, Hypercubes, Morgan Kaufman Publishers, San Mateo, CA, USA, 1992, ISBN 1558601171, 978-1558601178.

[7] M. Brazil, R. Graham, D. Thomas, M. Zachariasen, On the history of the Euclidean Steiner tree problem, Arch. Hist. Exact Sci. 68 (3) (2014) 327-354, ISSN 0003-9519, doi:10.1007/s00407-013-0127-z.

[8] C.E. Leiserson, Fat-trees: universal networks for hardware-efficient supercomputing, IEEE Trans. Comput. C-34 (1985) 892-901, doi:10.1109/TC.1985.6312192.

[9] T.H. Cormen, C.E. Leiserson, R.L. Rivest, C. Stein, Introduction to Algorithms, MIT Press, Cambridge, MA, USA, 2009, ISBN 0262033844, 978-0262033848.

[10] IPv4 AS Core: Visualizing IPv4 and IPv6 Internet Topology at a Macroscopic Scale in 2013, URL http://www.caida.org/research/topology/as_core_network/.

[11] L. Stockmeyer, U. Vishkin, Simulation of parallel random access machines by circuits, SIAM J. Comput. 13 (1984) 409-422, doi:10.1137/0213027.

[12] PCI-SIG Specifications, URL http://www.pcisig.com/specifications/.

[13] IEEE Standard 802.3-2012: Ethernet, URL http://standards.ieee.org/findstds/standard/802.3-2012.html.

[14] IEEE Standard 1394-2008: High Performance Serial Bus, URL http://standards.ieee.org/findstds/standard/1394-2008.html.

[15] Universal Serial Bus (USB), URL http://www.usb.org/home.

[16] Y.-K. Kwok, I. Ahmad, Static scheduling algorithms for allocating directed task graphs to multiprocessors, ACM Comput. Surv. 31 (1999) 406-471, doi:10.1145/344588.344618.

[17] S. Pande, D.P. Agrawal, Compiler Optimizations for Scalable Parallel Systems: Languages, Compilation Techniques, and Run Time Systems, Springer verlag, Berlin, Germany, 2001, ISBN 3540419454, 978-3540419457.

[18] M. Herlihy, N. Shavit, The Art of Multiprocessor Programming, Morgan Kaufman Publishers, Waltham, MA, USA, 2013, ISBN 0123973376, 978-0123973375.

[19] N.R. Adiga, M.A. Blumrich, D. Chen, P. Coteus, A. Gara, M.E. Giampapa, P. Heidelberger, S. Singh, B.D. Steinmacher-Burow, T. Takken, M. Tsao, P. Vranas, Blue Gene/L Torus interconnection network, IBM J. Res. Dev. 49 (2005) 265-276.

[20] The Cray XT5 System Highlights, URL www.cray.com/Assets/PDF/products/xt/CrayXT5Brochure.pdf.

[21] Y. Akima, Y. Takagi, T. Inoue, S. Hiramoto, T. Shimizu, The Tofu Interconnect, in: Proceedings of 19th IEEE Symposium on High Performance Interconnects, 2011, pp. 87-94.

[22] S. Hauck, A. DeHon, Reconfigurable Computing: The Theory and Practice of FPGA-Based Computation, Morgan Kaufman Publishers, Burlington, MA, USA, 2008, ISBN 0123705223, 978-0123705228.

[23] R. Vaidyanathan, J.L. Trahan, Dynamic Reconfiguration: Architectures and Algorithms, Kluwer Academic Publishers, New York, NY, USA, 2004, ISBN 0306481898, 978-0306481895.

[24] H. Attiya, J. Welch, Distributed Computing: Fundamentals, Simulations and Advanced Topics (2nd edition), John Wiley Interscience, Hoboken, NJ, USA, 2004, ISBN 0-471-453242.

[25] N.A. Lynch, Distributed Algorithms, Morgan Kaufmann Publishers Inc., San Francisco, CA, USA, 1996, ISBN 1558603484.

[26] M.D. Hill, M.R. Marty, Amdahl's law in the multicore era, IEEE Comput. 41 (2008) 33-38, doi:10.1109/MC.2008.209.

[27] M.A. Suleman, Y.N. Patt, E. Sprangle, A. Rohillah, A. Ghuloum, D. Carmean, Asymmetric Chip Multiprocessors: Balancing Hardware Efficiency and Programmer Efficiency (TR-HPS-2007-001), 2007, URL http://hps.ece.utexas.edu/pub/TR-HPS-2007-001.pdf.

[28] S. Aluru, N. Futamura, K. Mehrotra, Parallel biological sequence comparison using prefix computations, J. Parallel Distrib. Comput. 63 (2003) 264-272, doi:10.1016/S0743-7315(03)00010-8.

[29] G.E. Blelloch, Prefix sums and their applications, in: J.H. Reif (Ed.), Synthesis of Parallel Algorithms, Morgan Kaufman Publishers, San Francisco, CA, USA, ISBN 155860135X, 978-1558601352, 1993, pp. 35-60.

[30] H.P. Dharmasena, R. Vaidyanathan, The mesh with binary tree networks: an enhanced mesh with low bus-loading, J. Interconnect. Netw. 05 (2004) 131-150, doi:10.1142/S0219265904001064.

[31] J. Jájá, An Introduction to Parallel Algorithms, Addison Wesley Publishing Co., Reading, MA, USA, 1992, ISBN 0201548569, 978-0201548563.

[32] P.M. Kogge, H.S. Stone, A parallel algorithm for the efficient solution of a general class of recurrence equations, IEEE Trans. Comput. C-22 (1973) 786-793, doi:10.1109/TC.1973.5009159.

[33] R.E. Ladner, M.J. Fischer, Parallel prefix computation, J. ACM 27 (1980) 831-838, doi: 10.1145/322217.322232.

[34] N. Abramson, The ALOHA system—another alternative for computer communications, in: Proceedings of the Fall Joint Computer Conference, AFIPS Press, 1970, pp. 281-285, URL http://en.wikipedia.org/wiki/ALOHAnet.

[35] D.R. Kowalski, A. Pelc, Leader election in ad hoc radio networks: a keen ear helps, J. Comput. Syst. Sci. 79 (2013) 1164-1180, doi:10.1016/j.jcss.2013.04.003.

[36] J.L. Hennessy, D.A. Patterson, Computer Architecture: A Quantitative Approach, Morgan Kaufman Publishers, Waltham, MA, USA, 2011, ISBN 012383872X, 978-0123838728.

[37] R. Vaidyanathan, P. Vinukonda, A.C. Lessing, Pipelined execution of windowed image computations, J. Netw. Comput. 3 (2013) 75-97.

Networks and MPI for cluster computing

Ryan E. Grant* and Stephen L. Olivier*

Sandia National Laboratories[a]

Relevant core courses: CS2, DS/A, Systems.

Relevant parallel and distributed computing topics: Cluster computing, Message passing, Single program, multiple data, Bulk synchronous parallel, Communication algorithms, MIPS/FLOPS, LINPACK, Distributed memory, Partitioned global address space languages, Synchronization.

Learning outcomes: Students will become aware of the existence of message passing paradigms for cluster computing. They will understand the concept of collective communication and the need for unique identifiers for each computational process. The concept of supercomputing and the unique concerns of operating large-scale systems will be introduced.

Context for use: These topics should be introduced along with shared memory parallel computing as a replacement for or a complement to shared memory. They can be used to complement any discussion of machine parallelism by representing that individual computing nodes can then be leveraged for further multinode parallelism.

This chapter offers insights into the practice of cluster computing and super-computing for instructors, while covering the technical details needed to explain the concepts to computer science/computer engineering students. It includes guidance on how and when to introduce these topics to students within the parallel and distributed computing curriculum, as well as some suggested classroom activities that can be used to enhance student classroom participation.

[a]Sandia National Laboratories is a multiprogram laboratory managed and operated by Sandia Corporation, a wholly owned subsidiary of Lockheed Martin Corporation, for the U.S. Department of Energy's National Nuclear Security Administration under contract DE-AC04-94AL85000. SAND Report Number 2013-10652P.

This chapter begins with an introductory essay explaining the key concepts of message passing in cluster computing, along with some common misperceptions. This essay focuses on a real-world application context, relating the theoretical concepts to examples of practice that can be used in a classroom setting.

The material following the essay details additional technical information needed to teach cluster computing topics at a core computer science level. This material will cover all the required knowledge for an instructor aiming to provide a Bloom classification of K to C for cluster computing and message passing concepts in core computer science courses. We also provide an advanced concepts section that briefly discusses topics best introduced in advanced-level elective courses along with the relevant technical information needed to teach such subjects. Some of this advanced material may also be introduced by the instructor for enrichment proposes in core-level courses.

6.1 WHY MESSAGE PASSING/MPI?

Vocabulary:

Node—an individual computing system that is part of a cluster (e.g., a rack server or a workstation).

Nonuniform memory access—a memory architecture configuration in which costs to access different parts of memory are not equal.

Message Passing Interface (MPI)—a standard way of exchanging data (via messages) between cooperating compute nodes.

Message passing is the current standard programming model for multi-compute node parallel computing systems. The idea of message passing has existed for many years. The idea of message-based networks formed the basis for what we now know as the Internet. The Internet and other wide area networks work using packetized messages, which are interpreted as either a stream of data (Transmission Control Protocol (TCP)) or as independent messages (User Datagram Protocol (UDP)). The Message Passing Interface (MPI) is a messaging middleware that provides a standard way of communicating via messages with a given group of communication partners. It defines what form the messages passed should take, and allows the target of the messages to determine where the message was sent from, whether it has been delivered in order, what process it was meant to be delivered to, and where it should be placed in memory when it arrives. It provides the features needed to develop very large parallel code using efficient message exchanges that can even be used between compute nodes with different architectures (e.g., big endian versus little endian). It provides collective operations, such as Broadcast, Gather, and Scatter, which allows efficient communication of computational results for parallel code. MPI is supported on many different platforms, and by many different vendors, providing a single interface for code development that is portable between many different types of systems.

Message passing techniques before the introduction of MPI were not standardized, and several methods existed. This led to code portability issues, as not all methods were supported on all platforms. For example, some platforms supported Parallel Virtual Machine middleware, while others supported independently developed message passing libraries such as LAM (Local Area Multicomputer). Several other message passing middleware packages also existed, which while incompatible, shared the same goal of providing a message passing interface. Starting in the mid 1990s the developers of these message passing approaches decided to work together to combine the best aspects of their solutions into a standard. Many industry vendors and academic researchers came together to publish the first MPI standard in 1996. MPI-1, as it came to be known, was popular for many years, and was widely adopted. However, the standard was not perfect, and as it aged it failed to address some of the state-of-the-art work being done on high-performance networks. The MPI standardization body was rejuvenated with new members and began to meet again to discuss a new MPI version, MPI-2. Continuing work on MPI by many different groups culminated in the release of MPI-3 in 2013. MPI has been embraced by the high-performance computing (HPC) community as the premier method of internode communications, and runs on virtually all of the top supercomputers in the world today.

The platforms that run MPI are typically a cluster of homogeneous systems (nodes) that work cooperatively on large computational tasks. Many of the top supercomputers in the world as of this writing use MPI to communicate between many computational nodes, connected together with very high speed networks (some custom-built), while using readily available enterprise class server components. Supercomputers can use a combination of typical x86 general-purpose CPUs as well as lighter-weight accelerator cores, typically a graphics processing unit (GPU) or lightweight general-purpose cores.

The bulk synchronous parallel (BSP) programming model is fully supported by MPI. This model has been used for many years as the standard for large-scale scientific computational code. It allows many processes to compute sections of a problem solution with the computation progressing in a series of "supersteps," each ending with a communication among all of the participating processes (even if it is just a barrier to keep the processes synchronized at a coarse level).

An alternative architecture to cluster computing with MPI is a shared memory system. Designing large shared memory systems can be very difficult, and designing a shared memory system that contains millions of cores would be impractical. The MPI programming model combined with cluster computing offers a much more economical solution to large-scale processing, as it can take advantage of commonly available servers, which can be supplemented with high-performance networking hardware. The use of high-performance networks is key to many computational problems as low-latency, high-bandwidth MPI communication is key to good performance for many MPI programs.

MPI is a commonly accepted method of message passing in between nodes of a cluster. However, it may not be the perfect solution for intranode communication/

concurrency. Shared memory optimization for MPI processes is a well-researched topic, but MPI is not ideal for dynamically adjusting program concurrency during computation. To benefit from many parallel threads of execution during specific parallel regions of code, other multithreading techniques can be used. This combination of a local concurrency method and MPI is referred to as MPI+X. At the time of writing, the exact method of local concurrency that will be used in future supercomputers is unknown. Some examples of current methods include OpenMP and Cilk.

Given the relationship between MPI and shared memory local concurrency methods, MPI can be introduced alongside discussions on shared memory. It can also be discussed in the context of networks, especially if the students have already been introduced to shared memory and local concurrency. This can be a motivation for why high-speed networks are such an important component of large-scale systems. MPI can also be addressed whenever process synchronization is discussed, with the networking delay being accounted for, and the ramifications that this has on the performance of synchronization operations. Finally, a very appropriate time to discuss MPI is in a course of data structures and algorithms (DS/A) when discussing collective operations (Broadcast, multicast, Scatter/Gather).

The basic concepts of message passing can be illustrated to students using examples from their own lives (instant messaging, passing paper notes, e-mail when working in a group). These examples typically represent point-to-point communications (one node to another). A proven, effective method of teaching collective operations (in the context of MPI or not) is to have students perform the jobs of actors in the system. For example, to illustrate a Broadcast or multicast, the instructor can hand out small pieces of paper to some students. A reduce operation can occur by collecting the pieces and computing their sum. This activity provides a great visual reference, and students typically have good retention of the ideas, particularly if they are involved.

6.1.1 SHARED MEMORY CACHE COHERENT NONUNIFORM MEMORY ACCESS ARCHITECTURE DOES NOT EXTEND TO AN EXTREME SCALE

Distributed shared memory schemes (e.g., Cluster OpenMP) are difficult to scale to large systems. This is due to the overhead of keeping the many individual processors in the system observing the same memory space. For example, when accessing shared memory in a distributed scheme, one must make sure that the memory being accessed has not been updated elsewhere. This requires that either all memory updates must be pushed to all of the processors, or that some method be used to determine if the shared memory being read is current (i.e., polling other processors that can access that memory). A distributed memory scheme can also lead to performance inefficiencies due to data placement. For instance, if one CPU is accessing memory at a far-away location, it may significantly slow the progress of that CPU. It may be possible to migrate that shared memory to the CPU most in need of it, but this too has overhead. Distributed shared memory systems may not be able to inform an application of when memory is remote, making it difficult for the application to understand when memory accesses will be fast (local) or slow (remote). All of these factors combine to make distributed shared memory schemes difficult to design and implement. As such, many existing approaches, such as Cluster OpenMP, are not widely adopted in the cluster computing/supercomputing community.

Message passing helps to avoid some of the data placement performance inefficiencies of distributed shared memory schemes by explicitly exposing the locality of data. While an application may not always know what other MPI processes are running on the same node, the locality of the memory that the MPI process is working with is generally known. Remote memory locations require explicit message passing in order to access them, and therefore the programmer is aware of data locality.

Shared memory processing for local node computing is widely regarded as beneficial for cluster computing. Unlike the distributed shared memory case, the locality of the memory to the CPUs and smaller ranges for possible memory latencies make this approach very practical. When combined with multithreading techniques, shared memory processing within a cluster node is a powerful parallel processing tool. Approaches such as OpenMP allow the creation of many threads for a parallel portion of application code, with easy methods of indicating the parallelism required and the memory sharing parameters. Because this shared memory multithreading model is confined to a local compute node, this scales well as each node is essentially a separate system from the local shared memory point of view. Of course, shared memory can also be used by other cluster computing parallel programming interfaces such as MPI. Most MPI implementations are optimized to use shared memory to pass messages between processes on a local node. Current (MPI-3.0) implementations make it difficult to dynamically adjust the amount of parallelism while an application is running. Therefore, MPI is typically combined with other approaches such as OpenMP for local concurrency with message passing between the MPI processes.

This can be conceptualized for students as workers (processes or threads) on different machines that need to exchange data at certain points in the job. A useful analogy is that of students working together in the same room who can easily discuss the problem they are working to solve and exchange data (shared memory) and that same group working with other groups that are not in the same location (distributed memory). While message passing is the dominant remote node cluster communication technique, there may be situations in which the performance penalty of current-day distributed shared memory versus MPI is acceptable in order to present the whole cluster as one large shared memory computer for ease of programming.

This topic can be introduced when discussing single program, multiple data (SPMD) in CS2 and DS/A, and is also relevant when discussing shared memory. It is important to include this material in any discussion of distributed shared memory. An in-depth understanding of message passing is not required, but a good learning goal is to make students aware that message passing exists, and that while distributed shared memory methods exist, message passing is the dominant paradigm. It is also appropriate to recap in parallel programming and perhaps in advanced architecture courses.

6.1.2 MESSAGE PASSING PROVIDES SCALABILITY FOR "GRAND CHALLENGE" PROBLEMS

Answering many of the great scientific questions of the twenty-first century will require large interconnected systems that can work together. One of the keys to designing future-generation cluster computing systems is extreme scalability. As core counts of large clusters exceed 1 million, the overhead incurred to manage millions of simultaneous processes can become onerous. Therefore, it is important to design communication middleware that can scale to millions of processes. MPI has demonstrated that it is capable of scaling to 1 million cores [1]. However, scalability of communication middleware must be supported by scalable networking hardware. For example, if a typical connection-based networking transport is used, the overhead of maintaining communication state for each process to every other process can consume significant amounts of resources. Connectionless networking transports alleviate this issue, but require additional mechanisms to ensure that messages can reach their target processes, given that no or very little communication state information is maintained.

Assuming that a scalable underlying network is available, message passing allows one to logically approach application design at million-process scales. With use of MPI ranks, each process can be assigned a portion of work easily. This approach provides scalability by allowing good application code to efficiently manage communication. Good application code minimizes global synchronization and allows communication/computation overlap by asynchronously processing communication operations while computation is ongoing. Programming such applications is not an easy task, and requires expert programming specialists that have detailed knowledge of not only programming but also of lower-level software environments and even hardware. Large computing systems also require dedicated teams of technicians to keep them operational. Alternatives to traditional "big iron" systems exist, but they may not be scalable for all problems.

Need more tightly coupled systems than distributed computing efforts

Distributed computing efforts that utilize the Internet and individual consumer devices with "donated" compute cycles are a good fit for a subset of problems. For efforts such as SETI@home [2], which uses volunteers' personal computers to look for evidence of extraterrestrial communication, it is an excellent fit. The problem they solve is very large, but the data and the processing of the data is not dependent on the state of the whole system. In other words, a home computer can work on a piece of the dataset collected by SETI without interacting with other computers working on other pieces. The result of one computation is not dependent on the output from another. Therefore, this model fits quite well with using many home computers (even gaming consoles) connected to the Internet to perform parallel computations in a reasonable amount of time.

Many large scientific problems require that all participating processes combine the results of their calculations before proceeding to the next step of the computation.

For example, consider a physics simulation of many molecules. Each molecule exerts a force on all of the others in the system. Consequently, in the simulation of the whole system, each molecule simulated needs to know the position and velocity of each other molecule in order to calculate its own position and velocity. This simulation proceeds in discrete "time steps." In every time step all of the computing systems need to exchange some information. If a single system falls behind, then all of the others must wait for it to complete its calculation before they can proceed with the next time step. Such a simulation is impractical to perform at a great scale and speed in a loosely coupled distributed computing paradigm.

Time delays introduced by the physical distribution of the compute systems and slow interconnection networks make the coordinated use of many distributed home computers impractical. Widely distributed computations also typically require more effort to secure them, and are subject to potentially malicious behavior when they are driven by public volunteers. Different hardware architectures and system performance variations also make coordinated-dependency-laden computations impractical.

This material is appropriate for CS2, DS/A, and a course on systems when discussing cluster computing and clouds/grids. Students may already be aware of projects such as Folding@home and SETI@home, and may even be volunteers with the said projects. By introducing the pros and cons of distributed computing, one can easily demonstrate to students why large homogeneous private supercomputers are still useful.

When teaching this material, one must keep in mind that cluster computing applications are typically latency sensitive. Scalability in a cluster computing context refers to the maximum speedup that can be obtained. Adding additional resources, such as compute cores or entire nodes, may not increase speedup for many scientific applications, as it simply adds more processes waiting for a key resource. This is illustrative of why distributed systems over a wide area may be inherently limited in their scalability, owing to the high latency of long-distance networks. For example, typical network latencies over the Internet can range from tens to hundreds of milliseconds. In contrast, high-speed networks for cluster computers can have latencies below 1 μs.

6.1.3 SPMD MODEL ENABLES REASONING ABOUT AND PROGRAMMING *O*(MILLION) PROCESS PROGRAMS

Vocabulary:

Single program, multiple data (SPMD)—a parallelism technique where many processes of a single program work on different input datasets in order to complete processing quickly.

Dividing the work on a very large problem and executing it in the same way on many individual nodes is a reasonable way to approach programming at very high process counts. This approach, called single program, multiple data (SPMD) allows reasoning about thousands, hundreds of thousands, and even millions of simultaneous processes. However, programming applications for very large process counts is not trivial. There are many additional concerns that must be taken into account when using extreme numbers of processes as functions that were previously reasonable (e.g., collective operations) become increasingly expensive as the process count rises. Synchronization between processes becomes a performance bottleneck as the percentage of execution time spent in communication between processes both for collectives and synchronization collectives such as barriers increases. Shared resource contention is also a concern, in that there are many requesters for limited numbers of resources, and the amount of time waiting to use shared resources increases on an individual process basis. A good analogy to explain this concept to students is thinking about the lines at an amusement park. When there are a few thousand people in the park, everything runs smoothly, but if the population booms to a million people, everything comes to a halt quickly. Unlike the obvious items such as the capacity of the rides, other concerns come into play, such as the width of the walkways. In the given analogy, the crowded walkways are equivalent to an overloaded network and the massive lines at the rides are equivalent to the contention for shared resources such as file systems or shared memory (especially if the shared memory is distributed and needed by multiple processes at once). This is very much like the extra concerns that must be taken into account with large numbers of simultaneous processes on a computing system.

The key advantage of the SPMD model is that it allows a structured approach to performing a massive job. Although other concerns must be considered, the fundamental idea behind the approach is that a single code base can run from one process up to 1 million processes. This provides easy scalability from a programmatic point of view, and simplifies maintenance of the code. While a naïvely written MPI program *might* be able to be run with many simultaneous processes, its performance would be disappointing. The SPMD model provides the tools for expressing a massively parallel program, but does not guarantee that the said program is useful/has good performance.

This material is intended to introduce students to thinking about the challenges of scaling these approaches to extreme scales. Although the answers to the questions the students are asked by this material may be outside the scope of the curriculum, they are meant to stimulate independent thought on the topic. This is an excellent topic to introduce to students near the end of a lecture to spur students to think outside the classroom about what they have just learned and the depth of the topic of parallelism.

The following are suggested questions for students to consider:

How do you debug a program with 1 million processes?

Answer: This is only possible with lightweight distributed debugging tools such as the Stack Trace Analysis Tool (STAT). Such tools use lightweight tracing and distributed processing of the data. Using a 1-to-N approach is not feasible at these scales given the amount of data being processed.

What kind of applications can take advantage of such a system?

Answer: Not all applications can take advantage of massive parallelism. The applications that can best leverage massive parallelism are weak scaling applications. Weak scaling applications scale their problem size to the number of processes available, while strong scaling applications keep the given problem sizes but attempt to distribute that problem over more resources. Obviously, strong scaling applications have upper limits on the amount of parallelism that is practical for a given problem. Once the problem has been sufficiently divided into small enough chunks, further dividing it is either impossible or leads to performance issues as the amount of communication versus the amount of computation increases.

Given the size of the system, failures of individual nodes will happen, how will this affect performance?

Answer: Failures, whether they be hardware or software based, can greatly impact performance. Methods to avoid having catastrophic loss, such as checkpoint/ restart (which saves and restores application state), are effective at preventing complete job loss, but incur overheads. With very large systems, failures can occur regularly (once or multiple times per day), and therefore checkpointing is required for large long-running jobs to ensure that they can run to completion. Stopping the program execution and saving all required data and state to a persistent storage apparatus requires heavy use of the system interconnect and pauses the job during the entire operation (assuming there is a coordinated checkpointing scheme). Individual system performance impact will depend on how quickly such checkpoints can be taken (network performance and persistent storage capabilities) along with how often they need to be performed (related to how reliable the system is).

This material can be introduced when introducing SPMD in CS2; alternatively it can also be introduced when covering communication algorithms in DS/A.

6.1.4 HPC IN THE CLOUD COMPARED WITH TRADITIONAL HPC

HPC in the cloud uses the commercial cloud model as a basis for the hardware used for HPC code. The virtualization model used in cloud computing introduces additional overhead over the traditional private cluster model. An illustration of this is provided in Figure 6.1

In addition, the minimal service level guarantees provided by the cloud model may be insufficient for an HPC application's needs. Another major performance concern for HPC in the cloud is the presence of other jobs running in the cloud that may interfere with the resource-hungry HPC applications. This can also affect the performance of other jobs in the cloud as the HPC applications consume large amounts of resources, particularly network resources. Current HPC cloud implementations are stand-alone systems much like a traditional cluster. HPC in the

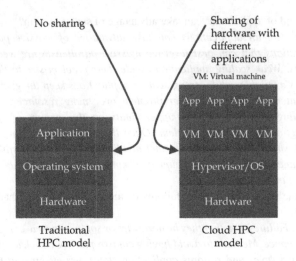

FIGURE 6.1

Traditional HPC compared with the cloud HPC model. OS, operating system.

cloud requires huge amounts of resources, and typically needs very high performance networking hardware. As such, creating an HPC-capable cloud computer requires significant investment in high-performance interconnects, and this infrastructure may not be practical for use throughout a general-use cloud that spends most of its time on non-HPC jobs.

The cloud may be an excellent solution for consumers who require only intermittent or marginal amounts of HPC capability. An example of this is small to medium-sized companies that can make use of HPC for simulations, but cannot justify the large investment required for dedicated HPC hardware. The cloud also provides the benefit of offering up-to-date hardware, and paying only for resources when they are being utilized. These benefits of and drawbacks to HPC in the cloud versus traditional HPC show that while HPC in the cloud will broaden access to HPC capabilities, some historical users of supercomputers (e.g., large corporations, the government, and the military) are unlikely to move to a cloud computing platform, both for performance requirements and for the sensitivity of the applications and data being used.

Cluster computing is well suited to HPC. The local nature of the hardware and the exclusivity of the system to a limited number of users is ideal for peak performance. The main drawback to this approach is mostly economic. Cluster-based supercomputers are very expensive both to procure and to operate. Supercomputers routinely consume millions of dollars' worth of energy every year, regardless of their utilization, and require teams of highly skilled technicians to keep them operational. In many cases, traditional cluster computing remains the method of choice for the largest consumers of HPC. Smaller clusters are also accessible to many organizations, and while cloud and grid computing may be attractive in some scenarios, many groups choose to operate private cluster computers.

In this section we have described the strengths and weaknesses of several different models for HPC. It is suggested this material be introduced as a pros and cons discussion in CS2 and DS/A, when the approaches are first mentioned. By contrasting the benefits of each approach, one can also discuss the differences between them.

6.2 THE MESSAGE PASSING CONCEPT

The message passing paradigm is a powerful concept for problem solving from small clusters to extreme-scale supercomputers. Two main communication mechanisms are provided: point-to-point and collective communications. Point-to-point communication allows pairwise data exchanges, while a collective communication coordinates data exchange and synchronization across many processes in a single operation.

6.2.1 POINT-TO-POINT COMMUNICATION

Basic idea of communicating processes
Vocabulary:

> Communicating sequential processes—a model of concurrent computation in which independent processes exchange messages to communicate with each other

A fundamental need in shared-memory programming for all but the most trivial of problems is to properly protect or order reads and writes of shared variables. The mechanisms provided by multithreading languages and libraries—for example, locks, critical sections, and flush operations—can be difficult to use without introducing data races. The contrasting conceptual foundation for message passing is the idea of communicating sequential processes.[1] A collection of independent processes is created, each with a distinct memory space. Two processes may run on two cores of the same multiprocessor chip (e.g., on a student's laptop), different chips on a common motherboard, or on different racks connected by cable links. Data is exchanged between processors by the sending and receiving of messages. The distinction between programming models for multithreading and message passing is of primary importance and can be discussed in the context of operating system processes and threads, or in the context of different concurrent algorithms and data structures.

Unique addresses for each process
Vocabulary:

> Message Passing Interface (MPI)—a standard application programming interface (API) for message passing programs.

---

[1] Students may benefit from reading the seminal paper by Hoare [3].

Rank—a unique integer process identifier.

Communicator—a group of processes.

To pass messages between processes, each process must have a unique identifier. Unique identifiers are established and distributed among the processes, allowing any process to communicate with any other process. In the ubiquitous MPI standard, the identifier is known as the process rank. The rank space is an ordered set of nonnegative integers, enabling algorithms to communicate in a particular order.

Communication groups, called communicators, can be defined in order to partition the possible destinations that processes can send to. Only processes that belong to a communicator can send to other processes in that communicator. This is a very useful concept when multiple MPI instances need to be used simultaneously. An example use case is a library that uses MPI operating at the same time as an MPI application. For the library and application not to receive each other's MPI messages, one can separate them out into separate communicators, ensuring that messages sent by the library will never be received by the application, and vice versa. Each of these communicator groups described is an intracommunicator, meaning that they communicate only among their group. It is also possible to create an intercommunicator, one that allows communication between intracommunicators. This approach is useful to provide both private message passing between processes of a library/application and also communication between the communicator groups. The hierarchical structure of this arrangement controls how the two communicators pass messages between themselves, which allows comprehensible communication between MPI jobs.

In some cases the need for a defined communicator is unnecessary. For example, an application may not expect to be interoperable with other message passing applications/libraries. In this case, a communicator spanning all active processes may be appropriate. MPI defines this communicator as MPI_COMM_WORLD, and in practice, many applications use MPI_COMM_WORLD as their communicator.

Send-receive pairs illustrated by an example

A point-to-point communication in the message passing model requires both the initiator and the target of the message to explicitly participate in the communication of messages. Because a single executable from the same source code is launched on each process, the role of each process is typically specified by indexing the rank with statements. The following is a basic example.[2]

The example code below and Figure 6.2 illustrate the classic game of telephone. The process with rank 0 comes up with a number, which is then passed to the next

---

[2]In this example and those that follow, a simplified API is used rather than the full MPI calls to simplify the examples and emphasize the core ideas. The complete forms of MPI_Send() and MPI_Recv() calls are given later. For more information and other complete API calls, consult the MPI standard [4].

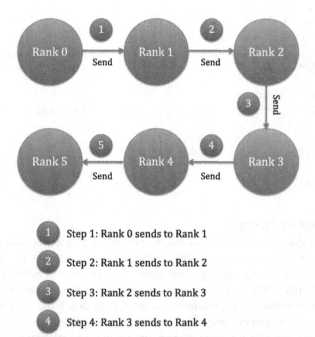

1 — Step 1: Rank 0 sends to Rank 1

2 — Step 2: Rank 1 sends to Rank 2

3 — Step 3: Rank 2 sends to Rank 3

4 — Step 4: Rank 3 sends to Rank 4

5 — Step 5: Rank 4 sends to Rank 5

FIGURE 6.2

Point-to-point communication example.

rank, and from then on to the next rank, and so on. Note the importance of the ordering of the receive and send calls. A given rank must first receive the number before sending it onward. There is no ambiguity in this ordering. This program requires $O(P)$ time, where P is the number of processes. Challenge students to think about how they might write a message passing program to perform the same task in $O(\log P)$ time. How long would the program take if rank 0 sent a message to each of the other ranks? While it may seem that such an approach could require only constant time, in practice this is not the case. In Section 6.2.2, this communication pattern, Broadcast, is shown to have a collective routine in the MPI with an efficient underlying implementation.

```
int my_rank;
int num_ranks;
int magic_number;
comm my_communicator;

init(&my_rank, &num_ranks, my_communicator);
```

```
if (my_rank == 0)
   magic_number = rand();
else
   receive(my_rank-1, my_rank, &magic_number, my_communicator);

if (my_rank < num_ranks - 1)
   send(my_rank+1, my_rank, &magic_number, my_communicator);

printf("Rank %d received magic number %d.\n", my_rank,
       magic_number);

finalize();
```

Using buffers for storage

In contrast to shared memory multithreading programming models, message passing programs do not have shared variables. Instead, all data transfer is accomplished through the sending and receiving of messages. The data passed between processors is stored in buffers. When buffers are used to receive messages, the order in which they are written into the target machine's memory must match the order in which the messages were sent. For the case of a 1 million or more process application, keeping buffers for each possible communicating partner is impractical. Some algorithms are designed to limit the number of communication partners. Another way to mitigate the impact of space limitations is to combine message passing with multithreading, such that several threads executing on adjacent cores communicate through only one MPI process. This hybrid parallel programming model is described further in Section 6.4.1.

Point-to-point communications and message size

When point-to-point messages are sent, buffers are not kept for each communicating partner, and those buffers that are reserved cannot handle very large message sizes. Consequently, for performance reasons, a number of smaller buffers will typically be maintained by a message passing implementation in order to quickly service incoming messages with preallocated buffers. There are specific reasons why registering memory on message arrival is impractical for high-performance networks, which are explored in more detail in Section 6.3.3.

To exploit these preregistered buffers, message passing implementations can use an "eager" protocol to send messages immediately to the target without first ensuring that buffer space exists on the remote side. It is possible that no buffer space (or at least one suitable for the message) exists, and the message passing implementation would have to drop the message and negotiate with the source to allocate sufficient buffer space for the message. Alternatively, above a given message threshold, it may be advantageous not to attempt an "eager" message transmission but instead to negotiate via handshake messages with the target to determine that appropriate buffer space is allocated to the message before its transmission. This scheme is typically called a "rendezvous" protocol. An eager protocol is best suited to small messages, while a rendezvous protocol is best suited to large messages. Consequently, a reasonable message passing library implementation can use both protocols by switching from the eager protocol to the rendezvous protocol at a message size threshold determined through appropriate tuning.

Figure 6.3 illustrates a bandwidth curve that represents the protocol switching that can take place inside a message passing library. For small messages the eager curve is superior, and therefore it is used. When the rendezvous curve eventually overtakes the eager curve for larger message sizes, the implementation can switch to take advantage of the superior rendezvous performance.

Complete forms of `MPI_Send()` **and** `MPI_Recv()` **and message tags**
The preceding examples used simplified syntax for the message passing calls to focus on the basics of the paradigm. The following are the complete forms of the `MPI_Send()` and `MPI_Recv()` calls:

```
MPI_Send ( void*        data,
           int          count,
           MPI_Datatype datatype,
           int          destination,
           int          tag,
           MPI_Comm     communicator )
```

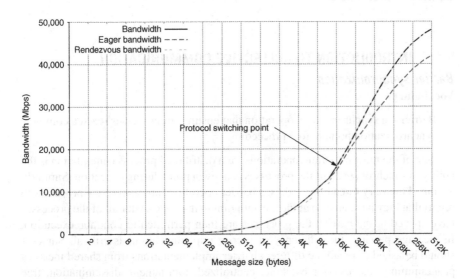

FIGURE 6.3

Point-to-point protocol switching from eager to rendezvous.

```
MPI_Recv ( void*        data,
           int          count,
           MPI_Datatype datatype,
           int          source,
           int          tag,
           MPI_Comm     communicator,
           MPI_Status*  status )
```

The first two arguments of the MPI_Send() call are straightforward: a pointer to the data buffer and the amount of data being sent. The third argument specifies the data type. The MPI standard defines basic data types corresponding to C primitive types such as MPI_INT and MPI_DOUBLE, but user-defined data types may also be specified. The next arguments are the destination rank and an integer tag. The tag value may be used by the programmer to distinguish the data being sent, especially since MPI does not guarantee the ordering of messages. For example, the user may choose to use the tag value 32 to designate the result of a particular calculation. The last argument is the communicator.

The arguments of the MPI_Recv() call mirror those of MPI_Send(). The first four arguments are the data buffer, the amount of data being received, the data type, and the source rank. The fifth argument is the tag, which on the receive side directs the MPI implementation to match the receive call to an incoming message sent with the specified tag value. Following the communicator is an MPI_Status pointer, which we will not discuss here.

6.2.2 INTRODUCTION TO COLLECTIVE COMMUNICATION
Barrier synchronization
Vocabulary:

Barrier—a synchronization operation that ensures all processes reach a common synchronization point before proceeding.

One of the most important operations for a distributed process computation is the ability to synchronize all of the processes at a given point during execution. Similarly to shared memory threading models, a barrier operation forces all of the processes to report that they have arrived at the barrier point in the code. After all of the processes have arrived at the barrier, the processes are then permitted to continue execution. In message passing, the efficiency of barrier implementations is critical. Students should be asked to recall the different barrier implementations from shared memory programming courses—for example, centralized, tournament, dissemination, tree barriers—and consider their implementation in the message passing model. Even with a very efficient implementation, barrier operations often limit the performance of applications that use them frequently on large-scale machines.

Other types of collectives
Vocabulary:

Collective operation—communication routines than involve all processes.

A barrier is called a collective operation because all processes, rather than a single send-receive pair, participate. Many other types of collective operations exist as well, Broadcast (one to all), Gather (get data from all other processes), Reduce (combines values from all processes into a single value, e.g., an addition), and All-to-all (every process broadcasts). Figure 6.4 shows examples of collective operations.

Consider the earlier example of the "telephone game," in which a value originating from one process is transmitted to all the other processes. The Broadcast collective can be used to do this transmission through a single call, as shown below:

```
int my_rank;
int num_ranks;
int magic_number;
comm my_communicator;

init(&my_rank, &num_ranks, my_communicator);

if (my_rank == 0)
    magic_number = rand();

broadcast(&magic_number, 0, my_communicator);

printf("Rank %d received magic number %d.\n", my_rank,
       magic_number);

finalize();
```

The arguments to the call specify the data and the process from which the value originates, process 0 in this case. In contrast to the earlier example using explicit send and receive calls, this program's use of the Broadcast collective is more concise and places the burden of orchestrating the message passing to accomplish the Broadcast on the message passing implementation rather than the programmer. A common implementation of the Broadcast collective is a tree-based transmission of the Broadcast data, and the implementation may be optimized and tuned for the underlying communication system architecture and the size of the data.

Now consider the problem of summing a large set of numbers stored in several files. Suppose each process sums the numbers contained in one of the files. Finally, the total sum can be calculated by combining the local sums from all processes. The following example shows an implementation of this strategy using the Gather collective:

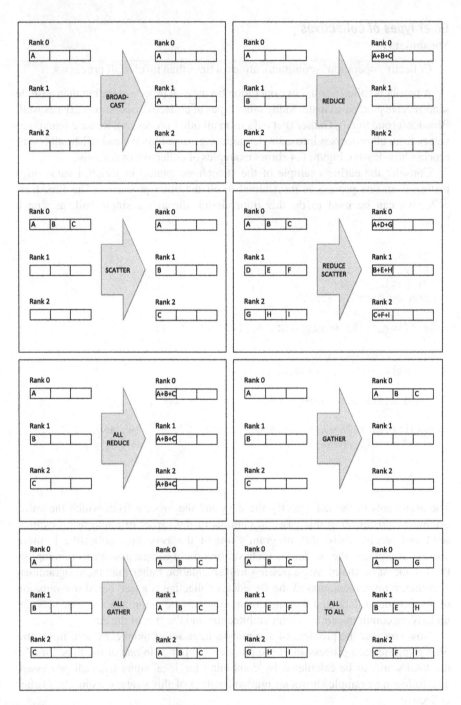

FIGURE 6.4

Collective operations for message passing programs.

```
int my_rank, num_ranks;
long n;
long i;
double *data;
long global_sum = 0, my_sum = 0;
long *local_sums;
comm my_communicator;

init(&my_rank, &num_ranks, my_communicator);

get_data_from_file(data, n, my_rank);

for (i = 0; i < n; i++)
   my_sum += data[i];

if (my_rank == 0)
   local_sums = (long *) (sizeof(int)*num_ranks);

Gather(&my_sum, local_sums, 0, my_communicator);

if (my_rank == 0)
{
   for (i = 0; i < num_ranks; i++)
      global_sum += local_sum[i];

   printf("The sum of the numbers is %d.\n", global_sum);

   free(local_sums);
}

finalize();
```

The example assumes that the function `get_data_from_file` allocates space for the data and populates it with values read from a file corresponding to its rank—for example, `data7.txt`. The Gather collective places all the local sums into an space allocated on process 0, which then combines the local sums. The Reduce collective can be used to eliminate the need for the last step, as shown in the code below:

```
int my_rank, num_ranks;
long n;
long i;
double *data;
long global_sum = 0, my_sum = 0;
comm my_communicator;

init(&my_rank, &num_ranks, my_communicator);

get_data_from_file(data, n, my_rank);
```

```
for (i = 0; i < n; i++)
    my_sum += data[i];

Reduce(&my_sum, &global_sum, SUM, 0, my_communicator);

if (my_rank == 0)
    printf("The sum of the numbers is %d.\n", global_sum);

finalize();
```

Upon the completion of the Reduce collective, the global sum resides in the global_sum variable on process 0.

Note that some collectives are composed from simpler collectives. For example, All-Gather gets data from all processes as in a Gather operation, then sends the collected data to all processors as in a Broadcast. Students can consider how collectives could be used to solve problems such as sorting or creating a histogram from a set of values.

Suggested classroom activity

Collectives can be more easily understood by conducting a classroom exercise where students serve as proxies for processes. For example, the instructor can write numbers on sticky notes and distribute them to the students in the front row of the lecture hall. This demonstrates a Broadcast. The students can then easily illustrate an all-gather or all-reduce operation by having one student collect the values from the other students (and perhaps sum them).

Collective communication can be discussed in DS/A when discussing Broadcast/multicast and Scatter/Gather.

6.2.3 BSP MODEL ILLUSTRATED WITH A SIMPLE EXAMPLE

Vocabulary:

Bulk synchronous processing (BSP)—a model of parallel computation in which at each step all processes compute independently, then communicate, then synchronize.

Many parallel applications follow a BSP model: they compute and exchange data during a "superstep" and then synchronize through a barrier. Figure 6.5 illustrates a BSP superstep. The need for synchronization can be illustrated to students through the following example. Imagine that the interactions of many molecules are simulated, and such a simulation is done in time steps. At the end of each time step, the forces on each molecule determine its direction and velocity. The direction and velocity of each molecule influence the forces acting on all of the other molecules. To proceed to the next time step in the simulation, all of the data about each molecule's velocity and direction need to be exchanged among the processes, and only then do they have the data required to proceed to the force calculations in the next time step.

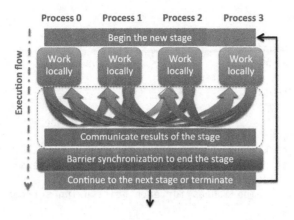

FIGURE 6.5

A BSP superstep.

The example code below represents an extremely simplified BSP program. It computes temperatures at a given point in a grid from the neighboring temperatures. The grid points are divided among the processes, as shown in Figure 6.6. The code computes the values for all of the points in the process's assigned portion of the array and then exchanges information about temperatures at its array boundaries with other processes. At the end of each iteration, the processes synchronize through a barrier call to ensure that all of the processes have successfully exchanged boundary temperature data before proceeding to the next time step. It is worth noting that this example is extremely simplified, and the complexity in the `compute_temp()` and `exchange_boundary_temps()` functions should not be overlooked.

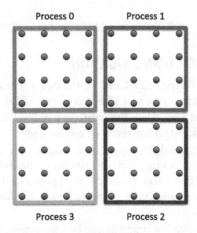

FIGURE 6.6

Example division of grid points among processes in the BSP temperature program.

```
int my_rank;
int num_ranks;
comm my_communicator;
int temperature[][];
int num_temps_x, num_temps_y;
int time_steps;
int requested_time_steps;

init(&my_rank, &num_ranks, my_communicator);
temps_per_rank = num_temps_x/num_ranks;
for (time_steps=0; time_steps < requested_time_steps;
     time_steps++) {
  /* compute temperatures for each point using surrounding
     points */
  for (x=temps_per_rank*my_rank; x < temps_per_rank*my_rank +
       temps_per_rank; x++) {
    for (y=0; y < num_temps_y; y++) {
      compute_temp(temperature[x,y]);
    }
  }
  /* exchange the results that might be needed by other
     processes */
  exchange_boundary_temps(&temperatures,my_communicator);
  /* synchronize all of the processes before continuing to the
     next iteration */
  barrier(&my_rank, my_communicator);
}

printf("done temperature simulation");
finalize();
```

This topic should be covered in DS/A as per the curriculum.

6.2.4 NONBLOCKING COMMUNICATION

This section has thus far presented only blocking/synchronous communication. Blocking means that when a receive call is made, the API does not return until the request is fulfilled. Therefore, when the message passing library returns a result to the application, either the target has received the message or a message has arrived, depending on whether the call is a send or a receive call. An alternative type of communication uses nonblocking or asynchronous communication. Such calls are typically denoted in MPI as Isend and Irecv, as opposed to the usual send and recv calls. Asynchronous communication requires that there is some method of achieving independent network progress.

Independent communication progress can be implemented in a variety of ways. First, the communication can be completely off-loaded to hardware. In this case, the program can initiate communication through API calls, which immediately return.

The program can then inquire about the completion of outstanding communication operations with other progress-checking API calls. This same basic concept can also be used for a software solution to communication progress. In the software case, the progression is handled by a separate execution thread. There can be a progression thread for each main process, or the progression thread can be shared by multiple main processes.

Asynchronous communication is important for performance, as one can avoid the idling of processes as they wait for communication to finish, doing no useful work while waiting. By returning from communication calls immediately, before the actual communication has finished, the CPU can continue to do useful work during the time period that the communication is taking place. This requires some extra care when programming applications that can use nonblocking communication. At some point the application will need to check if outstanding communication operations are complete, and, should the operations not be complete, it may still have to wait for the communication to finish before proceeding. For example, consider the case illustrated in the code below. In this code, the objective is to compute the sum of all of the elements in an array, and then add randomized noise to a different local array. To parallelize this operation, several different processes work on their own sections of the arrays. Once the summation is complete, the results are sent to the root (rank 0) process for final summation. During this final summation, the other nonroot nodes would sit idle during communication. However, with asynchronous communication, they could be doing useful work on the other array. Once the work on the second array has been done, the processes need to use the result from the first-array summation. Therefore, they need to wait until the asynchronous receive of the results is complete. Should the computation have exceeded the time needed for the communication to finish, the wait function will return immediately. It is also possible to use test functions, which are similar to wait except that they return immediately. This may be used to compute only while a communication is outstanding.

```
int my_rank, num_ranks;
comm my_communicator;
long n;
long i;
double *data;
double *data2;
long global_sum = 0, local_sum = 0;

init(&my_rank, &num_ranks, my_communicator);

get_data_from_file(data, n, my_rank);

for (i = 0; i < n; i++)
    local_sum += data[i];
```

```
send(root, my_rank, &local_sum, my_communicator);

irecv(root, my_rank, &global_sum, &request, my_communicator);

/* Add a small random number to our second array elements */
for (i=0; i < n; i++)
    data2[i] += rand() % 100000;

wait(&request);

/* Now work with the returned global sum */

for (i=0; i < n; i++)
    data2[i] += global_sum;

finalize();
```

The example for computation-communication overlap above results in the execution time behavior illustrated in Figure 6.7. The overlapping of computation and communication results in a time saving equivalent to T_{comp2} for this example.

The details of asynchronous/nonblocking communication are appropriate for more advanced courses, but a good learning goal for this material in core courses is that the students are made aware of the possibility of independent communication progress. This can be mentioned along with the BSP model in DS/A (with the goal of a Bloom K classification).

6.3 HIGH-PERFORMANCE NETWORKS

Vocabulary:

Remote direct memory access (RDMA)—a method of writing to another system's memory directly over a network.
InfiniBand—a popular type of high-performance network [5].
iWARP—RDMA-capable Ethernet [6].
Cray networks (Gemini and Aires)—custom high-performance networks developed for Cray supercomputers [7].
Portals—an RDMA network specification from Sandia National Laboratories [8] that has been implemented in the Cray SeaStar line of networks (predecessor to Gemini and Aries).
Myrinet (Myri 10G)—an RDMA-capable network produced by Myricom [9].

Several different high-performance networks are available today. The most popular, based on their use in the top 500 supercomputers in the world, are InfiniBand and Ethernet (both gigabit and 10 Gb). However, the highest-ranked supercomputers typically use other high-performance networks. In some cases the networks are custom designed for a single supercomputer or a supercomputer model line. For

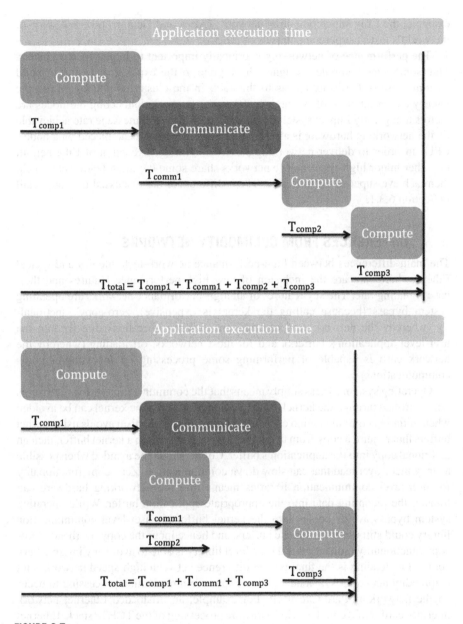

FIGURE 6.7

Computation-communication overlap execution comparison.

example, the Cray supercomputing networks (Aries and Gemini) powered some of the world's fastest supercomputers as of 2015.

The performance of networking is critically important to large supercomputers. That some supercomputer designers have gone to the expense and time to build custom network hardware attests to this fact. In the cluster computing world, the latency and bandwidth of the high-performance network connecting the nodes are factors that greatly impact system performance. The overall message rate achievable by the networking hardware is also important, as is the overhead placed on a node's CPUs in order to deliver networking services. With the exception of Ethernet, all the other major high-performance networks share some common features that help them achieve superior performance. These differences are discussed in more detail in Section 6.3.1.

6.3.1 DIFFERENCES FROM COMMODITY NETWORKS

The main differences between high-performance network technologies and typical Ethernet hardware are the inclusion of new high-performance features and their base signaling rate. The key features of all high-performance networks are operating system bypass (because calling the kernel is expensive), zero-copy functionality (whereby the network card can perform memory operations directly into the user-level application's buffers), and for most networks, off-loading (whereby the network card is capable of performing some processing on incoming/outgoing communications).

Operating system bypass simply means that the communication software/driver is not controlled through the kernel. Thus, a context switch to the kernel can be avoided when initiating communication calls. In addition, this mechanism avoids using kernel buffers that require a copy from the networking hardware into a kernel buffer, then an additional copy into the application's buffer. Copies should be avoided when possible as they incur overhead that can slow down communication. Zero-copy functionality for user-level communication libraries means that the networking hardware can transfer the incoming data into the appropriate application buffer. While operating system bypass avoids copies into the kernel buffers, a user-level communication library could still use intermediate buffers, and hence incur the copy overhead. Zero-copy functionality indicates that a user-level library is able to avoid any intermediary copies. Off-loading is the final typical difference between high-speed networks and commodity networks. Off-loading allows some communication processing to occur on the networking hardware itself. For example, an off-loaded Ethernet network interface card (NIC) could provide hardware processing of the TCP/IP stack. Ethernet is not typically used in the top high-performance clusters. Figure 6.8 illustrates why this is the case. The non-Ethernet high-performance network stack completely bypasses the operating system, avoiding a context switch from the application to the kernel. The number of memory copies performed for the traditional networking stack is shown to point out that several memory copies need to occur that are not needed for the high-performance networking stack.

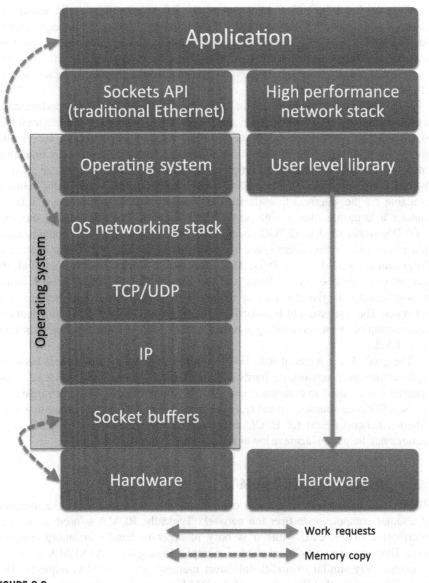

FIGURE 6.8

Comparison of networking stacks—traditional versus operating system bypass.

Compared with high-performance networks, Ethernet exhibits significant differences in performance. For example, for the InfiniBand high-performance interconnect, data rates circa 2015 are 96.97 Gb/s and submicrosecond latencies are possible. The fastest widely available Ethernet technology has a data rate of 10 Gb/s and latencies of approximately 5 μs. More typical 1 Gb Ethernet has latencies of tens of microseconds (20-50 μs).

It is helpful for students to understand the difference in the performance requirements of HPC versus traditional networking. A good in-class activity is to discuss the ping times from students' laptops to a departmental server and notice the multiple order of magnitude difference between those communication latencies and the requirements for a high-performance network. Students can also use the latest high-performance networking hardware specifications (typically publicly available on the Internet) to estimate the amount of time that it would take to transfer a large file over a high-performance network. For example, to transmit a DVD's worth of data (2.7GB) over a 56 Gb/s interconnect, the students must first convert the interconnect speed to gigabytes—(56 Gb/s)/8 = 7 GB/s—so a full DVD transfer would take 0.386 s. This gives a real-world example that students can relate to their everyday lives, and the experiences they have with existing networks and will give them an appreciation of the power of high-performance networks. The discussion of high-performance networks is intended to augment the introduction of cluster computing and explain why high-performance interconnects are needed.

The goal of this material is to briefly outline some of the differences between high-performance networking hardware and typical commercial hardware. This material can be used to enhance classroom discussion of networking or in elective courses. For core courses, a good learning goal is to make students aware that non-Ethernet networks exist for HPC/cluster computing and that they have advanced features that help them achieve lower latency and higher bandwidth.

6.3.2 INTRODUCTION TO RDMA

RDMA is a mechanism to allow a compute node to access directly the memory of another compute node over the network. Typically, RDMA is used to prevent interruption of the CPU while it is busy in order to handle incoming network data. There are a variety of methods for implementing RDMA. RDMA works in a manner very similar to traditional direct memory access (DMA) requests. The main difference is that the initiator of the DMA request is another system, and the request must be sent over a network to the remote DMA controller. An example of this scenario is illustrated in Figure 6.9

RDMA is typically accomplished via the queue-pair model. The queue-pair model uses connected pairs of queues at both the origin and the target. Each process has a send queue (SQ) as well as a receive queue (RQ). The SQ and RQ can be populated by work queue elements (WQEs, typically pronounced "wookies"). Each of these elements corresponds to a communication task. The results of these

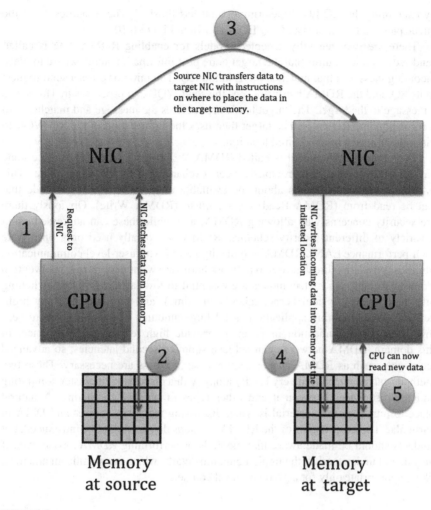

FIGURE 6.9

RDMA overview.

operations can be placed in a completion queue (CQ), also called an event queue (EQ) in some RDMA designs. The host processes that use the RDMA device can both post WQEs to the SQ/RQ and read/remove items from the CQ/EQ. This design allows the processes/threads using the network to post elements describing messages to be sent or received to the local networking hardware and then return to working on other tasks. The network hardware attempts to make independent progress without the need for the application to call into a library in order to allow communication to progress. The application can check on the progress that has been made at any time by examining the CQ/EQ to determine what has finished. The basic design of the queue pairs and the associated CQ/EQ is shown in Figure 6.10

There are two generally accepted models for enabling RDMA, one is called send-recv, and it requires that the target node post information about where to place incoming messages that match a WQE in the RQ. The initiator posts a send request to its SQ, and the RDMA hardware sees the send WQE and processes it. This sends a message to the target. The target hardware receives the message and matches it to a corresponding RQ entry. The target then uses the information in the RQ WQE to place the message in the desired location.

The other RDMA model is called RDMA Write/Read, where the source node has information that has previously been exchanged with the target node. This information contains details about the available memory on the target node that can be read from (RDMA Read) or written to (RDMA Write). Obviously there are security concerns with allowing RDMA, and while these can addressed using a variety of different security schemes, RDMA is typically used only on private high-performance LANs. RDMA is typically paired with user-level communication libraries (providing direct access to network hardware without requiring intervention from the kernel). These techniques are essential to low latency (context switching into an operating system kernel takes some time), and throughput. Many high-performance computing applications send huge amounts of data and require very low latency communication in order to provide high levels of performance. In this domain, RDMA networks can achieve submicrosecond latencies, so advanced techniques such as RDMA and operating system bypass are necessary. These two methods can be introduced very briefly along with a discussion of cluster computing and the differences between it and other types of parallel computing. A natural place to introduce this material is when discussing memory accesses and DMA in particular. The exact details of the RDMA methods do not have to be introduced, but students should be made aware that methods of performing RDMAs exist, even if they do not understand all the implementation details, which are significant and most likely appropriate only for a graduate-level course.

6.3.3 MAIN MEMORY AND RDMA

The DMA engines on RDMA-capable hardware may encounter issues on some machines when they are not capable of determining if a given virtual-to-physical address is still resident in physical memory. Memory pinning can resolve this issue by preventing the swapping of memory in pinned regions. This mechanism guarantees that whenever the DMA engine accesses the pinned memory region, it is modifying the intended memory locations. The cost of memory registration can be significant and impacts performance when done dynamically in code. Consequently, many high-performance messaging libraries (e.g., MPI) try to preregister memory, so that a pool of buffers can be used for low-latency communication. For large bulk data transfers, memory registration costs may be warranted. For very large transfers such costs

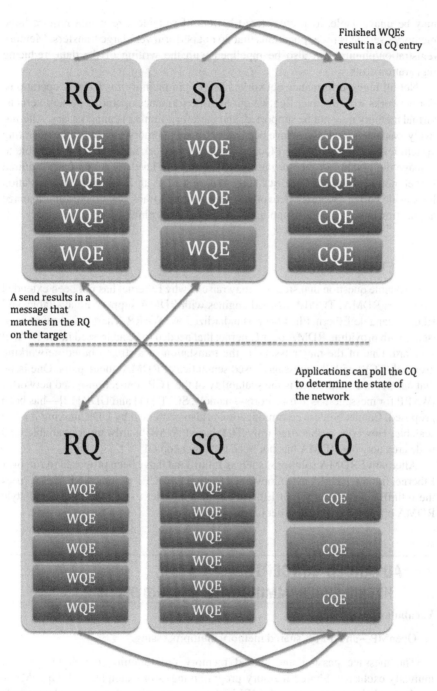

Finished WQEs result in a CQ entry

A send results in a message that matches in the RQ on the target

Applications can poll the CQ to determine the state of the network

FIGURE 6.10

The queue-pair model.

may be unavoidable, as preregistered buffers of suitable size would require large memory overheads for applications that do not perform very large transfers. Memory registration/pinning can also be pipelined with the writing of the data, reducing registration costs.

Not all high-performance networks need to pin memory for RDMA operations. For networks working over lightweight high-performance operating system kernels, virtual memory may not be supported, and therefore pinning is unnecessary. Alternatively, past network designs have been able to avoid memory pinning at the operating system level. The now defunct Quadrics QSNet network hardware [10] was able to manage the pinning of memory at the NIC hardware level. This approach required kernel modifications for Quadrics networks, as well as an NIC hardware translation look-aside buffer. Quadrics networks hardware could track page tables and manage application memory page swapping such that memory pinning was unnecessary.

6.3.4 ETHERNET RDMA

A reasonable question that students may raise is why Ethernet has not been extended to support RDMA. TCP/IP off-load engines with RDMA support are available, and RDMA-capable Ethernet has been standardized as iWARP. There are a number of issues with providing RDMA over Ethernet that needed to be addressed in the iWARP standard. One of the major issues is the translation of a stream-based networking protocol (TCP) with the message-based semantics of RDMA queue pairs. One issue that has not been addressed is the scalability of the TCP connection-based networks. iWARP for message-based transports—namely, SCTP [11] and UDP [12]—has been proposed. Connectionless communication is also addressed by UDP, making it more scalable. However, at this time only TCP-based iWARP hardware is available, and wide area network RDMA has not been broadly adopted.

Alternative RDMA solutions, such as InfiniBand, have been proposed to run over Ethernet frames. RDMA over Converged Ethernet (RoCE), pronounced "rocky," uses the InfiniBand stack on top of Ethernet frames in order to provide InfiniBand-style RDMA operations over Ethernet hardware [13].

6.4 ADVANCED CONCEPTS
6.4.1 HYBRID PROGRAMMING WITH MPI AND OPENMP
Vocabulary:

OpenMP—an API for shared memory multiprocessing.

The message passing and shared memory programming paradigms are not mutually exclusive. Shared memory programming—for example, with OpenMP—can be used simultaneously with MPI in the same program. A very simple example is one in which OpenMP is used to perform a parallel computation locally on a single compute node, and MPI is used to coordinate the work of many compute nodes. MPI could also explicitly pass messages between multiple processes on a single node through the network, and MPI can also be used to perform shared-memory-based message passing.

A key question that may be asked when introducing hybrid programming is why another API is needed when MPI can communicate through shared memory itself. The reason hybrid programming is useful is that shared memory APIs such as OpenMP are capable of handling threads dynamically (i.e., forking and joining threads). Creating new MPI processes on the fly is not trivial. Therefore, OpenMP is used in conjunction with MPI when it is desirable to have threads during a portion of the execution and large numbers of MPI processes are undesirable. Basically, when large amounts of concurrency are desired for only certain parallel portions of the code, hybrid programming can be a good solution. The addition of OpenMP avoids the need for MPI to spawn many more MPI processes, and the costly activity of managing unique IDs for each new process. Such extra MPI processes would also have to be involved in collective operations, when this may not be desirable. Instead a single MPI process per compute node can use OpenMP to create a number of worker threads for a particular parallel portion of code, then gather the result. The MPI processes can then exchange results if necessary (a second tier of concurrency), as shown in Figure 6.11, and illustrated in the idealized simulation example given below[3]:

```
for ( i = 0; i < NUM_SIMULATION_STEPS; i++ )
    #pragma omp parallel
    {
        #pragma omp for
            for ( j = 0; j < NUM_DATA; j++ )
                compute( j );
        #pragma omp master
            communicate_results();
    }
```

Consider executing the example above on a cluster of compute nodes in which each node has multiple processor cores available. A possible hybrid usage of message passing and OpenMP thread parallelism would be to have one MPI process per node, each with an associated team of OpenMP threads equal to the number of processor cores per node. In the example, each simulation step would begin with all threads performing the computation over the data in the inner loop in parallel. Following that compute phase, only the master thread of each MPI process communicates the results of all the threads to the other MPI processes.

This material is useful to summarize the shared memory and distributed memory topics in DS/A, and why they can both be used at the same time. It is appropriate to address this when discussing shared memory and also whenever discussing cluster

---

[3]The OpenMP directives used in this example assume familiarity with OpenMP, covered in courses on shared memory programming.

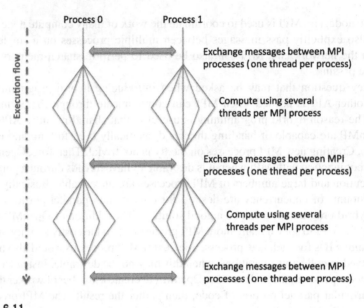

FIGURE 6.11

Hybrid programming using threads and MPI.

computing or message passing. Students should be aware that such approaches exist, and that hybrid programming is useful. At the core course level, students are not expected to understand the technical reasons why hybrid programming is useful, but a high-level understanding of the fact that shared memory approaches can better deal with dynamic concurrency than MPI would be desirable.

6.4.2 SUPERCOMPUTERS: ENABLING HPC

Vocabulary:

Graphics processing unit (GPU) aka , general purpose graphics processing unit (GPGPU)

Many of the top supercomputers are computing clusters. They are assembled from enterprise components, with high-performance (sometimes custom) networks. Individual computing nodes typically have large amounts of memory and multiple fast processors. Very high performance parallel file systems are needed to provide large datasets in a reasonable amount of time. Supercomputers typically use batch systems for job submission to accommodate the execution of multiple simultaneous workloads. Many supercomputers use accelerators such as GPUs and coprocessors to improve node-level performance. Supercomputers enable high-performance computing, which is a basis for many basic scientific investigations and discoveries.

The goal of supercomputers is to keep overheads as low as possible, thus keeping programs as close to the "metal" as possible. Effective systems minimize the number of software layers between the application and the hardware. As such, many supercomputers use modified operating systems. Current state-of-the-art approaches use lightweight kernels. Lightweight kernels have been in use for Department of Energy supercomputers for several years, and some supercomputer vendors provide lightweight kernels, such as Cray's CNK [14]. The goal of these operating systems is to reduce "operating system noise," which is slowdown introduced into a parallel system by the delay of processes (typically just a few) owing to their being swapped out of a core in order to service operating system tasks (e.g., daemons, scheduled tasks, etc.). Lightweight kernels can also be used to remove overhead due to operating system features that are not required for supercomputers.

The applications used on supercomputers are typically large, complex scientific codes. Many of these applications have been written using MPI, and there is significant momentum to continue to provide MPI support in future-generation systems. Radical new architectures occasionally force migration to new programming environments and methods, provided that the performance benefit from rewriting applications justifies the effort required. An example of this is the BlueGene supercomputers from IBM. BlueGene systems require a different programming technique in order to extract peak performance from the system. GPUs and coprocessors are introducing new programming models as well, and the programming of supercomputers is becoming increasingly complex. This is due to the exposure of more low-level hardware details than were required in previous-generation systems. For example, using a single homogeneous CPU architecture makes programming very large applications easier, as the application can use a single piece of code to run an operation on thousands of CPUs at the same time without issues surrounding the need for different instruction sets, nor any major difference in performance between the CPUs. Using accelerators that are not tightly integrated into the processor die requires mechanisms to move data efficiently to and from the accelerators.

Table 6.1 shows a historical summary of key supercomputers. It is interesting to note that until the 1990s supercomputers were not cluster-computer-type architectures. Since the 1990s, the top supercomputers have been primarily cluster-computing-type systems, with the latest supercomputers combining both traditional CPUs and accelerators. The most current information on the top supercomputers can be found at http://www.top500.org [15].

Supercomputers are a vital tool for many important scientific discoveries and important issues facing society. They are used for pharmaceutical research, genetics, climate modeling, weather prediction, fundamental physics and chemistry research, energy discovery, and complex system simulation. Increasingly powerful supercomputers both enhance the speed at which such problems can be solved, and increase the resolution and fidelity of the results. Some problems are so large that modern supercomputers are insufficient to solve them. For example, simulation of a human brain in real time is impossible with supercomputers circa 2015. Supercomputing is an important technology that will continue to enable cutting-edge scientific research

Table 6.1 Historical Supercomputer Performance

Name	Year	Processing (Flops)	CPU Cores	Memory
CDC 6600	1964	1×10^6	1 + 10 coprocessors	960 KB
Cray-2	1985	1.9×10^9	4	2 GB
ASCI Red	1997	1.3×10^{12}	9298	1.2 TB
RoadRunner	2008	1.02×10^{15}	6912 AMD CPUs (13,824 cores) + 12,960 Cell processors (116,640 cores)	104 TB
Titan	2012	17.59×10^{15}	18,688 + 18,688 GPUs (560,000 cores in total)	693.5 TB
Tianhe-2	2013	33.86×10^{15}	32,000 CPUs + 48,000 coprocessors (3.12 million cores in total)	1.34 PB

for the foreseeable future. It also helps to enhance individuals' daily lives through improved health care, new technologies, faster design, and of course, daily weather prediction.

The information presented here can be used by instructors as supplementary information to encourage students' interest in parallel and distributed computing. It can be introduced in DS/A and a course on systems when discussing cross-cutting topics, particularly cluster computing, power consumption, and fault tolerance, as these are key concerns for supercomputers. It can also be introduced wherever there is a desire for a real-world example of the potential benefits that parallelism and distributed computing provide and the impact that such technologies have on the world around us.

REFERENCES

[1] P. Balaji, D. Buntinas, D. Goodell, W. Gropp, S. Kumar, E. Lusk, R. Thakur, J.L. Träff, MPI on a million processors, in: Recent Advances in Parallel Virtual Machine and Message Passing Interface, Springer, Berlin, 2009, pp. 20-30.

[2] D.P. Anderson, J. Cobb, E. Korpela, M. Lebofsky, D. Werthimer, SETI @ home: an experiment in public-resource computing, Commun. ACM 45 (11) (2002) 56-61.

[3] C.A.R. Hoare, Communicating sequential processes, Commun. ACM 21 (8) (1978) 666-677, ISSN 0001-0782.

[4] MPI Forum, MPI: A Message-Passing Interface Standard. Version 3.0, 2012.

[5] InfiniBand Trade Association, InfiniBand Architecture Specification: Release 1.0, InfiniBand Trade Association, 2000.

[6] RDMA Consortium, Architectural Specifications for RDMA Over TCP/IP, 2005, URL http://www.rdmaconsortium.org.

[7] R. Alverson, D. Roweth, L. Kaplan, The Gemini system interconnect, in: 2010 IEEE 18th Annual Symposium on High Performance Interconnects (HOTI), IEEE, 2010, pp. 83-87.

[8] B.W. Barrett, R. Brightwell, R.E. Grant, S. Hemmert, K. Pedretti, K. Wheeler, K.D. Underwood, R. Reisen, A.B. Maccabe, T. Hudson, The Portals 4.0.2 Network Programming Interface, Sandia National Laboratories, 2014, Technical Report SAND2014-19568.

[9] N.J. Boden, D. Cohen, R.E. Felderman, A.E. Kulawik, C.L. Seitz, J.N. Seizovic, W.-K. Su, Myrinet: a gigabit-per-second local area network, Micro, IEEE 15 (1) (1995) 29-36.

[10] F. Petrini, W.-c. Feng, A. Hoisie, S. Coll, E. Frachtenberg, The Quadrics network: high-performance clustering technology, Micro, IEEE 22 (1) (2002) 46-57.

[11] M. Tsai, B. Penoff, A. Wagner, A hybrid MPI design using SCTP and iWARP, in: IEEE International Symposium on Parallel and Distributed Processing, 2008. IPDPS 2008, IEEE, 2008, pp. 1-8.

[12] R.E. Grant, M.J. Rashti, A. Afsahi, P. Balaji, RDMA capable iWARP over datagrams, in: IEEE International Symposium on Parallel & Distributed Processing Symposium (IPDPS), 2011, IEEE, 2011, pp. 628-639.

[13] D. Cohen, T. Talpey, A. Kanevsky, U. Cummings, M. Krause, R. Recio, D. Crupnicoff, L. Dickman, P. Grun, Remote direct memory access over the converged enhanced ethernet fabric: evaluating the options, in: 17th IEEE Symposium on High Performance Interconnects, 2009. HOTI 2009, IEEE, 2009, pp. 123-130.

[14] M. Giampapa, T. Gooding, T. Inglett, R.W. Wisniewski, Experiences with a lightweight supercomputer kernel: lessons Learned from Blue Gene's CNK, in: 2010 International Conference for High Performance Computing, Networking, Storage and Analysis (SC), IEEE, 2010, pp. 1-10.

[15] H. Meuer, E. Strohmaier, J. Dongarra, H. Simon, Top500 Supercomputing Sites, 2013, URL http://www.top500.org/.

For students

Fork-join parallelism with a data-structures focus

7

Dan Grossman*

*University of Washington**

Relevant core courses: Data structures and algorithms, Second programming course in the introductory sequence.

Relevant topics: Shared memory, Language extensions, Libraries, Task/thread spawning, Load balancing, Performance metrics, Speedup, Amdahl's law, Asymptotics, Time, Speedup, Bulk synchronous parallel/Cilk, Dependencies, Task graphs, Work, (Make)span, Divide and conquer (parallel aspects), Recursion (parallel aspects), Scan (parallel prefix), Reduction (map-reduce), Sorting, Why and what is parallel and distributed computing, Concurrency.

Learning outcomes: Students mastering the material in this chapter should be able to

- write small parallel programs in terms of explicit threads that communicate via shared memory and synchronize via fork and join;
- distinguish parallelism from concurrency control;
- identify computations that are reductions or maps that can be performed in parallel;
- analyze a fork-join computation in terms of work and span in general, and in particular be able to explain the linear work and logarithmic span of reductions and maps in the fork-join model;
- define Amdahl's law and use it to reason about the performance benefits of parallelism;
- reason about nontrivial parallel algorithms in an analogous way to how students in a conventional data structures and algorithms course can reason about sequential algorithms.

Context for use: This chapter and Chapter 8 complement each other. Both are designed to be used in an intermediate-advanced data-structures courses—the course that covers asymptotic complexity, balanced trees, hash tables, graph algorithms, sorting, etc., though some of the material has also been used in second programming courses. This chapter introduces a distinction between *parallelism* and *concurrency control (e.g., synchronization)* and then focuses on the former predominantly via *fork-join parallelism*. Chapter 8 focuses on concurrency control, predominantly via *mutual-exclusion locks*.

7.1 META-INTRODUCTION: AN INSTRUCTOR'S VIEW OF THIS MATERIAL

7.1.1 WHERE THIS MATERIAL FITS IN A CHANGING CURRICULUM

This chapter and Chapter 8 together introduce parallelism and concurrency control in the context of a data-structures course.

The case for teaching this material in a data-structures course:

There may be multiple natural places to introduce this material, but a "sophomore-level" data-structures course (after CS2 and a discrete-math course, but before a "senior-level" algorithms course) works very well. Here are some reasons:

- There is room: This chapter's author made room by removing 3 weeks of instruction on skew heaps, leftist heaps, binomial queues, splay trees, disjoint sets, and network flow. Some of the trimming was painful, and can be compensated for in a senior-level algorithms course, but all this material seems relatively less important. There was still plenty of room for essential data structures and related concepts such as asymptotic analysis, (simple) amortization, graphs, and sorting.
- Fork-join parallel algorithms are amenable to asymptotic analysis in terms of "work" and "span" over directed acyclic graphs (DAGs)—all concepts that fit very naturally in the course. Amdahl's law is fundamentally an asymptotic argument too.
- Ideas from sequential algorithms already in the course reappear with parallelism. For example, just as constant factors compel efficient quicksort implementations to switch to an $O(n^2)$ sort for small n, constant factors compel efficient parallel algorithms to switch to sequential algorithms for small problem sizes. Parallel sorting algorithms are also good examples of nontrivial parallelization.
- Many canonical examples for concurrent programming involve basic data structures: bounded buffers for condition variables, dictionaries for reader/writer locks, parallel unstructured graph traversals, etc. Making a data structure "thread-safe" is an ideal way to think about what it means to be "thread-safe."
- We already used Java in the course. Java 7's ForkJoin framework is excellent for teaching fork-join parallelism. Java's built-in support for threads, locks, and condition variables is sufficient for teaching synchronization.

On the other hand, instructors wishing to introduce message passing or distributed computation will have to consider whether it makes sense in this course. This chapter and Chapter 8 focus on shared memory, only mentioning other models. This is not to claim that shared memory is "better," only that it is an important model and a good one to start with pedagogically. There is also little emphasis on asynchrony and masking I/O latency. Such topics are probably better covered in a course on systems programming, though one could add them to the material in Chapter 8.

While most of the material in this chapter and Chapter 8 is not specific to a particular programming language, all examples and discussions use Java when a specific language is warranted. A C++ version of an earlier version of these materials is also available thanks to Steve Wolfman from the University of British Columbia. Porting to additional languages should be quite doable, and the author would be delighted to collaborate with people interested in doing so.

For more information on the motivation and context, see a SIGCSE 2012 paper coauthored with Ruth E. Anderson [1].

7.1.2 SIX THESES ON A SUCCESSFUL APPROACH TO THIS MATERIAL

In summary, this approach rests on several theses for how to teach this material:

1. Integrate it into a data-structures course.
2. Distinguish parallelism (using extra computational units to do more work per unit time) from concurrency control (managing access to shared resources). Teach parallelism first because it is easier and helps establish a nonsequential mindset.
3. Teach in a high-level language, using a library for fork-join parallelism. Teach how to use parallelism, threads, locks, etc. Do not teach how to implement them.
4. Conversely, do not teach in terms of higher-order parallel patterns such as maps and reduces. Mention these, but have students actually do the divide and conquer underlying these patterns.
5. Assume shared memory since one programming model is difficult enough.
6. Given the limited time and student background, do not focus on memory-hierarchy issues (e.g., caching), much like these issues are mentioned (e.g., with B trees) but rarely central in data-structures courses. (Adding a discussion should prove straightforward.)

7.1.3 HOW TO USE THESE MATERIALS—AND IMPROVE THEM

These materials were originally written for CSE332 at the University of Washington (http://courses.cs.washington.edu/courses/cse332/). They account for 3 weeks of a required 10-week course (the university uses a quarter system). There are also PowerPoint slides, homework assignments, and a programming project. In fact, this written text was the last aspect to be created—the first edition of the course succeeded without written material, and students reported parallelism to be their favorite aspect of the course.

The current home for all the materials is http://homes.cs.washington.edu/~djg/teachingMaterials. Feedback, information on typos, and suggestions for improvement are most welcome.

7.2 INTRODUCTION

7.2.1 MORE THAN ONE THING AT ONCE

In *sequential programming*, one thing happens at a time. Sequential programming is what most people learn first and how most programs are written. Probably every program you have written in Java (or a similar language) is sequential: execution starts at the beginning of `main` and proceeds one assignment/call/return/arithmetic operation at a time.

Removing the one-thing-at-a-time assumption complicates writing software. The multiple *threads of execution* (things performing computations) will somehow need to coordinate so that they can work together to complete a task—or at least not get in each other's way while they are doing separate things. This chapter and Chapter 8 cover basic concepts related to *multithreaded programming*—that is, programs where there are multiple threads of execution. We will cover the following:

- How to create multiple threads
- How to write and analyze divide-and-conquer algorithms that use threads to produce results more quickly (this chapter)
- How to coordinate access to shared objects so that multiple threads using the same data do not produce the wrong answer (Chapter 8)

A useful analogy is with cooking. A sequential program is like having one cook who does each step of a recipe in order, finishing one step before starting the next. Often there are multiple steps that could be done at the same time—if you had more cooks. But having more cooks requires extra coordination. One cook may have to wait for another cook to finish something. And there are limited resources: If you have only one oven, two cooks cannot bake casseroles at different temperatures at the same time. In short, multiple cooks present efficiency opportunities, but also significantly complicate the process of producing a meal.

Because multithreaded programming is so much more difficult, it is best to avoid it if you can. For most of computing's history, most programmers wrote only sequential programs. Notable exceptions were as follows:

- Programmers writing programs to solve such computationally large problems that it would take years or centuries for one computer to finish. So they would use multiple computers together.
- Programmers writing systems such as an operating system where a key point of the system is to handle multiple things happening at once. For example, you can have more than one program running at a time. If you have only one processor, only one program can *actually* run at a time, but the operating system still uses

threads to keep track of all the running programs and let them take turns. If the taking turns happens fast enough (e.g., 10 ms), humans fall for the illusion of simultaneous execution. This is called *time-slicing*.

Sequential programmers were lucky: since every 2 years or so computers got roughly twice as fast, most programs would get exponentially faster over time without any extra effort.

Around 2005, computers stopped getting twice as fast every 2 years. To understand why requires a course in computer architecture. In brief, increasing the clock rate (very roughly and technically inaccurately speaking, how quickly instructions execute) became infeasible without generating too much heat. Also, the relative cost of memory accesses can become too high for faster processors to help.

Nonetheless, chip manufacturers still plan to make exponentially more powerful chips. Instead of one processor running faster, they will have more processors. The next computer you buy will likely have at least four processors (also called *cores*) on the same chip, and the number of available cores will likely double every few years.

What would 256 cores be good for? Well, you can run multiple programs at once—for real, not just with time-slicing. But for an individual program to run any faster than with one core, it will need to do more than one thing at once. This is the reason that multithreaded programming is becoming more important. To be clear, *multithreaded programming is not new. It has existed for decades, and all the key concepts are just as old.* Before there were multiple cores on one chip, you could use multiple chips and/or use time-slicing on one chip—and both remain important techniques today. The move to multiple cores on one chip is "just" having the effect of making multithreading something that more and more software wants to do.

7.2.2 PARALLELISM VERSUS CONCURRENCY CONTROL

This chapter and Chapter 8 are organized around a fundamental distinction between *parallelism* and *concurrency control*. Unfortunately, the way we define these terms is not entirely standard (more common in some communities than in others), so you should not assume that everyone uses these terms precisely as we will. Nonetheless, most computer scientists agree that this distinction is important—we just disagree over the use of these English words.

Parallelism is about using additional computational resources to produce an answer faster.

As a canonical example, consider the trivial problem of summing up all the numbers in an array. We know no sequential algorithm can do better than $\Theta(n)$ time.[1]

---

[1] For those not familiar with "big-Θ notation," you can always read Θ as O, the more common "big-O notation." For example, if an algorithm is $\Theta(n)$, then it is also $O(n)$. The difference is that O provides only an upper bound, so, for example, an $O(n^2)$ algorithm is *also* an $O(n^3)$ algorithm and *might or might not* be an $O(n)$ algorithm. By definition, Θ is an upper and a lower bound: a $\Theta(n^2)$ algorithm is neither $\Theta(n^3)$ nor $\Theta(n)$. To provide more precise claims, this chapter uses Θ where appropriate.

Suppose instead we had four processors. Then hopefully we could produce the result roughly four times faster by having each processor add a quarter of the elements, and then we could just add these four partial results together with three more additions. $\Theta(n/4)$ is still $\Theta(n)$, but constant factors can matter. Moreover, when designing and analyzing a *parallel algorithm*, we should leave the number of processors as a variable, call it P. Perhaps we can sum the elements of an array in time $O(n/P)$ given P processors. As we will see, in fact the best bound under the assumptions we will make is $O(\log n + n/P)$.

In terms of our cooking analogy, parallelism is about using extra cooks (or utensils or pans or whatever) to get a large meal finished in less time. If you have a huge number of potatoes to slice, having more knives and more people is very helpful, but at some point adding more people stops helping because of all the communicating and coordinating you have to do: it is faster for me to slice one potato by myself than to slice it into fourths, give it to four other people, and collect the results.

Concurrency control is about correctly and efficiently controlling access by multiple threads to shared resources.

Suppose we have a dictionary implemented as a hash table with operations insert, lookup, and delete. Further suppose that inserting an item already in the table should update the key to map to the newly inserted value. Implementing this data structure for sequential programs is something we assume you can already do correctly. Now consider what might happen if different threads use the *same* hash table, potentially at the same time. Two threads might even try to insert the same key at the same time. What could happen? You would have to look at your sequential code carefully, but it is entirely possible that the same key might end up in the table twice. That is a problem since a subsequent delete with that key might remove only one of them, leaving the key in the dictionary.

To prevent problems such as this, concurrent programs use *synchronization primitives* to prevent multiple threads from *interleaving their operations* in a way that leads to incorrect results. Perhaps a simple solution in our hash table example is to make sure only one thread uses the table at a time, finishing an operation before another thread starts. But if the table is large, this is unnecessarily inefficient most of the time if the threads are probably accessing different parts of the table.

In terms of cooking, the shared resources could be something like an oven. It is important not to put a casserole in the oven unless the oven is empty. If the oven is not empty, we could keep checking until it is empty. In Java, you might naively write

```
while(true) {
    if(ovenIsEmpty()) {
        putCasseroleInOven();
        break;
    }
}
```

Unfortunately, code such as this is broken if two threads run it at the same time, which is the primary complication in concurrent programming. They might both see an empty oven and then both might put a casserole in it. We will need to learn ways to check the oven and put a casserole in it without any other thread doing something with the oven in the meantime.

Confusion over the terms "parallelism" and "concurrency"

An exciting aspect of multithreading is that it sits at the intersection of many traditional areas of computer science: algorithms, computer architecture, distributed computing, programming languages, and systems. However, different traditions have used various terms in incompatible ways, including the words *"parallelism"* and *"concurrency"* used to describe the main contrast between this chapter and Chapter 8.

As we have used them, parallelism is anything about gaining efficiency by doing multiple things at once, while concurrency is about all the issues that arise when different threads need to coordinate, share, and synchronize. This use of the terms is more common in the computer architecture and systems communities, particularly in recent years.

A more traditional use of the words, especially in the algorithms tradition, uses "parallelism" to describe when things *actually* happen at once and "concurrency" to describe when things *may* happen at once (e.g., if enough resources are available). This use of the terms makes a useful distinction within the realm of parallelism for gaining efficiency but leaves us without a one-word term for the collection of issues and techniques in Chapter 8.

In an attempt to make everyone happy (and with the risk of making everyone unhappy), this chapter and Chapter 8 will try to strike a balance. We will use "parallelism" for anything related to gaining efficiency by doing multiple things at once. For example, a parallel algorithm will describe what may happen at the same time, without necessarily considering how many threads can actually run at once. But we will avoid using "concurrency" to describe coordination, sharing, and synchronization. Instead, we will use the term *"concurrency control"* when we need a single term for controlling/limiting how multiple threads may interact, and we will use more specific terms related to coordination and synchronization when possible.

Comparing parallelism and concurrency control

We have emphasized here how parallelism and concurrency control are different. Is the problem one of using extra resources effectively, or is the problem one of preventing a bad interleaving of operations from different threads? It is all too common for a conversation to become muddled because one person is thinking about parallelism while the other is thinking about concurrency control.

In practice, the distinction between the two is not absolute. Many programs have aspects of each: how can we exploit parallelism while controlling access to shared resources? Suppose you had a huge array of values you wanted to insert into a hash table. From the perspective of dividing up the insertions among multiple threads, this is about parallelism. From the perspective of coordinating access to the hash table, this is about concurrency control. Also, parallelism does typically need some coordination: even when adding up integers in an array, we need to know when the different threads are finished with their chunk of the work.

We believe parallelism is an easier concept to start with than concurrency control. You probably found it easier to understand how to use parallelism to add up array elements than to understand why the while-loop for checking the oven was wrong. (And if you still do not understand the latter, do not worry, Chapter 8 will explain similar examples line-by-line.) So we will start with parallelism in this chapter, getting comfortable with multiple things happening at once. Then Chapter 8 will switch our focus to shared resources (using memory instead of ovens), learn many of the subtle problems that arise, and present programming guidelines to avoid them.

7.2.3 BASIC THREADS AND SHARED MEMORY

Before writing any multithreaded programs, we need some way to *make multiple things happen at once* and some way for those different things to *communicate*. Put another way, your computer may have multiple cores, but all the Java constructs you know are for sequential programs, which do only one thing at once. Before showing any Java specifics, we need to explain the *programming model*.

The model we will assume is *explicit threads* with *shared memory*. A *thread* is itself like a running sequential program, but one thread can create other threads that are part of the same program, and those threads can create more threads, etc. Two or more threads can communicate by writing and reading fields of the same objects. In other words, they share memory. This is only one model of parallel programming, but it is the only one we will use in this chapter. The next section briefly mentions other models that a full course on parallel programming would likely cover.

Conceptually, all the threads that have been started but not yet terminated are "running at once" in a program. In practice, they may not all be running at any particular moment:

- There may be more threads than processors. It is up to the Java implementation, with help from the underlying operating system, to find a way to let the threads "take turns" using the available processors. This is called *scheduling*, and is a major topic in operating systems. All we need to know is that it is not under the Java programmer's control: you create the threads, and the system schedules them.
- A thread may be waiting for something to happen before it continues. For example, the next section discusses the `join` primitive, where one thread does not continue until another thread has terminated.

Let us be more concrete about what a thread is and how threads communicate. It is helpful to start by enumerating the key pieces that a *sequential* program has *while it is running* (see also Figure 7.1):

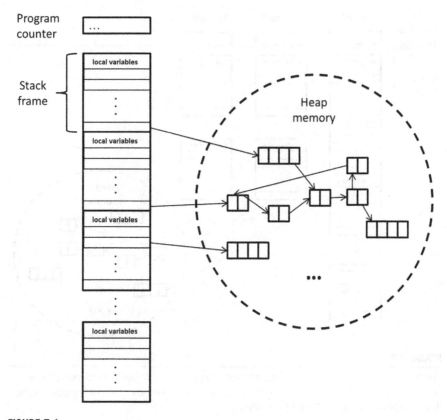

FIGURE 7.1

The key pieces of an executing sequential program: a program counter, a call stack, and a heap of objects. (There are also static fields of classes, which we can think of as being in the heap.)

1. One *call stack*, where each *stack frame* holds the local variables for a method call that has started but not yet finished. Calling a method pushes a new frame, and returning from a method pops a frame. Call stacks are why recursion is not "magic."
2. One *program counter*. This is just a low-level name for keeping track of what statement is currently executing. In a sequential program, there is exactly one such statement.
3. Static fields of classes.
4. Objects. An object is created by calling new, which returns a reference to the new object. We call the memory that holds all the objects the *heap*. This use of the word "heap" has nothing to do with the heap data structure used to implement priority queues. It is memory separate from the memory used for the call stack and static fields.

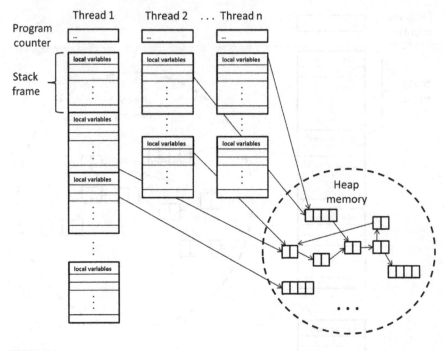

FIGURE 7.2

The key pieces of an executing multithreaded program: each thread has its own program counter and call stack, but objects in the heap may be shared by multiple threads. (Static fields of classes are also shared by all threads.)

With this overview of the sequential *program state*, it is much easier to understand threads:

Each thread has its own call stack and program counter, but all the threads share one collection of static fields and objects. (See also Figure 7.2.)

- When a new thread starts running, it will have its own new call stack. It will have one frame on it, which is *like* that thread's main, but it will not actually be main.
- When a thread returns from its first method, it terminates.
- Each thread has its own program counter and local variables, so there is no "interference" from other threads for these things. The way loops, calls, assignments to variables, exceptions, etc., work for each thread is just as you learned in sequential programming and is separate for each thread.
- What is different is how static fields and objects work. In sequential programming we know x.f = 42; y = x.f; always assigns 42 to the variable y. But now the object that x refers to might also have its f field written to by other threads, so we cannot be so sure.

In practice, even though all objects *could* be shared among threads, most are not. In fact, just as having static fields is often poor style, having lots of objects shared among threads is often poor style. But we need *some* shared objects because that is how threads communicate. If we are going to create parallel algorithms where helper threads run in parallel to compute partial answers, they need some way to communicate those partial answers to the "main" thread. The way we will do this is to have the helper threads write to some object fields that the main thread later reads.

We finish this section with some Java specifics for exactly how to create a new thread in Java. The details differ in different languages, and in fact most of this chapter uses a different Java library with slightly different specifics. In addition to creating threads, we will need other language constructs for coordinating them. For example, for one thread to read the result another thread wrote as its answer, the reader often needs to know the writer is finished. We will present such primitives as we need them.

To create a new thread in Java requires that you define a new class (step 1) and then perform two actions at run-time (steps 2-3):

1. Define a subclass of `java.lang.Thread` and override the `public` method `run`, which takes no arguments and has return type `void`. The `run` method will act like "main" for threads created using this class. It must take no arguments, but the example below shows how to work around this inconvenience.

2. Create an instance of the class you defined in step 1. That is, if you defined class `ExampleThread`, then use `new` to create an `ExampleThread` object. Note this does *not* yet create a running thread. It just creates an object of class `ExampleThread`, which is a subclass of `Thread`.

3. Call the `start` method of the object you created in step 2. This step does the "magic" creation of a new thread. That new thread will execute the `run` method of the object. Notice that you do *not* call `run`; that would just be an ordinary method call. You call `start`, which makes a new thread that runs `run`. The call to `start` "returns immediately" so the caller continues on, in parallel with the newly created thread running `run`. The new thread terminates when its `run` method finishes.

Here is a complete example of a useless Java program that starts with one thread and then creates 20 more threads:

```
class ExampleThread extends java.lang.Thread {
    int i;
    ExampleThread(int i) { this.i = i; }
    public void run() {
        System.out.println("Thread " + i + " says hi");
        System.out.println("Thread " + i + " says bye");
    }
}
```

```
class M {
  public static void main(String[] args) {
    for(int i=1; i <= 20; ++i) {
      ExampleThread t = new ExampleThread(i);
      t.start();
    }
  }
}
```

When this program runs, it will print 40 lines of output, one of which is

```
Thread 13 says hi
```

We cannot predict the order for these 40 lines of output. In fact, if you run the program multiple times, you will probably see the output appear in different orders on different runs. After all, each of the 21 separate threads running "at the same time" (conceptually, since your machine may not have 21 processors available for the program) can run in an unpredictable order. The main thread is the first thread, and then it creates 20 others. The main thread always creates the other threads in the same order, but it is up to the Java implementation to let all the threads "take turns" using the available processors. There is no guarantee that threads created earlier run earlier. Therefore, multithreaded programs are often *nondeterministic*, meaning their output can change even if the input does not. This is a main reason that multithreaded programs are more difficult to test and debug. Figure 7.3 shows two possible orders of execution, but there are many, many more.

So is any possible ordering of the 40 output lines possible? No. Each thread still runs sequentially. So we will always see `Thread 13 says hi` *before* the line `Thread 13 says bye` even though there may be other lines in-between. We might also wonder if two lines of output would ever be mixed, something like

```
Thread 13 Thread says 14 says hi hi
```

This is really a question of how the `System.out.println` method handles concurrency, and the answer happens to be that it will always keep a line of output together, so this would not occur. In general, concurrency introduces new questions about how code should and does behave.

We can also see how the example worked around the rule that `run` must override `java.lang.Thread`'s `run` method and therefore not take any arguments. The standard idiom is to pass any "arguments" for the new thread to the *constructor*, which then stores them in fields so that `run` can later access them. In this simple example, this trick is the only use of shared memory since the helper threads (the ones doing the printing) do not need to pass any other data to/from the main thread or each other.

It may not look like this is using shared memory, but it is: When the main thread calls `new ExampleThread(i)`, this is a normal call to a constructor. A new object is created and the main thread runs the constructor code, writing to the `i` field of the new

Example Run 1:	Example Run 2:
Thread 1 says hi	Thread 1 says hi
Thread 3 says hi	Thread 3 says hi
Thread 2 says hi	Thread 3 says bye
Thread 1 says bye	Thread 2 says hi
Thread 5 says hi	Thread 6 says hi
Thread 3 says bye	Thread 4 says hi
Thread 7 says hi	Thread 6 says bye
Thread 7 says bye	Thread 1 says bye
Thread 5 says bye	Thread 2 says bye
Thread 6 says hi	Thread 5 says hi
Thread 6 says bye	Thread 4 says bye
Thread 9 says hi	Thread 9 says hi
Thread 9 says bye	Thread 5 says bye
Thread 4 says hi	Thread 8 says hi
Thread 2 says bye	Thread 7 says hi
Thread 8 says hi	Thread 8 says bye
Thread 18 says hi	Thread 9 says bye
Thread 17 says hi	Thread 11 says hi
Thread 15 says hi	Thread 11 says bye
Thread 14 says hi	Thread 13 says hi
Thread 14 says bye	Thread 7 says bye
Thread 11 says hi	Thread 13 says bye
Thread 11 says bye	Thread 12 says hi
Thread 12 says hi	Thread 10 says hi
Thread 12 says bye	Thread 12 says bye
Thread 19 says hi	Thread 14 says hi
Thread 4 says bye	Thread 15 says hi
Thread 10 says hi	Thread 10 says bye
Thread 10 says bye	Thread 15 says bye
Thread 19 says bye	Thread 16 says hi
Thread 15 says bye	Thread 14 says bye
Thread 13 says hi	Thread 19 says hi
Thread 13 says bye	Thread 18 says hi
Thread 17 says bye	Thread 20 says hi
Thread 16 says hi	Thread 16 says bye
Thread 18 says bye	Thread 17 says hi
Thread 8 says bye	Thread 20 says bye
Thread 16 says bye	Thread 18 says bye
Thread 20 says hi	Thread 19 says bye
Thread 20 says bye	Thread 17 says bye

FIGURE 7.3

Two possible outputs from running the program that creates 20 threads that each print two lines.

object. Later, after the "magic" call to start, the new running thread is running the run method with this bound to the same object that the main thread wrote to. The helper thread then reads i, which just means this.i, and gets the value previously written by the main thread: shared-memory communication. See Figure 7.4.

As this example shows, shared-memory communication relies on aliasing. The t on some iteration of the for loop refers to the same object as this in one of the new threads' run method. Aliasing is often difficult to reason about, but it is the way we communicate in shared-memory multithreaded programs.

7.2.4 OTHER MODELS

While this chapter and Chapter 8 focus on using threads and shared memory to create parallelism, it would be misleading to suggest that this is the only model for parallel programming. Shared memory is often considered *convenient* because communication uses "regular" reads and writes of fields to objects. However, it is also considered *error-prone* because communication is implicit; it requires deep understanding of the code/documentation to know which memory accesses are doing interthread communication and which are not. The definition of shared-memory programs is also much subtler than many programmers think because of issues regarding *data races*, as discussed in Chapter 8 (Section 8.4.2).

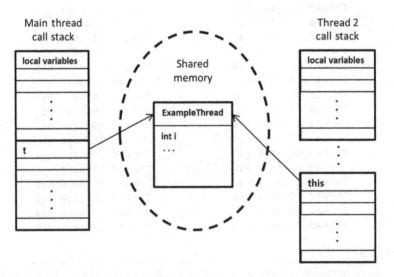

FIGURE 7.4

How we can use shared memory, specifically fields in a subclass of Thread, to pass data to a newly created thread.

Here are three well-known, popular alternatives to shared memory. As is common in computer science, no option is "clearly better." Different models are best suited to different problems, and any model can be abused to produce incorrect or unnecessarily complicated software. One can also build abstractions using one model on top of another model, or use multiple models in the same program. These are really different perspectives on how to describe parallel/concurrent programs.

Message passing is the natural alternative to shared memory. In this model, we have explicit threads, but they do not share objects. To communicate, there is a separate notion of a *message*, which sends a *copy* of some data to its recipient. Since each thread has its own objects, we do not have to worry about other threads wrongly updating fields. But we do have to keep track of different copies of things being produced by messages. When processors are far apart, message passing is likely a more natural fit, just like when you send e-mail and a copy of the message is sent to the recipient. Here is a visual interpretation of message passing:

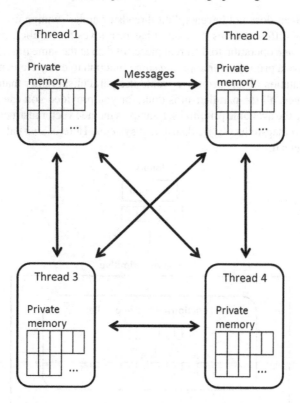

Dataflow provides more structure than having "a bunch of threads that communicate with each other however they want." Instead, the programmer uses primitives to create a DAG. A node in the graph performs some computation using inputs that arrive on its incoming edges. This data is provided by other nodes along their outgoing edges. A node starts computing when all of its inputs are available, something the implementation keeps track of automatically. Here is a visual interpretation of dataflow where different nodes perform different operations for some computation, such as "filter," "fade in," and "fade out":

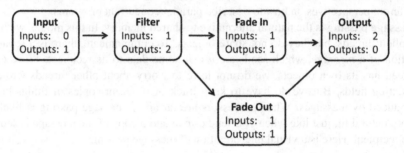

Data parallelism does not have explicit threads or nodes running different parts of the program at different times. Instead, it has primitives for parallelism that involve applying the *same* operation to different pieces of data at the same time. For example, you would have a primitive for applying some function to every element of an array. The implementation of this primitive would use parallelism rather than a sequential `for` loop. Hence, all the parallelism is done for you provided you can express your program using the available primitives. Examples include vector instructions on some processors and map-reduce-style distributed systems. Here is a visual interpretation of data parallelism:

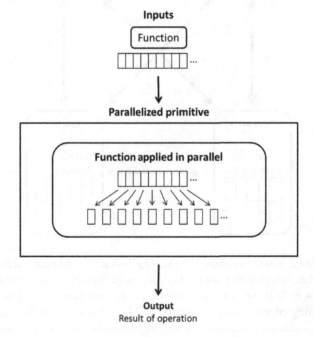

7.3 BASIC FORK-JOIN PARALLELISM

This section shows how to use threads and shared memory to implement simple parallel algorithms. The only synchronization primitive we will need is `join`, which causes one thread to wait until another thread has terminated. We begin with simple pseudocode and then show how using threads in Java to achieve the same idea requires a bit more work (Section 7.3.1). We then argue that it is best for parallel code to *not* be written in terms of the number of processors available (Section 7.3.2), and show how to use recursive divide and conquer instead (Section 7.3.3). Because Java's threads are not engineered for this style of programming, we switch to the Java ForkJoin framework, which is designed for our needs (Section 7.3.4). With all of this discussion in terms of the single problem of summing an array of integers, we then turn to other, similar problems, introducing the terminology of *maps* and *reduces* (Section 7.3.5) as well as data structures other than arrays (Section 7.3.6).

7.3.1 A SIMPLE EXAMPLE: OKAY IDEA, INFERIOR STYLE

Most of this section will consider the problem of computing the sum of an array of integers. An $O(n)$ sequential solution to this problem is trivial:

```
int sum(int[] arr) {
    int ans = 0;
    for(int i=0; i < arr.length; i++)
        ans += arr[i];
    return ans;
}
```

If the array is large and we have extra processors available, we can get a more efficient parallel algorithm. Suppose we have four processors. Then we could do the following:

- Use the first processor to sum the first quarter of the array and store the result somewhere
- Use the second processor to sum the second quarter of the array and store the result somewhere
- Use the third processor to sum the third quarter of the array and store the result somewhere
- Use the fourth processor to sum the fourth quarter of the array and store the result somewhere
- Add the four stored results and return that as the answer

This algorithm is clearly correct provided that the last step is started only after the previous four steps have finished. The first four steps can occur in parallel. More generally, if we have P processors, we can divide the array into P equal segments and have an algorithm that runs in time $O(n/P + P)$, where n/P is for the parallel part and P is for combining the stored results. Later we will see we can do better if P is very large, though that may be less of a practical concern.

In pseudocode, a convenient way to write this kind of algorithm is with a FORALL loop. A FORALL loop is like a for loop except it does all the iterations in parallel. Like for a regular for loop, the code after a FORALL loop does not execute until the loop (i.e., all its iterations) is finished. Unlike for the for loop, the programmer is "promising" that all the iterations can be done at the same time without them interfering with each other. Therefore, if one loop iteration writes to a location, then another iteration must not read or write to that location. However, it is fine for two iterations to read the same location: that does not cause any interference.

Here, then, is a pseudocode solution to using four processors to sum an array. Note it is essential that we store the four partial results in separate locations to avoid any interference between loop iterations.[2]

```
int sum(int[] arr) {
    results = new int[4];
    len = arr.length;
    FORALL(i=0; i < 4; ++i) {
        results[i] = sumRange(arr,(i*len)/4,((i+1)*len)/4);
    }
    return results[0] + results[1] + results[2] + results[3];
}
int sumRange(int[] arr, int lo, int hi) {
    result = 0;
    for(j=lo; j < hi; ++j)
        result += arr[j];
    return result;
}
```

Unfortunately, Java and most other general-purpose languages do not have a FORALL loop. (Java has various kinds of for loops, but all run all iterations on one thread.) We can encode this programming pattern explicitly using threads as follows:

1. In a regular for loop, create one thread to do each iteration of our FORALL loop, passing the data needed in the constructor. Have the threads store their answers in fields of themselves.
2. Wait for all the threads created in step 1 to terminate.
3. Combine the results by reading the answers out of the fields of the threads created in step 1.

---

[2]We must take care to avoid bugs due to integer-division truncation with the arguments to sumRange. We need to process each array element exactly once even if len is not divisible by 4. This code is correct; notice in particular that ((i+1)*len)/4 will always be len when i==3 because 4*len is divisible by 4. Moreover, we could write (i+1)*len/4 since * and / have the same precedence and associate from left to right. But (i+1)*(len/4) would *not* be correct. For the same reason, defining a variable int rangeSize = len/4 and using (i+1)*rangeSize would *not* be correct.

To understand this pattern, we will first show a *wrong* version to get the idea. That is a common technique in this chapter—learning from wrong versions is extremely useful—but wrong versions are always clearly indicated.

Here is our *wrong* attempt:

```
class SumThread extends java.lang.Thread {
    int lo; // fields for communicating inputs
    int hi;
    int[] arr;
    int ans = 0; // for communicating result
    SumThread(int[] a, int l, int h) {
      lo=l; hi=h; arr=a;
    }
    public void run() { // overriding, must have this type
      for(int i=lo; i<hi; i++)
        ans += arr[i];
    }
}
class C {
  static int sum(int[] arr) {
    int len = arr.length;
    int ans = 0;
    SumThread[] ts = new SumThread[4];
    for(int i=0; i < 4; i++) {
      ts[i] = new SumThread(arr,(i*len)/4,((i+1)*len)/4);
      ts[i].start();
    }
    for(int i=0; i < 4; i++) {
      ans += ts[i].ans;
    }
    return ans;
  }
}
```

The code above gets most of the pieces right. The sum method creates four instances of SumThread, which is a subclass of java.lang.Thread, and calls start on each of them. The SumThread constructor takes as arguments the data that the thread needs to do its job, in this case, the array and the range for which this thread is responsible. (We use a convenient convention that ranges *include* the low bound and *exclude* the high bound.) The SumThread constructor stores this data in fields of the object so that the new thread has access to them in the run method. (Typically run would pass the relevant data to helper methods, but here the problem is simple enough not to bother.)

Notice each SumThread object also has an ans field. This is shared memory for communicating the answer from the helper thread to the main thread. In particular, for the thread created on the ith iteration of the for loop in sum, the field this.ans is an alias for `ts[i].ans`. So the main thread can sum the four `ans` fields from the threads it created to produce the final answer.

The bug in this code has to do with synchronization: The main thread does not wait for the helper threads to finish before it sums the `ans` fields. Remember that `start` returns immediately—otherwise we would not get any parallelism. So the `sum` method's second `for` loop probably starts running before the helper threads are finished with their work. Having one thread (the main thread) read a field while another thread (the helper thread) is writing the same field is a bug, and here it would produce a wrong (too-small) answer. We need to delay the second `for` loop until the helper threads are finished.

There is a method in `java.lang.Thread`, and therefore in all its subclasses such as `SumThread`, that is just what we need. If one thread, in our case the main thread, calls the `join` method of a `java.lang.Thread` object, in our case one of the helper threads, then this call is blocked (i.e., does not return) unless/until the thread corresponding to the object has terminated. So we can add another `for` loop to `sum` in-between the two loops already there to make sure all the helper threads finish before we add together the results:

```
for(int i=0; i < 4; i++)
    ts[i].join();
```

Notice it is the main thread that is calling `join`, which takes no arguments. On the first loop iteration, the main thread will remain blocked until the first helper thread is finished. On the second loop iteration, the main thread will remain blocked until the second helper thread is finished. It is certainly possible that the second helper thread actually finished before the first thread. This is not a problem: a call to `join` when the helper thread has already terminated just returns right away (no blocking).

Essentially, we are using two `for` loops, where the first one creates helper threads and the second one waits for them all to terminate, to encode the idea of a FORALL loop. This style of parallel programming is called "fork-join parallelism." It is like we create a "(four-way in this case) fork in the road of execution" and send each helper thread down one path of the fork. Then we join all the paths of the fork back together and have the single main thread continue. Fork-join parallelism can also be *nested*, meaning one of the helper threads forks its own helper threads. In fact, we will soon argue that this is better style. The term "join" is common in different programming languages and libraries, though it is not the most descriptive English word for the concept.

It is common to combine the joining `for` loop and the result-combining `for` loop. Understanding why this is still correct helps understand the `join` primitive. So far we have suggested writing code like this in our `sum` method:

```
for(int i=0; i < 4; i++)
    ts[i].join();
for(int i=0; i < 4; i++)
```

```
        ans += ts[i].ans;
    return ans;
```

There is nothing wrong with the code above, but the following is also correct:

```
    for(int i=0; i < 4; i++) {
        ts[i].join();
        ans += ts[i].ans;
    }
    return ans;
```

Here we do not wait for all the helper threads to finish before we start producing the final answer. But we still ensure that the main thread does not access a helper thread's ans field until at least that helper thread has terminated.

There is one last Java-specific detail we need when using the join method defined in java.lang.Thread. This method can throw a java.lang.Interrupted Exception, so a method calling join will not compile unless it catches this exception or declares that it might be thrown. In many kinds of concurrent programming, it is bad style or even incorrect to ignore this exception, but for basic parallel programming like we are doing, this exception is a nuisance and will not occur. So we will say no more about it. Also, the ForkJoin framework we will use starting in Section 7.3.4 has a different join method that does not throw exceptions.

Here, then, is a complete and correct program.[3] There is no change to the SumThread class. This example shows many of the key concepts of fork-join parallelism, but Section 7.3.2 will explain why it is poor style and can lead to suboptimal performance. Sections 7.3.3 and 7.3.4 will then present a similar but better approach.

```
    class SumThread extends java.lang.Thread {
        int lo; // fields for communicating inputs
        int hi;
        int[] arr;
        int ans = 0; // for communicating result
        SumThread(int[] a, int l, int h) {
            lo=l; hi=h; arr=a;
        }
        public void run() { // overriding, must have this type
            for(int i=lo; i<hi; i++)
                ans += arr[i];
        }
    }
```

---

[3] Technically, for very large arrays, i*len might be too large, and we should declare one of these variables to have type long. We will ignore this detail throughout this chapter to avoid distractions, but long is a wiser choice when dealing with arrays that may be very large.

```
class C {
  static int sum(int[] arr)
       throws java.lang.InterruptedException {
    int len = arr.length;
    int ans = 0;
    SumThread[] ts = new SumThread[4];
    for(int i=0; i < 4; i++) {
      ts[i] = new SumThread(arr,(i*len)/4,((i+1)*len)/4);
      ts[i].start();
    }
    for(int i=0; i < 4; i++) {
      ts[i].join();
      ans += ts[i].ans;
    }
    return ans;
  }
}
```

7.3.2 WHY NOT USE ONE THREAD PER PROCESSOR?

Having now presented a basic parallel algorithm, we will argue that the approach the algorithm takes is poor style and likely to lead to unnecessary inefficiency. Do not despair: the concepts we have learned such as creating threads and using join will remain useful—and it was best to explain them using a too-simple approach. Moreover, many parallel programs have been written in this style, often because libraries such as those in Section 7.3.4 have not always been available. Fortunately, such libraries are now available on many platforms.

The problem with the previous approach was dividing the work into exactly four pieces. This approach assumes there are four processors available to do the work (no other code needs them) and that each processor is given approximately the same amount of work. Sometimes these assumptions may hold, but it would be better to use algorithms that do not rely on such brittle assumptions. The rest of this section explains in more detail why these assumptions are unlikely to hold and some partial solutions. Section 7.3.3 then describes the better solution that we advocate.

Different computers have different numbers of processors

We want parallel programs that effectively use the processors available to them. Using exactly four threads is a horrible approach. If eight processors are available, half of them will sit idle, and our program will be no faster than with four processors. If three processors are available, our four-thread program will take approximately twice as long as with four processors. If three processors are available and we rewrite our program to use three threads, then we will use resources effectively, and the result will be only about 33% slower than when we had four processors and four threads. (We will take one-third as much time as the sequential version compared with one-quarter as much time. And one-third corresponds to 33% slower than

one-quarter.) But we do not want to have to edit our code every time we run it on
a computer with a different number of processors.

A natural solution is a core software-engineering principle you should already
know: do not use constants where a variable is appropriate. Our sum method can take
as a parameter the number of threads to use, leaving it to some other part of the
program to decide the number. (There are Java library methods to ask for the number
of processors on the computer, for example, but we argue next that using that number
is often unwise.) It would look like this:

```
static int sum(int[] arr, int numThreads)
    throws java.lang.InterruptedException {
  int len = arr.length;
  int ans = 0;
  SumThread[] ts = new SumThread[numThreads];
  for(int i=0; i < numThreads; i++) {
    ts[i] = new SumThread(arr,(i*len)/numThreads,
                          ((i+1)*len)/numThreads);
    ts[i].start();
  }
  for(int i=0; i < numThreads; i++) {
    ts[i].join();
    ans += ts[i].ans;
  }
  return ans;
}
```

Note that you need to be careful with integer division not to introduce rounding errors
when dividing the work.

The processors available to part of the code can change

The second dubious assumption made so far is that every processor is available
to the code we are writing. But some processors may be needed by other programs
or even other parts of the same program. We have parallelism after all—maybe the
caller to sum is already part of some outer parallel algorithm. The operating system
can reassign processors at any time, even when we are in the middle of summing
array elements. It is fine to assume that the underlying Java implementation will try
to use the available processors effectively, but we should not assume four or even
numThreads processors will be available from the beginning to the end of running
our parallel algorithm.

We cannot always predictably divide the work into approximately equal pieces

In our sum example, it is quite likely that the threads processing equal-size chunks
of the array take approximately the same amount of time. They may not, due to
memory-hierarchy issues or other architectural effects, however. Moreover, more
sophisticated algorithms could produce a large *load imbalance*, meaning different

helper threads are given different amounts of work. As a simple example (perhaps too simple for it to actually matter), suppose we have a large `int[]` and we want to know how many elements of the array are prime numbers. If one portion of the array has more large prime numbers than another, then one helper thread may take longer.

In short, giving each helper thread an equal number of data elements is not necessarily the same as giving each helper thread an equal amount of work. And any load imbalance hurts our efficiency since we need to wait until all threads have finished.

A solution: Divide the work into smaller pieces

We outlined three problems above. It turns out we can solve all three with a perhaps counterintuitive strategy: *use substantially more threads than there are processors.* For example, suppose to sum the elements of an array we created one thread for each 1000 elements. Assuming a large enough array (size greater than 1000 times the number of processors), the threads will not all run at once since a processor can run at most one thread at a time. But this is fine: the system will keep track of what threads are waiting and keep all the processors busy. There is some overhead to creating more threads, so we should use a system where this overhead is small.

This approach clearly fixes the first problem: any number of processors will stay busy until the very end when there are fewer 1000-element chunks remaining than there are processors. It also fixes the second problem since we just have a "big pile" of threads waiting to run. If the number of processors available changes, that affects only how fast the pile is processed, but we are always doing useful work with the resources available. Lastly, this approach helps with the load imbalance problem: smaller chunks of work make load imbalance far less likely since the threads do not run as long. Also, if one processor has a slow chunk, other processors can continue processing faster chunks.

We can go back to our cutting-potatoes analogy to understand this approach: Rather than give each of four cooks (processors) a quarter of the potatoes, we have them each take a moderate number of potatoes, slice them, and then return to take another moderate number. Since some potatoes may take longer to cut than others (they might be dirtier or have more eyes), this approach is better balanced and is probably worth the cost of the few extra trips to the pile of potatoes—especially if one of the cooks might take a break (processor used for a different program) before finishing his/her pile.

Unfortunately, this approach still has two problems addressed in Sections 7.3.3 and 7.3.4:

1. We now have more results to combine. Dividing the array into four total pieces leaves $\Theta(1)$ results to be combined. Dividing the array into 1000-element chunks leaves `arr.length`/1000, which is $\Theta(n)$, results to be combined.

Combining the results with a sequential for loop produces an $\Theta(n)$ algorithm, albeit with a smaller constant factor. To see the problem even more clearly, suppose we go to the extreme and use one-element chunks—now the results combining reimplements the original sequential algorithm. In short, we need a better way to combine results.

2. Java's threads were not designed for small tasks such as adding 1000 numbers. They will work and produce the correct answer, but the constant-factor overheads of creating a Java thread are far too large. A Java program that creates 100,000 threads on a small desktop computer is unlikely to run well at all—each thread just takes too much memory, and the scheduler is overburdened and provides no asymptotic run-time guarantee. In short, we need a different implementation of threads that is designed for this kind of fork-join programming.

7.3.3 DIVIDE-AND-CONQUER PARALLELISM

This section presents the idea of divide-and-conquer parallelism using Java's threads. Then Section 7.3.4 switches to using a library where this programming style is actually efficient. This progression shows that we can understand all the ideas using the basic notion of threads even though in practice we need a library that is designed for this kind of programming.

The key idea is to *change our algorithm* for summing the elements of an array to use recursive divide and conquer. To sum all the array elements in some range from lo to hi, do the following:

1. If the range contains only one element, return that element as the sum. Else in parallel
   a. recursively sum the elements from lo to the middle of the range;
   b. recursively sum the elements from the middle of the range to hi.
2. Add the two results from the previous step.

The essence of the recursion is that steps 1a and 1b will themselves use parallelism to divide the work of their halves in half again. It is the same divide-and-conquer recursive idea as you have seen in algorithms such as mergesort. For sequential algorithms for simple problems such as summing an array, such fanciness is overkill. But for parallel algorithms, it is ideal.

As a small example (too small to actually want to use parallelism), consider summing an array with 10 elements. The algorithm produces the following tree of recursion, where the range [i,j) includes i and excludes j:

```
Thread: sum range [0,10)
  Thread: sum range [0,5)
    Thread: sum range [0,2)
```

```
        Thread: sum range [0,1) (return arr[0])
        Thread: sum range [1,2) (return arr[1])
        add results from two helper threads
    Thread: sum range [2,5)
        Thread: sum range [2,3) (return arr[2])
        Thread: sum range [3,5)
            Thread: sum range [3,4) (return arr[3])
            Thread: sum range [4,5) (return arr[4])
            add results from two helper threads
        add results from two helper threads
    add results from two helper threads
Thread: sum range [5,10)
    Thread: sum range [5,7)
        Thread: sum range [5,6) (return arr[5])
        Thread: sum range [6,7) (return arr[6])
        add results from two helper threads
    Thread: sum range [7,10)
        Thread: sum range [7,8) (return arr[7])
        Thread: sum range [8,10)
            Thread: sum range [8,9) (return arr[8])
            Thread: sum range [9,10) (return arr[9])
            add results from two helper threads
        add results from two helper threads
    add results from two helper threads
add results from two helper threads
```

The total amount of work done by this algorithm is $O(n)$ because we create approximately $2n$ threads and each thread either returns an array element or adds together results from two helper threads it created. Much more interestingly, if we have $O(n)$ processors, then this algorithm can run in $O(\log n)$ time, which is exponentially faster than the sequential algorithm. The key reason for the improvement is that the algorithm is combining results in parallel. The recursion forms a binary tree for summing subranges, and the height of this tree is $\log n$ for a range of size n. See Figure 7.5, which shows the recursion in a more conventional tree form where the number of nodes is growing exponentially faster than the tree height. With enough processors, the total running time corresponds to the tree *height*, not the tree *size*: this is the fundamental running-time benefit of parallelism. Later sections will discuss why the problem of summing an array has such an efficient parallel algorithm; not every problem enjoys exponential improvement from parallelism.

Having described the algorithm in English, seen an example, and informally analyzed its running time, we now consider an actual implementation with Java threads and then modify it with two important improvements that affect only constant factors, but the constant factors are large. Then the next section will show the "final" version, where we use the improvements and use a different library for the threads.

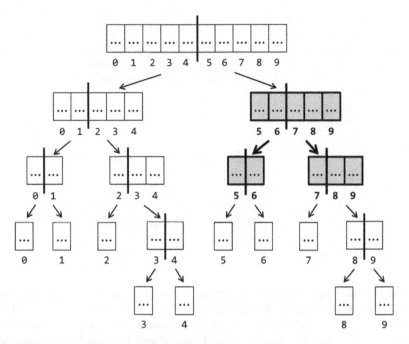

FIGURE 7.5

Recursion for summing an array where each node is a thread created by its parent. For example (see the shaded region), the thread responsible for summing the array elements from index 5 (inclusive) to index 10 (exclusive) creates two threads, one to sum the elements from index 5 to index 7 and the other to sum the elements from index 7 to index 10.

To start, here is the algorithm directly translated into Java, omitting some boilerplate such as putting the main sum method in a class and handling java.lang.InterruptedException.[4]

```
class SumThread extends java.lang.Thread {
    int lo; // fields for communicating inputs
    int hi;
    int[] arr;
    int ans = 0; // for communicating result
    SumThread(int[] a, int l, int h) { arr=a; lo=l; hi=h; }
    public void run() {
```

---

[4]For the exception, you cannot declare that run throws this exception because it overrides a method in java.lang.Thread that does not have this declaration. Since this exception is not going to be raised, it is reasonable to insert a catch statement and ignore this exception. The Java ForkJoin framework introduced in Section 7.3.4 does not have this problem; its join method does not throw checked exceptions.

```
    if(hi - lo == 1) {
      ans = arr[lo];
    } else {
      SumThread left  = new SumThread(arr,lo,(hi+lo)/2);
      SumThread right = new SumThread(arr,(hi+lo)/2,hi);
      left.start();
      right.start();
      left.join();
      right.join();
      ans = left.ans + right.ans;
    }
  }
}
int sum(int[] arr) {
  SumThread t = new SumThread(arr,0,arr.length);
  t.run();
  return t.ans;
}
```

Notice how each thread creates two helper threads left and right and then waits for them to finish. Crucially, the calls to left.start *and* right.start precede the calls to left.join *and* right.join. If, for example, left.join() came before right.start(), then the algorithm would have no effective parallelism whatsoever. It would still produce the correct answer, but so would the original, much simpler sequential program.

As a minor but important coding point, notice that the "main" sum method calls the run method directly. As such, this is an ordinary method call like you have used since you started programming; the caller and callee are part of the same thread. The fact that the object is a subclass of java.lang.Thread is relevant only if you call the "magic" start method, which calls run in a new thread.

In practice, code such as this produces far too many threads to be efficient. To add up four numbers, does it really make sense to create six new threads? Therefore, implementations of fork-join algorithms invariably use a *cutoff* below which they switch over to a sequential algorithm. Because this cutoff is a constant, it has no effect on the asymptotic behavior of the algorithm. What it does is eliminate the vast majority of the threads created, while still preserving enough parallelism to balance the load among the processors.

Here is code using a cutoff of 1000. As you can see, using a cutoff does not really complicate the code.

```
class SumThread extends java.lang.Thread {
  static int SEQUENTIAL_CUTOFF = 1000;
  int lo; // fields for communicating inputs
  int hi;
  int[] arr;
  int ans = 0; // for communicating result
  SumThread(int[] a, int l, int h) { arr=a; lo=l; hi=h; }
```

```
public void run(){
  if(hi - lo < SEQUENTIAL_CUTOFF) {
    for(int i=lo; i < hi; i++)
      ans += arr[i];
  } else {
    SumThread left = new SumThread(arr,lo,(hi+lo)/2);
    SumThread right= new SumThread(arr,(hi+lo)/2,hi);
    left.start();
    right.start();
    left.join();
    right.join();
    ans = left.ans + right.ans;
  }
}
}
int sum(int[] arr) {
  SumThread t = new SumThread(arr,0,arr.length);
  t.run();
  return t.ans;
}
```

Using cutoffs is common in divide-and-conquer programming, even for sequential algorithms. For example, it is typical for quicksort to be slower than an $O(n^2)$ sort such as insertion sort for small arrays ($n < 10$ or so). Therefore, it is common to have the recursive quicksort switch over to insertion sort for small subproblems. In parallel programming, switching over to a sequential algorithm below a cutoff is *the exact same idea*. In practice, the cutoffs are usually larger, with numbers between 500 and 5000 being typical.

It is often worth doing some quick calculations to understand the benefits of things such as cutoffs. Suppose we are summing an array with 2^{30} elements. Without a cutoff, we would use $2^{31} - 1$, (i.e., 2 billion) threads. With a cutoff of 1000, we would use approximately 2^{21} (i.e., 2 million) threads since the last 10 levels of the recursion would be eliminated. Computing $1 - 2^{21}/2^{31}$, we see we have eliminated 99.9% of the threads. Use cutoffs!

Our second improvement may seem anticlimactic compared with cutoffs because it reduces the number of threads by an additional factor of only 2. Nonetheless, it is worth seeing for efficiency especially because the ForkJoin framework in the next section performs poorly if you do not do this optimization "by hand." The key is to notice that all threads that create two helper threads are not doing much work themselves: they divide the work in half, give it to two helpers, wait for them to finish, and add the results. Rather than having all these threads wait around, we find it is more efficient to create *one helper thread* to do half the work and have the thread do the other half *itself*. Modifying our code to do this is easy since we can just call the run method directly, which recall is just an ordinary method call, unlike the "magic" start method.

```
class SumThread extends java.lang.Thread {
  static int SEQUENTIAL_CUTOFF = 1000;
  int lo; // fields for communicating inputs
  int hi;
  int[] arr;
  int ans = 0; // for communicating result
  SumThread(int[] a, int l, int h) { arr=a; lo=l; hi=h; }
  public void run(){
    if(hi - lo < SEQUENTIAL_CUTOFF) {
      for(int i=lo; i < hi; i++)
        ans += arr[i];
    } else {
      SumThread left = new SumThread(arr,lo,(hi+lo)/2);
      SumThread right= new SumThread(arr,(hi+lo)/2,hi);
      left.start();
      right.run();
      left.join();
      ans = left.ans + right.ans;
    }
  }
}
int sum(int[] arr) {
  SumThread t = new SumThread(arr,0,arr.length);
  t.run();
  return t.ans;
}
```

Notice how the code above creates two `SumThread` objects, but creates only one
helper thread with `left.start()`. It then does the right half of the work itself by
calling `right.run()`. There is only one call to `join` because only one helper thread
was created. The order here is still essential so that the two halves of the work are
done in parallel. Creating a `SumThread` object for the right half and then calling `run`
rather than creating a thread may seem odd, but it keeps the code from getting more
complicated and still conveys the idea of dividing the work into two similar parts that
are done in parallel.

Unfortunately, even with these optimizations, the code above will run poorly in
practice, especially if given a large array. The implementation of Java's threads is
not engineered for threads that do such a small amount of work as adding 1000
numbers: it takes much longer just to create, start running, and dispose of a thread.
The space overhead may also be prohibitive. In particular, it is not uncommon for a
Java implementation to preallocate the maximum amount of space it allows for the
call stack, which might be 2 MB or more. So creating thousands of threads could
use gigabytes of space. Hence, we will switch to the library described in the next
section for parallel programming. We will return to Java's threads when we learn
concurrency control in Chapter 8 because the synchronization operations we will use
work with Java's threads.

7.3.4 **THE JAVA FORKJOIN FRAMEWORK**

Java 7 includes classes in the `java.util.concurrent` package designed exactly for the kind of fine-grained fork-join parallel computing this chapter uses. In addition to supporting lightweight threads (which the library calls ForkJoin tasks) that are small enough that even 1 million of them should not overwhelm the system, the implementation includes a scheduler and run-time system with provably optimal expected-time guarantees, as described in Section 7.4. Similar libraries for other languages include Intel's Thread Building Blocks and Microsoft's Task Parallel Library for C#. The core ideas and implementation techniques go back much further to the Cilk language, an extension of C developed since 1994.

This section describes just a few practical details and library specifics. Compared with Java threads, the core ideas are all the same, but some of the method names and interfaces are different—in places more complicated and in others simpler. Naturally, we give a full example (actually two) for summing an array of numbers. The actual library contains many other useful features and classes, but we will use only the primitives related to forking and joining, implementing anything else we need ourselves.

For introductory notes on using the library and avoiding some difficult-to-diagnose pitfalls, see http://homes.cs.washington.edu/~djg/teachingMaterials/spac/grossmanSPAC_forkJoinFramework.html.

We first show a full program (minus a `main` method) that is as much as possible like the version we wrote using Java threads. We show a version using a sequential cutoff and only one helper thread at each recursive subdivision, though removing these important improvements would be easy. After discussing this version, we show a second version that uses Java's generic types and a different library class. This second version is better style, but is easier to understand after the first version. First version (inferior style):

```java
import java.util.concurrent.ForkJoinPool;
import java.util.concurrent.RecursiveAction;

class SumArray extends RecursiveAction {
    static int SEQUENTIAL_THRESHOLD = 1000;

    int lo;
    int hi;
    int[] arr;
    int ans = 0;
    SumArray(int[] a, int l, int h) { lo=l; hi=h; arr=a; }

    protected void compute() {
        if(hi - lo <= SEQUENTIAL_THRESHOLD) {
            for(int i=lo; i < hi; ++i)
                ans += arr[i];
        } else {
```

```
            SumArray left  = new SumArray(arr,lo,(hi+lo)/2);
            SumArray right = new SumArray(arr,(hi+lo)/2,hi);
            left.fork();
            right.compute();
            left.join();
            ans = left.ans + right.ans;
        }
    }
}
class Main {
    static final ForkJoinPool fjPool = new ForkJoinPool();
    static int sumArray(int[] array) {
        SumArray t = new SumArray(array,0,array.length);
        fjPool.invoke(t);
        return t.ans;
    }
}
```

While there are many differences compared with using Java's threads, the overall structure of the algorithm should look similar. Furthermore, most of the changes are just different names for classes and methods:

- Subclass `java.util.concurrent.RecursiveAction` instead of `java.lang.Thread`.
- The method that "magically" creates parallelism is called `fork` instead of `start`.
- The method that starts executing when a new thread begins is called `compute` instead of `run`. Recall these methods can also be called normally.
- (The method `join` is still called `join`.)

The small additions involve creating a `ForkJoinPool` and using the `invoke` method on it. These are just some details because the library is not built into the Java *language*, so we have to do a little extra to initialize the library and start using it. Here is all you really need to know:

- The entire program should have exactly one `ForkJoinPool`, so it makes sense to store it in a static field and use it for all the parallel algorithms in your program.
- Inside a subclass of `RecursiveAction`, you use `fork`, `compute`, and `join` just like we previously used `start`, `run`, and `join`. But outside such classes, you cannot use these methods, because if you use them, then the library will not work correctly. To "get the parallelism started," you instead use the `invoke` method of the `ForkJoinPool`. You pass to `invoke` a subclass of `RecursiveAction`, and that object's `compute` method will be called. Basically, use `invoke` once to start the algorithm and then `fork` or `compute` for the recursive calls. Conversely, do *not* use `invoke` from "inside" the library—that is, in `compute` or any helper methods it uses.

We will present one final version of our array-summing program to demonstrate one more class of the ForkJoin framework that you should use as a matter of style.

The RecursiveAction class is best only when the subcomputations do not produce a result, whereas in our example they do: the sum of the range. It is quite common not to produce a result—for example, a parallel program that increments every element of an array. So far, the way we have "returned" results is via a field, which we called ans.

Instead, we can subclass RecursiveTask instead of RecursiveAction. However, RecursiveTask is a generic class with one type parameter: the type of value that compute should return. Here is the full version of the code using this more convenient and less error-prone class, followed by an explanation:

Final, better version:

```
import java.util.concurrent.ForkJoinPool;
import java.util.concurrent.RecursiveTask;

class SumArray extends RecursiveTask<Integer> {
    static int SEQUENTIAL_THRESHOLD = 1000;

    int lo;
    int hi;
    int[] arr;
    SumArray(int[] a, int l, int h) { lo=l; hi=h; arr=a; }

    public Integer compute() {
        if(hi - lo <= SEQUENTIAL_THRESHOLD) {
            int ans = 0;
            for(int i=lo; i < hi; ++i)
                ans += arr[i];
            return ans;
        } else {
            SumArray left  = new SumArray(arr,lo,(hi+lo)/2);
            SumArray right = new SumArray(arr,(hi+lo)/2,hi);
            left.fork();
            int rightAns = right.compute();
            int leftAns = left.join();
            return leftAns + rightAns;
        }
    }
}
class Main {
    static final ForkJoinPool fjPool = new ForkJoinPool();
    static int sumArray(int[] array) {
        return fjPool.invoke(new SumArray(array,0,array.length));
    }
}
```

Here are the differences from the version that subclasses `RecursiveAction`:

- `compute` returns an object of whatever (object) type we want. Because `int` is not an object type, we write `Integer` instead. Java implicitly converts an `int` to/from an `Integer` in all the places it is needed in this program.
- The `join` method also returns the value returned by `compute` in the thread that is being joined to. Therefore, we do not need an `ans` field: we write `int leftAns = left.join()` to get the value that the thread bound to `left` returned from its `compute` method.
- The `invoke` method works similarly when passed a subclass of a `RecursiveTask` class: It returns the value of the `compute` method that is called.
- The class declaration of `SumArray` indicates that it extends `RecursiveTask<Integer>`. More generally, always put the same type between the angle brackets as the return type of `compute`.
- Because Java expressions are always evaluated from left to right, we could replace the last three lines of the `else` branch in `compute` with just `return right.compute() + left.join();`. But this is rather subtle—`left.join() + right.compute()` would destroy the parallelism—so we do not advise writing this shorter but less clear code.

If you are familiar with Java's generic types, this use of them should not be particularly perplexing. The library is also using static overloading for the `invoke` method. But as *users* of the library, it suffices just to follow the pattern in the example above.

Why is there `RecursiveAction` and `RecursiveTask`? The former is better style when there really is nothing to return; otherwise `RecursiveTask` is better. Both are actually implemented in terms of the same superclass inside the library. You can use that class directly, but it is less convenient.

Given the convenience of not needing a field for returning values, why not also provide the convenience of not needing fields to pass arguments (`arr`, `lo`, and `hi`)? That *would* be nice, but there just is not a particularly pleasant way to write such a library in Java. The ForkJoin framework is just a library; it cannot make any changes/extensions to the Java language. It uses some advanced Java features to be as convenient as it can be.

7.3.5 REDUCTIONS AND MAPS

It may seem that given all the work we did to implement something as conceptually simple as summing an array that fork-join programming is too complicated. To the contrary, many, many problems can be solved very much like we solved this one. Just as regular `for` loops took some getting used to when you started programming but now you can recognize exactly what kind of loop you need for all sorts of problems, divide-and-conquer parallelism often follows a small number of patterns. Once you know the patterns, most of your programs are largely the same.

For example, here are several problems for which efficient parallel algorithms look almost identical to summing an array:

- Count how many array elements satisfy some property (e.g., how many elements are the number 42).
- Find the maximum or minimum element of an array.
- Given an array of strings, compute the sum (or max, or min) of all their lengths.
- Find the leftmost array index that has an element satisfying some property.

Compared with summing an array, all that changes is the base case for the recursion and how we combine results. For example, to find the index of the leftmost 42 in an array of length n, we can do the following (where a final result of n means the array does not hold a 42):

- For the base case, return `lo` if `arr[lo]` holds 42 and `n` otherwise.
- To combine results, return the smaller number.

Implement one or two of these problems to convince yourself they are not any harder than what we have already done. Or come up with additional problems that can be solved the same way.

Problems that have this form are so common that there is a name for them: *reductions*, which you can remember by realizing that we take a collection of data items (in an array) and *reduce* the information down to a single result. As we have seen, the way reductions can work in parallel is to compute answers for the two halves recursively and in parallel and then merge these to produce a result.

However, we should be clear that *not every problem over an array of data can be solved with a simple parallel reduction*. To avoid getting into arcane problems, let us just describe a general situation. Suppose you have sequential code like the following:

```
interface BinaryOperation<T> {
    T m(T x, T y);
}
class C<T> {
    T fold(T[] arr, BinaryOperation<T> binop, T initialValue) {
        T ans = initialValue;
        for(int i=0; i < arr.length; ++i)
            ans = binop.m(ans,arr[i]);
        return ans;
    }
}
```

The name `fold` is conventional for this sort of algorithm. The idea is to start with `initialValue` and keep updating the "answer so far" by applying some binary function `m` to the current answer and the next element of the array.

Without any additional information about what `m` computes, this algorithm cannot be effectively parallelized since we cannot process `arr[i]` until we know the answer from the first `i-1` iterations of the `for` loop. A more humorous example of a procedure that cannot be sped up given additional resources is 9 women cannot make a baby in 1 month.

So what do we have to know about the BinaryOperation above in order to use a parallel reduction? All we need is that the operation is *associative*, meaning for all a, b, and c, $m(a, m(b, c))$ is the same as $m(m(a, b), c)$. Our array-summing algorithm is correct because $a + (b + c) = (a + b) + c$. Our find-the-leftmost-index-holding 42 algorithm is correct because *min* is also an associative operator.

Because reductions using associative operators are so common, we could write one generic algorithm that took the operator, and what to do for a base case, as arguments. This is an example of higher-order programming, and the fork-join framework has several classes providing this sort of functionality. Higher-order programming has many, many advantages (see the end of this section for a popular one), but when first *learning* a programming pattern, it is often useful to "code it up yourself" a few times. For that reason, we encourage writing your parallel reductions manually in order to see the parallel divide and conquer, even though they all really look the same.

Parallel reductions are not the only common pattern in parallel programming. An even simpler one, which we did not start with because it is just so easy, is a parallel *map*. A map performs an operation on each input element independently; given an array of inputs, it produces an array of outputs of the same length. A simple example is multiplying every element of an array by 2. An example using two inputs and producing a separate output is vector addition. Using pseudocode, we could write

```
int[] add(int[] arr1, int[] arr2) {
  assert(arr1.length == arr2.length);
  int[] ans = new int[arr1.length];
  FORALL(int i=0; i < arr1.length; i++)
    ans[i] = arr1[i] + arr2[i];
  return ans;
}
```

Coding up this algorithm in the ForkJoin framework is straightforward: Have the main thread create the ans array and pass it before starting the parallel divide and conquer. Each thread object will have a reference to this array but will write to different portions of it. Because there are no other results to be combined, subclassing RecursiveAction is appropriate. Using a sequential cutoff and creating only one new thread for each recursive subdivision of the problem remain important—these ideas are more general than the particular programming pattern of a map or a reduce.

Recognizing problems that are fundamentally maps and/or reduces over large data collections is a valuable skill that allows efficient parallelization. In fact, it is one of the key ideas behind Google's MapReduce framework and the open-source variant Hadoop. In these systems, the programmer just writes the operations that describe how to map data (e.g., "multiply by 2") and reduce data (e.g., "take the minimum"). The system then does all the parallelization, often using hundreds or thousands of computers to process gigabytes or terabytes of data. For this to work, the programmer must provide operations that have no side effects (since the order in which they occur is unspecified) and reduce operations that are associative (as we discussed). As parallel programmers, it is often enough for us to "write down the maps and reduces"—leaving it to systems such as the ForkJoin framework or Hadoop to do the actual scheduling of the parallelism.

7.3.6 DATA STRUCTURES BESIDES ARRAYS

So far we have considered only algorithms over one-dimensional arrays. Naturally, one can write parallel algorithms over any data structure, but divide-and-conquer parallelism requires that we can efficiently (ideally in $O(1)$ time) divide the problem into smaller pieces. For arrays, dividing the problem involves only $O(1)$ arithmetic on indices, so this works well.

While arrays are the most common data structure in parallel programming, balanced trees, such as AVL trees or B trees, also support parallel algorithms well. For example, with a binary tree, we can use a fork operation to process the left child and right child of each node in parallel. For good sequential cutoffs, it helps to have stored at each tree node the number of descendants of the node, something easy to maintain. However, for trees with guaranteed balance properties, other information—such as the height of an AVL tree node—should suffice.

Certain tree problems will not run faster with parallelism. For example, searching for an element in a balanced binary search tree takes $O(\log n)$ time with or without parallelism. However, maps and reduces over balanced trees benefit from parallelism. For example, summing the elements of a binary tree takes $O(n)$ time sequentially, where n is the number of elements, but with a sufficiently large number of processors, the time is $O(h)$, where h is the height of the tree. Hence, tree balance is even more important with parallel programming: for a balanced tree $h = \Theta(\log n)$ compared with the worst case $h = \Theta(n)$.

For the same reason, parallel algorithms over regular linked lists are typically poor. Any problem that requires reading all n elements of a linked list takes time $\Omega(n)$ regardless of how many processors are available. (Fancier list data structures such as skip lists are better for exactly this reason—you can get to all the data in $O(\log n)$ time.) Streams of input data, such as from files, typically have the same limitation: it takes linear time to read the input, and this can be the bottleneck for the algorithm.

There can still be benefit to parallelism with such "inherently sequential" data structures and input streams. Suppose we had a map operation over a list but each operation was itself an expensive computation (e.g., decrypting a significant piece of data). If each map operation took time $O(x)$ and the list had length n, doing each operation in a separate thread (assuming, again, no limit on the number of processors) would produce an $O(x+n)$ algorithm compared with the sequential $O(xn)$ algorithm. But for simple operations such as summing or finding a maximum element, there would be no benefit.

7.4 ANALYZING FORK-JOIN ALGORITHMS

As with any algorithm, a fork-join parallel algorithm should be correct and efficient. This section focuses on the latter, even though the former should always be one's first concern. For efficiency, we will focus on asymptotic bounds and analyzing algorithms that are not written in terms of a fixed number of processors. That is, just as the size of the problem n will factor into the asymptotic running time, so will the number of processors P. The ForkJoin framework (and similar libraries in other languages) will give us an optimal expected-time bound for any P. This section explains what that bound is and what it means, but we will not discuss *how* the framework achieves it.

We then turn to discussing Amdahl's law, which analyzes the running time of algorithms that have both sequential parts and parallel parts. The key and depressing upshot is that programs with even a small sequential part quickly stop getting much benefit from running with more processors.

Finally, we discuss Moore's "law" in contrast to Amdahl's law. While Moore's law is also important for understanding the progress of computing power, it is not a mathematical theorem like Amdahl's law.

7.4.1 WORK AND SPAN

Defining work and span

We define T_P to be the time a program/algorithm takes to run if there are P processors available during its execution. For example, if a program was the only one running on a quad-core machine, we would be particularly interested in T_4, but we want to think about T_P more generally. We will reason about the general T_P in terms of T_1 and T_∞:

- T_1 is called the *work*. By definition, this is how long it takes the algorithm to run on one processor. More intuitively, it is just the total of all the running time of all the pieces of the algorithm: we have to do all the work before we are finished, and there is exactly one processor (no parallelism) to do it. In terms of fork-join, we can think of T_1 as doing one side of the fork and then the other, though the total T_1 does not depend on how the work is scheduled.
- T_∞ is called the *span*, though other common terms are the *critical path length* and *computational depth*. By definition, this is how long it takes the algorithm to run on an unlimited number of processors. Notice this is *not* necessarily $O(1)$ time; the algorithm still needs to do the forking and combining of results. For example, under our model of computation—where creating a new thread and

adding two numbers are both $O(1)$ operations—the algorithm we developed is asymptotically optimal with $T_\infty = \Theta(\log n)$ for an array of length n.

We need a more precise way of characterizing the execution of a parallel program so that we can describe and compute the work, T_1, and the span, T_∞. We will describe a program execution as a DAG,[5] where we have the following:

- Nodes are pieces of work the program performs. Each node will be a constant—that is, $O(1)$—amount of work that is performed sequentially. So T_1 is asymptotically just the number of nodes in the DAG.
- Edges represent that the source node must finish before the target node begins—that is, there is a *computational dependency* along the edge. This idea lets us visualize T_∞: with unlimited processors, we would immediately start every node as soon as its predecessors in the graph had finished. Therefore, T_∞ is just the length of the longest path in the DAG.

Figure 7.6 shows an example DAG and the longest path, which determines T_∞.

If you have studied combinational hardware circuits, this model is strikingly similar to the DAGs that arise in that setting. For circuits, *work* is typically called the *size* of the circuit, (i.e., the amount of hardware), and *span* is typically called the *depth* of the circuit, (i.e., the time, in units of "gate delay," to produce an answer).

With basic fork-join divide-and-conquer parallelism, the execution DAGs are quite simple: The $O(1)$ work to set up two smaller subproblems is one node in the DAG. This node has two outgoing edges to two new nodes that start doing the two subproblems. (The fact that one subproblem might be done by the same thread

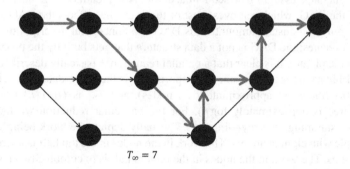

$T_\infty = 7$

FIGURE 7.6

An example DAG and the path (see the thicker arrows) that determines its span.

---

[5]A directed acyclic graph (DAG; the word "graph" here is the name for a data structure and does not mean a chart for presenting data) is a set of nodes and edges between pairs of nodes where each edge has a direction (a *source* that it starts from and a *target* that it ends at). Furthermore, the graph is acyclic, which means you cannot start at any node, follow edges from the source to the target, and get back to the starting node.

is not relevant here. Nodes are not threads: they are $O(1)$ pieces of work.) The two subproblems will lead to their own DAGs. When we join on the results of the subproblems, that creates a node with incoming edges from the last nodes for the subproblems. This same node can do an $O(1)$ amount of work to combine the results. (If combining results is more expensive, then it needs to be represented by more nodes.)

Overall, then, the DAG for a basic parallel reduction would look like this:

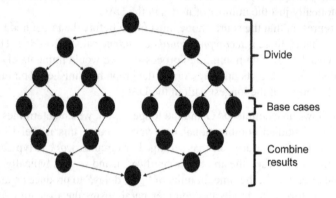

The root node represents the computation that divides the array into two equal halves. The bottom node represents the computation that adds together the two sums from the halves to produce the final answer. The base cases represent reading from a one-element range assuming no sequential cutoff. A sequential cutoff "just" trims out levels of the DAG, which removes most of the nodes but affects the DAG's longest path by "only" a constant amount. This DAG is a conceptual description of how a program executes; the DAG is not a data structure that gets built by the program.

From the picture, it is clear that a parallel reduction is basically described by two balanced binary trees whose size is proportional to the input data size. Therefore T_1 is $O(n)$ (there are approximately $2n$ nodes), and T_∞ is $O(\log n)$ (the height of each tree is approximately $\log n$). For the particular reduction we have been studying—summing an array—Figure 7.7 visually depicts the work being done for an example with eight elements. The work in the nodes in the top half is to create two subproblems. The work in the nodes in the bottom half is to combine two results.

The DAG model of parallel computation is much more general than for simple fork-join algorithms. It describes all the work that is done and the earliest that any piece of that work could begin. To repeat, T_1 and T_∞ become simple graph properties: the number of nodes and the length of the longest path, respectively.

Defining speedup and parallelism

Having defined work and span, we can use them to define some other terms more relevant to our real goal of reasoning about T_P. After all, if we had only one processor, then we would not study parallelism, and having infinite processors is impossible.

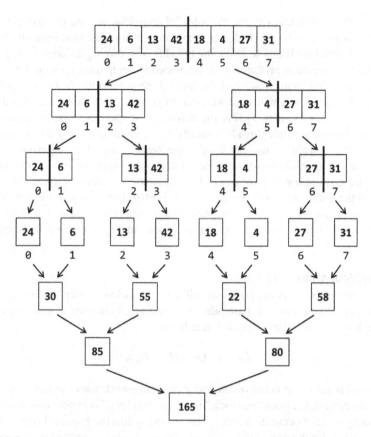

FIGURE 7.7

Example execution DAG for summing an array.

We define the *speedup* on P processors to be T_1/T_P. It is basically the ratio of how much faster the program runs given the extra processors. For example, if T_1 is 20 s and T_4 is 8 s, then the speedup for $P = 4$ is 2.5.

You might naively expect a speedup of 4, or more generally P for T_P. In practice, such a *perfect speedup* is rare because of several issues including the overhead of creating threads and communicating answers among them, memory-hierarchy issues, and the inherent computational dependencies related to the span. In the rare case that doubling P cuts the running time in half (i.e., doubles the speedup), we call it *perfect linear speedup*. In practice, this is not the absolute limit; one can find situations where the speedup is even higher even though our simple computational model does not capture the features that could cause this.

It is important to note that reporting only T_1/T_P can be "dishonest" in the sense that it often overstates the advantages of using multiple processors. The reason is that T_1 is the time it takes to run the *parallel algorithm* on one processor, but this algorithm is likely to be much slower than an algorithm designed sequentially. For example, if someone wants to know the benefits of summing an array with parallel fork-join, that person is probably most interested in comparing T_P with the time for the sequential for loop. If we call the latter S, then the ratio S/T_P is usually the speedup of interest and will be lower, due to constant factors such as the time to create recursive tasks, than T_1/T_P, the definition of speedup. One measure of the overhead of using multiple threads is simply T_1/S, which is usually greater than 1.

As a final definition, we call T_1/T_∞ the *parallelism* of an algorithm. It is a measure of how much improvement one could possibly hope for since it should be at least as great as the speedup for any P. For our parallel reductions where the work is $\Theta(n)$ and the span is $\Theta(\log n)$, the parallelism is $\Theta(n/\log n)$. In other words, there is exponential available parallelism (n grows exponentially faster than $\log n$), meaning with enough processors we can hope for an exponential speedup over the sequential version.

The ForkJoin framework bound

Under some important assumptions we will describe below, algorithms written using the ForkJoin framework, in particular the divide-and-conquer algorithms in this chapter, have the following *expected* time bound:

$$T_P \quad \text{is} \quad O(T_1/P + T_\infty).$$

The bound is *expected* because internally the framework uses randomness, so the bound can be violated from "bad luck," but such "bad luck" is exponentially unlikely, so it simply will not occur in practice. This is exactly like the expected-time running-time guarantee for the sequential quicksort algorithm when a pivot element is chosen randomly. Because this chapter does not describe the framework's implementation, we will not see where the randomness arises.

Notice that, if we disregard constant factors, this bound is optimal: given only P processors, no framework can expect to do better than T_1/P or better than T_∞. For small P, the term T_1/P is likely to be dominant, and we can expect roughly linear speedup. As P grows, the span becomes more relevant, and the limit on the run-time is more influenced by T_∞.

Constant factors can be relevant, and it is entirely possible that a hand-crafted parallel algorithm in terms of some fixed P could do better than a generic library that has no idea what sort of parallel algorithm it is running. But just like we often use asymptotically optimal data structures even if hand-crafted ones for our task might be a little faster, using a library such as this is often an excellent approach.

Thinking in terms of the program-execution DAG, we find it rather amazing that a library can achieve this optimal result. While the program is running, it is the framework's job to choose among all the threads that *could* run next (they are not blocked waiting for some other thread to finish) and assign P of them to processors. For simple parallel reductions, the choice hardly matters because all paths to the bottom of the DAG are about the same length, but for arbitrary DAGs it seems important to work on the longer paths. Yet a much greedier algorithm that just picks randomly among the available threads will do only a constant factor worse. But this is all about the library's internal scheduling algorithm (which is not actually totally random) and we, as library users, can just rely on the bound provided.

However, as mentioned above, the bound holds only under a couple of assumptions. The first is that all the threads you create to do subproblems do approximately the same amount of work. Otherwise, if a thread with much more work to do is scheduled very late, other processors will sit idle waiting for this laggard to finish. The second is that all the threads do a small but not tiny amount of work. This again helps with load balancing. The documentation for the library suggests aiming for approximately 5000 basic computational steps (additions, method calls, etc.) and that the exact figure can be off by a factor of 10 or so without problem. In other words, just avoid threads that do millions of operations as well as threads that do dozens.

To summarize, as a user of a library like this, your job is to pick a good parallel algorithm, implement it in terms of divide and conquer with a reasonable sequential cutoff, and analyze the expected run-time in terms of the bound provided. The library's job is to give this bound while trying to maintain low constant-factor overheads. While this library is particularly good for *this* style of programming, this basic division is common: application writers develop good algorithms and rely on some underlying *thread scheduler* to deliver reasonable performance.

7.4.2 AMDAHL'S LAW

So far we have analyzed the running time of a parallel algorithm. While a parallel algorithm could have some "sequential parts" (a part of the DAG where there is a long linear sequence of nodes), it is common to think of an execution in terms of some entirely parallel parts (e.g., maps and reductions) and some entirely sequential parts. The sequential parts could simply be algorithms that have not been parallelized, or they could be inherently sequential, such as reading in input. As this section shows, even a little bit of sequential work in your program drastically reduces the speedup once you have a significant number of processors.

This result is really a matter of very basic algebra. It is named after Gene Amdahl, who first articulated it. Though almost all computer scientists learn it and understand it, it is all too common to forget its implications. It is, perhaps, counterintuitive that just a little nonparallelism has such a drastic limiting effect on speedup. But it is a fact, so learn and remember Amdahl's law!

With that introduction, here is the full derivation of Amdahl's law: Suppose the work T_1 is 1—that is, the total program execution time on one processor is 1 "unit time." Let S be the portion of the execution that cannot be parallelized, and assume the rest of the execution $(1 - S)$ gets perfect linear speedup on P processors for any P. Notice this is a charitable assumption about the parallel part equivalent to assuming the span is $O(1)$. Then,

$$T_1 = S + (1 - S) = 1,$$
$$T_P = S + (1 - S)/P.$$

Notice all we have assumed is that the parallel portion $(1 - S)$ runs in time $(1 - S)/P$. Then, the speedup, by definition, is

$$T_1/T_P = 1/(S + (1 - S)/P),$$

which is Amdahl's law. As a corollary, the parallelism is just the simplified equation as P goes to ∞:

$$T_1/T_\infty = 1/S.$$

The equations may look innocuous until you start plugging in values. For example, if 33% of a program is sequential, then 1 billion processors can achieve a speedup of at most 3. That is just common sense: they cannot speed up one-third of the program, so even if the rest of the program runs "instantly," the speedup is only 3.

The "problem" is when we expect to get twice the performance from twice the computational resources. If those extra resources are processors, this works only if most of the execution time is spent running parallel computations. Adding a second or third processor can often provide significant speedup, but as the number of processors grows, the benefit quickly diminishes.

Recall that from 1980 to 2005 the processing speed of desktop computers doubled approximately every 18 months. Therefore, 12 years or so was long enough to buy a new computer and have it run an old program 100 times faster. Now suppose that instead in 12 years we have 256 processors rather than one processor but all the processors have the same speed. What percentage of a program would have to be perfectly parallelizable in order to get a speedup of 100? Perhaps a speedup of 100 given 256 cores seems easy? Plugging the data into Amdahl's law, we find need

$$100 \leq 1/(S + (1 - S)/256).$$

Solving for S reveals that at most 0.61% of the program can be sequential.

Given depressing results such as these—and there are many (hopefully you will draw some possible-speedup plots as homework exercises)—it is tempting to give up on parallelism as a means to performance improvement. While you should never forget Amdahl's law, you should also not entirely despair. Parallelism does provide real speedup for performance-critical parts of programs. You just do not get to speed up *all* of your code by buying a faster computer. More specifically, there are two common work-arounds to the fact of life that is Amdahl's law:

1. We can find new parallel algorithms. Given enough processors, it is worth parallelizing something (reducing span) even if it means more total computation (increasing work). Amdahl's law says that as the number of processors grows, span is more important than work. This is often described as "scalability matters more than performance," where "scalability" means additional processors

improves execution time and "performance" means run-time on a small number of processors. In short, large amounts of parallelism can change your algorithmic choices.

2. We can use the parallelism to solve new or bigger problems rather than solving the same problem faster. For example, suppose the parallel part of a program is $O(n^2)$ and the sequential part is $O(n)$. As we increase the number of processors, we can increase n with only a small increase in the running time. One area where parallelism is very successful is computer graphics (animated movies, video games, etc.). Compared with years ago, it is not so much that computers are rendering the same scenes faster; it is that they are rendering more impressive scenes with more pixels and more accurate images. In short, parallelism can enable new things (provided those things are parallelizable of course) even if the old things are limited by Amdahl's law.

7.4.3 COMPARING AMDAHL'S LAW AND MOORE'S LAW

There is another "law" relevant to computing speed and the number of processors available on a chip. Moore's law, named after its inventor, Gordon Moore, states that the number of transistors per unit area on a chip doubles roughly every 18 months. That increased transistor density used to lead to faster processors; now it is leading to more processors.

Moore's law is an observation about the semiconductor industry that has held for decades. The fact that it has held for so long is entirely about empirical evidence—people look at the chips that are sold and see that they obey this law. Actually, for many years it has been a self-fulfilling prophecy: chip manufacturers expect themselves to continue Moore's law, and they find a way to achieve technological innovation at this pace. There is no inherent mathematical theorem underlying it. Yet we expect the number of processors to increase exponentially for the foreseeable future.

On the other hand, Amdahl's law is an irrefutable fact of algebra.

7.5 FANCIER FORK-JOIN ALGORITHMS: PREFIX, PACK, SORT

This section presents a few more sophisticated parallel algorithms. The intention is to demonstrate (a) sometimes problems that seem inherently sequential turn out to have efficient parallel algorithms, (b) we can use parallel-algorithm techniques as building blocks for other larger parallel algorithms, and (c) we can use asymptotic complexity to help decide when one parallel algorithm is better than another. The study of parallel algorithms could take an entire course, so we will pick just a few examples that represent some of the many key parallel-programming patterns.

As is common when studying algorithms, we will not show full Java implementations. It should be clear at this point that one could code up the algorithms using the ForkJoin framework even if it may not be entirely easy to implement more sophisticated techniques.

7.5.1 PARALLEL PREFIX SUM

Consider this problem: given an array of n integers input, produce an array of n integers output, where output[i] is the sum of the first i elements of input. In other words, we are computing the sum of *every* prefix of the input array and returning all the results. This is called the *prefix-sum problem*.[6] Figure 7.8 shows an example input and output. A $\Theta(n)$ sequential solution is trivial:

```
int[] prefix_sum(int[] input) {
  int[] output = new int[input.length];
  output[0] = input[0];
  for(int i=1; i < input.length; i++)
    output[i] = output[i-1] + input[i];
  return output;
}
```

It is not at all obvious that a good parallel algorithm—say, one with $\Theta(\log n)$ span—exists. After all, it seems we need output[i-1] to compute output[i]. If so, the span will be $\Theta(n)$. Just as a parallel reduction uses a totally different algorithm than the straightforward sequential approach, there is also an efficient parallel algorithm for the prefix-sum problem. Like many clever data structures and algorithms, it is not something most people are likely to discover on their own, but it is a useful technique to know.

The algorithm works in two passes. We will call the first pass the "up" pass because it builds a binary tree from bottom to top. We first describe the resulting

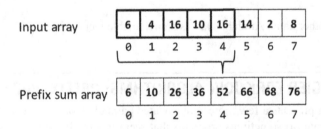

FIGURE 7.8

Example input and output for computing a prefix sum. Notice the sum of the first five elements is 52.

---

[6]It is common to distinguish the inclusive sum (the first i elements) from the exclusive sum (the first i - 1 elements); we will assume inclusive sums are desired.

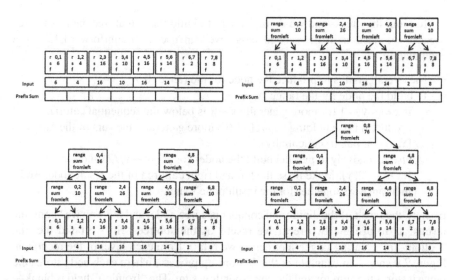

FIGURE 7.9

Example of the first pass of the parallel prefix-sum algorithm: the overall result (bottom right) is a binary tree where each node holds the sum of a range of elements of the input. Each node holds the index range for which it holds the sum (two numbers for the two end points) and the sum of that range. At the lowest level, we write *r* for range and *s* for sum just for formatting purposes. The fromleft field is used in the second pass. We can build this tree bottom-up with $\Theta(n)$ work and $\Theta(\log n)$ span because a node's sum is just the sum of its children.

tree, and then explain how it can be produced via a fork-join computation. Figure 7.9 shows an example.

- Every node holds the sum of the integers for some range of the `input` array.
- The root of the tree holds the sum for the entire range $[0, n)$.[7]
- A node's left child holds the sum for the left half of the node's range, and the node's right child holds the sum for the right half of the node's range. For example, the root's left child is for the range $[0, n/2)$, and the root's right child is for the range $[n/2, n)$.
- Conceptually, the leaves of the tree hold the sum for one-element ranges. So there are *n* leaves. In practice, we would use a sequential cutoff and have the leaves store the sum for a range of, say, approximately 500 elements.

---

[7] As before, we describe ranges as including their left end but excluding their right end.

To build this tree—and we do mean here to build the actual tree data structure[8] because we need it in the second pass—we can use a straightforward fork-join computation:

- The overall goal is to produce the node for the range $[0, n)$.
- To build the node for the range $[x, y)$,
  - if $x == y - 1$ (or more generally $y - x$ is below the sequential cutoff), produce a node holding input[x] (or more generally the sum of the range $[x, y)$ computed sequentially).
  - else recursively in parallel build the nodes for $[x, (x + y)/2)$ and $[(x + y)/2, y)$. Make these the left and right children of the result node. Add their answers together for the result node's sum.

In short, the result of the divide and conquer is a tree node, and the way we "combine results" is to use the two recursive results as the subtrees. So we build the tree "bottom-up," creating larger subtrees as we return from each level of the recursion. Figure 7.9 shows an example of this bottom-up process, where each node stores the range it stores the sum for and the corresponding sum. The "fromleft" field is blank—we use it in the second pass.

Convince yourself this algorithm is $\Theta(n)$ work and $\Theta(\log n)$ span.

Now we are ready for the second pass called the "down" pass, where we use this tree to compute the prefix sum. The essential trick is that we process the tree from top to bottom, *passing "down" as an argument the sum of the array indices to the left of the node*. Figure 7.10 shows an example. Here are the details:

- The argument passed to the root is 0. This is because there are no numbers to the left of the range $[0, n)$, so their sum is 0.
- The argument passed to a node's left child is the same argument passed to the node. This is because the sum of the numbers to the left of the range $[x, (x + y)/2)$ is the sum of the numbers to the left of the range $[x, y)$.
- The argument passed to a node's right child is the argument passed to the node *plus* the sum stored at the node's left child. This is because the sum of the numbers to the left of the range $[(x + y)/2, y)$ is the sum to the left of x plus the sum of the range $[x, (x + y)/2)$. This is why we stored these sums in the up pass!

When we reach a leaf, we have exactly what we need: output[i] is input[i] plus the value passed down to the ith leaf. Convincing yourself this algorithm is correct

---

[8] As a side note, if you have seen an array-based representation of a complete tree—for example, with a binary-heap representation of a priority queue—then notice that *if* the array length is a power of 2, then the tree we build is also complete and therefore amenable to a compact array representation. The length of the array needs to be $2n - 1$ (or less with a sequential cutoff). If the array length is not a power of 2 and we still want a compact array, then we can either act as though the array length is the next larger power of 2 or use a more sophisticated rule for how to divide subranges so that we always build a complete tree.

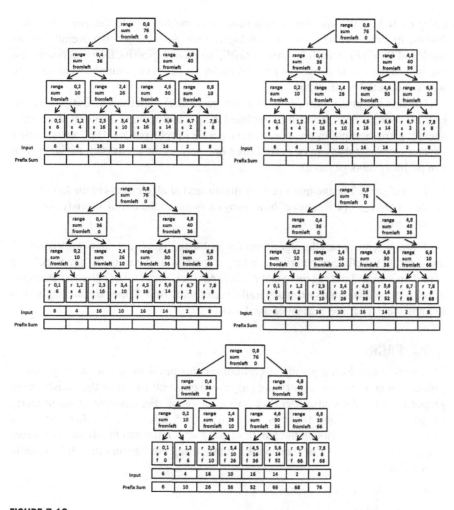

FIGURE 7.10

Example of the second pass of the parallel prefix-sum algorithm. Starting with the result of the first pass and a "fromleft" value at the root of 0, we proceed down the tree filling in fromleft fields in parallel, propagating the same fromleft value to the left-child and the fromleft value plus the left-child's sum to the right-value. At the leaves, the fromleft value plus the (1-element) sum is precisely the correct prefix-sum value. This pass is $\Theta(n)$ work and $\Theta(\log n)$ span.

will likely require working through Figure 7.10 in detail or creating your own short example while drawing the binary tree.

　　This second pass is also amenable to a parallel fork-join computation. When we create a subproblem, we just need the value being passed down and the node it is being passed to. We just start with a value of 0 and the root of the tree. This pass, like the first one, is $\Theta(n)$ work and $\Theta(\log n)$ span. So the algorithm overall is $\Theta(n)$ work and $\Theta(\log n)$ span. It is *asymptotically* no more expensive than computing just the sum of the whole array. The parallel-prefix problem, surprisingly, has a solution with exponential parallelism!

Perhaps the prefix-sum problem is not particularly interesting. But just as our original sum-an-array problem exemplified the parallel-reduction pattern, the prefix-sum problem exemplifies the more general parallel-prefix pattern. Here are two other general problems that can be solved the same way as the prefix-sum problem (you can probably think of more):

- Let output[i] be the minimum (or maximum) of all elements to the left of i.
- Let output[i] be a count of how many elements to the left of i satisfy some property.

Moreover, many parallel algorithms for problems that are not "obviously parallel" use a parallel-prefix computation as a helper method. It seems to be "the trick" that comes up over and over again to make things parallel. Section 7.5.2 gives an example, developing an algorithm on top of parallel prefix sum. We will then use *that* algorithm to implement a parallel variant of quicksort.

7.5.2 PACK

This section develops a parallel algorithm for this problem: given an array input, produce an array output containing only those elements of input that satisfy some property, and in the same order they appear in input. For example, if the property is "greater than 10" and input is {17,4,6,8,11,5,13,19,0,24}, then output is {17,11,13,19,24}. Notice the length of output is unknown in advance but never longer than input. A $\Theta(n)$ sequential solution using our "greater than 10" example is as follows:

```
int[] greaterThanTen(int[] input) {
    int count = 0;
    for(int i=0; i < input.length; i++)
        if(input[i] > 10)
            count++;
    int[] output = new int[count];
    int index = 0;
    for(int i=0; i < input.length; i++)
        if(input[i] > 10)
            output[index++] = input[i];
    assert(index==count);
    return output;
}
```

Writing a generic version is really no more difficult; as in Section 7.3.5, it amounts to a judicious use of generics and higher-order programming. In general, let us call this pattern a *pack* operation, adding it to our patterns of maps, reduces, and prefixes. However, the term "pack" is not standard, nor is there a common term to the knowledge of the author. "Filter" is also descriptive, but underemphasizes that the order is preserved.

This problem looks difficult to solve with effective parallelism. Finding which elements should be part of the output is a trivial map operation, but knowing what output index to use for each element requires knowing how many elements to the left are also greater than 10. But that is exactly what a prefix computation can do!

We can describe an efficient parallel pack algorithm almost entirely in terms of helper methods using patterns we already know. For simplicity, we describe the algorithm in terms of three steps, each of which is $\Theta(n)$ work and $\Theta(\log n)$ span; in practice it is straightforward to do the first two steps together in one fork-join computation:

1. Perform a parallel map to produce a *bit vector* where a 1 indicates the corresponding input element is greater than 10. So for
   {17,4,6,8,11,5,13,19,0,24}, this step produces {1,0,0,0,1,0,1,1,0,1}.
2. Perform a parallel prefix sum on the bit vector produced in the previous step.
   Continuing our example produces {1,1,1,1,2,2,3,4,4,5}.
3. The array produced in the previous step provides the information that a final parallel map needs to produce the packed output array. In pseudocode, calling the result of step 1 bitvector and the result of step 2 bitsum, we have

```
int output_length = bitsum[bitsum.length-1];
int[] output = new int[output_length];
FORALL(int i=0; i < input.length; i++) {
    if(bitvector[i]==1)
        output[bitsum[i]-1] = input[i];
}
```

Note it is also possible to do step 3 using only bitsum and not bitvector, which would allow step 2 to do the prefix sum *in place*, updating the bitvector array. In either case, each iteration of the FORALL loop either does not write anything or writes to a different element of output than every other iteration.

Just as prefix sum was surprisingly useful for pack, pack turns out to be surprisingly useful for more important algorithms, including a parallel variant of quicksort.

7.5.3 PARALLEL QUICKSORT

Recall that sequential quicksort is an in-place sorting algorithm with $O(n \log n)$ best- and expected-case running time. It works as follows:

1. Pick a pivot element ($O(1)$).
2. Partition the data into ($O(n)$)
   (a) elements less than the pivot

(b) the pivot

(c) elements greater than the pivot.

3. Recursively sort the elements less than the pivot.

4. Recursively sort the elements greater than the pivot.

Let us assume for simplicity the partition is roughly balanced, so the two recursive calls solve problems of approximately half the size. If we write $R(n)$ for the running time of a problem of size n, then, except for the base cases of the recursion, which finish in $O(1)$ time, we have $R(n) = O(n) + 2R(n/2)$ due to the $O(n)$ partition and two problems of half the size.[9] When the running time is $R(n) = O(n) + 2R(n/2)$, this works out to be $O(n \log n)$, but we do not show the derivation of this fact here. Moreover, if pivots are chosen randomly, the expected running time remains $O(n \log n)$. For simplicity, the analysis below will continue to assume the chosen pivot is magically exactly the median. As with sequential quicksort, the expected-time asymptotic bounds are the same if the pivot is chosen uniformly at random, but the proper analysis under this assumption is more mathematically intricate.

How should we parallelize this algorithm? The first obvious step is to perform steps 3 and 4 in parallel. This has no effect on the work, but changes the running time for the span to $R(n) = O(n) + 1R(n/2)$ (because we can solve the two problems of half the size simultaneously), which works out to be $O(n)$. Therefore, the parallelism, T_1/T_∞, is $O(n \log n)/O(n)$—that is, $O(\log n)$. While this is an improvement, it is a far cry from the exponential parallelism we have seen for algorithms up to this point. Concretely, it suggests an infinite number of processors would sort billions of elements dozens of times faster than one processor. This is okay, but underwhelming.

To do better, we need to parallelize the step that produces the partition. The sequential partitioning algorithm uses clever swapping of data elements to perform the in-place sort. To parallelize it, we will sacrifice the in-place property. Given Amdahl's law, this is likely a good trade-off: use extra space to achieve additional parallelism. All we will need is one more array of the same length as the input array.

To partition the elements into our new extra array, all we need are two pack operations: one into the left side of the array and one into the right side. In particular, do the following:

- Pack all elements less than the pivot into the left side of the array: if x elements are less than the pivot, put this data at positions 0 to $x - 1$.
- Pack all elements greater than the pivot into the right side of the array: if x elements are greater than the pivot, put this data at positions $n - x$ to $n - 1$.

The first step is exactly like the pack operation we saw earlier. The second step just works down from the end of the array instead of up from the beginning of the array. After performing both steps, we have one spot left for the pivot between the two partitions. Figure 7.11 shows an example of performing two parallel pack operations to partition the elements.

---

[9]The more common notation is $T(n)$ instead of $R(n)$, but we will use $R(n)$ to avoid confusion with work T_1 and span T_∞.

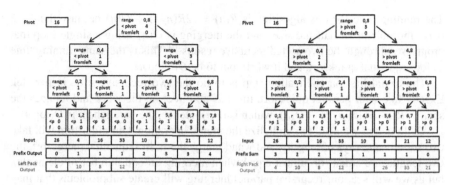

Input	26	4	16	33	10	8	21	12
Prefix Output	0	1	1	1	2	3	3	4
Left Pack Output	4	10	8	12				

Input	26	4	16	33	10	8	21	12
Prefix Sum	3	2	2	2	1	1	1	0
Right Pack Output	4	10	8	12		26	33	21

FIGURE 7.11

Example using two pack operations to partition in parallel.

Each of the two pack operations is $O(n)$ work and $O(\log n)$ span. The fact that we look at each element twice, once to decide if it is less than the pivot and once to decide if it is greater than the pivot, is only a constant factor more work. Also note that the two pack operations can be performed in parallel, though this is unnecessary for the asymptotic bound.

After completing the partition, we continue with the usual recursive sorting (in parallel) of the two sides. Rather than create another auxiliary array, the next step of the recursion can reuse the original array. Sequential mergesort often uses this same space-reuse trick.

Let us now reanalyze the asymptotic complexity of parallel quicksort using our parallel (but not in-place) partition and, for simplicity, assuming pivots always divide problems exactly in half. The work is still $R(n) = O(n) + 2R(n/2) = O(n \log n)$, where the $O(n)$ now includes the two pack operations. The span is now $R(n) = O(\log n) + 1R(n/2)$ because the span for the pack operations is $O(\log n)$. This turns out to be (again, not showing the derivation) $O(\log^2 n)$, not as good as $O(\log n)$, but much better than the $O(n)$ (in fact, $\Theta(n)$) we had with a sequential partition. Hence, the available parallelism is proportional to $n \log n / \log^2 n = n / \log n$, an exponential speedup.

7.5.4 PARALLEL MERGESORT

As a final parallel algorithm, we develop a parallel version of mergesort. As with quicksort, achieving a little parallelism is trivial, but achieving a lot of parallelism requires much more cleverness. We first recall the sequential mergesort algorithm, which always has running time $O(n \log n)$ and is not in place:

1. Recursively sort the left half and right half of the input.
2. Merge the sorted results into a new sorted array by repeatedly moving the smallest not-yet-moved element into the new array.

The running time for this algorithm is $R(n) = 2R(n/2) + O(n)$ because there are two subproblems of half the size, and the merging is $O(n)$ using a single loop that progresses through the two sorted recursive results.[10] This is the same running time as for sequential quicksort, and it works out to be $O(n \log n)$.

The trivial first parallelization step is to do the two recursive sorts in parallel. Exactly like with parallel quicksort, this has no effect on the work and reduces the span to $R(n) = 1R(n/2) + O(n)$, which is $O(n)$. Hence, the parallelism is $O(\log n)$.

To do better, we need to parallelize the merge operation. Our algorithm will take two sorted subarrays of length x and y and merge them. In sequential mergesort, the two lengths are equal (or almost equal when merging an odd number of elements), but as we will see, our recursive parallel merging will create subproblems that may need to merge arrays of different lengths. The algorithm is as follows[11]:

- Determine the median element of the larger array. this is just the element in the middle of its range, so this operation is $O(1)$.
- Use binary search to find the position j in the smaller array such that all elements to the left of j are less than the larger array's median. Binary search is $O(\log m)$, where m is the length of the smaller array.
- Recursively merge the left half of the larger array with positions 0 to j of the smaller array.
- Recursively merge the right half of the larger array with the rest of the smaller array.

The total number of elements this algorithm merges is $x+y$, which we will call n. The first two steps are $O(\log n)$ since n is greater than the length of the array on which we do the binary search. That leaves the two subproblems, which are not necessarily of size $n/2$. That best-case scenario occurs when the binary search ends up in the middle of the smaller array. The worst-case scenario is when it ends up at one extreme—that is, all elements of the smaller array are less than the median of the larger array or all elements of the smaller array are greater than the median of the larger array.

But we now argue that the worst-case scenario is not that bad. The larger array has at least $n/2$ elements—otherwise it would not be the larger array. And we always split the larger array's elements in half for the recursive subproblems. So each subproblem has at least $n/4$ (half of $n/2$) elements. So the worst-case split is $n/4$ and $3n/4$. That turns out to be "good enough" for a large amount of parallelism for the merge operation. The full analysis of the recursive algorithm is a bit intricate, so we just mention a few salient facts here.

Because the worst-case split is $n/4$ and $3n/4$, the worst-case span is $R(n) = R(3n/4)+O(\log n)$: the $R(n/4)$ does not appear because it can be done in parallel with the $R(3n/4)$ and is expected to finish first (and the $O(\log n)$ is for the binary search).

---

[10] As with the analysis for parallel quicksort, we are writing $R(n)$ instead of the more common $T(n)$ to avoid confusion with our notation for work and span.

[11] The base case, disregarding a sequential cutoff, is when x and y are both 1 or less, in which case merging is trivially $O(1)$.

$R(n) = R(3n/4) + O(\log n)$ works out to be $O(\log^2 n)$ (which is not obvious and we do not show the derivation here). The work is $R(n) = R(3n/4) + R(n/4) + O(\log n)$, which works out to be $O(n)$ (again omitting the derivation).

Recall this analysis was just for the merging step. Adding $O(\log^2 n)$ span and $O(n)$ work for merging back into the overall mergesort algorithm, we get a span of $R(n) = 1R(n/2) + O(\log^2 n)$, which is $O(\log^3 N)$, and a work of $R(n) = 2R(n/2) + O(n)$, which is $O(n \log n)$. While the span and resulting parallelism is $O(\log n)$ worse than for parallel quicksort, it is a worst-case bound compared with quicksort's expected case.

ACKNOWLEDGMENTS

I deserve no credit for the material in this chapter. If anything, my role was simply to distill decades of wisdom from others down to 3 weeks of teaching core concepts and integrate the result into a data-structures course. When in doubt, I stuck with the basic and simplest topics and examples.

I was particularly influenced by Guy Blelloch and Charles Leiserson in terms of teaching parallelism before synchronization and emphasizing divide-and-conquer algorithms that do not consider the number of processors. Doug Lea and other developers of Java's ForkJoin framework provided a wonderful library that, with some hand-holding, is usable by sophomores. Larry Snyder was also an excellent resource for parallel algorithms.

Feedback from Ruth Anderson, Kim Bruce, Kristian Lieberg, Tyler Robison, Cody Schroeder, and Martin Tompa helped improve explanations and remove typos. Tyler and Martin deserve particular mention for using these notes when they were very new. James Fogarty made many useful improvements to the presentation slides that accompany this material. Steve Wolfman created a C++ version of the material.

Nicholas Shahan created almost all the images and diagrams in this chapter which make the accompanying explanations much better.

I have had enlightening and enjoyable discussions on "how to teach this stuff" with too many researchers and educators over the last few years to list them all, but I am grateful to them.

This work was funded in part via grants from the United States National Science Foundation and generous support, financial and otherwise, from Intel Labs university collaborations.

REFERENCE

[1] D. Grossman, R.E. Anderson, Introducing parallelism and concurrency in the data structures course, in: 43rd SIGCSE Technical Symposium on Computer Science Education, Raleigh, NC, 2012.

Shared-memory concurrency control with a data-structures focus

8

Dan Grossman*

*University of Washington**

Relevant core courses: Data structures and algorithms, Second programming course in the introductory sequence.

Relevant parallel and distributed computing topics: Shared memory, Language extensions, Libraries, Task/thread spawning, Synchronization, Critical regions, Concurrency defects, Memory models, Nondeterminism.

Learning outcomes: Students mastering the material in this chapter should be able to

- use locks to implement critical sections correctly;
- identify the need for critical sections and the incorrect results that can arise if a lock is omitted or the wrong lock is used in a concurrent program;
- distinguish data races as a distinct notion from a bad interleaving even though both arise from too little synchronization;
- follow basic guidelines for easier concurrent programming, such as avoiding mutable thread-shared state where possible and following consistent protocols for what locks protect what data;
- define deadlock and explain why a consistent order on lock acquisition avoids it;
- explain the purpose of reader/writer locks and condition variables.

Context for use: This chapter and Chapter 7 complement each other. Both are designed to be used in an intermediate-advanced data-structures course—the course that covers asymptotic complexity, balanced trees, hash tables, graph algorithms, sorting, etc.—though some of the material has also been used in second programming courses. While Chapter 7 focuses on parallelism for efficiency, this chapter focuses on concurrency control, predominantly via *mutual-exclusion locks*.

8.1 INTRODUCTION

This chapter complements Chapter 7 in terms of the conceptual distinction between parallelism and concurrency control presented in Section 7.2. Chapter 7 focused on fork-join parallelism using the shared-memory programming model. This chapter uses the same programming model, but leaves fork-join parallelism behind to focus on concurrency control, which is about correctly and efficiently controlling access by multiple threads to shared resources.

We will still have threads and shared memory. We will use Java's built-in threads (java.lang.Thread). The "shared resources" will be memory locations (fields of objects) used by more than one thread. We will learn how to write code that provides properly synchronized access to shared resources even though it may not be known in what order the threads may access the data. In fact, multiple threads may *try* to access and/or modify the data at the same time. We will see when this cannot be allowed and how programmers must use programming-language features to avoid it. The features we will focus on involve *mutual-exclusion locks*, introduced in Section 8.3.2.

Here are some simple high-level examples of shared resources where we need to control concurrent access:

1. We are writing banking software where we have an object for each bank account. Different threads (e.g., one per bank teller or ATM) deposit funds in or withdraw funds from various accounts. What happens if two threads try to manipulate the same account at the same time?
2. We have a hash table storing a cache of previously retrieved results. For example, maybe the table maps patients to medications they need to be given. What happens if two threads try to insert patients—maybe even the same patient—at the same time? Could we end up with the same patient in the table twice? Could that cause other parts of the program to indicate double the appropriate amount of medication for the patient?
3. Suppose we have a *pipeline*, which is like an assembly line, where each *stage* is a separate thread that does some processing and then gives the result to the subsequent stage. To pass these results, we could use a queue where the result-provider enqueues items that the result-receiver dequeues. So an n-stage pipeline would have $n - 1$ queues; one queue between each pair of adjacent stages. What happens if an enqueue operation and a dequeue operation happen at the same time? What happens if a dequeue operation is attempted when there are no elements in the queue (yet)? In sequential programming, dequeuing from an empty queue is typically an error. In concurrent programming, we may prefer instead to *wait* until another thread enqueues something.

8.2 THE PROGRAMMING MODEL

As the examples above hint at, in concurrent programming we have multiple threads that are "largely doing their own thing" but occasionally need to coordinate since they are accessing shared resources. It is like different cooks working in the same kitchen—easy if they are using different utensils and stove burners, but more difficult if they need to share things. The cooks may be working toward a shared goal such as producing a meal, but while they are each working on a different recipe, the shared goal is not the focus.

In terms of programming, the basic model comprises multiple threads that are running in a mostly uncoordinated way. We might create a new thread when we have something new to do. The operations of each thread are *interleaved* (running alongside, before, after, or at the same time) with operations of other threads. This is very different from fork-join parallelism. In fork-join algorithms, one thread creates a helper thread to solve a specific subproblem, and the creating thread waits (by calling join) for the other thread to finish. Here, we may have four threads processing bank-account changes as they arrive. While it is unlikely that two threads would access the same account at the same time, it is possible, and we must be correct in this case.

One thing that makes these sorts of programs very difficult to debug is that the bugs can be very unlikely to occur. If a program exhibits a bug and you rerun the program another million times with the same inputs, the bug may not appear again. This is because what happens can depend on the order in which threads access shared resources, which is not entirely under programmer control. It can depend on how the threads are *scheduled* onto the processors—that is, when each thread is chosen to run and for how long, something that is decided *automatically* (when debugging, it often feels *capriciously*) by the implementation of the programming language, with help from the operating system. Therefore, how a program executes is *nondeterministic*, and the outputs may depend not only on the inputs but also on scheduling decisions not visible to or controllable by the programmer. Because testing concurrent programs is so difficult, it is exceedingly important to design them well using well-understood design principles (see Section 8.5) from the beginning.

As an example, suppose a bank-account class has methods deposit and withdraw. Suppose the latter throws an exception if the amount to be withdrawn is larger than the current balance. If one thread deposits money into the account and another thread withdraws money from the account, then whether the withdrawing thread throws an exception could depend on the order in which the operations occur. And that is still assuming all of one operation finishes before the other starts. In upcoming sections, we will learn how to use *locks* to ensure the operations themselves are not interleaved, but even after we have ensured this, the program can still be nondeterministic.

As a contrast, we can see how fork-join parallelism as covered in Chapter 7 made it relatively easy to avoid having two threads access the same memory at the same time. Consider a simple parallel reduction such as summing an array. Each thread accesses a disjoint portion of the array, so there is no sharing like there potentially is with bank accounts. The sharing is with fields of the thread objects: One thread initializes fields (like the array range) before creating the helper thread. Then the helper thread may set some result fields that the other thread reads after the helper thread terminates. The *synchronization* here is accomplished entirely via (1) thread creation (not calling start or fork until the correct fields are written) and (2) join (not reading results until the other thread has terminated). But in this chapter, this form of synchronization is not applicable because we will not wait for another thread to finish running before accessing a shared resource such as a bank account.

It is worth asking why anyone would use this difficult programming model. It would certainly be simpler to have one thread that does everything we need to do. There are several reasons:

- *Parallelism:* Unlike in the carefully chosen algorithms in Chapter 7, it may well be that a parallel algorithm needs to have different threads accessing some of the same data structures in an unpredictable way. For example, we could have multiple threads search through a graph, only occasionally crossing paths.
- *Responsiveness:* Many programs, including operating systems and programs with user interfaces, want/need to respond to external events quickly. One way to do this is to have some threads doing the program's expensive computations while other threads are responsible for "listening for" events such as buttons being clicked or typing occurring. The listening threads can then (quickly) write to some fields that the computation threads later read.
- *Processor utilization:* If one thread needs to read data from disk (e.g., a file), this will take a very long time relatively speaking. In a conventional single-threaded program, the program will not do anything for the milliseconds it takes to get the information. But this is enough time for another thread to execute millions of instructions. So by having other threads, the program can do useful work while waiting for I/O. This use of multithreading is called *masking (or hiding) I/O latency*.
- *Failure/performance isolation:* Sometimes having multiple threads is simply a more convenient way to structure a program. In particular, when one thread throws an exception or takes too long to compute a result, it affects only what code is executed by that thread. If we have multiple independent pieces of work, some of which might (as a consequence of a bug, a problem with the data, or some other reason) cause an exception or run for too long, the other threads can still continue executing. There are other approaches to these problems, but threads often work well.

It is common to hear that threads are useful *only* for performance. This is true only if "performance" includes responsiveness and isolation, which stretches the definition of performance.

8.3 SYNCHRONIZATION WITH LOCKS
8.3.1 THE NEED FOR SYNCHRONIZATION

This section presents in detail an initial example to demonstrate why we should prevent multiple threads from simultaneously performing operations on the same memory. We will focus on showing *possible interleavings* that produce the wrong answer. However, the example also has *data races*, which Section 8.4 explains must be prevented. We will show that using "ordinary" Java features to try to prevent bad interleavings simply does not work. Instead, we will learn to use *locks*, which are primitives provided by Java and other programming languages that provide what we need. We will not learn how to *implement* locks, since the techniques use low-level features more central to courses in operating systems and computer architecture.

Consider the following code for a BankAccount class:

```
class BankAccount {
  private int balance = 0;
  int getBalance() {
    return balance;
  }
  void setBalance(int x) {
    balance = x;
  }
  void withdraw(int amount) {
    int b = getBalance();
    if(amount > b)
      throw new WithdrawTooLargeException();
    setBalance(b - amount);
  }
  // ... other operations like deposit, etc.
}
```

This code is correct in a single-threaded program. But suppose we have two threads: one calls x.withdraw(100), and the other calls y.withdraw(100). The two threads could truly run at the same time on different processors. Or they may run one at a time, but the *thread scheduler* might stop one thread and start the other at any point, switching between them any number of times. Still, in many scenarios it is not a problem for these two method calls to execute concurrently:

- If x and y are not aliases, meaning they refer to distinct bank accounts, then there is no problem because the calls are using different memory. This is like two cooks using different pots at the same time.
- If one call happens to finish before the other starts, then the behavior is like in a sequential program. This is like one cook using a pot and then another cook using the same pot. When this is not the case, we say the calls *interleave*. Note that interleaving can happen even with one processor because a thread can be *preempted* at any point, meaning the thread scheduler stops the thread and runs another one.

So let us consider two interleaved calls to withdraw on the same bank account. We will "draw" interleavings using a vertical timeline (earlier operations closer to the top) with each thread in a separate column. There are many possible interleavings since even the operations in a helper method like getBalance can be interleaved with operations in other threads. But here is one incorrect interleaving. Assume initially the balance field holds 150 and both withdrawals are passed 100. Remember that each thread executes a different method call with its own "local" variables b and amount but the calls to getBalance and setBalance are, we assume, reading/writing the one balance field of the *same* object.

```
Thread 1                              Thread 2
--------                              --------
int b = getBalance();
// b holds 150
                                      int b = getBalance();
                                      if(amount > b)
                                        throw new ...;
                                      // now set balance to 50
                                      setBalance(b - amount);
if(amount > b) // no exception
  throw new ...;
setBalance(b - amount);
```

If this interleaving occurs, the resulting balance will be 50, and no exception will be thrown. But two withdraw operations were supposed to occur—there *should* be an exception. Somehow we "lost" a withdraw, which would not make the bank happy. The problem is that balance changed after Thread 1 retrieved it and stored it in b.

When first learning concurrent programming, there is a natural tendency to attempt to fix this sort of problem in a way that does not work. It is tempting to rearrange or repeat operations to try to avoid using "stale" information such as the value in b. Here is a *wrong* idea:

```
void withdraw(int amount) {
  if(amount > getBalance())
    throw new WithdrawTooLargeException();
  // maybe balance changed, so get the new balance
  setBalance(getBalance() - amount);
}
```

The idea above is to call getBalance() a second time to get any updated values. But there is *still* the potential for an incorrect interleaving. Just because setBalance(getBalance() - amount) is on one line in our source code does not mean it happens all at once. This code still (a) calls getBalance, then (b) subtracts amount from the result, then (c) calls setBalance. Moreover (a) and (c) may consist of multiple steps. In any case, the balance can change between (a) and (c), so we have not really accomplished anything except we might now produce a negative balance without raising an exception.

The sane way to fix this sort of problem, which arises whenever we have concurrent access to shared memory that might change (i.e., the contents are *mutable*), is to enforce *mutual exclusion*: allow only one thread to access any particular account at a time. The idea is that a thread will "hang a do-not-disturb sign" on the account before it starts an operation such as withdraw and not remove the sign until it is finished. Moreover, all threads will check for a "do-not-disturb sign" before trying to hang a sign and perform an operation. If such a sign is there, a thread will *wait* until there is no sign so that it can be sure it is the only one performing an operation on the bank account. Crucially, the act of "checking there is no sign hanging and then hanging a sign" has to be done "all at once" or, to use the common terminology, *atomically*. We call the work done "while the sign is hanging" a *critical section*; it is critical that such operations are not interleaved with other conflicting ones. (Critical sections often have other technical requirements, but this simple informal definition will suffice for our purposes.)

Here is one *wrong* way to try to implement this idea (you should never write code that tries to do this manually, but it is worth understanding why it is *wrong*):

```
class BankAccount {
  private int balance = 0;
  private boolean busy = false;
  void withdraw(int amount) {
    while(busy) { /* spin-wait */ }
    busy = true;
    int b = getBalance();
    if(amount > b)
      throw new WithdrawTooLargeException();
    setBalance(b - amount);
    busy = false;
  }
  // deposit would spin on same boolean
}
```

The idea is to use the busy variable as our do-not-disturb sign. All the other account operations would use the busy variable in the same way so that only one operation occurs at a time. The while loop is perhaps a little inefficient since it would be better not to do useless work and instead be notified when the account is "available" for another operation, but that is not the real problem. The busy variable does not work, as this interleaving shows:

```
Thread 1                     Thread 2
--------                     --------
while(busy) { }
                             while(busy) { }
busy = true;
                             busy = true;
int b = getBalance();
                             int b = getBalance();
                             if(amount > b)
                               throw new ...;
                             setBalance(b - amount);
if(amount > b)
  throw new ...;
setBalance(b - amount);
```

Essentially we have the same problem with busy that we had with balance: we can check that busy is false, but then it might be set to true before we have a chance to set it to true ourselves. We need to check there is no do-not-disturb sign *and* put our own sign up while *we still know there is no sign*. Hopefully you can see that using a variable to see if busy is busy is only going to push the problem somewhere else again.

To get out of this conundrum, we rely on *synchronization primitives* provided by the programming language. These typically rely on special hardware instructions that can do a little bit more "all at once" than just read or write a variable. That is, they give us the *atomic* check for no sign and hang a sign that we want. This turns out to be enough to implement mutual exclusion properly. The particular kind of synchronization we will use is *locking*.

8.3.2 LOCKS

We can define a *mutual-exclusion lock*, also known as just a *lock* (or sometimes called a *mutex*), as an abstract datatype designed for concurrency control and supporting three operations:

(1) new creates a new lock that is initially "not held."
(2) acquire takes a lock and blocks the calling thread until the lock is currently "not held" (this could be right away—that is, not blocking at all, since the lock might already be not held). It sets the lock to "held" and returns.
(3) release takes a lock and sets it to "not held."

This is exactly the "do-not-disturb" sign we were looking for, where the acquire operation blocks the thread's execution (does not return) until the caller is the thread that most recently hung the sign. It is up to the lock implementation to ensure that it always does the right thing no matter how many acquires and/or releases different threads perform simultaneously. For example, if there are three acquire operations at the same time for a "not held" lock, one will "win" and return immediately, while the other two will be blocked. When the "winner" calls release, one other thread will get to hold the lock next, and so on.

The description above is a general notion of what locks are. Section 8.3.3 will describe how to use the locks that are part of the Java language. But using the general idea, we can write this *pseudocode* (Java does not actually have a Lock class), which is almost correct (i.e., still *wrong* but close to correct):

```
class BankAccount {
  private int balance = 0;
  private Lock lk = new Lock();
  ...
  void withdraw(int amount) {
    lk.acquire(); /* may block */
    int b = getBalance();
    if(amount > b)
```

```
        throw new WithdrawTooLargeException();
      setBalance(b - amount);
      lk.release();
    }
    // deposit would also acquire/release lk
  }
```

Though we show only the withdraw operation, remember that all operations accessing balance and whatever other fields the account has should acquire and release the lock held in lk. That way only one thread will perform any operation on a particular account at a time. Interleaving a withdraw and a deposit, for example, is incorrect. If any operation does not use the lock correctly, it is like threads calling that operation are ignoring the do-not-disturb sign. Because each account uses a different lock, different threads can still operate on different accounts at the same time. But because locks work correctly to enforce the invariant that at most one thread holds any given lock at a time, we have the mutual exclusion we need for each account. If instead we used one lock for all the accounts, then we would still have mutual exclusion, but we could have worse performance since threads would be waiting unnecessarily.

What, then, is wrong with the pseudocode? The biggest problem occurs if amount > b. In this case, an exception is thrown, and therefore the lock is not released. So no thread will ever be able to perform another operation on this bank account, and any thread that attempts to do so will be blocked *forever* waiting for the lock to be released. This situation is like someone leaving the room through a window without removing the do-not-disturb sign from the door, so nobody else ever enters the room.

A fix in this case would be to add lk.release() in the branch of the if statement before the throw statement. But more generally we have to worry about any exception that might be thrown, even while some other method called from within the critical section is executing or because of a null-pointer or array-bounds violation. So more generally it would be safer to use a catch statement or finally statement to make sure the lock is always released. Fortunately, as Section 8.3.3 describes, when we use Java's locks instead of our pseudocode locks, this will not be necessary.

A second problem, also not an issue in Java, is subtler. Notice that withdraw calls getBalance and setBalance while holding the lock for the account. These methods might also be called directly from outside the bank-account implementation, assuming they are public. Therefore, they should also acquire and release the lock before accessing the account's fields such as balance. But if withdraw calls these helper methods *while holding the lock*, then as we have described it, the thread would be blocked forever—waiting for "some thread" to release the lock when in fact the thread itself already holds the lock.

There are two solutions to this problem. The first solution is more difficult for programmers: we can define two versions of getBalance and setBalance. One would acquire the lock and one would assume the caller already holds it. The latter could be private, perhaps, though there are any number of ways to manually keep track in the programmer's head (and hopefully documentation!) what locks the program holds where.

The second solution is to change our definition of the `acquire` and `release` operations so that it is okay for a thread to (re)acquire a lock it already holds. Locks that support this are called *reentrant locks*. (The name fits well with our do-not-disturb analogy.) To define reentrant locks, we need to adjust the definitions for the three operations by adding a *count* to track how many times the current holder has reacquired the lock (as well as the identity of the current holder):

- `new` creates a new lock with no current holder and a count of 0.
- `acquire` blocks the calling thread if there is a current holder *different from the calling thread*. If the current holder is the thread calling it, `acquire` increments the counter and does not block the thread. If there is no current holder, `acquire` sets the current holder to the calling thread.
- `release` releases the lock (sets the current holder to "none") only if the count is 0. Otherwise, it decrements the count.

In other words, a lock is released when the number of `release` operations by the holding thread equals the number of `acquire` operations.

8.3.3 LOCKS IN JAVA

The Java language has built-in support for locks that is different from the pseudocode in the previous section, but is easy to understand in terms of what we have already discussed. The main addition to the language is a synchronized statement, which looks like this:

```
synchronized (expression) {
    statements
}
```

Here, `synchronized` is a keyword. Basically, the *syntax* is just like a `while` loop using a different keyword, but this is *not* a loop. Instead it works as follows:

1. The `expression` is evaluated. It must produce (a reference to) an object—not `null` or a number. This object is treated as a lock. In Java, *every object is a lock* that any thread can acquire or release. This decision is a bit strange, but is convenient in an object-oriented language, as we will see.
2. The synchronized statement acquires the lock—that is, the object that is the result of step 1. Naturally, this may block the calling thread until the lock is available. Locks are reentrant in Java, so the statement will not block a thread that already holds the lock.
3. After the lock has been successfully acquired, the `statements` are executed.
4. When control leaves the `statements`, the lock is released. This happens either when the final } is reached *or* when the program "jumps out of the statement" via an exception, a `return`, a `break`, or a `continue`.

Step 4 is the other unusual thing about Java locks, but it is quite convenient. Instead of there being an explicit release statement, the release happens implicitly at the ending }. More importantly, the lock is still released if an exception causes the thread not to finish the statements. Naturally, statements can contain arbitrary Java code: method calls, loops, other synchronized statements, etc. The only shortcoming is that there is no way to release the lock *before* reaching the ending }, but it is rare that you want to do so.

Below is an implementation of our bank-account class using synchronized statements as you might expect. However, this example is *unusual style* and is *not encouraged*. The key thing to notice is that any object can serve as a lock, so for the lock we simply create an instance of Object, the built-in class that is a superclass of every other class.

```
class BankAccount {
  private int balance = 0;
  private Object lk = new Object();
  int getBalance() {
    synchronized (lk) {
      return balance;
    }
  }
  void setBalance(int x) {
    synchronized (lk) {
      balance = x;
    }
  }
  void withdraw(int amount) {
    synchronized (lk) {
      int b = getBalance();
      if(amount > b)
        throw new WithdrawTooLargeException();
      setBalance(b - amount);
    }
  }
  // deposit and other operations would also use
  // synchronized(lk)
}
```

Because locks are reentrant, it is no problem for withdraw to call setBalance and getBalance. Because locks are automatically released, the exception in withdraw is not a problem.

While it may seem naturally good style to make lk a private field since it is an implementation detail (clients need not care *how* instances of BankAccount provide mutual exclusion), this choice prevents clients from writing their own critical sections involving bank accounts. For example, suppose a client wants to double an account's balance. In a sequential program, another class could include this correct method:

```
void doubleBalance(BankAccount acct) {
  acct.setBalance(acct.getBalance()*2);
}
```

But this code is subject to a bad interleaving: the balance might be changed by another thread after the call to getBalance. If lk were instead public, then clients could use it—and the convenience of reentrant locks—to write a proper critical section:

```
void doubleBalance(BankAccount acct) {
  synchronized(acct.lk) {
    acct.setBalance(acct.getBalance()*2);
  }
}
```

There is a simpler and more idiomatic way, however: Why create a new Object and store it in a public field? Remember any object can serve as a lock, so it is more convenient, and the custom in Java, to use the instance of BankAccount itself (or in general, the object that has the fields relevant to the synchronization). So we would remove the lk field entirely like this (there is one more slightly shorter version coming):

```
class BankAccount {
  private int balance = 0;
  int getBalance() {
    synchronized (this) {
      return balance;
    }
  }
  void setBalance(int x) {
    synchronized (this) {
      balance = x;
    }
  }
  void withdraw(int amount) {
    synchronized (this) {
      int b = getBalance();
      if(amount > b)
        throw new WithdrawTooLargeException();
      setBalance(b - amount);
    }
  }
  // deposit and other operations would also use
  // synchronized(this)
}
```

All we are doing differently is using the object itself (referred to by the keyword this) rather than a different object. Of course, all methods need to agree on what lock they are using. Then a client could write the doubleBalance method like this:

```
void doubleBalance(BankAccount acct) {
  synchronized(acct) {
    acct.setBalance(acct.getBalance()*2);
  }
}
```

In this way, doubleBalance acquires the same lock that the methods of acct do, ensuring mutual exclusion. That is, doubleBalance will not be interleaved with other operations on the same account.

Because this idiom is so common, Java has one more shortcut to save you a few keystrokes. When an entire method body should be synchronized on this, we can omit the synchronized statement and instead put the synchronized keyword in the method declaration before the return type. This is just a shorter way of saying the same thing. So our *final version* looks like this:

```
class BankAccount {
  private int balance = 0;
  synchronized int getBalance() {
    return balance;
  }
  synchronized void setBalance(int x) {
    balance = x;
  }
  synchronized void withdraw(int amount) {
    int b = getBalance();
    if(amount > b)
      throw new WithdrawTooLargeException();
    setBalance(b - amount);
  }
  // deposit and other operations would also be
  // declared synchronized
}
```

There is no change to the doubleBalance method. It must still use a synchronized statement to acquire acct.

While we have built up to our final version in small steps, in practice it is common to have classes defining shared resources consisting of all synchronized methods. This approach tends to work well provided that critical sections access only the state of a single object. For some other cases, see the guidelines in Section 8.5.

Finally, note that the synchronized statement is far from the only support for concurrency control in Java. In Section 8.7.2, we will show Java's support for *condition variables*. The package java.util.concurrent also has many library classes useful for different tasks. For example, you almost surely should not implement your own concurrent hash table or queue since carefully optimized correct implementations are already provided. In addition to concurrent data structures, the standard library also has many features for controlling threads. A standard reference (an entire book!) is *Java Concurrency in Practice* by Goetz et al. [1]

8.4 RACE CONDITIONS: BAD INTERLEAVINGS AND DATA RACES

A *race condition* is a mistake in your program (i.e., a bug) such that whether the program behaves correctly or not depends on the order in which the threads execute. The reason for the name is a bit difficult to describe: the idea is that the program will "happen to work" if certain threads during program execution "win the race" to do their next operation before some other threads do their next operations. Race conditions are very common bugs in concurrent programming that, by definition, do not exist in sequential programming. This section defines two kinds of race conditions and explains why you must avoid them. Section 8.5 describes programming guidelines that help you do so.

One kind of race condition is a *bad interleaving*, sometimes called a *higher-level race* (to distinguish it from the second kind). Section 8.1 showed some bad interleavings and this section will show several more. The key point is that "what is a bad interleaving" *depends entirely on what you are trying to do*. Whether or not it is okay to interleave two bank-account withdraw operations depends on some specification of how a bank account is supposed to behave.

A *data race* is a specific kind of race condition that is better described as a "simultaneous access error" although nobody uses that term. There are two kinds of data races:

(1) When one thread might *read* an object field at the same moment as another thread *writes* the same field.

(2) When one thread might *write* an object field at the same moment as another thread *writes* the same field.

Notice it is *not an error* for two threads to both *read* the same object field at the same time.

As Section 8.4.2 explains, *your programs must never have data races even if it looks like a data race would not cause an error—if your program has data races, the execution of your program is allowed to do very strange things.*

To better understand the difference between bad interleavings and data races, consider the final version of the BankAccount class from Section 8.3. If we accidentally omit the synchronized keyword from the withdraw definition, the program will have many bad interleavings, such as the first one we considered in Section 8.3. But since getBalance and setBalance are still synchronized, there are no data races: Every piece of code that reads or writes balance does so while holding the appropriate lock. So there can never be a simultaneous read/write or write/write of this field.

Now suppose withdraw is synchronized but we accidentally omitted synchronized from getBalance. Data races now exist, and the program is wrong regardless of what a bank account is supposed to do. Figure 8.1 depicts an example that meets our definition: two threads reading/writing the same field at potentially the same time. (If both threads were writing, it would also be a data race.) Interestingly, simultaneous calls to getBalance do *not* cause a data race because simultaneous reads are not an error. But if one thread calls getBalance at the same time as another thread calls setBalance, then a data race occurs. Even though setBalance is synchronized, getBalance is not, so they might read and write balance at the same time. If your program has data races, it is infeasible to reason about what might happen.

8.4.1 BAD INTERLEAVINGS: AN EXAMPLE WITH STACKS

A useful way to reason about bad interleavings is to think about *intermediate states* that other threads must not "see." Data structures and libraries typically have *invariants* necessary for their correct operation. For example, a size field may need to store the correct number of elements in a data structure. Operations typically violate invariants temporarily, restoring the invariant after making an appropriate change. For example, an operation might add an element to the structure *and* increment the size field. No matter what order is used for these two steps, there is an intermediate state where the invariant does not hold. In concurrent programming, our synchronization strategy often amounts to using mutual exclusion to ensure that

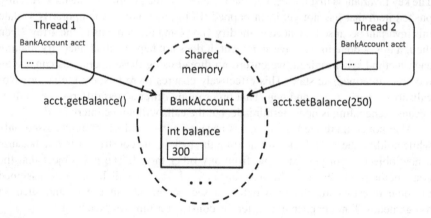

FIGURE 8.1

Visual depiction of a data race: two threads accessing the same field of the same object, at least one of them writing the field, without synchronization to ensure the accesses cannot happen "at the same time."

no thread can observe an invariant-violating intermediate state produced by another thread. What invariants matter for program correctness depends on the program.

Let us consider an extended example using a basic implementation of a bounded-size stack. (This is not an interesting data structure; the point is to pick a small example so we can focus on the interleavings. Section 8.7.2 discusses an alternative to throwing exceptions for this kind of structure.)

```java
class Stack<E> {
  private E[] array;
  private int index = 0;
  Stack(int size) {
    array = (E[]) new Object[size];
  }
  synchronized boolean isEmpty() {
    return index==0;
  }
  synchronized void push(E val) {
    if(index==array.length)
      throw new StackFullException();
    array[index++] = val;
  }
  synchronized E pop() {
    if(index==0)
      throw new StackEmptyException();
    return array[--index];
  }
}
```

The key invariant is that if index>0 then index-1 is the position of the most recently pushed item that has not yet been popped. Both push and pop temporarily violate this invariant because they need to modify index and the contents of the array. Even though this is done in one Java statement, it does not happen all at once. By making each method synchronized, we ensure no thread using these operations can see an incorrect intermediate state. This effectively ensures there is some global order of calls to isEmpty, push, and pop. That order might differ across different executions because scheduling is nondeterministic, but the calls will not be interleaved.

Also notice there are no data races because array and size are accessed only while holding the this lock. Not holding the lock in the constructor is fine because a new object is not yet reachable from any other thread. The new object that the constructor produces (i.e., the new instance of Stack) will have to be assigned to some thread-shared location before a second thread can use it, and such an assignment will not happen until after the constructor finishes executing.[1]

---

[1]This would not necessarily be the case if the constructor did something such as someObject.f = this;, but doing such things in constructors is usually a bad idea.

Now suppose we want to implement a new operation for our stack called `peek` that returns the newest not-yet-popped element in the stack without popping it. (This operation is also sometimes called `top`.) A correct implementation would be as follows:

```
synchronized E peek() {
   if(index==0)
       throw new StackEmptyException();
   return array[index-1];
}
```

If we omit the `synchronized` keyword, then this operation would cause data races with simultaneous `push` or `pop` operations.

Consider instead this alternative also-correct implementation:

```
synchronized E peek() {
  E ans = pop();
  push(ans);
  return ans;
}
```

This version is perhaps worse style, but it is certainly correct. It also has the advantage that this approach could be taken by a helper method outside the class where the first approach could not since `array` and `index` are private fields:

```
class C {
  static <E> E myPeekHelper(Stack<E> s) {
      synchronized (s) {
        E ans = s.pop();
        s.push(ans);
        return ans;
      }
  }
}
```

Notice this version could not be written if stacks used some private inaccessible lock. Also notice that it relies on reentrant locks. However, we will consider instead this *wrong* version where the helper method omits its own synchronized statement:

```
class C {
  static <E> E myPeekHelperWrong(Stack<E> s) {
      E ans = s.pop();
      s.push(ans);
      return ans;
  }
}
```

Notice this version has no data races because the `pop` and `push` calls still acquire and release the appropriate lock. Also notice that `myPeekHelperWrong` uses the stack operators exactly as it is supposed to. Nonetheless, it is incorrect because a `peek` operation is not supposed to modify the stack. While the *overall result* is the same stack if the code runs without interleaving from other threads, the code produces an *intermediate state* that other threads should not see or modify. This intermediate state would not be observable in a single-threaded program or in our correct version that made the entire method body a critical section.

To show why the wrong version can lead to incorrect behavior, we can demonstrate interleavings with other operations such that the stack does the wrong thing. Writing out such interleavings is good practice for reasoning about concurrent code and helps determine what needs to be in a critical section. In our small example, `myPeekHelperWrong` causes race conditions with all other stack operations, including itself.

`myPeekHelperWrong` **and** `isEmpty`:

If a stack is not empty, then `isEmpty` should return `false`. Suppose two threads share a stack `stk` that has one element in it. If one thread calls `isEmpty` and the other calls `myPeekHelperWrong`, the first thread can get the wrong result:

```
Thread 1                      Thread 2 (calls myPeekHelperWrong)
--------                      ----------------------------------
                              E ans = stk.pop();
boolean b = isEmpty();
                              stk.push(ans);
                              return ans;
```

Figure 8.2 shows how this interleaving produces the wrong result when the stack has one element. Notice there is nothing wrong with what "Java is doing" here. It is the programmer who wrote `myPeekHelperWrong` such that it does not behave like a `peek` operation should. Yet the code that gets the wrong answer is `isEmpty`, which is another reason debugging concurrent programs is difficult.

`myPeekHelperWrong` **and** `push`:

Another key property of stacks is that they return elements in last in, first out order. But consider this interleaving, where one of Thread 1's `push` operations happens in the middle of a concurrent call to `myPeekHelperWrong`.

```
Thread 1                      Thread 2 (calls myPeekHelperWrong)
--------                      ----------------------------------
stk.push(x);
                              E ans = stk.pop();
stk.push(y);
                              stk.push(ans);
                              return ans;
E z = stk.pop();
```

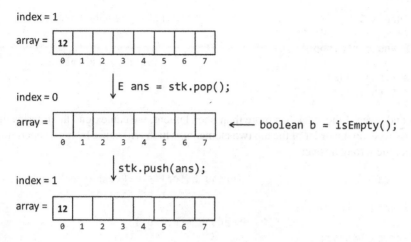

FIGURE 8.2

A bad interleaving for a stack with a peek operation that is incorrect in a concurrent program.

This interleaving has the effect of reordering the top two elements of the stack, so z ends up holding the wrong value.

myPeekHelperWrong **and** pop:

   Similarly to the previous example, a pop operation (instead of a push) that views the intermediate state of myPeekHelperWrong can get the wrong (not last in, first out) answer:

```
Thread 1                    Thread 2 (calls myPeekHelperWrong)
--------                    ----------------------------------
stk.push(x);
stk.push(y);
                            E ans = stk.pop();

E z = stk.pop();
                            stk.push(ans);
                            return ans;
```

myPeekHelperWrong **and** myPeekHelperWrong:

   Finally, two threads both calling myPeekHelperWrong causes race conditions. First, if stk initially has one element, then a bad interleaving of the two calls could raise a StackEmptyException, which should happen only when a stack has zero elements:

```
Thread 1                          Thread 2 (calls myPeekHelperWrong)
--------                          ----------------------------------
E ans = stk.pop();
                                  E ans = stk.pop(); // exception!
stk.push(ans);
return ans;
```

Second, even if the stack has more than one element, we can extend the interleaving above to swap the order of the top two elements, which will cause later pop operations to get the wrong answer.

```
Thread 1                          Thread 2 (calls myPeekHelperWrong)
--------                          ----------------------------------
E ans = stk.pop();
                                  E ans = stk.pop();
stk.push(ans);
return ans;
                                  stk.push(ans);
                                  return ans;
```

In general, bad interleavings can involve any number of threads using any operations. The defense is to define large enough critical sections such that every possible thread schedule is correct. Because push, pop, and isEmpty are synchronized, we do not have to worry about calls to these methods being interleaved with each other. To implement peek correctly, the key insight is to realize that its intermediate state must not be visible, and therefore we need its calls to pop and push to be part of *one* critical section instead of two separate critical sections. As Section 8.5 discusses in more detail, making your critical sections large enough—but not too large—is an essential task in concurrent programming.

8.4.2 DATA RACES: WRONG EVEN WHEN THEY LOOK RIGHT

This section provides more detail on the rule that data races—simultaneous read/write or write/write of the same field—must be avoided even if it "seems like" the program would be correct anyway.

For example, consider the Stack implementation from Section 8.4.1, and suppose we omit synchronization from the isEmpty method. Given everything we have discussed so far, doing so seems okay, if perhaps a bit risky. After all, isEmpty reads only the index field, and since all the other critical sections write to index at most once, it cannot be that isEmpty observes an intermediate state of another critical section: it would see index either before or after it was updated—and both possibilities remain when isEmpty is properly synchronized.

Nonetheless, omitting synchronization introduces data races with concurrent push and pop operations. As soon as a Java program has a data race, it is extremely difficult to reason about what might happen. (The author of this chapter is genuinely unsure if the stack implementation is correct with isEmpty unsynchronized.) In the

C++11 standard, it is *impossible* to do such reasoning: any program with a data race is as wrong as a program with an array-bounds violation. So data races must be avoided. The rest of this section gives some indication as to *why* and a little more detail on *how* to avoid data races.

Inability to reason in the presence of data races

Let us consider an example that is simpler than the stack implementation but is so simple that we will not motivate why anyone would write code like this:

```
class C {
    private int x = 0;
    private int y = 0;

    void f() {
        x = 1; // line A
        y = 1; // line B
    }
    void g() {
        int a = y; // line C
        int b = x; // line D
        assert(b >= a);
    }
}
```

Suppose we have two threads operating on the same instance of C, one calling f and the other calling g. Notice f and g are not synchronized, leading to potential data races on fields x and y. Therefore, the assertion in g can fail. But there is no interleaving of operations that justifies the assertion failure! Here we prove that all interleavings are correct. Then Section 8.4.2 explains why the assertion can fail anyway.

- If a call to g begins after at least one call to f has ended, then x and y are both 1, so the assertion holds.
- Similarly, if a call to g finishes before any call to f begins, then x and y are both 0, so the assertion holds.
- So we need only concern ourselves with a call to g that is interleaved with the first call to f. One way to proceed is to consider all possible interleavings of the lines marked A, B, C, and D and show the assertion holds under all of them. Because A must precede B and C must precede D, there are only six such interleavings: ABCD, ACBD, ACDB, CABD, CADB, and CDAB. Manual inspection of all six possibilities completes the proof.
  A more illuminating approach is a proof by contradiction: Assume the assertion fails, meaning !(b>=a). Then a==1 and b==0. Since a==1, line B happened before line C. Since (1) A must happen before B, (2) C must happen before D, and (3) "happens before" is a transitive relation, so A must happen before D. But then b==1, and the assertion holds.

There is nothing wrong with the proof except its assumption that we can reason in terms of "all possible interleavings" or that everything happens in certain orders. We can reason this way *only* if the program has no data races.

Partial explanation of why data races are disallowed

To understand fully why one cannot always reason in terms of interleavings requires taking courses in compilers and/or computer architecture.

Compilers typically perform *optimizations* to execute code faster without changing its meaning. If we required compilers to never change the possible interleavings, then it would be too difficult for compilers to be effective. Therefore, language definitions allow compilers to do things such as execute line B above before line A. Now, in this simple example, there is no reason why the compiler *would* do this reordering. The point is that it is *allowed to*, and in more complicated examples with code containing loops and other features there are reasons to do so. Once such a reordering is allowed, the assertion is allowed to fail. Whether it will ever do so depends on exactly how a particular Java implementation works.

Similarly, in hardware, there is not *really* one single shared memory containing a single copy of all data in the program. Instead there are various caches and buffers that let the processor access some memory faster than other memory. As a result, the hardware has to keep track of different copies of things and move things around. As it does so, memory operations might not become "visible" to other threads in the order they happened in the program. As with compilers, requiring the hardware to expose all reads and writes in the exact order they happen is considered too onerous from a performance perspective.

To be clear, compilers and hardware cannot just "do whatever they want." All this reordering is *completely hidden from you*, and you never need to worry about it *if* you avoid data races. This issue is irrelevant in single-threaded programming because with one thread you can never have a data race.

The grand compromise

One way to summarize the previous section is in terms of a "grand compromise" between programmers who want to be able to reason easily about what a program might do and compiler/hardware implementers who want to implement things efficiently and easily:

- The programmer promises not to write data races.
- The implementers promise that if the programmer does his/her job, then the implementation will be indistinguishable from one that does no reordering of memory operations. That is, it will preserve the illusion that all memory operations are interleaved in a global order.

Why is this compromise the state of the art rather than a more extreme position of requiring the implementation to preserve the "interleaving illusion" even in the presence of data races? In short, it would make it much more difficult to develop compilers and processors. And for what reason? Just to support programs with data races, which are almost always bad style and difficult to reason about anyway! Why go to so much trouble just for ill-advised programming style? On the other hand, if your program accidentally has data races, it might be more difficult to debug.

Avoiding data races

To avoid data races, we need synchronization. Given Java's locks, which we already know about, we could rewrite our example from Section 8.4.2 as follows:

```
class C {
   private int x = 0;
   private int y = 0;

   void f() {
     synchronized(this) { x = 1; } // line A
     synchronized(this) { y = 1; } // line B
   }
   void g() {
     int a, b;
     synchronized(this) { a = y; } // line C
     synchronized(this) { b = x; } // line D
     assert(b >= a);
   }
}
```

In practice you might choose to implement each method with one critical section instead of two, but using two is still sufficient to eliminate data races, which allows us to reason in terms of the six possible interleavings, which ensures the assertion cannot fail. It would even be correct to use two different locks, one to protect x (lines A and D) and another to protect y (lines B and C). The bottom line is that by avoiding data races, we can reason in terms of interleavings (ignoring reorderings) because we have fulfilled our obligations under the grand compromise.

There is a second way to avoid data races when writing tricky code that depends on the exact ordering of reads and writes of fields. Instead of using locks, we can declare fields to be *volatile*. By *definition*, accesses to volatile fields *do not count as data races*, so programmers using volatiles are still upholding their end of the grand compromise. In fact, this definition is the reason that volatile is a keyword in Java—and the reason that until you study concurrent programming you will probably not encounter it. Reading/writing a volatile field is less efficient than reading/writing a regular field, but is more efficient than acquiring and releasing a lock. For our example, the code looks like this:

```
class C {
   private volatile int x = 0;
   private volatile int y = 0;

   void f() {
     x = 1; // line A
```

```
        y = 1; // line B
      }
    void g() {
      int a = y; // line C
      int b = x; // line D
      assert(b >= a);
    }
  }
```

Volatile fields are typically used only by concurrency experts. They can be convenient when concurrent code is sharing only a single field. Usually with more than one field you need critical sections longer than a single memory access, in which case the right tool is a lock, not a volatile field.

A more likely example

Since the previous discussion focused on a strange and unmotivated example (who would write code such as f and g?), this section concludes with a data-race example that would arise naturally.

Suppose we want to perform some expensive iterative computation—for example, rendering a really ugly monster for a video game—until we have achieved a perfect solution or another thread informs us that the result is "good enough" (it is time to draw the monster) or no longer needed (the video-game player has left the room with the monster). We could have a Boolean stop field that the expensive computation checks periodically:

```
class MonsterDraw {
  boolean stop = false;
  void draw(...) {
    while(!stop) {
      ... keep making uglier ...
    }
    ...
  }
}
```

Then one thread would execute draw and other threads could set stop to true as necessary. Notice that doing so introduces data races on the stop field. Even though this programming approach is wrong, with most Java implementations it will probably work. But if it does not, it is the programmer's fault. Worse, the code might work for a long time, but when the Java implementation changes or the compiler is run with different pieces of code, the idiom might stop working. Most likely what would happen is the draw method would never "see" that stop was changed, and it would not terminate.

The simplest "fix" to the code above is to declare stop volatile. However, many concurrency experts would consider this idiom poor style and would recommend learning more about Java's thread library, which has built-in support for having one thread "interrupt" another one. Java's concurrency libraries are large with built-in support for many coding patterns. This is just one example of a pattern where using the existing libraries is "the right thing to do," but we do not go into the details of the libraries in this chapter.

8.5 CONCURRENCY PROGRAMMING GUIDELINES

This section does not introduce any new primitives for concurrent programming. Instead, we acknowledge that writing correct concurrent programs is difficult—just saying "here is how locks work, try to avoid race conditions but still write efficient programs" would leave you ill-equipped to write nontrivial multithreaded programs. Over the decades that programmers have struggled with shared memory and locks, certain guidelines and strategies have proven useful. Here we sketch some of the most widely agreed upon approaches to getting your synchronization correct. Following them does not make concurrency easy, but it does make it much easier. We focus on how to design/organize your code, but related topics such as how to use tools to test and debug concurrent programs are also important.

8.5.1 CONCEPTUALLY SPLITTING MEMORY INTO THREE PARTS

Every memory location in your program (e.g., an object field) should meet *at least one* of the following three criteria:

1. It is *thread-local*: only one thread ever accesses it.
2. It is *immutable*: (after being initialized,) it is only read, never written.
3. It is *synchronized*: locks are used to ensure there are no race conditions.

Put another way, memory that is thread-local or immutable is irrelevant to synchronization. You can ignore it when considering how to use locks and where to put critical sections. So the more memory you have that is thread-local or immutable, the easier concurrent programming will be. It is often worth changing the data structures and algorithms you are using to ones that have less sharing of mutable memory, leaving synchronization only for the unavoidable communication among threads. It cannot be emphasized enough that each memory location needs to meet at least one of the three conditions above to avoid race conditions, and if it meets either of the first two (or both), then you do not need locks.

So a powerful guideline is to make as many objects as you can immutable or thread-local or both. Only when doing so is ineffective for your task do you need to figure out how to use synchronization correctly. Therefore, we next consider ways to make more memory thread-local and then consider ways to make more memory immutable.

More thread-local memory

Whenever possible, do not share resources. Instead of having one resource, have a separate (copy of the) resource for each thread. For example, there is no need to have one shared `Random` object for generating pseudorandom numbers, since it will be just as random for each thread to use its own object. Dictionaries storing already computed results can also be thread-local: this has the disadvantage that one thread will not insert a value that another thread can then use, but the decrease in synchronization is often worth this trade-off.

Note that because each thread's call stack is thread-local, there is never a need to synchronize on local variables. So using local variables instead of object fields can help where possible, but this is good style anyway, even in single-threaded programming.

Overall, the vast majority of objects in a typical concurrent program should and will be thread-local. It may not seem that way in this chapter, but only because we are focusing on the shared objects, which are the difficult ones. In conclusion, do not share objects unless those objects really have the *explicit purpose* of enabling shared-memory communication among threads.

More immutable memory

Whenever possible, do not update fields of objects: make new objects instead. This guideline is a key tenet of *functional programming*. Even in single-threaded programs, it is often helpful to avoid mutating fields of objects because other too-often-forgotten-about references to that object (i.e., *aliases*) will "see" any mutations performed.

Let us consider a small example that demonstrates some of the issues. Suppose we have a dictionary such as a hash table that maps student IDs to names where the name class is represented like this:

```
class Name {
  public String first;
  public String middle;
  public String last;
  public Name(String f, String m, String l) {
    first  = f;
    middle = m;
    last   = l;
  }
  public String toString() {
    return first + " " + middle + " " + last;
  }
}
```

Suppose we want to write a method that looks up a student by ID in some table and returns the name, but using a middle-name initial instead of the full middle name. The following direct solution is probably the *best style*:

```
Name n = table.lookup(id);
return n.first + " " + n.middle.charAt(0) + " " + n.last;
```

Notice that the computation is almost the same as that already done by `toString`. So if the computation were more complicated than just a few string concatenations, it would be tempting and arguably reasonable to try to reuse the `toString` method. This approach is a *bad idea*:

```
Name n = table.lookup(id);
n.middle = n.middle.substring(0,1);
return n.toString();
```

While this code produces the right answer, it has the *side effect* of changing the name's `middle` field. Worse, the `Name` object is *still in the table*. Actually, this depends on how the `lookup` method is implemented. We assume here it returns a reference to the object in the table, rather than creating a new `Name` object. If `Name` objects are not mutated, then returning an alias is simpler and more efficient. Under this assumption, the full middle name for some student has been *replaced* in the table by the middle initial, which is presumably a bug.

In a *single-threaded program*, the following work-around is correct but *poor style*:

```
Name n = table.lookup(id);
String m = n.middle;
n.middle = m.substring(0,1);
String ans = n.toString();
n.middle = m;
return ans;
```

Again, this is total overkill for our example, but the idea makes sense: undo the side effect before returning.

But if the table is shared among threads, the *approach above is wrong*. Simultaneous calls using the same ID would have data races. Even if there were no data races, there would be interleavings where other operations might see the intermediate state where the `middle` field held only the initial. The point is that for shared memory, you cannot perform side effects and undo them later: later is too late in the presence of concurrent operations. This is a major reason that the functional-programming paradigm is even more useful with concurrency.

The solution is to make a copy of the object and, if necessary, mutate the (thread-local) copy. So this *works*:

```
Name n1 = table.lookup(id);
Name n2 = new Name(n1.first, n1.middle.substring(0,1),
             n1.last);
return n2.toString();
```

Note that it is no problem for multiple threads to look up the same `Name` object at the same time. They will all *read* the same fields of the same object they all have aliases to it, but simultaneous reads never lead to race conditions. It is like multiple pedestrians reading the same street sign at the same time: they do not bother each other.

8.5.2 APPROACHES TO SYNCHRONIZATION

Even after the use of thread-local and immutable objects has been maximized, there will remain some shared resources among the threads (else threads have no way to communicate). The remaining guidelines suggest ways to think about correctly synchronizing access to these resources.

Guideline 0: Avoid data races.

Use locks to ensure that two threads never simultaneously read/write or write/write the same field. While guideline 0 is *necessary* (see Section 8.4.2), it is not *sufficient* (see Section 8.4.1 and other examples of wrong programs that have no data races).

Guideline 1: Use consistent locking.

For each location that needs synchronization, identify a lock that is always held when accessing that location. If some lock *l* is always held when memory location *m* is read or written, then we say that *l guards* the location *m*. It is extremely good practice to document (e.g., via comments) for each field needing synchronization what lock guards that location. For example, the most common situation in Java would be "this guards all fields of instances of the class."

Note that each location would have exactly one guard, but one lock can guard multiple locations. A simple example would be multiple fields of the same object, but any mapping from locks to locations is okay. For example, perhaps all nodes of a linked list are protected by one lock. Another way to think about consistent locking is to imagine that all the objects needing synchronization are *partitioned*. Each piece of the partition has a lock that guards all the locations in the piece.

Consistent locking is *sufficient* to prevent data races, but is *not sufficient* to prevent bad interleavings. For example, the extended example in Section 8.4.1 used consistent locking.

Consistent locking is *not necessary* to prevent data races nor bad interleavings. It is a guideline that is typically the default assumption for concurrent code, violated only when carefully documented and for good reason. One good reason is when the program has multiple conceptual "phases" and all threads globally coordinate when the program moves from one phase to another. In this case, different phases can use different synchronization strategies.

For example, suppose in an early phase multiple threads are inserting different key-value pairs into a dictionary. Perhaps there is one lock for the dictionary and all threads acquire this lock before performing any dictionary operations. Suppose that at some point in the program the dictionary becomes fixed, meaning no more insertions or deletions will be performed on it. Once all threads *know* this point has been reached (probably by reading some other synchronized shared-memory object to make sure that all threads are finished adding to the dictionary), it would be correct to perform subsequent lookup operations *without synchronization* since the dictionary has *become immutable*.

Guideline 2: Start with coarse-grained locking and move to finer-grained locking only if contention is hurting performance.

This guideline introduces some new terms. *"Coarse-grained locking"* means using fewer locks to guard more objects—for example, one lock for an entire dictionary or for an entire array of bank accounts would be coarse-grained. Conversely, *"fine-grained locking"* means using more locks, each of which guards fewer memory locations. For example, using a separate lock for each bucket in a chaining hash table or a separate lock for each bank account would be fine-grained. The terms "coarse-grained" and "fine-grained" do not have a strict dividing line: we can really only say that one locking strategy is "more coarse-grained" or "more fine-grained" than another one. That is, *locking granularity* is really a continuum, where one direction is coarser and the other direction is finer.

Coarse-grained locking is typically easier. After acquiring just one lock, we can access many different locations in a critical section. With fine-grained locking, operations may end up needing to acquire multiple locks (using nested synchronized statements). It is easy to forget to acquire a lock or to acquire the wrong lock. It also introduces the possibility of deadlock (Section 8.6).

But coarse-grained locking leads to threads waiting for other threads to release locks unnecessarily—that is, in situations when no errors would result if the threads proceeded concurrently. In the extreme, the coarsest strategy would have just one lock for the entire program! Under this approach, it is obvious what lock to acquire, but no two operations on shared memory can proceed in parallel. Having one lock for many, many bank accounts is probably a bad idea because with enough threads there will be multiple threads attempting to access bank accounts at the same time and they will be unable to. *"Contention"* describes the situation where threads are blocked waiting for each other: They are *contending* (in the sense of competing) for the same resource, and this is hurting performance. If there is little contention (it is rare that a thread is blocked), then coarse-grained locking is sufficient. When contention becomes problematic, it is worth considering finer-grained locking, realizing that changing the code without introducing race conditions is difficult. A good execution profiler[2] should provide information on where threads are most often blocked waiting for a lock to be released.

Guideline 3: Make critical sections large enough for correctness but no larger. Do not perform I/O or expensive computations within critical sections.

The granularity of critical sections is completely orthogonal to the granularity of locks (guideline 2). Coarse-grained critical sections are "large" pieces of code, whereas fine-grained critical sections are "small" pieces of code. However, what

---

[2]A profiler is a tool that reports where a run of a program is spending time or other resources.

matters is *not* how many lines of code a critical section occupies, but how long a critical section takes to execute (longer means larger) and how many shared resources such as memory locations it accesses (more means larger).

If you make your critical sections too short, you are introducing more possible interleavings and potentially incorrect race conditions. For example, compare

```
synchronized(lk) { /* do first thing */ }
/* do second thing */
synchronized(lk) { /* do third thing */ }
```

with

```
synchronized(lk) {
    /* do first thing */
    /* do second thing */
    /* do third thing */
}
```

The first version has smaller critical sections. Smaller critical sections lead to less contention. For example, other threads can use data guarded by lk while the code above is doing the "second thing." But smaller critical sections expose more states to other threads. Perhaps only the second version with one larger critical section is correct. This guideline is therefore a tough one to follow because it requires moderation: make critical sections no longer or shorter than necessary.

Basic operations such as assignment statements and method calls are so fast that it is almost never worth the trouble of splitting them into multiple critical sections. However, expensive computations inside critical sections should be avoided wherever possible for the obvious reason that other threads may end up blocked waiting for the lock. Remember, in particular, that reading data from disk or the network is typically orders of magnitude slower than reading memory. Long running loops and other computations should also be avoided.

Sometimes it is possible to reorganize code to avoid long critical sections by repeating an operation in the (hopefully) rare case that it is necessary. For example, consider this large critical section that replaces a table entry by performing some computation on its old value:

```
synchronized(lk) {
    v1 = table.lookup(k);
    v2 = expensive(v1);
    table.remove(k);
    table.insert(k,v2);
}
```

We assume the program is incorrect if this critical section is any smaller: We need other threads to see either the old value in the table or the new value. And we need to compute v2 using the current v1. So this variation would be *wrong*:

```
synchronized(lk) {
  v1 = table.lookup(k);
}
v2 = expensive(v1);
synchronized(lk) {
  table.remove(k);
  table.insert(k,v2);
}
```

If another thread updated the table to map k to some v3 while this thread was executing expensive(v1), then we would not be performing the correct computation. In this case, either the final value in the table should be v3 (if that thread ran second) or the result of expensive(v3) (if that thread ran first), but never v2.

However, this more complicated version would *work* in this situation, under the *caveat* described below:

```
boolean loop_done = false;
while(!loop_done) {
  synchronized(lk) {
    v1 = table.lookup(k);
  }
  v2 = expensive(v1);
  synchronized(lk) {
    if(table.lookup(k)==v1) {
      loop_done = true;
      table.remove(k);
      table.insert(k,v2);
    }
  }
}
```

The essence of the trick is the second critical section. If table.lookup(k)==v1, then we know what expensive(v1) would compute, having already computed it! So the critical section is small, but does the same thing as our original large critical section. But if table.lookup(k)!=v1, then our precomputation did useless work and the while loop starts over. If we expect concurrent updates to be rare, then this approach is a "good performance bet" while still correct in all cases.

As promised, there is an important caveat to be mentioned. This approach does *not* ensure the table entry for key k was unmodified during the call to expensive. There could have been any number of concurrent updates, removals, insertions, etc., with this key. All we know is that when the second critical section executes, the key k has value v1. Maybe it was unchanged or maybe it was changed and then changed back.

In our example, we assumed it did not matter. There are many situations where it *does* matter, and in such cases checking the value is wrong because it does not ensure the entry has not been modified. This is known as an "A-B-A" problem, meaning the value started as A, changed to B, and changed back to A, causing some incorrect code to conclude, wrongly, that it was never changed.

Guideline 4: Think in terms of what operations need to be *atomic*. Determine a locking strategy after you know what the critical sections are.

An operation is *atomic*, as in indivisible, if it executes either entirely or not at all, with no other thread able to observe that it has partly executed.[3] Ensuring necessary operations appear to be atomic is exactly why we have critical sections. Since this is the essential point, this guideline recommends thinking first in terms of what the critical sections are *without thinking about locking granularity*. Then, once the critical sections are clear, how to use locks to implement the critical sections can be the next step.

In this way, we ensure we actually develop the software we want—the correct critical sections—without being distracted prematurely by the implementation details of how to do the locking. In other words, think about atomicity (using guideline 3) first and the locking protocol (using guidelines 0, 1, and 2) second.

Unfortunately, one of the most difficult aspects of lock-based programming is when software needs changing. When new critical sections are needed in "version 2.0" of a program, it may require changing the locking protocol, which in turn will require carefully modifying the code for many other already working critical sections. Section 8.6 even includes an example where there is really no good solution. Nonetheless, following guideline 4 makes it easier to think about why and how a locking protocol may need changing.

Guideline 5: Do not implement your own concurrent data structures. Use carefully tuned ones written by experts and provided in standard libraries.

Widely used libraries for popular programming languages already contain many reusable data structures that you should use whenever they meet your needs. For example, there is little reason in Java to implement your own hash table since the `Hashtable` class in the standard library has been carefully tuned and tested. For concurrent programming, the advice to "reuse existing libraries" is even more important, precisely because writing, debugging, and testing concurrent code is so difficult. Experts who devote their lives to concurrent programming can write tricky fine-grained locking code once and the rest of us can benefit. For example, the `ConcurrentHashMap` class implements a hash table that can be safely used by multiple threads with very little contention. It uses some techniques more advanced than those discussed in this chapter, but clients of the library have such trickiness hidden from them. For basic things such as queues and dictionaries, do not implement your own.

If standard libraries are so good, then why learn about concurrent programming at all? For the same reason that educated computer scientists need a basic understanding of sequential data structures in order to pick the right ones and use them correctly

---

[3]In the databases literature, this would be called "atomic and *isolated*," but it is common in concurrent programming to conflate these two ideas under the term "atomic."

(e.g., designing a good hash function), concurrent programmers need to understand how to debug and performance-tune their use of libraries (e.g., to avoid contention).

Moreover, standard libraries do not typically handle all the necessary synchronization for an application. For example, ConcurrentHashMap does not support atomically removing one element and inserting two others. If your application needs to do that, then you will need to implement your own locking protocol to synchronize access to a shared data structure. Understanding race conditions is crucial. While the examples in this chapter consider race conditions on simple data structures such as stacks, larger applications using standard libraries for concurrent data structures will still often have bad interleavings at higher levels of abstraction.

8.6 DEADLOCK

There is another common concurrency bug that you must avoid when writing concurrent programs: if a collection of threads are blocked forever, all waiting for another thread in the collection to do something (which it will not because it is blocked), we say the threads are *deadlocked*. Deadlock is a different kind of bug from a race condition, but unfortunately preventing a potential race condition can cause a potential deadlock and vice versa. Deadlocks typically result only with some, possibly rare, thread schedules (i.e., like race conditions they are nondeterministic). One advantage compared with race conditions is that it is easier to tell a deadlock occurred: some threads never terminate because they are blocked.

As a canonical example of code that could cause a deadlock, consider a bank-account class that includes a method to transfer money to another bank account. With what we have learned so far, the following *wrong* code skeleton looks reasonable:

```
class BankAccount {
    ...
    synchronized void withdraw(int amt) { ... }
    synchronized void deposit(int amt) { ... }
    synchronized void transferTo(int amt, BankAccount a) {
        this.withdraw(amt);
        a.deposit(amt);
    }
}
```

This class uses a fine-grained locking strategy where each account has its own lock. There are no data races because the only methods that directly access any fields are (we assume) synchronized like withdraw and deposit, which acquire the correct lock. More subtly, the transferTo method appears atomic. For another thread to see the intermediate state where the withdrawal has occurred but not the deposit would require operating on the withdrawn-from account. Since transferTo is synchronized, this cannot occur.

Nonetheless, there are interleavings of two `transferTo` operations where neither one ever finishes, which is clearly not desired. For simplicity, suppose x and y are static fields each holding a `BankAccount`. Consider this interleaving in pseudocode:

```
Thread 1: x.transferTo(1,y)      Thread 2: y.transferTo(1,x)
--------------------------       ---------------------------
acquire lock for x
withdraw 1 from x
                                 acquire lock for y
                                 withdraw 1 from y
                                 block on lock for x
block on lock for y
```

In this example, one thread transfers money from one account (call it "A") to another (call it "B") while the other thread transfers money from B to A. With just the wrong interleaving, the first thread holds the lock for A and is blocked on the lock for B, while the second thread holds the lock for B and is blocked on the lock for A. So both are waiting for a lock to be released by a thread that is blocked. They will wait forever.

More generally, a deadlock occurs when there are threads $T_1, T_2, ..., T_n$ such that

- for $1 \le i \le (n-1)$, T_i is waiting for a resource held by T_{i+1};
- T_n is waiting for a resource held by T_1.

In other words, there is a cycle of waiting.

Returning to our example, there is, unfortunately, no obvious way to write an atomic `transferTo` method that will not deadlock. Depending on our needs, we could write the following:

```
void transferTo(int amt, BankAccount a) {
  this.withdraw(amt);
  a.deposit(amt);
}
```

All we have done is make `transferTo` not be synchronized. Because `withdraw` and `deposit` are still synchronized methods, the only negative effect is that an intermediate state is potentially exposed: another thread that retrieved the balances of the two accounts in the transfer could now "see" the state where the withdrawal had occurred but not the deposit. If that is okay in our application, then this is a sufficient solution. If it is not, another approach would be to resort to coarse-grained locking where all accounts use the same lock.

Both of these approaches avoid deadlock because they ensure that no thread ever holds more than one lock at a time. This is a sufficient but not necessary condition for avoiding deadlock because it cannot lead to a cycle of waiting. A much more flexible sufficient-but-not-necessary strategy that subsumes the often-unworkable "only one lock at a time strategy" works as follows: for all pairs of locks x and y, either do not have a thread ever (try to) hold both x and y simultaneously *or* have a globally agreed upon order, meaning either x is always acquired before y or y is always acquired before x.

This strategy effectively defines a conceptual partial order on locks and requires that a thread tries to acquire a lock only if all locks currently held by the thread (if any) come earlier in the partial order. It is merely a programming convention that the entire program must get right.

To understand how this ordering idea can be useful, we return to our `transferTo` example. Suppose we wanted `transferTo` to be atomic. A simpler way to write the code that still has the deadlock problem we started with is as follows:

```
void transferTo(int amt, BankAccount a) {
  synchronized(this) {
    synchronized(a) {
      this.withdraw(amt);
      a.deposit(amt);
    }
  }
}
```

Here we make explicit that we need the locks guarding both accounts, and we hold those locks throughout the critical section. This version is easier to understand, and the potential deadlock—still caused by another thread performing a transfer to the accounts in reverse order—is also more apparent. (Note that a deadlock involving more threads is also possible. For example, Thread 1 could transfer money from A to B, thread 2 from B to C, and thread 3 from C to A.)

There are two locks for the critical section to acquire. If all threads acquired these locks in the same order, then no deadlock could occur. In our deadlock example where one thread calls `x.transferTo(1,y)` and the other calls `y.transferTo(1,x)`, this is exactly what goes wrong: one acquires x before y and the other acquires y before x. We want one of the threads to acquire the locks in the other order.

In general, there is no clear way to do this, but sometimes our data structures have some unique identifier that lets us pick an arbitrary order to prevent deadlock. Suppose, as is the case in actual banks, that every `BankAccount` already has an `acctNumber` field of type `int` that is distinct from every other `acctNumber`. Then we can use these numbers to require that threads always acquire locks for bank accounts in increasing order. (We could also require decreasing order, the key is that all code agrees on one way or the other.) We can then write `transferTo` like this:

```
class BankAccount {
  ...
  private int acctNumber; // must be unique
  void transferTo(int amt, BankAccount a) {
    if(this.acctNumber < a.acctNumber)
      synchronized(this) {
        synchronized(a) {
          this.withdraw(amt);
          a.deposit(amt);
```

```
            }
          }
      else
        synchronized(a) {
          synchronized(this) {
            this.withdraw(amt);
            a.deposit(amt);
          }
        }
    }
  }
```

While it may not be obvious that this code prevents deadlock, it should be obvious that it follows the strategy described above. And *any* code following this strategy will not deadlock because we cannot create a cycle if we acquire locks according to the agreed-upon partial order.

In practice, methods such as `transferTo` where we have two instances of the same class are a difficult case to handle. Even in the Java standard library it does not always work well: The `StringBuffer` class has an `append` method that is subject to race conditions (bad interleavings) because the only way to avoid it would be to create a possible deadlock. With no clear, efficient solution (buffers do not have unique identifiers like bank accounts), the documentation for `StringBuffer` indicates that clients of the library must use their own synchronization to prevent calls to `append` from interleaving with other methods that change the contents or size of a `StringBuffer`.

Fortunately, there are other situations where preventing deadlock amounts to fairly simple rules about the order in which locks are acquired. Here are two examples:

(1) If you have two different types of objects, you can order the locks by the types of data they protect. For example, the documentation could state, "When moving an item from the hash table to the work queue, never try to acquire the queue's lock while holding the hash table's lock (the other order is acceptable)."

(2) If you have an acyclic data structure such as a tree, you can use the references in the data structure to define the locking order. For example, the documentation could state, "If holding a lock for a node in the tree, do not acquire other nodes' locks unless they are descendants in the tree."

8.7 ADDITIONAL SYNCHRONIZATION PRIMITIVES

So far, the synchronization primitives we have seen are (reentrant) locks, `join`, and volatile fields. This section describes two more useful primitives—reader/writer locks and condition variables—in detail, emphasizing how they provide facilities that basic locks do not. Then Section 8.7.3 briefly mentions some other primitives.

8.7.1 **READER/WRITER LOCKS**

This chapter has emphasized multiple times that it is *not* an error for multiple threads to read the same information at the same time. Simultaneous reads of the same field by any number of threads is not a data race. Immutable data does not need to be accessed from within critical sections. But as soon as there might be concurrent writes, we have used locks that allow only one thread at a time. *This is unnecessarily conservative.* Considering all the data guarded by a lock, it would be fine to allow multiple simultaneous *readers* of the data provided that any *writer* of the data does so exclusively—that is, while there are neither concurrent readers nor writers. In this way, we still prevent any data race or bad interleaving resulting from read/write or write/write errors. A real-world (or at least online) analogy could be a webpage: it is fine for many people to read the same page at the same time, but there should be at most one person editing the page, during which nobody else should be reading or writing the page.

As an example where this would be useful, consider a dictionary such as a hash table protected by a single lock (i.e., simple, coarse-grained locking). Suppose that lookup operations are common, but insert or delete operations are very rare. As long as lookup operations do not actually mutate any elements of the dictionary, it is fine to allow them to proceed in parallel, and doing so avoids unnecessary contention.[4] When an insert or delete operation does arrive, it would need to be blocked until there were no other operations active (lookup operations or other operations that mutate the dictionary), but (a) that is rare and (b) that is what we expect from coarse-grained locking. In short, we would like to support simultaneous concurrent reads. Fine-grained locking might help with this, but only indirectly and incompletely (it still would not help with reads of the same dictionary key), and it is much more difficult to implement.

Instead a *reader/writer lock* provides exactly what we are looking for as a primitive. It has an interface different from that of a regular lock: A reader/writer lock is acquired either "to be a reader" or "to be a writer." The lock allows multiple threads to hold the lock "as a reader" at the same time, but allows only one to hold it as a writer and only if there are no holders as readers. In particular, here are the operations:

- `new` creates a new lock that initially has "0 readers and 0 writers."
- `acquire_write` blocks the thread that calls it if there are currently any readers or writers, else it makes the lock "held for writing."
- `release_write` returns the lock to its initial state.

---

[4] A good question is why lookup operations *would* mutate anything. To *clients* of the data structure, no mutation should be apparent, but there are data-structure techniques that *internally* modify memory locations to improve asymptotic guarantees. Two examples are move-to-front lists and splay trees. These techniques conflict with using reader/writer locks as described in this section, which is another example of the disadvantages of mutating shared memory unnecessarily.

- `acquire_read` blocks the calling thread if the lock is currently "held for writing," else it increments the number of readers.
- `release_read` decrements the number of readers, which may or may not return the lock to its initial state.

A reader/writer lock will block an `acquire_write` or `acquire_read` operation as necessary to maintain the following invariants, where we write $|r|$ and $|w|$ for the number of threads holding the lock for reading and writing, respectively:

- $0 \leq |w| \leq 1$, i.e., $|w|$ is 0 or 1,
- $|w| * |r| = 0$, i.e., $|w|$ is 0 or $|r|$ is 0.

Note that the name "reader/writer lock" is really a misnomer. Nothing about the definition of the lock's operations has anything to do with reading or writing. A better name might be a *"shared/exclusive lock"*: Multiple threads can hold the lock in "shared mode," but only one can hold it in "exclusive mode" and only when no threads hold it in "shared mode." It is up to the programmer to use the lock correctly—that is, to ensure that it is okay for multiple threads to proceed simultaneously when they hold the lock for reading. And the most sensible way to ensure this is to read from memory but not write to it.

Returning to our dictionary example, using a reader/writer lock is entirely straightforward: The lookup operation would acquire the coarse-grained lock for reading, and other operations (insert, delete, resize, etc.) would acquire it for writing. If these other operations are rare, there will be little contention.

There are a few details related to the semantics of reader/writer locks worth understanding. To learn how a particular library resolves these questions, you need to read the documentation. First, some reader/writer locks give *priority* to writers. This means that an "acquire for writing" operation will succeed before any "acquire for reading" operations that *arrive later*. The "acquire for writing" still has to wait for any threads that *already* hold the lock for reading to release the lock. This priority can prevent writers from *starving* (blocking forever) if readers are so common or have long enough critical sections that the number of threads wishing to hold the lock for reading is never 0.

Second, some libraries let a thread *upgrade* itself from being a reader to being a writer without releasing the lock. Upgrading might lead to deadlock though if multiple threads try to upgrade themselves.

Third, just like regular locks, a reader/writer lock may or may not be reentrant.[5] Aside from the case of upgrading, this is an orthogonal issue.

Java's synchronized statement supports only regular locks, not reader/writer locks. But Java's standard library has reader/writer locks, such as the class `ReentrantReadWriteLock` in the `java.util.concurrent.locks` package. The interface is slightly different than with synchronized statements (you have to be

---

[5]Recall reentrant locks allow the same thread to "acquire" the lock multiple times and hold the lock until the equal number of release operations.

careful to release the lock even in the case of exceptions). It is also different from the operations we described above. Methods `readLock` and `writeLock` return objects that then have `lock` and `unlock` methods. So "acquire for writing" could look like `lk.writeLock().lock()`. One advantage of this more complicated interface is that some library could provide some clients with only one of the "read lock" or the "write lock," thereby restricting which operations the clients can perform.

8.7.2 CONDITION VARIABLES

Condition variables are a mechanism that lets threads *wait* (block) until another thread *notifies* them that it might be useful to "wake up" and try again to do whatever could not be done before waiting. (We assume the thread that waited chose to do so because some *condition* prevented it from continuing in a useful manner.) It can be awkward to use condition variables correctly, but most uses of them are within standard libraries, so arguably the most useful thing is to understand when and why this wait/notification approach is desirable.

To understand condition variables, consider the canonical example of a *bounded buffer*. A bounded buffer is just a queue with a maximum size. Bounded buffers that are shared among threads are useful in many concurrent programs. For example, if a program is conceptually a pipeline (an assembly line), we could assign some number of threads to each stage and have a bounded buffer between each pair of adjacent stages. When a thread in one stage produces an object for the next stage to process, it can enqueue the object in the appropriate buffer. When a thread in the next stage is ready to process more data, it can dequeue the object from the same buffer. From the perspective of this buffer, we call the enqueuers *producer threads* (or just *producers*) and the dequeuers *consumer threads* (or just *consumers*).

Naturally, we need to synchronize access to the queue to make sure each object is enqueued/dequeued exactly once, there are no data races, etc. One lock per bounded buffer will work fine for this purpose. More interesting is what to do if a producer encounters a full buffer or a consumer encounters an empty buffer. In single-threaded programming, it makes sense to throw an exception when encountering a full or empty buffer since this is an unexpected condition that cannot change. But here:

- If the thread simply waits and tries again later, a producer may find the queue no longer full (if a consumer has dequeued an object) and a consumer may find the queue no longer empty (if a producer has enqueued an object).
- It is not unexpected to find the queue in a "temporarily bad" condition for continuing. The buffer is for managing the transfer of data and it is entirely natural that at some point the producers might get slightly ahead (filling the buffer and wanting to enqueue more data) or the consumers might get slightly ahead (emptying the buffer and wanting to dequeue more data).

The fact that the buffer is bounded is useful. Not only does it save space, but it ensures the producers will not get too far ahead of the consumers. Once the buffer is full, we want to stop running the producer threads since we would rather use our processors to run the consumer threads, which are clearly not running enough or are taking longer. So we really do want waiting threads to stop using computational resources so the threads that are not stuck can get useful work done.

With just locks, we can write a version of a bounded buffer that never results in a wrong answer, but it will be *inexcusably inefficient* because threads will not stop using resources when they cannot proceed. Instead they keep checking to see if they can proceed:

```
class Buffer<E> {
    // not shown: an array of fixed size for the queue with two
    // indices for the front and back, along with methods
    // isEmpty() and isFull()
    void enqueue(E elt) {
        while(true) {
            synchronized(this) {
                if(!isFull()) {
                    ... do enqueue as normal ...
                    return;
                }
            }
        }
    }
    E dequeue() {
        while(true) {
            synchronized(this) {
                if(!isEmpty()) {
                    E ans = ... do dequeue as normal ...
                    return ans;
                }
            }
        }
    }
}
```

The purpose of condition variables is to avoid this *spinning*, meaning threads checking the same thing over and over again until they can proceed. This spinning is particularly bad because it causes contention for exactly the lock that other threads need to acquire in order to do the work before the spinners can do something useful. Instead of constantly checking, the threads could "sleep for a while" before trying again. But how long should they wait? Too little waiting slows the program down because of wasted spinning. Too much waiting slows the program down because threads that could proceed are still sleeping.

It would be best to have threads "wake up" (unblock) exactly when they might usefully continue. In other words, if producers are blocked on a full queue, wake them up when a dequeue operation occurs, and if consumers are blocked on an empty queue, wake them up when an enqueue operation occurs. This cannot be done correctly with just locks, which is exactly why condition variables exist.

In Java, just like every object is a lock, every object is *also* a condition variable. So we will first explain condition variables as extra methods that every object has. (Quite literally, the methods are defined in the `Object` class.) We will see later that while this setup is often convenient, associating (only) one condition variable with each lock (the same object) is not always what you want. There are three methods:

(1) `wait` should be called only while holding the lock for the object. (Typically, the call is to `this.wait` so the lock `this` should be held.) The call will atomically (a) block the thread, (b) release the lock, and (c) register the thread as "waiting" to be notified. (This is the step you cannot reasonably implement on your own; there has to be no "gap" between the lock release and registering for notification else the thread might "miss" being notified and never wake up.) When the thread is later woken up, it will reacquire the same lock before `wait` returns. (If other threads also seek the lock, then this may lead to more blocking. There is no guarantee that a notified thread gets the lock next.) Notice the thread then continues as part of a *new critical section*; the entire point is that the state of shared memory has changed in the meantime while it did not hold the lock.

(2) `notify` wakes up *one* thread that is blocked on this condition variable (i.e., has called `wait` on the same object). If there are no such threads, then `notify` has no effect, but this is fine. (And this is why there has to be no "gap" in the implementation of `wait`.) If there are multiple threads blocked, there is no guarantee which one is notified.

(3) `notifyAll` is like `notify` except it wakes up all the threads blocked on this condition variable.

The term "*wait*" is standard, but the others differ in different languages. Sometimes "*notify*" is called "*signal*" or "*pulse.*" Sometimes "*notifyAll*" is called "*broadcast*" or "*pulseAll.*"

Below is a *wrong* use of these primitives for our bounded buffer. It is close enough to correct get the basic idea. Identifying the bugs is essential for understanding how to use condition variables correctly.

```
class Buffer<E> {
    // not shown: an array of fixed size for the queue with two
    // indices for the front and back, along with methods
    // isEmpty() and isFull()
    void enqueue(E elt) {
        synchronized(this) {
            if(isFull())
                this.wait();
            ... do enqueue as normal ...
```

```
            if(... buffer was empty (i.e., now has 1 element) ...)
               this.notify();
         }
      }
   E dequeue() {
      synchronized(this) {
         if(isEmpty())
            this.wait();
         E ans = ... do dequeue as normal ...
         if(... buffer was full (i.e., now has room for 1
            element) ...)
            this.notify();
         return ans;
      }
   }
}
```

enqueue waits if the buffer is full. Rather than spinning, the thread will consume
no resources until it is awakened. While waiting, it does not hold the lock (per the
definition of wait), which is crucial so other operations can finish. On the other hand,
if the enqueue puts one item into an empty queue, it needs to call notify in case there
are dequeuers waiting for data. dequeue is symmetric. Again, this is the *idea*—wait
if the buffer cannot handle what you need to do and notify other threads that might be
blocked after you change the state of the buffer—but this code has two serious bugs.
It may not be easy to see them because thinking about condition variables takes some
getting used to.

The first bug is that we have to account for the fact that after a thread is notified
that it should try again, but before it actually tries again, the buffer can undergo other
operations by other threads. That is, there is a "gap" between the notification and
when the notified thread actually reacquires the lock to begin its new critical section.
Here is an example of a bad interleaving with the enqueue in Thread 1 doing the
wrong thing (a symmetric example exists for dequeue):

```
Initially the buffer is full (so Thread 1 blocks)

Thread 1 (enqueue)   Thread 2 (dequeue)    Thread 3 (enqueue)
------------------   ------------------    ------------------
if(isFull())
   this.wait();
                     ... do dequeue ...
                     if(... was full ...)
                        this.notify();
                                           if(isFull())
                                           (not full: don't wait)
                                              ... do enqueue ...

... do enqueue ... (wrong!)
```

Thread 3 "snuck in" and refilled the buffer before Thread 1 ran again; hence, Thread 1 adds an object to a full buffer, when what it should do is wait again. The fix is that Thread 1, after (implicitly) reacquiring the lock, must again check whether the buffer is full. A second `if` statement does not suffice because if the buffer is full again, Thread 1 will wait and need to check a third time after being awakened and so on. Fortunately, we know how to check something repeatedly until we get the answer we want: a `while` loop. So this version fixes this bug, but is still *wrong*:

```
class Buffer<E> {
    // not shown: an array of fixed size for the queue with two
    // indices for the front and back, along with methods
    // isEmpty() and isFull()
    void enqueue(E elt) {
        synchronized(this) {
            while(isFull())
                this.wait();
            ... do enqueue as normal ...
            if(... buffer was empty (i.e., now has 1 element) ...)
                this.notify();
        }
    }
    E dequeue() {
        synchronized(this) {
            while(isEmpty())
                this.wait();
            E ans = ... do dequeue as normal ...
            if(... buffer was full (i.e., now has room for 1
              element) ...)
                this.notify();
            return ans;
        }
    }
}
```

The only change is using a `while` loop instead of an `if` statement for deciding whether to wait. *Calls to* `wait` *should always be inside* `while` *loops that recheck the condition.* Not only is this in almost every situation the right thing to do for your program, but technically for obscure reasons Java is allowed to notify (i.e., wake up) a thread even if your program does not! So it is mandatory to recheck the condition since it is possible that nothing changed. This is still much better than the initial spinning version because each iteration of the `while` loop corresponds to being notified, so we expect very few iterations (probably one).

Unfortunately, the version of the code above is still wrong. It does not account for the possibility of multiple threads being blocked due to a full (or empty) buffer. Consider this interleaving:

```
Initially the buffer is full (so Threads 1 and 2 block)

Thread 1 (enqueue) Thread 2 (enqueue)  Thread 3 (two dequeues)
------------------ ------------------  -----------------------
while(isFull())
   this.wait();
                     while(isFull())
                        this.wait();
                                         ... do dequeue ...
                                         this.notify();

                                         ... do dequeue ...
                                         // no notification!
```

Sending one notification on the first dequeue was fine at that point, but that still left a thread blocked. If the second dequeue happens before any enqueue, no notification will be sent, which leaves the second blocked thread waiting when it should not wait.

The simplest solution in this case is to change the code to use notifyAll instead of notify. That way, whenever the buffer becomes nonempty, *all* blocked producers know about it and similarly whenever the buffer becomes nonfull, *all* blocked consumers wake up. If there are n blocked threads and there are no subsequent operations such as the second dequeue above, then $n - 1$ threads will simply become blocked again, but at least this is correct. So this is *right*:

```
class Buffer<E> {
   // not shown: an array of fixed size for the queue with two
   // indices for the front and back, along with methods
   // isEmpty() and isFull()
   void enqueue(E elt) {
      synchronized(this) {
         while(isFull())
            this.wait();
         ... do enqueue as normal ...
         if(... buffer was empty (i.e., now has 1 element) ...)
            this.notifyAll();
      }
   }
   E dequeue() {
      synchronized(this) {
         while(isEmpty())
            this.wait();
         E ans = ... do dequeue as normal ...
         if(... buffer was full (i.e., now has room for 1
            element) ...)
            this.notifyAll();
```

```
        return ans;
    }
  }
}
```

If we do not expect very many blocked threads, this notifyAll solution is reasonable. Otherwise, it causes a lot of probably wasteful waking up (just to have $n - 1$ threads probably get blocked again). Another tempting solution *almost* works, but of course "almost" means "wrong." We could have every enqueue and dequeue call this.notify, not just if the buffer had been empty or full. (In terms of the code, just replace the if statements with calls to this.notify().) In terms of the interleaving above, the first dequeue would wake up one blocked enqueuer, and the second dequeue would wake up another one. If no thread is blocked, then the notify call is unnecessary but does no harm.

The reason this is incorrect is subtle, but here is one scenario where the wrong thing happens. For simplicity, assume the size of the buffer is 1 (any size will do, but larger sizes require more threads before there is a problem).

1. Assume the buffer starts empty.
2. Then two threads T_1 and T_2 get blocked trying to dequeue an item.
3. Then one thread T_3 enqueues an item (filling the buffer) and calls notify. Suppose this wakes up T_1.
4. But before T_1 reacquires the lock, another thread T_4 tries to enqueues an item and gets blocked (because the buffer is still full).
5. Now T_1 runs, emptying the buffer and calling notify, *but in a stroke of miserable luck this wakes up T_2 instead of T_4.*
6. T_2 will see an empty buffer and wait again. So now T_2 and T_4 are blocked even though T_4 should enqueue an item that T_2 could then dequeue.

The way to fix this problem is to use *two condition variables*—one for producers to notify consumers and one for consumers to notify producers. But we need both condition variables to be "associated with" the same lock, since we still need all producers and consumers to use one lock to enforce mutual exclusion. This is why Java's choice to associate one condition variable with every lock is somewhat strange. However, the Java standard library has a ReentrantLock class that is more flexible. It has a newCondition method that lets you associate as many condition variables as you want with the same lock. You then call wait and notify on these separate condition objects. In other languages and libraries, it is common for locks and condition variables to be separate things entirely, leaving it up to the programmer to manually associate each condition variable with a lock.

In any case, condition variables are

- important: Concurrent programs need ways to have threads wait without spinning until they are notified to try again. Locks are not the right tool for this.
- subtle: Bugs are more difficult to reason about, and the correct programming idioms are less intuitive than with locks.

In practice, condition variables tend to be used in very stylized ways. Moreover, it is rare that you need to use condition variables explicitly rather than using a library that internally uses condition variables. For example, the Java standard library already has a class `java.util.concurrent.ArrayBlockingQueue<E>` that is exactly what we need for a bounded buffer. (It uses the names `put` and `take` rather than `enqueue` and `dequeue`.) It is good to know that any blocking caused by calls to the library will be efficient thanks to condition variables, but we do not need to write or understand the condition-variable code.

8.7.3 OTHER PRIMITIVES

Locks and condition variables are not the only synchronization primitives. For one, do not forget `join` from Chapter 7, which synchronizes two threads in a particular way and is very convenient when it is the appropriate tool. You may encounter other primitives as you gain experience with concurrent programming. Your experience learning about locks should make it much easier to learn other constructs. Key things to understand when learning about synchronization are as follows:

- What interleavings does a primitive prevent?
- What are the rules for using a primitive correctly?
- What are the standard idioms where a primitive proves most useful?

Another common exercise is to implement one primitive in terms of another, perhaps inefficiently. For example, it is possible to implement `join` in terms of locks: The helper thread can hold a lock until just before it terminates. The `join` primitive can then (try to) acquire and immediately release this lock. Such an *encoding* is poor style if `join` is provided directly, but it can help understand how `join` works and can be useful if you are in a setting where only locks are provided as primitives.

Here is an incomplete list of other primitives you may encounter:

- *Semaphores* are rather low-level mechanisms where two operations, called *P* and *V* for historical reasons, increment or decrement a counter. There are rules about how these operations are synchronized and when they block the calling thread. Semaphores can be easily used to implement locks as well as barriers.
- *Barriers* are a bit more like `join` and are often more useful in parallel programming closer in style to the problems studied in Chapter 7. When threads get to a barrier, they become blocked until *n* of them (where *n* is a property of the barrier) reach the barrier. Unlike `join`, the synchronization is not waiting for *one* other thread to *terminate*, but rather is waiting for *n* other threads to *get to the barrier*.
- *Monitors* provide synchronization that corresponds more closely to the structure of your code. Like an object, they can encapsulate some private state and provide some entry points (methods). As synchronization, the basic idea is that only one thread can call any of the methods at a time, with any others waiting. This is *very* much like an object in Java where all the methods are synchronized on the `this`

lock, which is exactly Java's standard idiom. Therefore, it is not uncommon for Java's locks to be called "monitors." We did not use this term because the actual primitive Java provides is a reentrant lock even though the common idiom is to code up monitors using this primitive.

ACKNOWLEDGMENTS

I deserve no credit for the material in this chapter. If anything, my role was simply to distill decades of wisdom from others down to 3 weeks of teaching core concepts and integrate the result into a data-structures course. When in doubt, I stuck with the basic and simplest topics and examples.

The treatment of shared-memory synchronization is heavily influenced by decades of operating-systems courses, but with the distinction of ignoring all issues of scheduling and synchronization implementation. Moreover, the emphasis on the need to avoid data races in high-level languages is frustratingly underappreciated despite the noble work of memory-model experts such as Sarita Adve, Hans Boehm, and Bill Pugh.

Feedback from Ruth Anderson, Kim Bruce, Kristian Lieberg, Tyler Robison, Cody Schroeder, and Martin Tompa helped improve explanations and remove typos. Tyler and Martin deserve particular mention for using these notes when they were very new. James Fogarty made many useful improvements to the presentation slides that accompany this material. Steve Wolfman created a C++ version of the material.

Nicholas Shahan created almost all the images and diagrams in this chapter, which make the accompanying explanations much better.

I have had enlightening and enjoyable discussions on "how to teach this stuff" with too many researchers and educators over the last few years to list them all, but I am grateful to them.

This work was funded in part via grants from the US National Science Foundation and generous support, financial and otherwise, from Intel Labs university collaborations.

REFERENCE

[1] B. Goetz, T. Peierls, J. Bloch, J. Bowbeer, D. Lea, D. Holmes, Java Concurrency in Practice, Addison-Wesley, Reading, 2006, ISBN 0321349601.

Parallel computing in a Python-based computer science course

Thomas H. Cormen*
Dartmouth College*

Relevant core courses: This material applies to a CS1 or a CS2 course.

Relevant parallel and distributed computing topics: Shared memory; vector model; reduction; scan; segmented operations; analysis of algorithms; sorting; quicksort.

Learning outcomes:

1. Break down a complex computation (quicksort) into individual parallel operations.
2. See how to perform reductions and scans in parallel.
3. Understand costs of parallel operations in a shared-memory environment.
4. Gain practice in using parallel operations.
5. Understand how to analyze an asymptotic running time that is the sum of two different terms, each of which may dominate.
6. If students are sufficiently advanced, analyze the trade-offs between sequential and parallel computing.
7. Learn how to write code in a parallel style using Python.
8. If necessary, learn about Python's lambda construct and how to design Python functions that take a variable number of parameters. This material is not covered in this chapter, as there are many resources elsewhere for it.

Suggested student background: Students should know

1. basic aspects of Python programming,
2. how to analyze simple code using O notation,
3. how to understand, write, and analyze running times of recursive functions,
4. (recommended) Python's `lambda` construct and the $*$ operator to gather and scatter function parameters.

Context for use: This material is designed for a CS1 or CS2 course. Some of the material might be too advanced for certain CS1 courses, depending on the students. For example, at Dartmouth College, our CS1 course draws from the general student population, and not from just the technically oriented students. Several of the nontechnical students have had trouble understanding this material. A course that draws primarily from technical students should be able to incorporate this material.

The programming material here is based on Python, because that is what we teach in our CS1 course at Dartmouth College. The material should be adaptable to other programming languages, but the treatment here sticks to Python.

The model is a shared-memory machine with multiple processors, but the programming style derives from Blelloch's work [1, 2] on the vector model and scan operations. All operations are on Python lists, and scan operations (also known as prefix computations) figure heavily.

All code is provided, except the code for unsegmented parallel partitioning and the code for parallel quicksort; the code for these functions is provided in a supplement. Students should implement these functions in an assignment. Implementing unsegmented parallel partitioning is a good warm-up assignment for implementing full parallel quicksort.

9.1 PARALLEL PROGRAMMING

Suppose that we want to write code that takes advantage of a computer with multiple processors and a shared memory, which is the simplest parallel computer to program. Computer scientists have developed several ways to program such machines. Rather than fixing on any particular one, we will write code that "looks" parallel (we will see what that means a little later) and would be easy to convert to true parallel code on a real parallel system, but that runs sequentially on our own laptops.

Let us imagine that we have at our disposal p processors, each of which can access a common, shared memory. We will assume that each processor can access any variable, any object, any item of any list, etc. To avoid the havoc that would occur when multiple processors try concurrently to change the value of the same variable, we will consider only programs in which that does not occur. In particular, we will partition our data among the p processors, so that for an n-item list, each processor is responsible for n/p items. We will always assume that if $n > p$, then n is a multiple of p, and we will consistently use m to equal n/p.

9.1.1 PARALLELIZABLE LOOPS

From a programming point of view, we will call a for-loop that runs for at most p iterations, in which the result of each iteration has no effect on other iterations, *parallelizable*. We can imagine each of the at most p iterations running on its own processor *in parallel* (i.e., concurrently), so that if each iteration takes time t, all the iterations together take only time $O(t)$, rather than the $O(pt)$ time they would take if we ran them sequentially. For example, if each iteration of a parallelizable for-loop takes constant time, then the for-loop takes constant time when run in parallel. If that for-loop is operating on a list of n items, then in order for all iterations to run in parallel, we must have $n \leq p$. On the other hand, if $n > p$, then a parallelizable for-loop has to work on n/p items per processor, so that the best we could hope for from the parallelizable for-loop would be $O(n/p)$ time (or, equivalently, $O(m)$ time).

Let us make this idea more concrete. Suppose we have three lists, a, b, and c, each of length p, and we want to add the corresponding items of a and b into the corresponding item of c. Here is a simple for-loop that does the job:

```
for i in range(p):
    c[i] = a[i] + b[i]
```

This for-loop is parallelizable, since each iteration has no effect on other iterations. Thus, because each iteration takes constant time, if we have p processors, then this for-loop runs in constant time—that is, $O(1)$ time—in parallel.

Now suppose that each of the lists a, b, and c has n items, where $n > p$, so that $m > 1$. Then here are nested for-loops that add the corresponding items of a and b into the corresponding item of c:

```
# This outer for-loop is parallelizable.
for i in range(p):
    # This inner for-loop is not parallelizable.
    for j in range(m):
        c[i*m + j] = a[i*m + j] + b[i*m + j]
```

The idea here is that processor 0 is responsible for the m indices 0 to $m-1$, processor 1 is responsible for the m indices m to $2m - 1$, processor 2 is responsible for the m indices $2m - 1$ to $3m-1$, and so on. More generally, processor i, for $i = 0, 1, 2, \ldots, p-1$, is responsible for the m indices $im, im+1, im+2, \ldots, im+(m-1)$. We can parallelize the outer for-loop, so that each processor performs its $m = n/p$ iterations of the inner for-loop in parallel with the other processors, but these m iterations of the inner for-loop run sequentially on the processor. Since each iteration of the inner for-loop takes constant time, this computation runs in $O(m)$ time in parallel.

9.1.2 BARRIERS

Many parallel computations get to a point where no processor should proceed until all processors have arrived at the same point. By analogy, think of what happens when several people dine together at a restaurant: nobody starts the next course until everyone has finished the current course. When all processors need to arrive at the same point in a parallel computation, we call that a **barrier**. We will assume that we have a function barrier, which takes no parameters, and returns only once all processors have called it.

There are several ways to implement a barrier, but we will not go into them here. We will count the number calls to `barrier` when we analyze parallel running times, however. We will assume that the time for each barrier call is given by the parameter β.

9.1.3 OUTLINE

We will work our way up to performing a parallel version of the quicksort algorithm [3, Chapter 7]. The approach we use draws heavily from Blelloch's work [1, 2] on the vector model and scan operations.

We start by seeing how to perform reduction and scan operations in parallel. We then add parallel meld and permute operations, which give us the operations we need to partition a list in parallel, with a result similar to that produced by sequential quicksort. To perform all the recursive steps on quicksort, we introduce segmented operations, and then modify our partitioning procedure to work with segmented operations.

Python code appears for most, but not all, of the operations in this chapter. We omit Python code for partitioning and for the full parallel quicksort because these programs make for excellent exercises.

This chapter closes by analyzing the trade-offs between sequential and parallel implementations of reduction and scan operations.

9.2 PARALLEL REDUCTION

A *reduction* operation applies an associative operator to the items of a list, giving the single result of applying the operator. For example, a plus-reduction on a list x with n items gives the value $x[0] + x[1] + x[2] + \cdots + x[n-2] + x[n-1]$. (Recall that an associative operator—let us call it $\oplus$ to keep it generic—satisfies the property that $(a \oplus b) \oplus c = a \oplus (b \oplus c)$ for any operands a, b, and c.)

At first glance, you might think that computing the plus-reduction on a list is inherently sequential, because we have to first sum $x[0]+x[1]$, and then add in $x[2]$, then add in $x[3]$, and so on. But because the operation we are performing—addition in this case—is associative, we can add values in other orders. For example, we could first compute $x[0]+x[1]+x[2]+\cdots+x[n/2-1]$, and we could compute $x[n/2]+x[n/2 + 1]+x[n/2 + 2]+\cdots+x[n-1]$, and we could then sum these two results to give the plus-reduction of the entire list. In other words, instead of parenthesizing our additions as $((\cdots((x[0] + x[1]) + x[2]) + \cdots + x[n-2]) + x[n-1])$, we could parenthesize them as $(x[0] + x[1] + x[2] + \cdots + x[n/2-1]) + (x[n/2] + x[n/2 + 1] + x[n/2 + 2] + \cdots + x[n-1])$, where we can further parenthesize the sums $(x[0] + x[1] + x[2] + \cdots + x[n/2-1])$ and $(x[n/2] + x[n/2 + 1] + x[n/2 + 2] + \cdots + x[n-1])$ however we choose.

In our code, we will use two global variables:

- p: the number of processors
- m: the number of items per processor—that is, n/p

9.2.1 REDUCING IN PARALLEL WHEN $n \leq p$

The function `simple_reduce` in Listing 9.1 shows how we can compute a reduction on a list x with $n \leq p$ items in parallel. The parameter `op` is a Python function that computes some associative function of two parameters, and the parameter `ident` is the identity for the operation `op`. For example, if `op` is a function that adds two numbers, then `ident` would be 0, and if `op` is a function that multiplies two numbers, then `ident` would be 1. We need the identity in case the list is empty.

```python
# Return the reduction of all values in an n-item list x. The
# parameter op is a two-parameter function for the reduction. The
# parameter ident is the identity for op, in case the list is empty.
# Assumes that n <= p, where p is the number of processors. The
# reduction takes O(beta log n) time in parallel.
def simple_reduce(x, op, ident):
    n = len(x)

    if n == 0:
        return ident # empty list
    elif n == 1:
        return x[0] # base case: only one value
    else:
        # Create a new list, subproblem, of half the size, rounding
        # up if n is odd.
        half = (n+1) / 2
        subproblem = [None] * half

        # Using a parallelizable for-loop, combine pairs of values
        # in x into subproblem.
        for i in range(half-1):
            subproblem[i] = op(x[2*i], x[2*i+1])

        # Need special code to handle the last one or two values in
        # x, in case n is odd.
        if n % 2 == 0:
            subproblem[half-1] = op(x[2*half-2], x[2*half-1])
        else:
            subproblem[half-1] = x[2*half-2]

        barrier()

        # Return the reduction of the subproblem. This recursive
        # call is on a problem of half the size.
        return simple_reduce(subproblem, op, ident)
```

LISTING 9.1

The function `simple_reduce`.

Instead of breaking the problem down as we did above, `simple_reduce` works as follows. We create a new list, `subproblem`, of half the size. That is, `subproblem` has size $n/2$, represented by the variable `half`, except that we round up when n is odd by computing `half = (n+1) / 2`, using integer division. We then combine consecutive pairs of values of x into `subproblem` using the operator `op`. For example, if `op` is addition, then `subproblem[0]` equals `x[0] + x[1]`, `subproblem[1]` equals `x[2] + x[3]`, `subproblem[2]` equals `x[4] + x[5]`, and so on. The function `simple_reduce` uses special code to handle the case when n is odd, in which case the last item of `subproblem` gets just the last value of x. Observe that the reduction of x must equal the reduction of `subproblem`. Hence, we simply recurse on `subproblem`, passing `subproblem` to the recursive call of `simple_reduce`, and we return the result of the recursive call. The base cases occur when the length of the list is 1, in which case we just return the value of `x[0]`, and when the list is empty, where we return the identity `ident` for the operation.

Pictorially, Figure 9.1 shows how a single step of the recursion works on a list with the values 2, 3, 4, 2, 3, 6, 5, 2 and the operation of addition, and Figure 9.2 shows how the entire recursion unfolds.

To analyze this function, we observe that the for-loop is parallelizable. Why? The computation in each iteration—filling in `subproblem[i]`—is independent of the computation in all other iterations. Since $n \leq p$ and we have p processors, we can execute this for-loop in constant time in parallel. Thus, each recursive call takes constant time in parallel, plus the time for the recursive call. The number of recursive

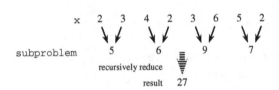

FIGURE 9.1

A single recursive call in `simple_reduce`.

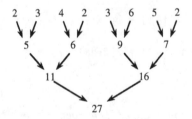

FIGURE 9.2

All recursive calls in `simple_reduce`.

calls is $O(\log n)$, since we (approximately) halve n in each call. (After $O(\log n)$ recursions, we get down to a problem size of 1. Rounding up $n/2$ when n is odd does not affect the number of recursive calls in terms of O notation.)

Notice the call to the `barrier` function immediately preceding the recursive call. Why do we need it? Each processor must have computed its portion of the reduction before that result is given to a recursive call. Referring to Figure 9.2, we see in the first call of `simple_reduce`, processor 0 adds 2 and 3, producing 5; processor 1 adds 4 and 2, producing 6; processor 2 adds 3 and 6, producing 9; and processor 3 adds 5 and 2, producing 7. In the second call of `simple_reduce` (the first call made recursively), processor 0 adds 5 and 6, producing 11; and processor 1 adds 9 and 7, producing 16. Now, in order for processor 0 to add 5 and 6, the values 5 and 6 must have already been produced. Although processor 0 produces the 5, it is processor 1 that produces the 6, and so processor 0 should not execute the recursive call until processor 1 has completed its original call. Similarly, for processor 1 to add 9 and 7, these values must have been produced by processors 2 and 3 in the original call. The call of `barrier` ensures that all processors have produced the values needed for a recursive call before the recursive call occurs.

We have $O(\log n)$ recursive calls, and each recursive call takes constant time per processor, plus β for the call to `barrier`. Thus, we can perform a reduction operation in parallel in $O(\beta \log n)$ time.

9.2.2 REDUCING IN PARALLEL WHEN $n > p$

Now, what about when $n > p$? The `reduce` function, in Listing 9.2, handles this case. Note that `reduce` is a built-in Python function that performs a reduction operation sequentially on a Python list; by redefining it, we perform the reduction in parallel. The idea is to create a list `reductions` of length p and have each processor combine its own portion of m items into one position of `reductions`. Then we can call `simple_reduce` on `reductions` to produce the reduction of the entire list.

Let us look at the `do_in_parallel` function in Listing 9.3. It takes as its first parameter a function `f`, and then it takes a tuple `params`, which comprises the gathered parameters for the function `f`. The function `do_in_parallel` runs two nested loops. The outer loop, with the header `for i in range(p)`, emulates running in parallel on p processors. The inner loop, with the header `for j in range(m)`, works on each item in processor i. By "working on each item," we mean calling the function `f` on each item j in processor i.

Now we can understand how `reduce` works. By passing to `do_in_parallel` the parameters `reduce_one`, `reductions`, `x`, and `op`, it calls `reduce_one` once for each combination of `i` and `j`, where $i = 0, 1, 2, \ldots, p - 1$ and $j = 0, 1, 2, \ldots, m - 1$. And `reduce_one` just combines `x[i*m + j]` into `reductions[i]`, using the operator `op`. For example, if `op` is addition, then `reduce_one` adds `x[i*m + j]` into `reductions[i]`. Get used to the expression `something[i*m + j]`; it denotes the jth item in processor i's portion of the list `something`.

```
# Return the reduction of all values in an n-item list x. The
# parameter op is a two-parameter function for the reduction. The
# parameter ident is the identity for op, in case the list is empty.
# Assumes that there are p processors, n > p, m = n / p, and
# processor i works on x[i*m] through x[i*m + m-1]. Takes O(m + beta
# log p) time in parallel.
def reduce(x, op, ident):
    # Create a list for reducing the values in each processor.
    reductions = [ident] * p

    # Using a parallelizable outer for-loop, reduce the values in
    # each processor's portion of x. With p processors, this loop
    # takes O(m) time.
    do_in_parallel(reduce_one, reductions, x, op)
    barrier()

    # Now we have a list of p reductions, so just return what the
    # recursive reduce function returns. This call takes O(beta log
    # p) time in parallel with p processors.
    return simple_reduce(reductions, op, ident)

# Perform one step of a reduction within processor i, combining the
# jth item in processor i into reductions[i].
def reduce_one(i, j, reductions, x, op):
    reductions[i] = op(reductions[i], x[i*m + j])
```

LISTING 9.2

The functions `reduce` and `reduce_one`.

```
# Function for performing a computation in parallel. Assumes that
# there are p processors that can operate independently and in
# parallel, and that each processor has m items from each list it
# operates on. The parameter f is the name of a function that
# operates on item j in processor i, and params gives the parameters
# for f. params should not include i and j, because these variables
# are loop variables within do_in_parallel.
def in_parallel(f, *params):
    # Call f for each i and j. The outer loop on i can run in
    # parallel, but the inner loop on j cannot.
    for i in range(p):
        for j in range(m):
            f(i, j, *params)
```

LISTING 9.3

The function `do_in_parallel`.

(Recall that processor 0 gets the first m items, processor 1 gets the next m items, and so on.)x

After the call to `do_in_parallel` has finished, `reductions[i]` has the reduction of all the values for which processor i is responsible: `x[i*m]` through `x[i*m + (m−1)]`. Remember that `reductions` has exactly p items, which we need to reduce. After `barrier` has been called to make sure that all processors have computed their own reductions, a call to `simple_reduce` does the trick, and `reduce` returns what `simple_reduce` returns.

Now we can analyze the parallel running time of `reduce`. The function `do_in_parallel` takes $O(m)$ parallel time, since each processor can combine its m items in $O(m)$ time. Then there is a single call to `barrier`, taking $O(\beta)$ time. As we have seen, the call to `simple_reduce` takes $O(\beta \log p)$ time. The total parallel time for `reduce`, therefore, comes to $O(m + \beta + \beta \log p)$. The middle term, β, is dominated by the $\beta \log p$ term, and so we can drop it. Remembering that $m = n/p$, we have a parallel running time of $O(n/p + \beta \log p)$. When $n/p > \beta \log_2 p$, the n/p term dominates the running time, and we get the best parallel speedup possible. When $\beta \log_2 p > n/p$, then n/p must be quite small: divide both sides by β and then raise both sides to be powers of 2, getting $p > 2^{n/(\beta p)}$, so we are not too disappointed that the running time is not $O(n/p)$; $O(\beta \log p)$ is still very good.

Going back to the code for a moment, we see that although the function `reduce_one` has parameters i and j, we do not include these parameters in the call to `do_in_parallel`. That is because `do_in_parallel` provides them as the parameters to its nested loops. We will see this pattern frequently in the parallel code that we develop.

9.3 PARALLEL SCANNING

A *scan* operation is somewhat like a reduction in that we wish to apply an associative operator—again, let us call it $\oplus$—to all items in a list. Unlike a reduction, which produces one answer, a scan operation on an n-item list `x[0..n−1]` produces n answers. In particular, if the result of the scan operation is in the n-item list `result`, then `result[i]` equals `x[0]` $\oplus$ `x[1]` $\oplus$ `x[2]` $\oplus \cdots \oplus$ `x[i−2]` $\oplus$ `x[i−1]`. That is, the ith position of the result should hold the combination of `x[0]` through `x[i−1]`. What about `result[0]`? It should hold the identity for the associative operator. For example, in a plus-scan, `result[0]` should equal 0.

We call this type of scan an *exclusive scan*, since the value of `result[i]` does not include `x[i]`. In an *inclusive scan*, `result[i]` equals the sum of `x[0]` through `x[i]` (not `x[i−1]`). We focus on the exclusive scan for two reasons. First, if we have the result of an exclusive scan, it is easy enough to combine `x[i]` into each position i to get the result of an inclusive scan. We cannot necessarily go backward, because not all associative operators have an inverse for every operand. (For example, matrix multiplication is associative, but if A, B, and C are matrices, and C equals the matrix product $A \times B$, we cannot necessarily determine B given A and C, since A might not be invertible or even square.) Second, exclusive scans have more practical applications than inclusive scans. We will see good applications of exclusive scans later.

Now, *this* operation looks inherently sequential. It would certainly be easy enough to compute it sequentially, given the identity ident for the function op:

```
result[0] = ident

for i in range(1, n):
    result[i] = op(result[i-1], x[i-1])
```

Seeing this computation makes us think that we need to compute result[i-1] before computing result[i]. Therefore, we would think that we have to compute result[0], then result[1], then result[2], and so on. That is a sequential computation, and it would take $O(n)$ time.

9.3.1 SCANNING IN PARALLEL WHEN $n \leq p$

Believe it or not, we can perform a scan operation in $O(\beta \log n)$ time when $n \leq p$. In other words, scanning is no harder than reduction, even though scanning seems inherently sequential.

Let us take an example of a plus-scan, where the list x has the values 2, 3, 4, 2, 3, 6, 5, 2. We expect the result to be 0, 2, 5, 9, 11, 14, 20, 25. Figure 9.3 shows a schematic drawing of the process, and Listing 9.4 gives the Python code for the function simple-scan.

We first combine consecutive pairs of values of x into a list subproblem, exactly as we did in the recursive simple_reduce function. As in simple_reduce, the list subproblem has $n/2$ items, rounding up if n is odd. In our example, subproblem has the values 5, 6, 9, 7. As in simple_reduce, we recurse on subproblem, but now we call simple_scan recursively, not simple_reduce. The recursive call is on a problem half the size. We assign the result to a list named recursive_result. In our example, recursive_result has the values 0, 5, 11, 20.

Let us think about the situation after we return from the recursive call. For even indices i, recursive_result[i/2] holds the combination (in our example, the sum) of all values in x[0] through x[i-1], and that is exactly what we want in

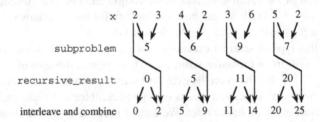

FIGURE 9.3

How to perform a scan operation in parallel.

```
# Return a list of n values, whose ith value is the reduction of all
# values in the first i-1 items of x under an operation op, and
# whose 0th value is the identity ident for op. Assumes that n <= p,
# where p is the number of processors. Takes O(beta log n) time in
# parallel.
def simple_scan(x, op, ident):
    # Create a list to hold the result of the scan.
    n = len(x)
    result = [None] * n

    if n == 1:
        result[0] = ident # base case: only one value
    else:
        # Create a new list, subproblem, of half the size, rounding
        # up if n is odd.
        half = (n+1) / 2
        subproblem = [None] * half

        # Using a parallelizable for-loop, combine pairs of values
        # in x into subproblem.
        for i in range(half-1):
            subproblem[i] = op(x[2*i], x[2*i+1])

        # Need special code to handle the last one or two values in
        # x, in case n is odd.
        if n % 2 == 0:
            subproblem[half-1] = op(x[2*half-2], x[2*half-1])
        else:
            subproblem[half-1] = x[2*half-2]

        barrier()

        # Having created a subproblem of half the size, recurse on
        # it.
        recursive_result = simple_scan(subproblem, op, ident)

        # Now, for even values of i, recursive_result[i/2] holds the
        # reduction of all values from x[0] through x[i-1], so
        # that's what we want in result[i]. For odd values of i,
        # recursive_result[i/2] holds the reduction of all values
        # from x[0] through x[i-2], so that result[i] should get the
        # combination of recursive_result[i/2] and x[i-1]. This
        # for-loop is parallelizable.
        for i in range(n):
            if i % 2 == 0:
                result[i] = recursive_result[i/2]
            else:
                result[i] = op(recursive_result[i/2], x[i-1])

        barrier()

    return result
```

LISTING 9.4

The function `simple_scan`.

the *i*th position of the result. Having created a list `result` of length *n*, we simply set `result[i]` = `recursive_result[i/2]` for even values of *i*. For odd values of *i*, `recursive_result[i/2]` holds the combination of all values in `x[0]` through `x[i-2]`, and so combining `x[i-1]` to `recursive_result[i/2]` gives us what we want in `result[i]`. We can think of filling in the `result` list as interleaving and combining, where we take the values in `recursive_result` and copy them into the even-indexed positions of `result`, and we combine the values of `recursive_result` into odd-indexed values of `x`, putting the sums into the odd-indexed positions of `result`.

When you look at the code in `parallel_scan`, you see that both for-loops are parallelizable. Therefore, the analysis is the same as for the `parallel_reduce` function, and we get that the parallel running time is just $O(\beta \log n)$. We have succeeded in parallelizing the scan operation!

9.3.2 SCANNING IN PARALLEL WHEN $n > p$

The `scan` function in Listing 9.5 handles the case when $n > p$. We start by performing a scan on the values in each processor's portion of the list `x`, placing the results into the list `result`. Processor *i* is responsible for the sublist from `x[i*m]` through `x[i*m + m−1]`, and so we want `result[i*m + j]` to hold `x[i*m]` $\oplus$ `x[i*m + 1]` $\oplus$ `x[i*m + 2]` $\oplus \cdots \oplus$ `x[i*m + j−1]`, and `result[i*m]` should hold `ident`, the identity for the operation `op`. We perform this scan by calling `do_in_parallel`, passing the function `scan_body`. When `j` is 0, `scan_body` just puts `ident` into the *j*th position of `result` in processor *i*; otherwise, it combines the result in the $(j − 1)$st position of processor *i* with the value of `x` in the $(j − 1)$st position of processor *i*. As we saw with reducing, the call to `do_in_parallel` takes $O(m)$ time in parallel.

We are not finished, however. We need to combine into each item of `result` the combination of values in all previous processors. In other words, we want to combine into `result[i*m + j]`, for $j = 0, 1, 2, \ldots, m − 1$, the value `x[0]` $\oplus$ `x[1]` $\oplus$ `x[2]` $\oplus \cdots \oplus$ `x[i*m − 1]`. We create a list `prior_reductions` of length *p*, where `prior_reductions[i]` will eventually have the combination of all the values belonging to processors 0 through $i−1$. Initially, `prior_reductions[i]` gets the sum of all of processor *i*'s values by assigning to it `result[i*m + m−1]` $\oplus$ `x[i*m + m−1]` (recall that `result[i*m + m−1]` has `x[i*m]` $\oplus$ `x[i*m + 1]` $\oplus$ `x[i*m + 2]` $\oplus \cdots \oplus$ `x[i*m + m−2]`, so that combining `x[i*m + m−1]` gives the combination of all of processor *i*'s portion of `x`). We then call `simple_scan` on `prior_reductions`, assigning the result into `processor_scan`, so that `processor_scan[i]` holds the combination of all the values belonging to processors 0 through $i − 1$. The call to `simple_scan` takes $O(\beta \log p)$ time.

Once we have `processor_scan` the way we want it, we just combine `processor_scan[i]` into each value in processor *i*'s portion of `result`. Again, we need to perform a computation for each of the *m* items in each processor, and so we call `do_in_parallel`, passing the function `accumulate`, to do the job in $O(m)$ parallel time.

```
# Return a list of n values, whose ith value is the reduction of all
# values in the first i-1 items of x under an operator op, and whose
# 0th value is the identity ident. Assumes that there are p
# processors, n > p, m = n / p, and processor i works on x[i*m]
# through x[i*m + m-1]. Takes O(m + beta log p) time in parallel.
def scan(x, op, ident):
    # Create a list to hold the result of the scan.
    n = m * p
    result = [ident] * (m * p)

    # In parallel, perform a scan on the values in each processor's
    # portion of x, so that result[i*m + j] has the reduction of the
    # values in x[i*m] through x[i*m + j-1] and result[i*m] has the
    # identity for op. With p processors, this loop takes O(m)
    # time.
    do_in_parallel(scan_body, result, x, op, ident)

    # Create a list, prior_reductions, where prior_reductions[i]
    # will hold the reduction of all the values in processor i's
    # portion of x.
    prior_reductions = [None] * p

    # Using a parallelizable for-loop, fill in prior_reductions.
    for i in range(p):
        prior_reductions[i] = op(result[i*m + m-1], x[i*m + m-1])
    barrier()

    # Perform a scan on prior_reductions, so that processor_scan[i]
    # will hold the reduction of all values in portions of x
    # belonging to processors 0 through i-1. This call takes O(beta
    # log p) time in parallel with p processors.
    processor_scan = simple_scan(prior_reductions, op, ident)

    # In parallel, combine processor_scan with the scan values
    # already computed.
    do_in_parallel(accumulate, result, processor_scan, op)
    barrier()

    return result

# Perform one step of a scan within processor i, combining the
# (j-1)st item in processor i into the result for the jth item in
# processor i.
def scan_body(i, j, result, x, op, ident):
    if j == 0:
        result[i*m + j] = ident
    else:
        result[i*m + j] = op(result[i*m + j-1], x[i*m + j-1])

# Given the result of the scan of all processors, "add" it into the
# jth result in processor i.
def accumulate(i, j, result, prior, op):
    result[i*m + j] = op(prior[i], result[i*m + j])
```

LISTING 9.5

The functions scan, scan_body, and accumulate.

As in the reduce function, the total parallel running time of scan works is $O(m + \beta \log p)$, or $O(n/p + \beta \log p)$.

9.3.3 INCLUSIVE SCANS IN PARALLEL

As claimed above, once we have the result of an exclusive scan, we can perform an inclusive scan by simply combining the result of the exclusive scan for position i with the value in x[i]. The inclusive_scan function, in Listing 9.6, calls scan to perform an exclusive scan, and then, in parallel, it combines the result of the exclusive scan with the corresponding value in x.

Because the parallel time for a call of tack_on is $O(m)$, the inclusive_scan function takes $O(m + \beta \log p)$ time, just like scan.

```
# Inclusive scan version of scan. Returns a list of n values, whose
# ith value is the reduction of all values in the first i items of a
# under an operator op, and whose 0th value is the identity ident.
# Assumes that there are p processors, n > p, m = n / p, and
# processor i works on x[i*m] through x[i*m + m-1]. Takes O(m + beta
# log p) time in parallel.
def inclusive_scan(x, op, ident):
    result = scan(x, op, ident)
    do_in_parallel(tack_on, result, x, op)
    barrier()
    return result

# Perform one step of turning an exclusive scan into an inclusive
# scan. Given the result of an exclusive scan in the jth item of
# result, processor i "adds" in the jth item of the original list x
# being scanned.
def tack_on(i, j, result, x, op):
    result[i*m + j] = op(result[i*m + j], x[i*m + j])
```
LISTING 9.6

The functions inclusive_scan and tack_on.

9.4 COPY-SCANS

In a *copy-scan*, we copy the value in x[0] to every position in the result. We will see that copy-scan is a surprisingly useful operation. For example, when partitioning for quicksort, we can use a copy-scan operation to copy the value of the pivot to all positions so that we can compare each value with the pivot in parallel. A copy-scan makes sense only as an inclusive scan, since there is no identity operator (and no reason that we would ever want to copy the value in the 0th position to everywhere *except* the 0th position).

9.4.1 COPY-SCANNING IN PARALLEL WHEN $n \leq p$

Unlike the other scan operations that we have seen, when $n \leq p$, we can perform a copy scan in constant parallel time, plus the time for a barrier. Why? Recall that we agreed we would design our algorithms so that two processors will not try to *write* into the same memory location simultaneously, but there is no reason that multiple processors cannot *read* from the same memory location simultaneously— as long as they all want to read the same value. And that is exactly what we want in a copy-scan. The simple_copy_scan function in Listing 9.7 runs in $O(\beta)$ parallel time.

```
# Return a list of n values, where each value is the value in x[0].
# Uses a parallelizable for-loop. Assumes that n <= p, where p is
# the number of processors. Takes O(beta) time in parallel.
def simple_copy_scan(x):
    n = len(x)
    result = [None] * n

    # This loop is parallelizable and runs in O(1) time if n <= p,
    # because we can read x[0] in parallel.
    for i in range(n):
        result[i] = x[0]
    barrier()

    return result
```
LISTING 9.7

The function simple_ copy_ scan.

9.4.2 COPY-SCANNING IN PARALLEL WHEN $n > p$

When $n > p$, we first perform a simple copy scan to copy the first value in processor 0 into all other processors, and then the usual loop structure copies this value throughout the list in parallel. The copy_scan function appears in Listing 9.8.

The copy_scan function takes $O(\beta)$ time in parallel for the call to simple_copy _scan and then $O(m + \beta)$ time in parallel for the call of do_in_parallel, for a total parallel time of $O(m + \beta)$.

```
# Return a list of n values, where each value is the value in
# x[0]. Assumes that processor i works on a[i*m] through a[i*m +
# m-1]. Assumes that there are p processors, n > p, m = n / p, and
# processor i works on x[i*m] through x[i*m + m-1]. Takes O(m +
# beta) time in parallel.
def copy_scan(x):
    # Create a list to hold the result of the scan.
    n = m * p
    result = [None] * n

    # Scan x[0] into each processor.
    copy = [None] * p
    copy[0] = x[0]
    copy = simple_copy_scan(copy)

    # Copy the result of scanning x[0] into each processor
    # throughout the processor's portion of the result.
    do_in_parallel(copy_body, result, copy)
    barrier()

    return result

# Perform one step of copying the result of a copy-scan into item j
# of the result in processor i.
def copy_body(i, j, result, copy):
    result[i*m + j] = copy[i]
```

LISTING 9.8

The functions copy_scan and copy_body.

9.5 PARTITIONING IN PARALLEL

Recall how quicksort relies on partitioning a list. In fact, that is really all that quicksort is: each recursive call partitions a sublist of the full list. We can parallelize quicksort by parallelizing partitioning. Scan operations are key, along with two other parallel operations, meld and permute, which we will see.

We will be using Boolean values quite a bit, but instead of True and False, it will be more convenient to use 1 and 0 instead, where 1 means True and 0 means False.

9.5.1 **MELD OPERATIONS**

A *meld* operation takes values from k lists, where $k \geq 2$, and combines them into a single list, according to k Boolean lists. This operation is best illustrated with an example. Here, we meld $k = 3$ lists—x, y, and z— holding values, according to k Boolean lists—a, b, and c:

index	0	1	2	3	4	5	6	7	8	9	10	11	12	13
a	0	0	**1**	**1**	**1**	0	0	**1**	0	0	**1**	**1**	**1**	**1**
x	0	0	**0**	**1**	**2**	3	3	**3**	4	4	**4**	**5**	**6**	**7**
b	**1**	0	0	0	0	0	**1**	0	0	0	0	0	0	0
y	**8**	9	9	9	9	9	**9**	10	10	10	10	10	10	10
c	0	**1**	0	0	0	**1**	0	0	**1**	**1**	0	0	0	0
z	10	**10**	11	11	11	**11**	12	12	**12**	**13**	14	14	14	14
result	8	10	0	1	2	11	9	3	12	13	4	5	6	7

If x[i] has a 1, then the *i*th position of the result gets x[i]; if b[i] has a 1, then the *i*th position of the result gets y[i]; and if c[i] has a 1, then the *i*th position of the result gets z[i]. Values of x, y, and z that go into the result are in boldface in the example above, as are the Boolean values that cause them to go there. We assume that for each position, exactly one of the Boolean lists holds a 1 in that position, as in the above example.

We can perform a meld operation in $O(km + \beta)$ time in parallel. The code for the meld function is in Listing 9.9. The input to the meld function is a little complicated. It is a list named lists, composed of k 2-tuples. The first item of each of the k 2-tuples is a list of n data items. The second item of each 2-tuple is a list of n 0/1 values, indicating whether the data in the corresponding position makes it into the result. So the parameter lists is a list of 2-tuples of lists! We can access the *h*th 2-tuple by lists[h]. We can access the data list in the *h*th 2-tuple by lists[h][0], and we can access the corresponding 0/1 list by lists[h][1]. And to access the data in item j of processor i in the *h*th list, we use lists[h][0][i*m + j]. Likewise, to access the corresponding 0/1 value, we use lists[h][1][i*m + j]. For our example above, the call would be meld([(x, a), (y, b), (z, c)]); the order of the tuples does not matter, so the call meld([(y, b), (z, c), (x, a)]) would produce the same result.

Notice that the function meld_operation, which is called for each $i = 0, 1, 2, \ldots, p - 1$ and $j = 0, 1, 2, \ldots, m - 1$, has a for-loop that runs for $h = 0, 1, 2, \ldots, k - 1$. Therefore, to fill in all m items of result in a given processor takes $O(km + \beta)$ parallel time. If k is a constant (3 in the example above), then the meld operation takes $O(m + \beta)$ time in parallel.

```
# Meld k 2-tuples together on p processors with m items per
# processor. lists is a list of k lists. Each of these 2-tuples
# consists of two lists. The first list contains data to be melded,
# and the second list has a 1 if the data in the corresponding
# position of the first list is to be melded, and 0 otherwise.
# Assumes that there are p processors, n > p, m = n / p, and
# processor i works on x[i*m] through x[i*m + m-1]. Takes O(mk +
# beta) time in parallel with p processors.
def meld(lists):
    n = m * p
    result = [None] * n
    k = len(lists)
    do_in_parallel(meld_operation, result, lists, k, m)
    barrier()
    return result


# Operation to store into the jth item of the result in processor i.
# Goes through all k 0/1 lists, and when it finds a 1 in the jth
# item of processor i, puts the data in the jth item of processor i
# into the result.
def meld_operation(i, j, result, lists, k, m):
    for h in range(k):
        if lists[h][1][i*m + j] == 1:
            result[i*m + j] = lists[h][0][i*m + j]
```

LISTING 9.9

The meld function.

9.5.2 PERMUTE OPERATIONS

A *permute* operation takes two lists—say, perm and x—and it produces a list result such that result[perm[i]] gets the value of x[i]. We assume that the perm list is a permutation (i.e., a rearrangement) of the indices $0, 1, 2, \ldots, n - 1$, so what we are really doing is permuting the values in the list x according to the indices in perm: perm[i] gives the index in result that x[i] goes to. For example, here is a permute operation that uses the result of melding in the previous example as the perm list:

index	0	1	2	3	4	5	6	7	8	9	10	11	12	13
perm	8	10	0	1	2	11	9	3	12	13	4	5	6	7
x	4	6	2	1	3	7	4	2	5	6	1	2	1	3
result	2	1	3	2	1	2	1	3	4	4	6	7	5	6

For example, because `perm[0]` is 8, the value 4 in `x[0]` appears in `result[8]`. Similarly, because `perm[1]` is 10, the value of `x[1]`, which is 6, appears in `result[10]`. And because `perm[4]` is 2, the 3 in `x[4]` appears in `result[2]`.

Listing 9.10 shows the Python code for the `permute` function. The permute operation runs in $O(m + \beta)$ time in parallel.

```
# Permute the list x according to the indices in the list perm. Copy
# x[i] into the perm[i]th position of the result. Assumes that
# there are p processors, n > p, m = n / p, and processor i works on
# x[i*m] through x[i*m + m-1]. Takes O(m + beta) time in parallel.
def permute(x, perm):
    n = m * p
    result = [None] * n
    do_in_parallel(permute_body, result, perm, x, m)
    barrier()
    return result


# Perform one step of permuting. Copies the value of x in the jth
# position of processor i into the index given by the jth position
# in processor i of perm.
def permute_body(i, j, result, perm, x, m):
    result[perm[i*m + j]] = x[i*m + j]
```

LISTING 9.10

The functions for `permute` and `permute_body`.

9.5.3 PARTITIONING

Now we can see how to partition in parallel. One difference from how to partition in the quicksort code that you have probably seen before is that we use the first item, not the last, as the pivot. Another difference is that we will make three partitions; in order from left to right: items less than the pivot, items equal to the pivot, and items greater than the pivot. Sequential quicksort would recurse on only the left and right partitions, not the middle partition, but when we work in parallel, it is easiest to recurse on all three partitions. We will show how to partition by example, using the list x from the previous example.

We will refer to performing operations "in parallel." That will mean "in as parallel a fashion as possible," typically taking parallel time $O(m + \beta \log p)$ to reduce or scan, and parallel time $O(m + \beta)$ to copy-scan, permute, or meld a constant number of lists.

Here is how to partition in parallel (refer to Figure 9.4 for a running example):

1. Copy-scan `x[0]` into a new list `pivot`, so that `pivot[i]` equals `x[0]` for all *i*. That way, we can compare all positions of x with the pivot in parallel.

index	0	1	2	3	4	5	6	7	8	9	10	11	12	13
x	4	6	2	1	3	7	4	2	5	6	1	2	1	3
pivot	4	4	4	4	4	4	4	4	4	4	4	4	4	4
less	0	0	1	1	1	0	0	1	0	0	1	1	1	1
eq	1	0	0	0	0	0	1	0	0	0	0	0	0	0
greater	0	1	0	0	0	1	0	0	1	1	0	0	0	0
less_scan	0	0	0	1	2	3	3	3	4	4	4	5	6	7
eq_scan	0	1	1	1	1	1	1	2	2	2	2	2	2	2
greater_scan	0	0	1	1	1	1	2	2	2	3	4	4	4	4
less_red	8	8	8	8	8	8	8	8	8	8	8	8	8	8
eq_red	2	2	2	2	2	2	2	2	2	2	2	2	2	2
eq_perm	8	9	9	9	9	9	9	10	10	10	10	10	10	10
greater_perm	10	10	11	11	11	11	12	12	12	13	14	14	14	14
perm	8	10	0	1	2	11	9	3	12	13	4	5	6	7
partitioned x	2	1	3	2	1	2	1	3	4	4	6	7	5	6

FIGURE 9.4

The steps in parallel partitioning.

2. In parallel, compute three Boolean lists: less[i] indicates whether
   x[i] < pivot[i]; eq[i] indicates whether x[i] = pivot[i]; and greater[i]
   indicates whether x[i] > pivot[i].
3. Perform a plus-scan on each of less, eq, and greater, and perform a
   plus-reduction on less and eq. Call the scan results less_scan, eq_scan, and
   greater_scan. Store the reduction results in less_red[0] and eq_red[0]
   (because we are going to copy-scan them).
   At this point, if x[i] is less than x[0] (the pivot), then less_scan[i] has the
   index of where we want to permute x[i]. If x[i] equals the pivot, then
   eq_scan[i] has the index of where we want to permute x[i], *but within the set
   of items equal to the pivot.* And if x[i] is greater than the pivot, then
   greater_scan[i] has the index of where we want to permute x[i], *but within
   the set of items greater than the pivot.*
4. Copy-scan less_red and eq_red. Add the result of copy-scanning less_red
   into eq_scan, item by item, giving eq_perm. Add the sum of the results of
   copy-scanning less_red and eq_red into greater_scan, item by item, giving
   greater_perm.
   Now if x[i] equals the pivot, then eq_perm[i] has the index of where we want
   to permute x[i] within the entire list, and if x[i] is greater than the pivot, then
   greater_scan[i] has the index of where we want to permute x[i] within the
   entire list.
5. Meld the lists less_scan, eq_perm, and greater_perm, using the Boolean lists
   less, eq, and greater. Call the resulting list perm, and this gives the index
   where each value of x[i] should go.

6. Permute the list x according to the indices in perm. The resulting list has the list x partitioned around the pivot x[0].

In the example, indices 0 through 7 of the partitioned list hold values of x that are less than the pivot 4; indices 8 and 9 hold values of x that equal the pivot 4; and indices 10 through 13 hold values of x that are greater than the pivot 4. Thus, we have successfully partitioned the list x.

9.5.4 ANALYSIS

Let us add up the costs of the steps:

Step		Parallel time
1.	Copy-scan the pivot	$O(m + \beta)$
2.	Compute less, eq, and greater	$O(m + \beta)$
3.	Plus-scan on less, eq, and greater	$O(m + \beta \log p)$
	Plus-reduce less and eq	$O(m + \beta \log p)$
4.	Copy-scan less_red and eq_red	$O(m + \beta)$
	Compute eq_perm and greater_perm	$O(m + \beta)$
5.	Meld	$O(m + \beta)$
6.	Permute	$O(m + \beta)$

The total cost of partitioning is dominated by the most "expensive" steps, which are steps 3 and 4. Thus, we can partition in parallel in only $O(m + \beta \log p)$ time.

9.6 PARALLEL QUICKSORT

Although partitioning is the key step in quicksort, partitioning just once is not enough. In quicksort, we have to partition at each step of the recursion, except for the base cases. One way to think of quicksort running in parallel on a list is to repeatedly partition the partitions until each partition contains only items with the same value.

For example, suppose that the initial list contains the valuesHere, the vertical bars

$$\left| \quad 4 \quad 6 \quad 2 \quad 1 \quad 3 \quad 7 \quad 4 \quad 2 \quad 5 \quad 6 \quad 1 \quad 2 \quad 1 \quad 3 \quad \right|$$

demarcate the start and end of the list, which is initially one big partition. If we partition around the pivot value 4, we get the following partitions: Next, partition

$$\left| \quad 2 \quad 1 \quad 3 \quad 2 \quad 1 \quad 2 \quad 1 \quad 3 \quad \right| \quad 4 \quad 4 \quad \left| \quad 6 \quad 7 \quad 5 \quad 6 \quad \right|$$

around the pivot value 2 in the first partition, around the pivot value 4 in the second partition, and around the pivot value 6 in the third partition. We get these partitions: At this point, every partition consists of only one value, and we have finished: the entire list has been sorted.

1	1	1	2	2	2	3	3	4	4	5	6	6	7

How do we keep track of the partitions? We use *segment bits* stored in a *segment list*. Let us call it seg. Then seg[i] is 1 if index *i* begins a segment, and it is 0 otherwise. Here is what seg and the data above, let us call it x, should look like before each step above:

index	0	1	2	3	4	5	6	7	8	9	10	11	12	13
seg	1	0	0	0	0	0	0	0	0	0	0	0	0	0
x	4	6	2	1	3	7	4	2	5	6	1	2	1	3
seg	1	0	0	0	0	0	0	0	1	0	1	0	0	0
x	2	1	3	2	1	2	1	3	4	4	6	7	5	6
seg	1	0	0	1	0	0	1	0	1	0	1	1	0	1
x	1	1	1	2	2	2	3	3	4	4	5	6	6	7

We can create *segmented scan* operations, which are just like the regular scan operations except that they treat each segment separately. For example, in the second seg and x lists above, here is what a segmented plus-scan would produce:

seg	1	0	0	0	0	0	0	0	1	0	1	0	0	0
x	2	1	3	2	1	2	1	3	4	4	6	7	5	6
result	0	2	3	6	8	9	11	12	0	4	0	6	13	18

How do we implement segmented scan operations? We will see a little later that we can implement them with unsegmented scans, if we think outside the box. We will also need segmented reductions. Once we have segmented scans and reductions, we can perform quicksort.

Here is how we perform one partitioning step in parallel (refer to Figure 9.5 for a running example):

1. In each segment, take the first item as the pivot in that segment, and copy-scan it throughout the segment. For example, let us start with the segments shown by seg and x in Figure 9.5. The segmented copy-scan gives the list pivot in the figure.

2. As in the unsegmented partitioning algorithm, compute three Boolean lists: less[i] indicates whether x[i] < pivot[i]; eq[i] indicates whether x[i] = pivot[i]; and greater[i] indicates whether x[i] > pivot[i].

index	0	1	2	3	4	5	6	7	8	9	10	11	12	13
seg	1	0	0	0	0	0	0	0	1	0	1	0	0	0
x	2	1	3	2	1	2	1	3	4	4	6	7	5	6
pivot	2	2	2	2	2	2	2	2	4	4	6	6	6	6
less	0	1	0	0	1	0	1	0	0	0	0	0	1	0
eq	1	0	0	1	0	1	0	0	1	1	1	0	0	1
greater	0	0	1	0	0	0	0	1	0	0	0	1	0	0
less_scan	0	0	1	1	1	2	2	3	0	0	0	0	0	1
eq_scan	0	1	1	1	2	2	3	3	0	1	0	1	1	1
greater_scan	0	0	0	1	1	1	1	1	0	0	0	0	1	1
less_red	3	3	3	3	3	3	3	3	0	0	1	1	1	1
eq_red	3	3	3	3	3	3	3	3	2	2	2	2	2	2
index_scan	0	0	0	0	0	0	0	0	8	8	10	10	10	10
less_perm	0	0	1	1	1	2	2	3	8	8	10	10	10	11
eq_perm	3	4	4	4	5	5	6	6	8	9	11	12	12	12
greater_perm	6	6	6	7	7	7	7	7	10	10	13	13	14	14
perm	3	0	6	4	1	5	2	7	8	9	11	13	10	12
partitioned x	1	1	1	2	2	2	3	3	4	4	5	6	6	7

FIGURE 9.5

How the steps of parallel partitioning in quicksort unfold.

3. Perform a segmented plus-scan on each of less, eq, and greater, and perform segmented plus-reductions on less and eq. Call the scan results less_scan, eq_scan, and greater_scan. Call the reduction results less_red and eq_red. Perform a segmented copy-scan on less_red and eq_red.
Now, if x[i] is less than pivot[i], then less_scan[i] has the index of where we want to permute x[i] *but within its current segment*. If x[i] equals pivot[i], then eq_scan[i] + less_red[i] has the index of where we want to permute x[i] *within its current segment*. And if x[i] is greater than pivot[i], then eq_scan[i] + less_red[i] + eq_red[i] has the index of where we want to permute x[i] *within its current segment*.

4. Perform a segmented copy-scan of the index, giving index_scan.

5. Add index_scan and less_scan, giving less_perm. Add index_scan, less_red, and eq_scan, giving eq_perm. Add index_scan, less_red, eq_red, and greater_scan, giving greater_perm.
Now less_perm gives the index *within the entire list* of where each item that is less than the corresponding pivot should go, eq_perm does the same for items

index	0	1	2	3	4	5	6	7	8	9	10	11	12	13
seg	1	0	0	0	0	0	0	0	1	0	1	0	0	0
less_red	3	3	3	3	3	3	3	3	0	0	1	1	1	1
eq_red	3	3	3	3	3	3	3	3	2	2	2	2	2	2
index_scan	0	0	0	0	0	0	0	0	8	8	10	10	10	10
partitioned x	1	1	1	2	2	2	3	3	4	4	5	6	6	7
eq_start	3	3	3	3	3	3	3	3	8	8	11	11	11	11
greater_start	6	6	6	6	6	6	6	6	10	10	13	13	13	13
new seg	1	0	0	1	0	1	0	0	1	0	1	1	0	1

FIGURE 9.6

How to compute the new segment bits in parallel after one parallel partitioning step of quicksort.

that equal their pivots, and greater_perm does the same for items greater than their pivots.

6. Meld the lists less_perm, eq_perm, and greater_perm, using the Boolean lists less, eq, and greater. Call the resulting list perm, and this gives the index *within the entire list* where each value of x[i] should go.

7. Permute the list x according to the indices in perm. The resulting list has each segment in x partitioned around the pivot in that segment.

8. As Figure 9.6 shows, to compute the new segment bits, add index_scan and less_red, giving eq_start. Add index_scan, less_red, and eq_red, giving greater_start. These values are the indices in which each new segment of values equal to the pivot and values greater than the pivot should start. Segments of values less than the pivot start where the original segments started. Make the new seg bits be 1 where index equals index_scan, eq_start, or greater_start, and 0 everywhere else.

9. This process repeats until the entire list has been sorted. To determine whether the entire list has been sorted, compute a Boolean list sorted such that sorted[i] equals (index[i] == 0) or (x[i−1] <= x[i]). (Notice that because the or operator is short-circuiting, no error occurs for $i = 0$.) Setting sorted[i] to 1 if index[i] is 0 makes it such that we do not need to compare the first value in the list with the value before it. Then just perform an and-reduction on sorted. If the and-reduction produces the value 1, then we have finished. Otherwise, keep going.

9.6.1 ANALYSIS

Let us see how long this quicksort algorithm takes. In the worst case, all the partition sizes are highly unbalanced, and sequential quicksort can take $O(n^2)$ time.

On average, however, the partition sizes are close enough to equal that sequential quicksort takes $O(n \log n)$ time to sort an n-item list. (See [3, Section 7.4] for a rigorous analysis.)

Suppose we were to draw a recursion tree for sequential quicksort, and suppose that the tree has d levels. Then the running time of sequential quicksort would be $O(nd)$. In the worst case, $d = n$, and on average d is $O(\log n)$.

For our parallel version, assuming that we can perform each segmented operation in $O(n/p + \beta \log p)$ parallel time (we will see how in the next section), each iteration takes $O(n/p + \beta \log p)$ time in parallel. Therefore, the total parallel running time is $O(d(n/p + \beta \log p))$.

Again, let us see how to interpret running times that have the sum of two terms (such as n/p and $\beta \log p$). One of the terms dominates the other, and in terms of O notation, that is the one that matters. For the moment, let us assume that $n/p \geq \beta \log p$, so the n/p term dominates. In the worst case, $d = n$, and the parallel running time is $O(n(n/p))$, or $O(n^2/p)$, and we have managed to reduce the sequential time by a factor of p. In the average case, d is $O(\log n)$, and parallel quicksort takes parallel time $O((n/p) \log n)$, or $O((n \log n)/p)$. Again we have reduced the sequential time by a factor of p. Given that we have p processors, having the parallel running time by a factor of p lower than the sequential running time is the best we can hope for.

What if $n/p < \beta \log p$? Then the parallel time is $O(d \beta \log p)$, or $O(n \beta \log p)$ in the worst case and $O((\log n)(\beta \log p))$ in the average case. In both cases, we trade a factor of n in the sequential time for a factor of $\beta \log p$ in the parallel time. That is a good trade except when $\beta \log p$ is in the narrow range $n/p < \beta \log p < n$.

9.7 HOW TO PERFORM SEGMENTED SCANS AND REDUCTIONS

To close the loop, we need to see how to perform segmented scan and reduction operations. The basic idea uses enhanced operators whose operands are tuples. We also have to be able to perform backward scans within segments.

9.7.1 SEGMENTED SCANS

We start with a basic segmented scan (not a segmented copy-scan, which we will see later) in the procedure `segmented_scan` in Listing 9.11. We will show how this function works by doing a max-scan on the list x shown in Figure 9.7, with the answer being the list `result`. Remember that scans are, by default, exclusive.

We are going to perform a segmented scan by performing an *un*segmented scan, but the operator we use in the unsegmented scan will be a strange one that combines op (the operator for the segmented scan) and the segment bits. In particular, this operator—let us call it @—takes two 2-tuples as operands and returns a 2-tuple. Each 2-tuple consists of a segment number and a value. So we can think of the operator @

```
# Perform a segmented exclusive scan operation on a list x of data,
# with a 0-1 list seg of segment bits. Like a regular scan, but
# restarts the scan for each position i such that seg[i] is 1.
# Assumes that seg[0] is 1. The parameter op gives the operation to
# perform, and the parameter ident is the identity for the
# operation. Assumes that there are p processors, n > p, m = n / p,
# and processor i works on x[i*m] through x[i*m + m-1]. Takes O(m +
# beta log p) time in parallel.
def segmented_scan(x, seg, op, ident):
    n = m * p

    # Do an inclusive plus-scan on the segment bits, calling the
    # result seg_number.
    seg_number = inclusive_scan(seg, add, 0)

    # Make a list of tuples whose ith item is the ith item in
    # seg_number and the ith item in x.
    tuples = [None] * n
    do_in_parallel(form_tuple, tuples, seg_number, x, m)
    barrier()

    # Do an exclusive scan on tuples.
    tuple_scan = scan(tuples, segmented_op(op), (0, ident))

    # Where the ith item in seg is 1, the result of the segmented
    # scan is the identity. Elsewhere, the result is the second
    # part of each tuple in tuple_scan.
    result = [None] * n
    do_in_parallel(unform_tuple, result, seg, tuple_scan, ident, m)
    barrier()

    return result

# Form a tuple of the segment number and value in x.
def form_tuple(i, j, tuples, seg_number, x, m):
    tuples[i*m + j] = (seg_number[i*m + j], x[i*m + j])

# After having scanned the tuples, use the identity where a segment
# starts. Use the second value in the tuple everywhere else.
def unform_tuple(i, j, result, seg, tuple_scan, ident, m):
    if seg[i*m + j] == 1:
        result[i*m + j] = ident
    else:
        result[i*m + j] = tuple_scan[i*m + j][1]
```

LISTING 9.11

The functions segmented_scan, form_tuple, and unform_tuple.

index	0	1	2	3	4	5	6	7	8
seg	1	0	0	1	0	0	0	1	0
x	5	7	6	3	9	4	5	2	6
result	$-\infty$	5	7	$-\infty$	3	9	9	$-\infty$	2

FIGURE 9.7

The result of a segmented max-scan on a list x.

as computing $(c[0], c[1]) = (a[0], a[1])@(b[0], b[1])$. Here, $c[0]$, $a[0]$, and $b[0]$ are segment numbers. We will also require that $a[0] \leq b[0]$.

The functions `segmented_operation` and `segmented_op` in Listing 9.12 give the rule for computing @. There is a ton going on in these few lines of code, so let us take it slowly. The idea is that `segmented_op` implements the @ operator. Given the operator `op` that we are doing the segmented scan on, `segmented_op` returns another function, which is unnamed and takes just the parameters `a` and `b`, assumed to be 2-tuples of the form described above. By using the <u>lambda</u> form of Python, we build `op` into this function. So `segmented_op` returns a modified form of `segmented_operation` in which `op` is built-in.

```
# Perform a segmented operation on two tuples, a and b. The first
# item in each tuple is a segment number, and the second item in
# each tuple is a value. op is the operation to perform.
# Assumption: a's segment number is less than or equal to
# b's segment number. If a's segment number is strictly less than
# b's segment number, then the result is b. Otherwise, the segment
# numbers must be equal, and the result is a tuple comprising this
# segment number and the operator op applied to a's value and b's
# value.
def segmented_operation(a, b, op):
    if a[0] < b[0]:
        return b
    else:
        return (a[0], op(a[1], b[1]))

# Return a function on two tuples, a and b, performing a segmented
# operation op. This operation, op, is built into the returned
# function. The function returned may be called later on.
def segmented_op(op):
    return lambda a, b: segmented_operation(a, b, op)
```

LISTING 9.12

The functions `segmented_operation` and `segmented_op`.

index	0	1	2	3	4	5	6	7	8
seg	1	0	0	1	0	0	0	1	0
x	5	7	6	3	9	4	5	2	6
seg_number	1	1	1	2	2	2	2	3	3
tuples	(1, 5)	(1, 7)	(1, 6)	(2, 3)	(2, 9)	(2, 4)	(2, 5)	(3, 2)	(3, 6)
tuple_scan	$(0, -\infty)$	(1, 5)	(1, 7)	(1, 7)	(2, 3)	(2, 9)	(2, 9)	(2, 9)	(3, 2)
result	$-\infty$	5	7	$-\infty$	3	9	9	$-\infty$	2

FIGURE 9.8

The steps in implementing a segmented max-scan from unsegmented operations.

Think of it this way. Let us name the function returned by segmented_op by assigning it to f, where op is max: f = segmented_op(max). Then we can call f(a, b), where a and b are our 2-tuples, and f returns a 2-tuple.

How does segmented_operation work? It first checks to see whether b's segment number is greater than a's segment number. If it is, then it just returns the 2-tuple b. Otherwise, the two segment numbers must be equal (recall that we require a's segment number to be less than or equal to b's segment number, so if a's segment number is not less than b's segment number, then the two segment numbers must be equal), and the 2-tuple returned has this segment number as the first component and op(a[1], b[1]) as the second component.

The idea behind segmented_operation is that if a and b are from the same segment, then we just perform op on the values in a and b. If they are in different segments, however, then b must be in a segment numbered higher than a's segment. That means b is starting a new segment, and we want to restart the scan just as if b were at index 0.

Now let us see, in Figure 9.8, how segmented_scan works on our above example to perform a max-scan. The first step is to compute segment numbers. The first segment is number 1, the second segment is number 2, and so on. An *inclusive* plus-scan on the segment bits does the trick, creating the list seg_number.

Next, we form the 2-tuples of the segment number and value in x by calling do_in_parallel on the form_tuple function:

```
# Form a tuple of the segment number and value in x.
def form_tuple(i, j, tuples, seg_number, x, m):
    tuples[i*m + j] = (seg_number[i*m + j], x[i*m + j])
```

We call the resulting list tuples.

Now we do an exclusive scan on tuples, using the function returned by the call of segmented_op(op) as the function for the exclusive scan. Let us call the result tuple_scan. Where seg[i] equals 1, the result of the segmented scan is the identity for op, passed to segmented_scan as the parameter ident. Where seg[i] equals 0, the result is the second part of each tuple in tuple_scan; the segmented_op function effectively restarted the scan at the beginning of the segment. We call do_in_parallel on the function unform_tuple, which does exactly this:

```
# After having scanned the tuples, use the identity where a segment
# starts. Use the second value in the tuple everywhere else.
def unform_tuple(i, j, result, seg, tuple_scan, ident, m):
    if seg[i*m + j] == 1:
        result[i*m + j] = ident
    else:
        result[i*m + j] = tuple_scan[i*m + j][1]
```

And we get the result shown in result.

The time to perform segmented_scan is dominated by the calls to inclusive_scan and scan, one of each, for a parallel running time of $O(n/p + \beta \log p)$. (The calls to do_in_parallel and barrier just add another $O(n/p + \beta)$.)

9.7.2 SEGMENTED INCLUSIVE SCANS

Once we have exclusive segmented scans, segmented inclusive scans are easy. We just use the tack_on function from Listing 9.6:

```
# Like segmented_scan, but performs an inclusive scan.
def segmented_inclusive_scan(x, seg, op, ident):
    result = segmented_scan(x, seg, op, ident)
    do_in_parallel(tack_on, result, x, op)
```

Like segmented_scan, the segmented_inclusive_scan function takes $O(n/p + \beta \log p)$ parallel time.

9.7.3 SEGMENTED COPY-SCANS

To perform a segmented copy-scan, we can think of performing a segmented inclusive scan using a copy operator:

```
# Operation for a segmented copy-scan. Always returns the first of
# its two parameters.
def copy(a, b):
    return a
```

The only problem is that we do not really have an identity for the copy operation. So we can perform a segmented copy-scan by first doing a segmented scan with a copy operator and then just putting the original value back where segment bits are 1. The code appears in Listing 9.13. Here is how it works for our example. After calling segmented_scan, we have

index	0	1	2	3	4	5	6	7	8
seg	1	0	0	1	0	0	0	1	0
x	5	7	6	3	9	4	5	2	6
result	None	5	5	None	3	3	3	None	2

And then after calling `do_in_parallel` to perform `segmented_copy_scan_body`, we have

index	0	1	2	3	4	5	6	7	8
seg	1	0	0	1	0	0	0	1	0
x	5	7	6	3	9	4	5	2	6
result	5	5	5	3	3	3	3	2	2

Once again, the segmented version of this operation has the same parallel running time, $O(n/p + \beta \log p)$, as its unsegmented counterpart.

```
# Perform a segmented copy—scan operation on a list x of data, with
# a 0—1 list seg of segment bits. Like a regular copy—scan, but
# restarts the scan for each position i such that seg[i] is 1.
# Assumes that seg[0] is 1. Assumes that there are p processors, n
# > p, m = n / p, and processor i works on x[i*m] through x[i*m +
# m—1]. Takes O(m + beta log p) time in parallel.
def segmented_copy_scan(x, seg):
    result = segmented_scan(x, seg, copy, None)
    do_in_parallel(segmented_copy_scan_body, result, seg, x, m)
    barrier()
    return result

# Where seg[i] is 1, just copy x[i] into result[i].
def segmented_copy_scan_body(i, j, result, seg, x, m):
    if seg[i*m + j] == 1:
        result[i*m + j] = x[i*m + j]
```

LISTING 9.13

The functions `segmented_copy_scan` and `segmented_copy_scan_body`.

9.7.4 SEGMENTED REDUCTIONS

To perform a segmented reduction, perform a segmented *inclusive* scan, and then perform a *backward* segmented copy-scan on the result. This operation places the result of each segmented reduction into all the items in its segment.

How do we perform a backward segmented copy-scan? It is *almost* enough to just reverse the lists x and seg, perform a normal (forward) copy-scan, and then reverse the result. Again, using vertical bars to delineate segments (you will see in a moment why we are not showing seg), we would get something like this:

x	5	7	6	3	9	4	5	2	6
reversed x	6	2	5	4	9	3	6	7	5
copy-scan	6	6	5	5	5	5	6	6	6
reverse again	6	6	6	5	5	5	5	6	6

That example gives the idea, but we cannot just reverse seg to indicate the start of each segment. Reversing seg places a 1 in the *last* position of each segment, not the first position:

seg	1	0	0	1	0	0	0	1	0
x	5	7	6	3	9	4	5	2	6

reversed seg	0	1	0	0	0	1	0	0	1
reversed x	6	2	5	4	9	3	6	7	5

Observe, however, that if position i ends a segment, then position $i + 1$ must start the next segment. To create the correct segment bits for the reversed version of x, therefore, we just need to shift the reversed segment bits one position to the right, filling the vacated bit at index 0 with a 1.

Listing 9.14 shows code to shift a list in parallel by a given number of positions, indicated by the parameter amount, and filling vacated positions with the value given by the parameter fill. If amount is positive, the shift is to the right, and if amount is negative, the shift is to the left. Listing 9.14 also gives the code to reverse a list in parallel. So now a backward segmented copy-scan is easy:

```
# Like segmented_copy_scan, but copies the last item in each
# segment throughout the segment.
def backward_segmented_copy_scan(x, seg):
    return reverse(segmented_copy_scan(reverse(x),
        shift(reverse(seg), 1, 1)))
```

And so is a segmented reduction:

```
# Perform a segmented reduction operation, copying the result
# of the reduction within each segment throughout the segment. The
# reduction operator is op, and the identity value for op is
# ident. Assumes that there are p processors, n > p, m = n / p, and
# processor i works on x[i*m] through x[i*m + m-1]. Takes O(m +
# beta log p) time in parallel.
def segmented_reduce(x, seg, op, ident):
    return backward_segmented_copy_scan(segmented_inclusive_scan(x,
        seg, op, ident), seg)
```

```
# Return a list that is the same as list x, but with all items
# shifted to the right by amount positions. If amount is negative,
# then shift to the left. Fill in evacuated positions with the
# parameter fill. Assumes that there are p processors, n > p, m = n
# / p, and processor i works on x[i*m] through x[i*m + m-1]. Takes
# O(m + beta) time in parallel.
def shift(x, amount, fill):
    n = m * p
    result = [None] * n
    do_in_parallel(shift_body, result, x, amount, fill, n, m)
    barrier()
    return result
def shift_body(i, j, result, x, amount, fill, n, m):
    index = i*m + j
    if index < amount or index >= n + amount:
        result[index] = fill
    else:
        result[index] = x[index - amount]


# Return the reverse of a list x. Assumes that there are p
# processors, n > p, m = n / p, and processor i works on x[i*m]
# through x[i*m + m-1]. Takes O(m + beta) time in parallel.
def reverse(x):
    n = m * p
    result = [None] * n
    do_in_parallel(reverse_body, result, x, n, m)
    barrier()
    return result


def reverse_body(i, j, result, x, n, m):
    index = i*m + j
    partner_index = n - index - 1
    result[partner_index] = x[index]
```

LISTING 9.14

Functions for shifting and reversing a list in parallel.

The shift and reverse functions take $O(n/p + \beta)$ parallel time, and so the parallel running time for segmented_reduce is the same as for segmented_inclusive_scan and segmented_copy_scan: $O(n/p + \beta \log p)$.

9.8 COMPARING SEQUENTIAL AND PARALLEL RUNNING TIMES

What are the trade-offs between parallel and sequential computation? Given the additional complexity of parallel computing, when does it pay to compute in parallel instead of sequentially? In this section, we will perform a simple analysis for reduction and scan operations.

We will start with reductions where $n \leq p$. Let t be the time to perform one operation—that is, one call of the function op in simple_reduce, along with whatever overhead per loop iteration is incurred to call op repeatedly in either parallel or sequential code. Let h be the overhead per recursive call, which includes testing for the base cases, creating the list of half the size, handling the case in which n is odd, the barrier, and making the recursive call. Then the total time T_1^* to perform the reduction operation sequentially is

$$T_1^* = t(n - 1),$$

since the operation must be applied $n - 1$ times. The total time T_p to perform the reduction operation in parallel is

$$T_p = (t + h) \log n,$$

since each recursive call can perform all the calls to op in parallel. The parallel version is worthwhile when $T_p < T_1^*$, or

$$(t + h) \log n < t(n - 1).$$

Dividing both sides by t gives

$$(1 + h/t) \log n < n - 1.$$

Raising both sides to be powers of 2 gives

$$2^{(1+h/t) \log n} < 2^{n-1},$$

or

$$n^{1+h/t} < 2^{n-1}.$$

Let us look at some possible ratios of h/t. If $h/t = 5$, then $T_p < T_1^*$ for $n \geq 31$. If $h/t = 10$, then $T_p < T_1^*$ for $n \geq 68$, and if $h/t = 20$, then $T_p < T_1^*$ for $n \geq 154$.

The analysis is similar for scan operations when $n \leq p$. Now each recursive call of simple_scan performs the operation op twice in parallel and calls barrier twice, so

$$T_{\mathrm{p}} = 2(t+h)\log n.$$

The parallel version is worthwhile when $T_{\mathrm{p}} < T_1^*$, or

$$n^{2(1+h/t)} < 2^{n-1}.$$

Using the same h/t ratios as before—5, 10, and 20—we get that $T_{\mathrm{p}} < T_1^*$ for $n \geq 76$, 163, and 358, respectively.

Now let us look at reduction operations when $n > p$. The sequential time $T_1^* = t(n-1)$ remains unchanged, but the parallel time for p processors becomes

$$T_{\mathrm{p}} = tn/p + \beta + (t+h)\log p.$$

To keep things simple, we know that $\beta < h$, so let us bound T_{p} by

$$T_{\mathrm{p}} < tn/p + h + (t+h)\log p,$$

so when we divide both sides by t, we find that $T_{\mathrm{p}} < T_1^*$ when

$$n/p + h/t + (1 + h/t)\log p < n - 1.$$

If we hold the ratio h/t constant and increase the number p of processors, we find that the crossover point where T_{p} goes below T_1^* increases with p. For example, Figure 9.9 shows crossover points for $h/t = 5$, 10, and 20. Taking into account that the horizontal axes show $\log p$, we find these crossover points increase quite slowly with the number of processors.

For scan operations when $n > p$, there are two calls to do_in_parallel and two calls to barrier, and so the parallel time becomes

$$T_{\mathrm{p}} = 2(tn/p + \beta) + (t+h)\log p,$$

which we again bound by

$$T_{\mathrm{p}} < 2(tn/p + h) + (t+h)\log p.$$

Again dividing both sides by t, we get $T_{\mathrm{p}} < T_1^*$ when

$$2(n/p + h/t) + (1 + h/t)\log p < n - 1.$$

As with the reduction operation, if we hold the ratio h/t constant and increase the number p of processors, we once again find that the crossover point where T_{p} goes below T_1^* increases with p, now for $p \geq 8$. Figure 9.10 shows crossover points for $h/t = 5$, 10, and 20. Once again, the crossover points increase rather slowly with the value of p.

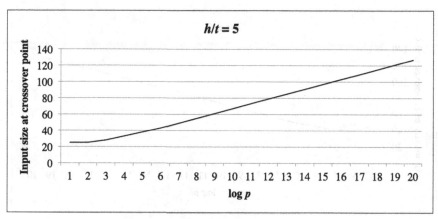

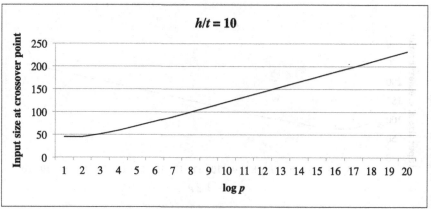

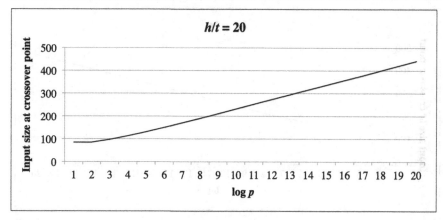

FIGURE 9.9

Input size n at crossover points for reduction operations at which $T_p < T_1^*$ for $h/t = 5, 10,$ and 20 when $n > p$.

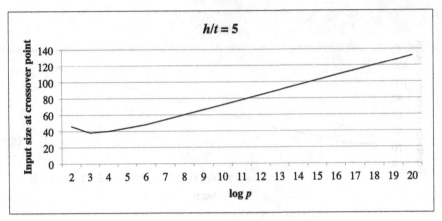

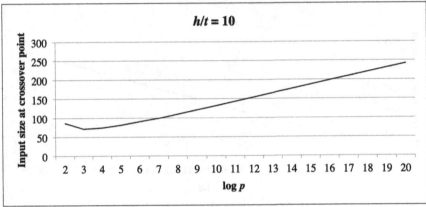

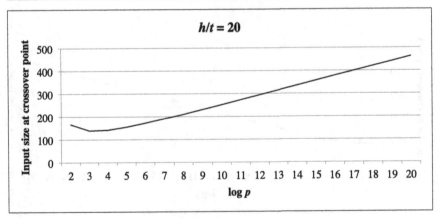

FIGURE 9.10

Input size n at crossover points for scan operations at which $T_p < T_1^*$ for $h/t = 5, 10,$ and 20 when $n > p$.

REFERENCES

[1] G.E. Blelloch, Scan Primitives and Parallel Vector Models, Ph.D. thesis, Massachusetts Institute of Technology, 1988.

[2] G.E. Blelloch, Vector Models for Data-Parallel Computing, The MIT Press, Cambridge, MA, 1990.

[3] T.H. Cormen, C.E. Leiserson, R.L. Rivest, C. Stein, Introduction to Algorithms, third ed., The MIT Press, Cambridge, MA, 2009.

Parallel programming illustrated through Conway's Game of Life

10

Victor Eijkhout*

*The University of Texas at Austin**

Relevant core courses: The student is supposed to have gone through CS1, with CS2 and DS/A preferred.

National Science Foundation/IEEE Computer Society Technical Committee on Parallel Processing curriculum topics: All topics have a Bloom classification of C unless otherwise noted.

Architecture topics

- Taxonomy: single instruction, multiple data (Section 10.2.1); multiple instruction, multiple data/single program, multiple data (Section 10.2.3)
- Pipelines: Section 10.2.1
- Dataflow: Section 10.2.3
- Graphics processing unit and single instruction, multiple thread: Section 10.2.1
- Multicore: Section 10.2.3
- Shared and distributed memory: Section 10.2.3
- Message passing: Section 10.2.3

Programming topics

- Single instruction, multiple data: Section 10.2.1

- Vector extensions: Section 10.2.1
- Shared and distributed memory: Section 10.2.3
- Single Program Multiple Data: Section 10.2.3; specifically CUDA (Section 10.2.1) and MPI (Section 10.2.3)
- Data parallel: Section 10.2.1
- Parallel loops: Section 10.2.2
- Data parallel for distributed memory: Section 10.2.3
- Data distribution: Section 10.3.1

Algorithm topics

- Model-based notions: dependencies and task graphs (Section 10.2.3)
- Communication: send/receive (Section 10.2.3)

Context for use: This chapter requires no knowledge of parallel programming; however, there will be a number of snippets of pseudocode in a Python-like

299

language, so exposure to at least one modern programming language (not necessarily Python) will be required.

Learning outcome: After study of this chapter, the student will have seen a number of basic concepts in parallel programming: data/vector/loop-based parallelism, as well as the basics of distributed memory programming and task scheduling. Graphics processing units are briefly touched upon. The student will have seen these concepts in enough detail to answer some basic questions.

10.1 INTRODUCTION

There are many ways to approach parallel programming. Of course you need to start with the problem that you want to solve, but after that there can be more than one algorithm for that problem, you may have a choice of programming systems to use to implement that algorithm, and finally you have to consider the hardware that will run the software. Sometimes people will argue that certain problems are best solved on certain types of hardware or with certain programming systems. Whether this is so is indeed a question worth discussing, but is hard to assess in all its generality.

In this tutorial we will look at one particular problem, Conway's *Game of Life* [1], and investigate how that is best implemented using different parallel programming systems and different hardware. That is, we will see how different types of parallel programming can all be used to solve the same problem. In the process, you will learn about most of the common parallel programming models and their characteristics.

This tutorial does not teach you to program in any particular system: you will deal only with *pseudocode* and will not run it on actual hardware. However, the discussion will go into detail on the implications of using different types of parallel computers.

(At some points in this discussion there will be references to the book *Introduction to High-Performance Scientific Computing* by the present author [2].)

10.1.1 CONWAY'S GAME OF LIFE

The Game of Life takes place on a two-dimensional board of *cells*. Each cell can be alive or dead, and it can switch its status from alive to dead or the other way around once per time interval, let us say 1 s. The rules for cells are as follows. In each time step, each cell counts how many live neighbors it has, where a neighbor is a cell that borders on it horizontally, vertically, or diagonally. Then

- if a cell is alive, and it has fewer than two live neighbors, it dies of loneliness;
- a live cell with more than three live neighbors dies of overcrowding;
- a live cell with two or three live neighbors lives on to the next generation;
- a dead cell with exactly three live neighbors becomes a live cell, as if by reproduction.

The "game" is that you create an initial configuration of live cells, and then stand back and see what happens.

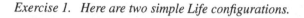

Exercise 1. Here are two simple Life configurations.

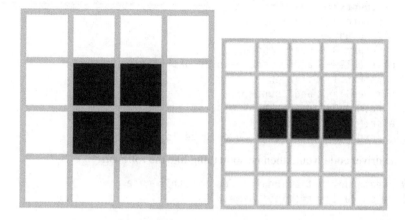

Go through the rules and show that the first figure is stationary, and the second figure morphs into something, then morphs back.

The Game of Life is hard to illustrate in a book, since it is so dynamic. If you search online you can find some great animations.

The rules of Life are very simple, but the results can be surprising. For instance, some simple shapes, called "gliders," seem to move over the board; others, called "puffers," move over the board, leaving behind other groups of cells. Some configurations of cells quickly disappear, others stay the same or alternate between a few shapes; for a certain type of configuration, called "garden of Eden," you can prove that it could not have evolved from an earlier configuration. Probably most surprisingly, Life can simulate, very slowly, a computer!

10.1.2 PROGRAMMING THE GAME OF LIFE

It is not hard to write a program for Life. Let us say we want to compute a certain number of time steps, and we have a square board of $N \times N$ cells. Also assume that we have a function life_evaluation that takes 3×3 cells and returns the updated status of the center cell[1]:

```
def life_evaluation( cells ):
  # cells is a 3x3 array
  count = 0
  for i in [0,1,2]:
    for j in [0,1,2]:
      if i!=1 and j!=1:
        count += cells[i,j]
```

---

[1] We use a quasi-Python syntax here, except that in arrays we let the upper bound be inclusive.

```
        return life_count_evaluation( cells[1,1],count )
    def life_count_evaluation( cell,count )
        if count<2:
            return 0 # loneliness
        elif count>3:
            return 0 # overcrowding
        elif cell==1 and (count==2 or count==3):
            return 1 # live on
        elif cell==0 and count==3:
            return 1 # spontaneous generation
        else:
            return 0 # no change in dead cells
```

The driver code would then be something like the following:

```
# create an initial board; we omit this code
life_board.create(final_time,N,N)

# now iterate a number of steps on the whole board
for t in [0:final_time-1]:
    for i in [0:N-1]:
        for j in [0:N-1]:
            life_board[t+1,i,j] =
                life_evaluation( life_board[t,i-1:i+1,j-1:j+1] )
```

where we do not worry too much about the edge of the board; we can, for instance, declare that points outside the range $0, \ldots, N - 1$ are always dead.

The above code creates a board for each time step, which is not strictly necessary. You can save yourself some space by creating only two boards:

```
life_board.create(N,N)
temp_board.create(N,N)

for t in [0:final_time-1]:
    life_generation( life_board,temp_board )

def life_generation( board,tmp ):
    for i in [0:N-1]:
        for j in [0:N-1]:
            tmp[i,j] = board[i,j]
    for i in [0:N-1]:
        for j in [0:N-1]:
            board[i,j] = life_evaluation( tmp[i-1:i+1,j-1:j+1] )
```

We will call this the basic *sequential implementation*, since it does its computation in a long sequence of steps. We will now explore parallel implementations of this algorithm. You will see that some look very different from this basic code.

Exercise 2. The second version used a whole temporary board. Can you come up with an implementation that uses just three temporary lines?

10.1.3 **GENERAL THOUGHTS ON PARALLELISM**

In the rest of this tutorial we will use various types of parallelism to explore coding the Game of Life. We start with data parallelism, based on the observation that each point in a Life board undergoes the same computation. Then we go on to task parallelism, which is necessary when we start looking at distributed memory programming on large clusters. But first we start with some basic thoughts on parallelism.

If you are familiar with programming, you will have read the above code fragments and agreed that this is a good way to solve the problem. You do one time step after another, and at each time step you compute a new version of the board, one line after another.

Most programming languages are very explicit about loop constructs: one iteration is done, and then the next, and the next, and so on. This works fine if you have just one processor. However, if you have some form of parallelism, meaning that there is more than one processing unit, you have to figure out which things really have to be done in sequence, and where the sequence is more an artifact of the programming language.

And by the way, *you* have to think about this yourself. In a distant past it was thought that programmers could write ordinary code, and the compiler would figure out parallelism. This has long proved impossible except in limited cases, so programmers these days accept that parallel code will look differently from sequential code, sometimes very much so.

So let us start looking at Life from a point of analyzing the parallelism. The Life program above used three levels of loops: one for the time steps, and two for the rows and columns of the board. While this is a correct way of programming Life, such explicit sequencing of loop iterations is not strictly necessary for solving the Game of Life problem. For instance, all the cells in the new board are the result of independent computations, and so they can be executed in any order, or indeed simultaneously.

You can view parallel programming as the problem of how to tell multiple processors that they can do certain things simultaneously, and other things only in sequence.

10.2 **PARALLEL VARIANTS**

We will now discuss various specific parallel realizations of Life.

10.2.1 **DATA PARALLELISM**

In the sequential reference code for Life we updated the whole board in its entirety before we proceeded to the next step. That is, we did the time steps sequentially. We also observed that, in each time step, all cells can be updated independently, and therefore in parallel. If parallelism comes in such small chunks, we call it *data*

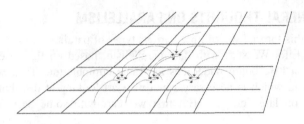

FIGURE 10.1

Illustration of data parallelism: all points of the board get the same update treatment.

parallelism or *fine-grained parallelism*: the parallelism comes from having lots of data points that are all treated identically. This is illustrated in Figure 10.1.

The fine-grained data parallel model of computing is known as single instruction, multiple data (SIMD): the same instruction is performed on multiple data elements. An actual computer will, of course, not have an instruction for computing a Life cell update. Rather, its instructions are things such as additions and multiplications. Thus, you may need to restructure your code a little for SIMD execution.

A parallel computer that is designed for doing lots of identical operations (on different data elements, of course) has certain advantages. For instance, there needs to be only one central instruction decoding unit that tells the processors what to do, so the design of the individual processors can be much simpler. This means that the processors can be smaller, more power efficient, and easier to manufacture.

In the 1980s and 1990s, SIMD computers existed, such as the MasPar and the Connection Machine. They were sometimes called *array processors* since they could operate on an array of data simultaneously, up to 2^{16} elements. These days, SIMD still exists, but in slightly different guises and on much smaller scale; we will now explore what SIMD parallelism looks like in current architectures.

Vector instructions

Modern processors have embraced the SIMD concept in an attempt to gain performance without complicating the processor design too much. Instead of operating on a single pair of inputs, you would load two or more pairs of operands, and execute multiple identical operations simultaneously.

Vector instructions constitute SIMD parallelism on a much smaller scale than the old array processors. For instance, Intel processors have had Streaming SIMD Extensions (SSE) instructions for quite some time; these are described as "two-wide" since they work on two sets of (double precision floating point) operands. The current generation of Intel vector instructions is called Advanced Vector Extensions (AVX), and they can be up to "eight-wide"; see Figure 10.2 for an illustration of four-wide instructions. Since with these instructions you can do four or eight operations per clock cycle, it becomes important to write your code such that the processor can actually use all that available parallelism.

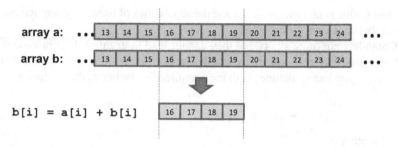

FIGURE 10.2

Four-wide vector instructions work on four operand pairs at the same time.

Now suppose that you are coding the Game of Life, which is SIMD in nature, and you want to make sure that it is executed with these vector instructions.

First of all the code needs to have the right structure. The original code does not have a lot of parallelism in the inner loop, where it can be exploited with vector instruction

```
for i in [0:N]:
  for j in [0:N]:
    count = 0
    for ii in {-1,0,+1}:
      for jj in {-1,0,+1}:
        if ii!=0 and jj!=0:
          count += board[i+ii,j+jj]
```

Instead, we have to exchange loops as

```
for i in [0:N]:
  for j in [0:N]:
    count[j] = 0
  for ii in {-1,0,+1}:
    for jj in {-1,0,+1}:
      if ii!=0 and jj!=0:
        for j in [0:N]:
          count[j] += board[i+ii,j+jj]
```

Note that the count variable now has become an array. This is one of the reasons that compilers are unable to make this transformation.

Regular programming languages have no way of saying "do the following operation with vector instructions." That leaves you with two options:

1. You can start coding in assembly language, or you can use your compiler's facility for using "in-line assembly."
2. You can hope that the compiler understands your code enough to generate the vector instructions for you.

The first option is no fun, and is beyond the capabilities of most programmers, so you will probably rely on the compiler.

Compilers are quite smart, but they cannot read your mind. If your code is too sophisticated, they may not figure out that vector instructions can be used. On the other hand, you can sometimes help the compiler. For instance, the operation

```
for i in [0:N]:
    count[i,j] += board[i,j+1]
```

can be written as

```
for ii in [0:N/2]:
    i = 2*ii
    count[i,j] += board[i,j+1]
    count[i+1,j] += board[i+1,j+1]
```

Here we perform half the number of iterations, but each new iteration comprises two old ones. In this version the compiler will have no trouble concluding that there are two operations that can be done simultaneously. This transformation of a loop is called *loop unrolling*, in this case, unrolling by 2.

Exercise 3. The second code is not actually equivalent to the first. (Hint: consider the case that N is odd.) How can you repair that code? One way of repairing this code is to add a few lines of "cleanup code" after the unrolled loop. Give the pseudocode for this.

Now consider the case of unrolling by 4. What does the unrolled code look like now? Think carefully about the cleanup code.

Vector pipelining

In the previous section you saw that modern CPUs can deal with applying the same operation to a sequence of data elements. In the case of vector instructions (above), or in the case of graphics processing units (GPUs; next section), these identical operations are actually done simultaneously. In this section we will look at *pipelining*, which is a different way of dealing with identical instructions.

Imagine a car being put together on an assembly line: As the frame comes down the line one worker puts on the wheels, another puts on the doors, another puts on the steering wheel, etc. Thus, the final product, a car, is gradually being constructed; since more than one car is being worked on simultaneously, this is a form of parallelism. And while it is possible for one worker to go through all these steps until the car is finished, it is more efficient to let each worker specialize in just one of the partial assembly operations.

We can have a similar story for computations in a CPU. Let us say we are dealing with floating point numbers of the form $a.b \times 10^c$. Now if we add 5.8×10^1 and 3.2×10^2, we

1. first bring them to the same power of ten: $0.58 \times 10^2 + 3.2 \times 10^2$,
2. do the addition: 3.88×10^2,
3. round to get rid of that last decimal place: 3.9×10^2.

So now we can apply the assembly line principle to arithmetic: we can let the processor do each piece in sequence, but a long time ago it was recognized that operations can be split up like that, letting the suboperations take place in different parts of the processor. The processor can now work on multiple operations at the same time: we start the first operation, and while it is under way we can start a second one, etc. In the context of computer arithmetic, we call this assembly line the *pipeline*.

If the pipeline has four stages, after the pipeline has been filled, there will be four operations partially completed at any time. Thus, the pipeline operation is roughly equivalent to, in this example, a fourfold parallelism. You would hope that this corresponds to a fourfold speedup; the following exercise lets you analyze this precisely.

Exercise 4. Assume that all the suboperations take the same amount of time t. If there are s suboperations (and assume s > 1), how much time does it take for one full calculation? And how much time does it take for two full calculations? Recognize that the time for two operations is less than twice the time for a single operation, since the second is started while the first is still in progress.

How much time does it take to do n operations? How much time would n operations take if the processor were not pipelined? What is the asymptotic improvement in speed of a pipelined processor over a nonpipelined one?

Around the 1970s the definition of a supercomputer was as follows: a machine with a single processor that can do floating point operations several times faster than other processors, as long as these operations are delivered as a stream of identical operations. This type of supercomputer essentially died out in the 1990s, but by that time microprocessors had become so sophisticated that they started to include pipelined arithmetic. So the idea of pipelining lives on.

Pipelining has similarities with array operations as described above: they both apply to sequences of identical operations, and they both apply the same operation to all operands. Because of this, pipelining is sometimes also considered SIMD.

GPUs

Graphics has always been an important application of computers, since everyone likes to look at pictures. With computer games, the demand for very fast generation of graphics has become even bigger. Since graphics processing is often relatively simple and structured, with, for instance, the same blur operation executed on each pixel, or the same rendering on each polygon, people have made specialized processors for doing just graphics. These can be cheaper than regular processors, since they only have to do graphics-type operations, and they take the load off the main CPU of your computer.

Wait. Did we just say "the same operation on each pixel/polygon"? That sounds a lot like SIMD, and in fact it is something very close to it.

Starting from the realization that graphics processing has a lot in common with traditional parallelism, people have tried to use GPUs for SIMD-type numerical computations. Doing so was cumbersome, until NVIDIA came out with the *Compute*

Unified Device Architecture (CUDA) language. CUDA is a way of explicitly doing data parallel programming: you write a piece of code called a *kernel*, which applies to a single data element. You then indicate a two-dimensional or three-dimensional grid of points on which the kernel will be applied.

In pseudo-CUDA, a kernel definition for the Game of Life and its invocation would look like the following:

```
kerneldef life_step( board ):
    i = my_i_number()
    j = my_j_number()
    board[i,j] = life_evaluation( board[i-1:i+1,j-1:j+1] )

for t in [0:final_time]:
    <<N,N>>life_step( board )
```

where the `<<N,N>>` notation means that the processors should arrange themselves in an $N \times N$ grid. Every processor has a way of telling its own coordinates in that grid.

There are aspects to CUDA that make it different from SIMD—namely, its threading—and for this reason NVIDIA uses the term "*single instruction, multiple thread*" (SIMT). We will not go into that here. The main purpose of this section was to remark on the similarities between GPU programming and SIMD array programming.

10.2.2 LOOP-BASED PARALLELISM

The above strategies of parallel programming were all based on assigning certain board locations to certain processors. Since the locations on the board can be updated independently, the processors can then all work in parallel.

There is a slightly different way of looking at this. Rather than going back to basics and reasoning about the problem abstractly, you can take the code of the basic, sequential, implementation of Life. Since the locations can be updated independently, the *iterations* of the loop are *independent* and can be executed in any order, or in fact simultaneously. So is there a way to tell the compiler that the iterations are independent, and let the compiler decide how to execute them?

The popular *OpenMP* system lets the programmer supply this information in comments:

```
def life_generation( board,tmp ):
    # OMP parallel for
    for i in [0:N-1]:
        for j in [0:N-1]:
            tmp[i,j] = board[i,j]
    # OMP parallel for
    for i in [0:N-1]:
        for j in [0:N-1]:
            board[i,j] = life_evaluation( tmp[i-1:i+1,j-1:j+1] )
```

The comments here state that both `for i` loops are parallel, and therefore their iterations can be executed by whatever parallel resources are available.

In fact, all N^2 iterations of the i,j loop nest are independent, which we express as

```
def life_generation( board,tmp ):
    # OMP parallel for collapse(2)
    for i in [0:N-1]:
        for j in [0:N-1]:
            tmp[i,j] = board[i,j]
```

This approach of annotating the loops of a naively written sequential implementation is a good way of getting started with parallelism. However, the structure of the resulting parallel execution may not be optimally suited to a given computer architecture. In the next section we will look at different ways of getting task parallelism, and why computationally it may be preferable.

10.2.3 COARSE-GRAINED DATA PARALLELISM

So far we have looked at implications of the fact that each cell in a step of Life can be updated independently. This view leads to tiny grains of computing, which are a good match to the innermost components of a processor core. However, if you look at parallelism on the level of the cores of a processor there are disadvantages to assigning small-grained computations randomly to the cores. Most of these have something to do with the way memory is structured: moving such small amounts of work around can be more costly than executing them (for a detailed discussion, see Section 1.3 in [2]). Therefore, we are motivated to look at computations in larger chunks than a single cell update.

For instance, we can divide the Life board into lines or square patches, and formulate the algorithm in terms of operations on such larger units. This is called *coarse-grained parallelism*, and we will look at several variants of it.

Shared memory parallelism

In the approaches to parallelism mentioned so far we have implicitly assumed that a processing element can actually get hold of any data element it needs. Or look at it this way: a program has a set of instructions, and so far we have assumed that any processor can execute any instruction.

This is certainly the case with multicore processors, where all cores can equally easily read any element from memory. We call this *shared memory*; see Figure 10.3.

In the CUDA example, each processing element essentially reasoned "this is my number, and therefore I will work on this element of the array" In other words, each processing element assumes that it can work on any data element, and this works because a GPU has a form of shared memory.

While it is convenient to program this way, it is not possible to make arbitrarily large computers with shared memory. The shared memory approaches discussed so far are limited by the amount of memory you can put in a single PC, at the moment

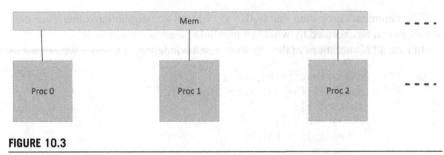

FIGURE 10.3

Shared memory: all processors access the same memory.

about 1 TB (which costs a lot of money!), or the processing power that you can associate with shared memory, at the moment around 48 cores.

If you need more processing power, you need to look at clusters, and "distributed memory programming."

Distributed memory parallelism

Clusters, also called *distributed memory* computers, can be thought of as a large number of PCs with network cabling between them. This design can be scaled up to a much larger number of processors than shared memory. In the context of a cluster, each of these PCs is called a *node*. The network can be *Ethernet* or something more sophisticated such as *Infiniband*.

Since all nodes work together, a cluster is in some sense one large computer. Since the nodes are also to an extent independent, this type of parallelism is called *multiple instruction, multiple data* (MIMD): each node has its own data, and executes its own program. However, most of the time the nodes will all execute the same program, so this model is often called single program, multiple data (SPMD); see Figure 10.4. The advantage of this design is that tying together thousands of processors allows you to run very large problems. For instance, the almost 13,000 processors of the Stampede supercomputer[2] (Figure 10.5) have almost 200 TB of memory. Parallel programming on such a machine is a little harder than what we discussed above. First of all we have to worry about how to partition the problem over this *distributed memory*. But more importantly, our above assumption that each processing element can get hold of every data element no longer holds.

It is clear that each cluster node can access its local problem data without any problem, but this is not true for the "remote" data on other nodes. In the former case the program simply reads the memory location; in the latter case accessing data is possible only because there is a network between the processors: in Figure 10.5 you can see yellow cabling connecting the nodes in each cabinet, and orange cabling

---

[2]Stampede has more than 6400 nodes, each with two Intel Sandy Bridge processors. Each node also has an Intel Xeon Phi coprocessor, but we do not count those for the moment.

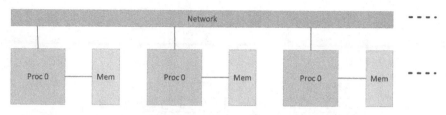

FIGURE 10.4

Distributed memory: every processor has its own memory and is connected to other processors through a network.

FIGURE 10.5

The Stampede supercomputer at the Texas Advanced Supercomputing Center.

overhead that connects the cabinets. Accessing data over the network probably involves an operating system call and accessing the network card, both of which are slow operations.

Distributed memory programming

By far the most popular way for programming distributed memory machines is by using the MPI library. This library adds functionality to an otherwise normal C or Fortran program for exchanging data with other processors. The name derives from the fact that the technical term for exchanging data between distributed memory nodes is *message passing*.

Let us explore how you would do programming with MPI. We start with the case that each processor stores the cells of a single line of the Life board, and that processor p stores line p. In that case, to update that line it needs the lines above and below it, which come from processors $p - 1$ and $p + 1$, respectively. In MPI terms, the processor needs to receive a message from each of these processors, containing the state of their line.

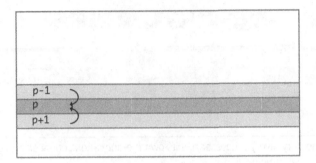

FIGURE 10.6

Processor p receives a line of data from $p-1$ and $p+1$.

Let us build up the basic structure of an MPI program. Throughout this example, keep in mind that we are working in SPMD mode: all processes execute the same program. As illustrated in Figure 10.6, a process needs to get data from its neighbors. The first step is for each process to find out what its number is, so that it can name its neighbors.

```
p = my_processor_number()
```

Then the process can actually receive data from those neighbors (we ignore complications from the first and the last line of the board here).

```
high_line = MPI_Receive(from=p-1,cells=N)
low_line = MPI_Receive(from=p+1,cells=N)
```

With this, it is possible to update the data stored in this process:

```
tmp_line = my_line.copy()
my_line = life_line_update(high_line,tmp_line,low_line,N)
```

(We omit the code for `life_line_update`, which computes the updated cell values on a single line.) Unfortunately, there is more to MPI than that. The commonest way of using the library is through *two-sided communication*, where for each receive action there is a corresponding send action: a process cannot just receive data from its neighbors, the neighbors have to send the data.

But now we recall the SPMD nature of the computation: if your neighbors send to you, you are someone else's neighbor and need to send to them. So the program code will contain both send and receive calls.

The following code is closer to the truth:

```
p = my_processor_number()

# send my data
my_line.MPI_Send(to=p-1,cells=N)
```

```
my_line.MPI_Send(to=p+1,cells=N)

# get data from neighbors
high_line = MPI_Receive(from=p-1,cells=N)
low_line = MPI_Receive(from=p+1,cells=N)
tmp_line = my_line.copy()

# do the local computation
my_line = life_line_update(high_line,tmp_line,low_line,N)
```

Since this is a general tutorial, and not a course in MPI programming, we will leave the example phrased in pseudo-MPI, ignoring many details. However, this code is still not entirely correct conceptually. Let us fix that.

Conceptually, a process would send a message, which disappears somewhere in the network, and goes about its business. The receiving process would at some point issue a receive call, get the data from the network, and do something with it. This idealized behavior is illustrated in the left half of Figure 10.7. Practice is different.

Suppose a process sends a large message, something that takes a great deal of memory. Since the only memory in the system is on the processors, the message has to stay in the memory of one processor, until it is copied to the other. We call this behavior *blocking communication*: a send call will wait until the receiving processor is indeed doing a receive call. That is, the sending code is blocked until its message is received.

But this is a problem: if every process p starts sending to $p-1$, everyone is waiting for someone else to do a receive call, and no one is actually doing a receive call. This sort of situation is called *deadlock*.

Exercise 5. Do you now see why the code fragment leads to deadlock? Can you come up with a clever rearrangement of the send and receive calls so that there is no deadlock?

Finding a "clever rearrangement" is usually not the best way to solve deadlock problems. A common solution is to use *nonblocking communication* calls. Here the send or receive instruction indicates to the system only the buffer with send data, or

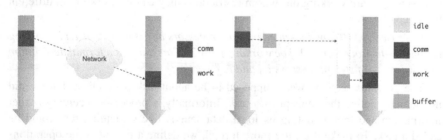

FIGURE 10.7

Illustration of "ideal" and "blocking" send calls.

the buffer in which to receive data. You then need a second call to ensure that the operation is actually completed.

In pseudocode, we have the following:

```
send( buffer1, to=neighbor1, result=request1 );
send( buffer2, to=neighbor2, result=request2 );
// maybe execute some other code
wait( request1 ); wait( request2 );
// make sure the operations are done
```

Task scheduling

All parallel realizations of Life you have seen so far were based on taking a single time step, and applying parallel computing to the updates in that time step. This was based on the fact that the points in the new time step can be computed independently. But the outer iteration has to be done in that order. Right?

Well...

Let us suppose you want to compute the board two time steps from now, without explicitly computing the next time step. Would that be possible?

Exercise 6. Life expresses the value in i,j *at time* $t + 1$ *as a simple function of the* 3×3 *patch* i-1:i+1,j-1:j+1 *at time t. Convince yourself that the value in* i,j *at* $t + 2$ *can be computed as a function of a* 5×5 *patch at t.*

Can you formulate rules for this update over two time steps? Are these rules as elegant as the old ones, just expressed in a count of live and dead cells? If you were to code the new rules as a case statement, how many clauses would there be? Let us not pursue this further....

This exercise makes an important point about dependence and independence. If the value at i,j depends on 3×3 previous points, and if each of these have a similar dependence, we can compute the value at i,j if we know 5×5 points two steps away, etc. The conclusion is that you do not need to finish a whole time step before you can start the next: for each point update only certain other points are needed, and not the whole board. If multiple processors are updating the board, they do not need to be working on the same time step. This is sometimes called *asynchronous computing*. It means that processors do not have to synchronize what time step they are working on: within restrictions they can be working on different time steps.

Exercise 7. Just how independent can processors be? If processor i,j is working on time t, can processor i+1,j be working on t+2? Can you give a formal description of how far out of step processors i,j and i',j' can be?

The previous sections were supposed to be about task parallelism, but we did not actually define the concept of a task. Informally, a processor receiving border information and then updating its local data sounds like something that could be called a task. To make it a little more formal, we define a task as some operations done on the same processor, plus a list of other tasks that have to be finished before this task can be finished.

This concept of computing is also known as *dataflow*: data flows as output of one operation to another; an operation can start executing when all its inputs are available. Another concept connected to this definition of tasks is that of a directed acyclic graph: the dependencies between tasks form a graph, and you cannot have cycles in this graph, otherwise you could never get started. . . .

You can interpret the MPI examples in terms of tasks. The local computation of a task can start when data from the neighboring tasks is available, and a task finds out about that from the messages from those neighbors coming in. However, this view does not add much information.

On the other hand, if you have shared memory, and tasks that do not all take the same amount of running time, the task view can be productive. In this case, we adopt a *master-worker model*: there is one master process that keeps a list of tasks, and there are a number of worker processors that can execute the tasks. The master executes the following program:

1. The master finds which running tasks have finished.
2. For each scheduled task, if it needs the data of a finished task, mark that the data is available.
3. Find a task that can now execute, find a processor for it, and execute it there.

The pseudocode for this is as follows:

```
while there_are_tasks_left():
    for r in running_tasks:
        if r.finished():
            for t in scheduled_tasks:
                t.mark_available_input(r)
    t = find_available_task()
    p = find_available_processor()
    schedule(t,p)
```

The master-worker model assumes that in general there are more available tasks than processors. In the Game of Life we can easily get this situation if we divide the board into more parts than there are processing elements. (Why would you do that? This mostly makes sense if you think about the memory hierarchy and cache sizes; see Section 1.3 in [2].) So with $N \times N$ divisions of the board and T time steps, we define the queue of tasks:

```
for t in [0:T]:
  for i in [0:N]:
    for j in [0:N]:
      task( id=[t+1,i,j],
        prereqs=[ [t,i,j],[t,i-1,j],[t,i+1,j] # et cetera
                ] )
```

Exercise 8.   *Argue that this model mostly makes sense on shared memory. Hint: if you were to execute this model on distributed memory, how much data would need to be moved in general when you start a task?*

10.3 ADVANCED TOPICS
10.3.1 DATA PARTITIONING

The previous sections approached parallelization of the Game of Life by taking the sequential implementation and the basic loop structure. For instance, in Section 10.2.3 we assigned a number of lines to each processor. This corresponds to a *one-dimensional partitioning* of the data. Sometimes, however, it is a good idea to use a two-dimensional one instead. (See Figure 10.8 for an illustration of the basic idea.) In this section you will get the flavor of the argument.

Suppose each processor stores one line of the Life board. As you saw in the previous section, to update that line it needs to receive two lines worth of data, and this takes time. In fact, receiving one item of data from another node is much slower than reading one item from local memory. If we inventory the cost of one time step in the distributed case, that comes down to

1. receiving $2N$ Life cells from other processors[3]; and
2. adding $8N$ values together to get the counts.

For most architectures, the cost of sending and receiving data will far outweigh the computation.

Let us now assume that we have N processors, each storing a $\sqrt{N} \times \sqrt{N}$ part of the Life board. We sometimes call this the processor's *subdomain*. To update this, a processor now needs to receive data from the lines above, under, and to the left and right of its part (we are ignoring the edge of the board here). That means four

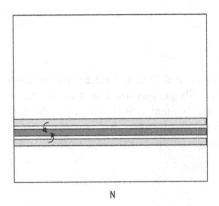
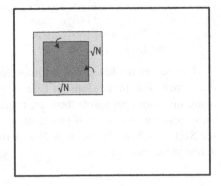

N

FIGURE 10.8

One-dimensional and two-dimensional distribution communication.

---

[3]For now we count only the transmission cost per item; there is also a one-time cost for each transmission, called the *latency*. For large enough messages, we can ignore this; for details, see Section 1.3.2 in [2].

messages, each of size $\sqrt{N} + 2$. On the other hand, the update takes $8N$ operations. For large enough N, the communication, which is slow, will be outweighed by the computation, which is much faster.

Our analysis here was very simple, based on having exactly N processors. In practice you will have fewer processors, and each processor will have a subdomain rather than a single point. However, a more refined analysis gives the same conclusion: a two-dimensional distribution is to be preferred over a one-dimensional one; see, for instance, Section 6.2.2.3 in [2] for the analysis of the matrix-vector product algorithm.

Let us do just a little analysis on the following scenario:

- You have a parallel machine where each processor has an amount M of memory to store the Life board.
- You can buy extra processors for this machine, thereby expanding both the processing power (in operations per second) and the total memory.
- As you buy more processors, you can store a larger Life board: we are assuming that the amount M of memory per processor is kept constant. (This strategy of scaling up the problem as you scale up the computer is called *weak scaling*. The scenario where you increase only the number of processors, keeping the problem fixed and therefore putting fewer and fewer Life cells on each processor, is called *strong scaling*.)

Let P be the number of processors, and let N the size of the board. In terms of the amount of memory M, we then have

$$M = N^2/P.$$

Let us now consider a one-dimensional distribution (left half of Figure 10.9). Every processor but the first and the last one needs to communicate two whole lines,

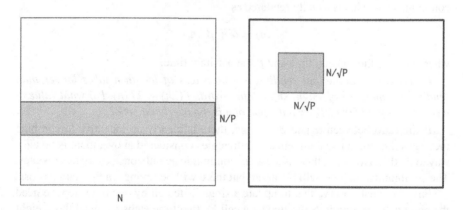

FIGURE 10.9

One-dimensional and two-dimensional distribution of a Life board meaning $2N$ elements. If you express this in terms of M, you find a formula that contains the variable P. This means that as you buy more processors, and can store a larger problem, the amount of communication becomes a function of the number of processors.

Exercise 9. Show that the amount of communication goes up with the number of processors. On the other hand, show that the amount of work stays constant, and that it corresponds to a perfect distribution of the work over the processors.

Now consider a two-dimensional distribution (right half of Figure 10.9). Every processor that is not on the edge of the board will communicate with eight other processors. With the four "corner" processors only a single item is exchanged.

Exercise 10. What is the amount of data exchanged with the processors left/right and top/bottom? Show that, expressed in terms of M, this formula does not contain the variable P. Show that, again, the work is constant in N and P.

The previous two exercises demonstrate an important point: different parallelization strategies can have different overhead and therefore different efficiencies. The one-dimensional distribution and the two-dimensional distribution both lead to a perfect parallelization of the work. On the other hand, with the two-dimension distribution the communication cost is constant, while with the one-dimensional distribution the communication cost goes up with the number of processors, so the algorithm becomes less and less efficient.

10.3.2 COMBINING WORK, MINIMIZING COMMUNICATION

In most of the above discussion we considered the parallel update of the Life board as one bulk operation that is executed in sequence: you do all communication for one update step, and then the communication for the next, etc.

Now, the time for a communication between two processes has two components: there is a start-up time (known as "latency"), and then there is a time per item communicated. This is usually rendered as

$$T(n) = \alpha + \beta \cdot n,$$

where the α is the start-up time and β the per-item time.

Exercise 11. Show that sending two messages of length n takes longer than sending one message of length $2n$, in other words $T(2n) < 2T(n)$. For what value of n is the overhead 50%? For what value of n is the overhead 10%?

If the ratio between α and β is large, there is clearly an incentive to combine messages. For the naive parallelization strategies considered above, there is no easy way to do this. However, there is a way to communicate only once every *two* updates. The communication cost will be larger, but there will be savings in the start-up cost.

First we must observe that to update a single Life cell by one time step we need the eight cells around it. So to update a cell by two time steps we need those eight cells plus the cells around them. This is illustrated in Figure 10.10. If a processor

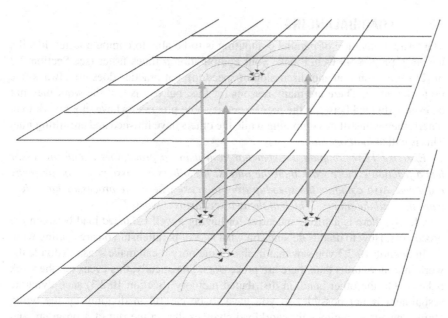

FIGURE 10.10

Two steps of Life updates.

has the responsibility for updating a subsection of the board, it needs the *halo region* around it. For a single update, this is a halo of width 1, and for two updates this is a halo of width 2.

Let us analyze the cost of this scheme. We assume that the board is square of size $N \times N$, and that there are $P \times P$ processors, so each processor is computing an $(N/P) \times (N/P)$ part of the board.

In the one-step-at-a-time implementation a processor

1. receives four messages of length N and four messages of length 1; and
2. then updates the part of the board it owns to the next time step.

To update its subdomain by two time steps, the following is needed:

1. Receive four messages of size $2N$ and four messages of size 4.
2. Compute the updated values at time $t + 1$ of the subdomain plus a locally stored border of thickness 1 around it.
3. Update precisely the owned subdomain to its state at $t + 2$.

So now you send slightly more data, and you compute a little more, but you save half the latency cost. Since communication latency can be quite high, this scheme can be faster overall.

10.3.3 **LOAD BALANCING**

The basic motivation of parallel computing is to be able to compute faster. Ideally, having p processors would make your computation p times faster (see Section 2.2 in [2] for a definition and discussion of speedup), but practice does not always live up to that ideal. There are many reasons for this, but one is that the work may not be evenly divided between the processors. If some processors have more work than others, they will still be computing while the others have finished and are sitting idle. This is called *load imbalance*.

Exercise 12. Compute the speedup from using p processors if one processor has a fraction ε more work than the others; the others are assumed to be perfectly balanced. Also compute the speedup from the case where one processor has ε less work than all the others. Which of the two scenarios is worse?

Clearly, there is a strong incentive for having a well-balanced load between the processors. How to do this depends on what sort of parallelism you are dealing with.

In Section 10.2.3 you saw that in shared memory it can make sense to divide the work into more units than there are processors. Statistically, this evens out the work balance. On the other hand, in distributed memory (Section 10.2.3) such dynamic assignment is not possible, so you have to be careful in dividing up the work. Unfortunately, sometimes the workload changes during the run of a program, and you want to rebalance it. Doing so can be tricky, since it requires problem data to be moved, and processors have to reallocate and rearrange their data structures. This is a very advanced topic, and not at all simple to do.

10.4 **SUMMARY**

In this chapter you have seen a number of parallel programming concepts through the example of the Game of Life. Like many scientific problems, you can view this as having parallelism on more than one level, and you can program it accordingly, depending on what sort of computer you have.

- The "data parallel" aspect of the Life board can be addressed with the vector instructions in even laptop processors.
- Just about every processor in existence is also pipelined, and you can express that in your code.
- A GPU can handle fairly fine-grained parallelism, so you would write a "kernel" that expresses the operations for updating a single cell of the board.
- If you have a multicore processor, which has shared memory, you can use a loop-based model such as OpenMP to parallelize the naive code.
- On both a multicore processor and distributed memory clusters you could process the Life board as a set of subboards, each of which is handled by a core or by a cluster node. This takes some rearranging of the reference code; in the distributed memory case you need to insert MPI library calls.

In all, you see that, depending on your available machine, some rearranging of the naive algorithm for Game of Life is needed. Parallelism is not a magic ingredient that you can easily add to existing code, it needs to be an integral part of the design of your program.

REFERENCES

[1] M. Gardner, Mathematical games—the fantastic combinations of John Conway's new solitaire game Life, Sci. Am. 223 (October 1970).
[2] V. Eijkhout, R. van de Geijn, E. Chow, Introduction to High Performance Scientific Computing, 2011. http://www.tacc.utexas.edu/~eijkhout/istc/istc.html

Appendix A: Chapters and topics

Sushil K. Prasad*, Anshul Gupta[†], Arnold L. Rosenberg[‡], Alan Sussman[§] and Charles C. Weems[¶]

Georgia State University* IBM Research[†] Northeastern University[‡] University of Maryland[§]
University of Massachusetts[¶]

The following tables list the parallel and distributed computing (PDC) topics covered in each chapter. The depth of coverage of each topic is indicated by the intended outcome of teaching that topic, expressed using Bloom's taxonomy of educational objectives:

K: Know the term
C: Comprehend so as to paraphrase/illustrate it
A: Apply it in some way

Chapter 2 Hands-On Parallelism

	Section			
PDC Concept	**2.3.1**	**2.3.2**	**2.3.3**	**2.3.4**
Concurrency	A	A	A	A
Why and what is PDC	A			
Time	C			
Communication	A		A	
Broadcast	A		A	
Nondeterminism		C		
Data races		A		
Synchronization		C		
Shared memory			K	A
Distributed memory				A

Chapter 3 Parallelism in Python

PDC Concept	Section			
	3.6	3.7	3.8	3.9
Concurrency	C			
Tasks and threads	A			
Decomposition into atomic tasks	A			
Sorting		A		
Message passing			A	
Synchronization			C	
Performance metrics			C	
Divide and conquer (parallel aspects)				A
Recursion (parallel aspects)				A

Chapter 4 Modules for Introducing Threads

PDC Concept	Section		
	4.1	4.2	4.3
Shared memory: compiler directives/pragmas			A
Shared memory: libraries		A	A
Task/thread spawning		A	A
Data parallel: parallel loops for shared memory			A
Synchronization: critical regions		A	
Concurrency defects: data races		C	C
Load balancing		C	C
Scheduling and mapping			K
Speedup		C	C

Chapter 5 PDC Concepts in Digital Logic

PDC Concept	Section					
	5.1	5.2	5.3	5.4	5.5	5.6
Concurrency, sequential/parallel		C	C	C	C	A
Interconnects, topologies	K	C	C			A
Performance measures (latency, scalability, efficiency, trade-offs)			K	C	C	C
Recursive decomposition, divide and conquer	K	C		A		
Prefix computation				C	A	
(A)synchrony			K		C	A

Chapter 5 PDC Concepts in Digital Logic–Cont'd

PDC Concept	Section					
	5.1	5.2	5.3	5.4	5.5	5.6
Pipelining					C	
Data hazards			K			
Buses, shared resources		K				K
Complexity, asymptotics	K					
Dependencies, task graphs			K			
Broadcast, multicast		K				
Reduction, convergecast		K			C	

Chapter 6 Networks and MPI

PDC Concept	Section			
	6.1	6.2	6.3	6.4
Programming single program, multiple data (SPMD)	C			
Performance issues, computation	K		K	K
Cluster	K	C	K	K
Grid/cloud	K			
Message passing	K	C		C
Why and what is PDC	K	K	K	K
Broadcast, multicast		K		

Chapter 7 Fork-Join Parallelism

PDC Concept	Section				
	7.1	7.2	7.3	7.4	7.5
Shared memory		C	A		
Language extensions		C	A		
Libraries			A		
Task/thread spawning		C	A		
Load balancing			K	C	
Performance metrics			K		
Speedup				C	A
Amdahl's law				A	
Asymptotics				A	
Time				A	A
Bulk synchronous parallel (BSP)/Cilk			A	A	A

Continued

Chapter 7 Fork-Join Parallelism–Cont'd

PDC Concept	Section				
	7.1	7.2	7.3	7.4	7.5
Dependencies				C	
Task graphs				K	
Work				A	A
(Make)span				A	A
Divide and conquer (parallel aspects)			A	A	A
Recursion (parallel aspects)			A		A
Scan (parallel-prefix)					C
Reduction (map-reduce)			A	A	A
Sorting					C
Why and what is PDC		A			
Concurrency		K			

Chapter 8 Shared-Memory Concurrency Control

PDC Concept	Section						
	8.1	8.2	8.3	8.4	8.5	8.6	8.7
Shared memory			A	A	A		C
Language extensions			C				C
Libraries							K
Synchronization			A	A	A		A
Critical regions			C	C	C		
Concurrency defects			A	A		A	
Memory models				C			
Nondeterminism		K	A	A			

Chapter 9 Parallel Computing in a Python-Based Course

PDC Concept	Section							
	9.1	9.2	9.3	9.4	9.5	9.6	9.7	9.8
Shared memory	C							
Parallel loops for shared memory	C	A	A	A	A	A	A	
Owner computes rule	C	A	A	A	A	A	A	
Time	C	A	A	A	A	A	A	A
PRAM	C	A	A	A	A	A	A	
Series-paralllel composition (barriers)	C							
Asymptotics		A	A	A	A	A	A	
Recursion		A	A					
Reduction		A			A	A	A	
Scan			A	A	A	A	A	
Sorting						A		

Chapter 10 Conway's Game of Life

PDC Concept	Section									
	10.1	10.2	10.3	10.4	10.5	10.6	10.7	10.8	10.9	10.10
Data parallelism, single instruction, multiple data (SIMD)	C									
Single program, multiple data (SPMD)	C			C			C	C		
CUDA, single instruction, multiple thread (SIMT)				C						
Vector extensions		C								
Pipelining			C							
Dataflow									C	
Task graphs									C	
Multicore						C	C	C		C
Shared versus distributed memory						C	C	C		C
Message passing					C					
Loop parallelism										
Data distribution										C

Index

Note: Page numbers followed by *f* indicate figures and *t* indicate tables.

Printed in the United States
By Bookmasters